Trust and Economic Learning

Trust and Economic Learning

Edited by

Nathalie Lazaric

Assistant Professor, University of Technology of Compiègne, France

Edward Lorenz

Professor, University of Technology of Compiègne, France

Edward Elgar

Cheltenham, UK • Northampton, MA, USA

Published by
Edward Elgar Publishing Limited
8 Lansdown Place
Cheltenham
Glos GL50 2HU
UK

Edward Elgar Publishing, Inc.
6 Market Street
Northampton
Massachusetts 01060
USA

A catalogue record for this book
is available from the British Library

Library of Congress Cataloguing in Publication Data

Trust and economic learning / edited by Nathalie Lazaric and Edward Lorenz.
Includes bibliographical references and index.
1. Economics—Moral and ethical aspects. 2. Trust. 3. Business ethics. I. Lazaric, Nathalie, 1965– . II. Lorenz, Edward, 1950–

HB72.T78 1998
330—DC21 97–31187
CIP

ISBN 1 85898 460 2

Printed and bound in Great Britain by Bookcraft (Bath) Ltd

Contents

Figures

Tables

Contributors

Bernard Baudruy, Economie des Changements Technologiques (ECT), University of Lyon II, France.

Benjamin Coriat, Centre de Recherche en Economie Industrielle (CREI), University of Paris XIII, Villetaneuse, France.

Jean-Claude Dupuy, Institut d'Economie Régionale, (IERT-LEREP), University of Social Sciences of Toulouse, Toulouse, France.

Amy Edmondson, Harvard Business School, Boston, MA, USA.

Dominique Foray, Institut pour le Management de la Recherche et de l'Innovation (IMRI), University of Paris-Dauphine, Paris, France.

Samira Guennif, Centre de Recherche en Economie Industrielle (CREI), University of Paris XIII, Villetaneuse, France.

Nathalie Lazaric, Département de Technologie et des Sciences de l'Homme, University of Technology of Compiègne, Compiègne, France.

Pierre Livet, Centre de Recherche en Epistémologie Appliquée (CREA), Ecole Polytechnique, Paris, France.

Edward Lorenz, Département de Technologie et des Sciences de l'Homme, University of Technology of Compiègne, Compiègne, France.

G.S. Mani, Department of Physics, University of Manchester, Manchester, England.

Luigi Marengo, Department of Economics, University of Trento, Trento, Italy.

Bertrand Moingeon, Département Stratégie et Politique d'Entreprise, Groupe HEC School of Management, Jouy-en-Josas, France.

André Orléan, Centre de Recherche en Epistémologie Appliquée (CREA), Ecole Polytechnique, Paris, France.

Bénédicte Reynaud, Centre de Recherche en Epistémologie Appliquée (CREA), Ecole Polytechnique, Paris, France.

Dorothée Rivaud-Danset, Centre de Recherche en Economie Industrielle (CREI), University of Paris XIII, Villetaneuse, France.

Mari Sako, Department of Industrial Relations, London School of Economics, London, England.

Pier Paolo Saviotti, Institut de la Recherhce Agronomique (SERD-INRA), University Pierre Mendès-France, Grenoble, France.

Hélène Tordjman, Centre de Recherche en Economie Industrielle (CREI), University of Paris XIII, Villetaneuse, France.

André Torre, Institut de la Recherche Agronomique, (LRDE-INRA), Corte, Corsica.

Introduction: The Learning Dynamics of Trust, Reputation and Confidence

Nathalie Lazaric and Edward Lorenz

In this Introduction, we focus on two related questions. The first question asks: is learning important for the emergence of trust and, if so, what are the distinctive features of this learning process? The second question reverses the order of inquiry and asks: does trust promote learning within or among organisations?

A number of the contributors to this book either argue explicitly, or can be interpreted as supporting the view, that trust among economic agents emerges through a particular type of learning process involving direct interaction among them.[1] The chapters in the volume, however, suggest caution in assimilating the emergence of trust to learning in general. Other types of learning process may give rise to related, though analytically distinct, beliefs or judgements. A number of the chapters argue that the learning processes underlying trust should be distinguished from those giving rise to the belief that an agent will always act in ways designed to preserve his good reputation.[2] Drawing on a distinction between trust and confidence developed by Rivaud-Danset (this volume), we shall also argue that the emergence of trust needs to be carefully distinguished from the collective learning dynamics giving rise to a 'state of confidence'.[3]

In response to the second question, we present a *prima facie* case for the view that trust is a necessary condition for organisational learning. This follows from the observation that organisational learning is marked by unanticipated contingencies and from the argument that in such circumstances individuals will be unwilling to commit their resources to a collective endeavour in the absence of trust. This view is supported by reference to empirical studies.

As will be apparent, our proposed answers to these questions reflect our particular definition of trust. Those readers dissatisfied with our semantics will probably remain unconvinced by our answers. In defence of our approach, we would argue, first, that what ultimately matters is not our particular choice of language but the pertinence of the distinctions we draw for the analysis of economic learning. Second, we would maintain that the orthodox economic approach, and notably the semantics of risk and subjective utility maximisation, are not fully adequate to this analysis. The analysis of trust is for us in part an exercise in developing a more appropriate semantics.

Our first task, then, is necessarily one of definition. After defining the general conditions under which trust becomes important for economic cooperation, we contrast the learning dynamics giving rise to trusting beliefs from those underlying a belief in reputation, and from those giving rise to a state of confidence. We then turn to the related question of why organisational learning depends upon trust.

NOTIONS OF TRUST

The contributors to this volume distinguish several notions or types of trust in analysing economic behaviour. One criterion used to define trust is that of degree or intensity. Livet and Reynaud (pp. 267–68), for example, draw the distinction between 'weak' and 'strong' trust, while Edmondson and Moingeon (p. 255) refer to different 'levels of trust' in organisational learning. The idea of degrees or intensity is also implicit in Sako's (pp. 26–27) distinction between 'contractual trust' and 'goodwill trust' in inter-firm relations, where the former refers to the 'expectation that promises will be kept' and the latter to 'the expectation that trading partners are committed to exploit new opportunities over and above what was promised'.

The notion of trust can also be defined according to whether it applies to bilateral relations or to relations among the members of a group involved in some collective action. This criterion is explicit in Livet and Reynaud's (pp. 277–79) notion of 'organisational trust', which is defined as a form of trust that depends on the members of a group involved in some collective endeavour holding the 'reasonable' belief that each is implicitly committed to it.[4]

Sako (p. 27) and Edmondson and Moingeon (p. 259) make a useful distinction between trust in the intentions of another and trust in their competencies. 'Competence trust' refers to the belief that our trading partners are *capable* of living up to their commitments, while 'intentions trust' refers to the belief that they *intend* to uphold their promises (Sako, p. 27). While competence trust and intentions trust are often related in practice, they are conceptually distinct. For example, after close observation we may come to believe fully in a trading partner's ability to undertake certain tasks, but nonetheless continue to harbour doubts about his honesty. In order to avoid confusion, we adopt the convention in this introductory chapter of always using the words 'competence trust' when referring to beliefs about another person's competencies. When the word trust appears without a qualifier it should be taken to refer to trust in the sense of belief about the intentions of another.

Given the multiple notions of trust proposed in this volume, it is appropriate to ask: is there an underlying common ground among them? We would argue that the following three conditions are common and provide the basis for a general definition of trust.[5] First, in each of its versions trust is identified with an agent's beliefs rather than with his behaviour or actions.[6] Second, trust refers to beliefs about the likely behaviour of another, or others, which matter for the trustor's decision-making. The trustor has to decide whether to make resources available for some form of cooperation or exchange with the trustee in a situation where, depending on how the trustee acts, the trustor will be better off or worse off than had the resources not been made available. This applies to contractual, goodwill and organisational trust. Third, trust pertains to situations where the complexity of the relationship, or the fact that it is marked by unanticipated contingencies, preclude having recourse to complete contingent contracts with third-party enforcement. This should not be taken to imply that the situation is such that formal contracts provide no guarantees on the behaviour of a trading partner, but rather that they cannot eliminate all uncertainty regarding the outcome. As Livet and Reynaud (p. 269) observe in discussing their notion of contractual trust, there is always the possibility that the incompleteness of the contract will allow one party to interpret its terms in an opportunistic manner.

While our proposed definition states that a belief in the efficacy of legally enforced contractual commitments cannot eliminate the problem of trust, it leaves open the possibility of reducing trust to some form of belief in reputation or to some form of confidence in the stability of macro-level arrangements. We consider first the differences between trust and reputation.

TRUST VERSUS REPUTATION

A number of the contributors to this volume argue that the emergence of trust depends on direct experience between the agents involved in a relationship (Coriat and Guennif, p. 54; Lazaric and Lorenz, p. 218; Edmondson and Moingeon, p. 261; Rivaud-Danset, p. 83; Sako, pp. 26, 35). This relational dimension of trust derives from condition (3) of our general definition. Complex relations marked by unanticipated contingencies encourage trading partners to develop a private language and to rely on implicit understandings which they rarely feel the need to articulate.[7] For this reason, it is often difficult for outsiders, who are not directly involved, to interpret the behaviour of the participants in an idiosyncratic trading relationship and to make useful judgements concerning their trustworthiness. The non-articulated nature of the knowledge which underlies trust means that trusting beliefs will not easily spread across a wider population of actors. In most cases the only way we can form a reasonable judgement concerning the trustworthiness of an individual is through what we have learned from our interactions with him. In so far as we feel capable of making such a judgement based on what we have observed of his interactions with others, this will be because we share his private language and can interpret the implicit dimensions of his commitments.

It is important to observe that trusting beliefs have an imprecise or open character due to the uncertain circumstances in which they become pertinent for decision-making. The commitment necessarily takes the form of, 'in circumstances yet to be fully defined I expect that my trading partner, or partners, will act in ways designed to improve my situation rather than worsen it'. This imprecise dimension of trust is well brought out in Sako's (p. 27) notion of goodwill trust as involving a willingness to go beyond explicitly enunciated commitments in furthering a cooperative arrangement.

The beliefs which underlie the force of reputation effects in economic exchange differ from trusting beliefs mainly on two grounds. First, they necessarily concern unambiguous commitments whose respect is readily observable by the wider community concerned. Second, they may display an impersonal or 'public goods' quality as opposed to the distinctly 'relational' quality of trusting beliefs. Consider first the unambiguous and observable nature of the commitments around which reputation is based. The basic idea in reputation arguments is that cooperation can be sustained between trading partners, even when reneging on one's commitments promises an immediate gain, in so far as each party to the transaction has a sufficient interest in maintaining their reputation for being honest with the wider community. The argument will only hold, however, if an agent's commitments are clear and unambiguous, and if compliance with them is easily observable by the entire community concerned. If this were not the case, it would be impossible for community members to make judgements as to the honesty of their potential partners and thus to enforce cooperative behaviour by threatening never to cooperate with an individual who had been observed reneging on his commitments. In the case of a contractual dispute they would be unable to make clear judgements as to whose claims are bogus, and this would clearly reduce the value to an individual involved in a contractual relation of always acting so as to maintain his good reputation.[8]

To appreciate the difference between a belief in reputation and trust, observe that the requirement that commitments or contractual terms be unambiguous and observable is clearly not respected in uncertain circumstances corresponding to condition (3) of our general definition of trust. This is for the simple reason that if a contingency is truly unanticipated, it will be impossible to specify *unambiguously* in advance what behaviour is expected in adapting to it.

Now turn to the impersonal aspect of belief in reputation. While reputation may attach to particular individuals, what often concerns us in business transactions is the reputation of the organisation or the firm. In this case reputation is bestowed with a public goods quality in the sense that an individual member of a firm can benefit from its good reputation even if he has not contributed to its construction.

To appreciate the public goods quality of reputation, consider David Kreps's (1990) game theoretic treatment of reputation and company culture. His basic conclusion is that in a series of transactions between a long-lived producer, B and a number of clients, Ai, the following strategy combination will induce the producer always to act so as to maintain his good reputation, given that he places sufficient value on future gains relative to present gains. The producer initially has a good reputation and starts out by keeping his commitments with the clients. Should the producer ever renege on his commitments with any of the clients, the entire community of potential clients refuses to transact with him in all future periods. Once a client gains a bad reputation, he always reneges on his commitments with any client that agrees to transact with him. In so far as the rate of time discount is such that the present discounted benefits of future cooperation are greater than the one time gain from reneging on one's commitments, it will be in the interest of the producer always to act so as to maintain his good reputation.[9]

The argument supposes that the producer is long-lived while the clients are short-lived. In practice, however, the owners and operators of firms have finite lives, and this, as Kreps (1990, p. 104) points out, poses a problem for the reputation argument since one can argue, by a logic of backward deduction, that cooperation will never get started. Since the clients know that reneging on one's commitments is the producer's dominant choice on the last move, none of them will be willing to transact with the producer on this move if it is reached. Since the producer knows this about the clients, he will have no interest in living up to his commitments on the next to last move in order to keep cooperation alive, and since the clients know this about the producer, none of them will have an interest in transacting with him on the next to last move should it be reached, and so on.

The reputation construction can be saved through the following arrangement. Call the producer firm 'B Associates' and suppose that when an associate retires he sells his place in the firm to an outsider. Suppose the clients adopt the strategy of transacting with any member of B Associates as long as the firm has never violated its commitments in the past, and of refusing to transact with any member of the firm if it has ever sullied its good reputation. With the standard conditions on the rate of time discount, the new associate will have an interest in acting so as to maintain the firm's established reputation for transacting fairly. Under these conditions, as Kreps (1990, p. 111) observes, the firm becomes a reputation bearer.

Kreps's argument makes clear that a belief in reputation may be impersonal in the sense that we may come to believe that an individual member of a firm will act in ways designed to uphold the firm's good reputation despite our lack of personal experience with him. In the game theoretic formulation of the problem presented above, the beliefs which underlie the force of reputation effects emerge instantaneously through the ability of potential trading partners to calculate the firm's net present discounted returns from always living up to its commitments. While this collapsing of a learning process into an instantaneous calculation is not realistic, the language of calculativeness is nonetheless appropriate. As we have observed, the enforcement of behaviour through reputation works because of the transparency of the situation. The firm's commitments must be unambiguous and its conformity to them easily observable. It must be apparent what the firm's longer-term interests are.

In comparison with the precise and calculate nature of the 'learning' which underlies reputation effects, the learning dynamics of trust display a distinctively incremental and provisional character. Trust is something which emerges gradually and which remains open to revision as experience accumulates and further knowledge is gained about a trading partner. Nothing precludes errors of judgement or that a provisional judgement of trust may turn to suspicion and mistrust. This lack of finality in judgements of trust relates to the limits of our rationality in a world characterised by surprise and unanticipated complexity.

Lazaric and Lorenz (pp. 222–23) point to the importance of direct interaction for judgements of trust in observing that firms contemplating long-term relations often begin with small initial commitments and then progressively risk larger commitments depending on the quality of the exchange. They describe how firms initiating a technological alliance or a partnership may explicitly put in place a 'step-by-step' procedure where the willingness of a partner to make further relation-specific investments depends on how the other has adapted to the unanticipated contingencies they have encountered.

Livet and Reynaud (pp. 274–75) make a similar point in their analysis of trust in organisational settings. They argue that an individual's judgement of trust for his fellow organisational members will be based not so much on what they say about their intentions, but on what they implicitly demonstrate about them in accepting the constraints involved in participating in some collective endeavour. Direct involvement with another helps an individual to undertake the imaginative act of reconstructing a scenario which may provide reasonable grounds for the judgement that the other is committed to the joint project.

Sako (p. 35) makes much the same point in pointing to the informational requirement of trust:

> Mutual trust between business organisations can be developed and sustained through intensive observation of each other's behaviour and performance. Such vigilance through access to information about each other's performance, processes and technology is required in order to engage in continuous improvement. Successfully exploiting opportunities for improvement would in turn be interpreted as a manifestation of 'goodwill' trust.

Although reputation does not amount to trust, it may be a condition for its development. Livet and Reynaud (p. 280) argue that explicit contractual commitments between an employer and an employee may provide the foundation upon which implicit commitments, which are the substance of trust, are established.[10] In a similar vein, Baudry (pp. 71–72) argues that contractually established incentives as well as the exercise of authority may be complementary to trust as mechanisms for ensuring coordination in vertical relations between a client and a subcontractor. The balance of importance between contract and authority will depend on the type of relationship, with a contract playing a relatively important part in what Baudry refers to as 'oblique quasi-integration', where the client seeks actively to involve the supplier in the design of the product. Trust, built up through personal relations and reciprocity over time, inevitably plays its role, however, because of the incompleteness of contracts (Baudry, p. 67).

Reputation, we would argue, can play an analogous role to explicit contracts in providing certain assurances for agents who are considering entering into a relationship marked by unanticipated contingencies. The assurances provided by a good reputation may encourage an agent to take the first step towards building up trust by committing some initial small amount of resources to the exchange. If the other party's reputation is bad, however, it is less likely that the kinds of exchange and learning experience that may ultimately lead to trust will be initiated.

STATES OF CONFIDENCE

Confidence, defined as an agent's belief concerning the future state of the economy (Rivaud-Danset, p. 79), can be most obviously distinguished from trust by the collective or institutional nature of the object of belief. Confidence pertains to such things as an agent's belief in the likely movement of stock prices, or in the probability that a technological standard will be universally adopted, or in the likelihood that the members of a community of producers will conform to certain norms of information-sharing.

It is common to argue for the self-reinforcing nature of a 'state of confidence', defined as a generalised belief among the members of a population concerning the future state of the economy. This, in our opinion, is an over-hasty conclusion which glosses over an important distinction. In exploring the learning dynamics giving rise to a state of confidence, it is important to distinguish between situations where a state of confidence is self-reinforcing due to some positive feedback mechanism between the collective state and individual belief, and situations where it is not self-reinforcing because some form of negative externalities leads to the expectation that cooperative arrangements may unravel. While real-life problems of coordination frequently combine these two types of situation, it is nonetheless useful for analytical purposes to distinguish between them.

Collective Learning with Self-Reinforcement

Perhaps the most well known economic model dealing with situations where the majority choice or opinion is self-reinforcing is Arthur's (1989) analysis of the adoption of competing technologies. The model depicts an infinitely growing population where at each point in time an individual adopter's probability of choosing, once and for all, one of the two available technologies depends on the relative frequencies of adoption. The majority choice tends to be self-reinforcing due to positive network externalities of adoption. Since the population grows to infinity, in the limit a random adopter will almost surely adopt one of the two available technologies with probability 1. Which one of the available technologies comes to dominate the economic scene, however, will depend on random events which determine the pattern of adoption in finite time (Dosi, Marengo and Fagiolo, 1996, pp. 40-41).[11]

One limitation of Arthur's model is that it abstracts from the problem that firms may lack the necessary competence effectively to adopt a technology. Saviotti and Mani (this volume) draw on nucleation theory to develop a framework for analysing the problem of technological transitions in which the absorptive capacity of the firm is explicitly considered. Self-reinforcement enters through the assumption that the probability a given firm will adopt the new technology is a positive function of the proportion of the population of firms having already made the transition. This can be seen as deriving from a form of network externalities, since the size of the population having adopted the new technology is seen to be directly related to the availability of the human resources which have the know-how to use it effectively.

A second limitation of Arthur's model is that there is no individual learning since firms are assumed to make once-and-for-all choices. While this may be the appropriate analogy for analysing irreversible investment decisions, it is not appropriate for modelling the reversible decision to believe that a particular state of the world will obtain. Orléan (this volume) develops a finite population model, more appropriate to the problem of confidence, in which myopic decision-makers use Bayes's rule to revise their beliefs periodically over two possible states of the world.[12] In revising their beliefs, it is assumed that individuals have access to two types of information: an imprecise signal (their private information) and the publicly announced frequency distribution of the population across the two possible states. The interesting case is when the two types of information are contradictory. An individual's choice will then depend on his degree of confidence in the majority opinion. By comparing situations where agents attribute more or less precision to the majority view, Orléan is able to show that imitative behaviour has an ambiguous impact on the efficiency of outcomes. While a certain degree of confidence in the majority opinion is efficient, because it is a way for boundedly rational individuals to take into account the private information of others,[13] above a certain threshold imitative behaviour is likely to give rise to a self-validating process where the majority choose incorrectly. Using an analogy from the literature on financial speculation, Orléan refers to such an outcome as a 'bubble'.

While Orléan's formal treatment allows him to explore the limit properties of the evolution of collective opinion,[14] it arguably does this at the expense of over-simplifying the representation of individual agents. This is evident in the assumption that agents uniformly revise the probabilities they attach to two well-defined states of the world according to some relatively uncomplicated heuristic such as Bayes's rule. Tordjman (this volume), in discussing the behaviour of heterogeneous traders on financial markets, argues for the pertinence of the 'representativeness' heuristic, in which likelihood judgements are based on a notion of the proximity or similarity of actual conditions to some stereotype. Stereotypes can be thought of as an archetypal representation of the problem under consideration, which are formed in part through collective processes of socialisation and education, and in part through individual experience. Heterogeneity is evident not only in the possibility that traders will attach different degrees of importance to the majority view, but also in their diverse representations of the market and in the varying criteria they use in judging similarity.

Judgements by representativeness are typically at odds with the predictions of Bayes's rule due to the bias of 'overconfidence', which can be defined as a tendency to be more confident in one's judgement than is warranted by the facts (Tordjman, p. 102). Drawing on Shiller's (1989) survey of the attitudes of private and institutional investors just after the October 1987 crash, Tordjman shows how overconfidence may enter into an explanation for the phenomenon of speculative euphoria and crashes. First, the traders questioned by Shiller reported being influenced by the behaviour of others, at least in part because they recognised that collective behaviour is at the origin of price movements. Second, in accounting for their behaviour, investors made frequent references to the 1929 crash and to the similarity of certain salient conditions in October 1987, such as a sudden fall in share prices, with those occuring before the 1929 crash. Third, many of the institutional traders expressed confidence in their ability to 'time the crash' and to go out of the market before the others. On this account, imitative behaviour may well give rise to speculative bubbles and to crashes. However, such behaviour would reflect less the judgement that others are better informed, than it would a tendency to attach too much importance to certain salient events, such as a reported fall in share prices, in combination with overconfidence in one's ability to guess the market.

Despite these differences of interpretation, the texts by Orléan and Tordjman converge in pointing to the myopic nature of the individual learning dynamics underlying the emergence of collective belief. In stressing limited foresight and progressive revision of beliefs, the learning processes they analyse have something in common with those we have argued characterise the emergence of trust. The differences, however, are equally salient. First, the quality of the information about others which bears upon a judgement of confidence is relatively coarse in nature compared with the intimate knowledge about another which underlies a judgement of trust. This is explicit in the model of Orléan, where individual beliefs are a function of the proportion of the population choosing a particular action. Second, the source of the uncertainty which precludes identifying the substantially rational choice appears to be different. In the case of trust, this uncertainty ultimately stems from the incompleteness of individual representations of the world which precludes comprehensive contracting with full anticipation of relevant contingencies. While Tordjman's analysis suggests that such incomplete representations characterise financial traders, a further source of uncertainty derives from the individual's imperfect understanding of the complex positive feedback mechanism linking the collective state to individual belief and choice. In the case of Tordjman's analysis, the imperfect understanding of the dynamic interaction between the macro state and micro-level choice may help to account for traders' tendency to base their opinion too readily on certain salient pieces of information, such as a reported drop in share prices.

Collective Learning in the Face of Negative Externalities

Economic analysis has rather less of interest to say about the emergence of a state of confidence in settings where there is a positive pay-off to free-riding. Perhaps this is because of the economist's conviction that when such negative strategic externalities are present, cooperative behaviour among a population of actors will not emerge or be sustained. This is the basic conclusion of the game theoretic analysis of such situations in terms of the finitely repeated prisoners' dilemma, where the dominance of defecting on the final move ensures, by a logic of backward induction, that cooperation never gets started. The analysis depends on the assumptions of complete information and common knowledge among the players, and for this reason one can argue that no real learning takes place. Players know the equilibrium before the game starts.[15]

One can introduce a limited form of learning by starting with the radically different assumption that players have no ability to anticipate the future and that they choose myopically among a fixed menu of choices according to some simple rule. The standard evolutionary game formulation of this approach, due to Maynard Smith (1982), has a large finite population distributed across a finite set of actions. In each period of play, each individual engages in a pairwise interaction with a randomly chosen opponent. The basic selection principle has strategies with higher pay-offs than the average pay-off for all strategies increasingly sampled in the population. As Boyer and Orléan (1995) observe, this can be interpreted as a gradual learning process where a proportion of the population abandons strategies that are observed *ex post* to give an inferior pay-off and switch to one of the higher earning strategies.

Some interesting work by Axelrod (1984) used this framework to test the stability of cooperation generated by the mutual adoption of the strategy 'tit-for-tat', which consists in always starting out by cooperating and then responding on the next move with the action that your opponent used in the previous move. The basic technique, following Maynard Smith, is to test whether this strategy is 'evolutionary stable' in the sense of being able to resist 'invasion' by the sudden appearance of a sufficiently small number of players adopting a mutant strategy, such as 'always defect' or 'periodically defect'.

More recent work (see Boyer and Orléan, 1995; Dupuy and Torre, this volume) draws on the approach developed by Foster and Young (1990) to strengthen the notion of an evolutionary stable equilibrium by introducing more 'noise' in the form of continuous stochastic mutations, which ensure that there is a positive probability that each member of the finite set of available strategies will be present among the population in each period. The model developed by Dupuy and Torre allows for individual learning by assuming that agents periodically revise their choice of strategy according to a rule which tells each agent to compare his current pay-off with the pay-offs of a small, randomly selected group of opponents, and to switch with positive probability to a strategy which has delivered a higher pay-off. Without entering into the details of their model, it qualifies in important respects Axelrod's conclusion concerning the evolutionary stable properties of 'tit-for-tat'. Their basic conclusion is that cooperation associated with the diffusion of 'tit-for-tat' is unlikely to emerge or to be sustained if the degree of openness of the system to outside mutant strategies is moderately high.

Dupuy and Torre are able to improve on this result by introducing a 'proximity' variable, which limits each individual's interactions to a small set of immediate neighbours. In terms of the logic of their model, proximity helps because it increases the likelihood of long sequences of interactions between pairs of interacting individuals.[16] Once the strategy of 'tit-for-tat' gets established in these small clusters, it tends to spread due to its key properties of forgiveness and reciprocity. The authors interpret their formal results as supporting the view that relations of proximity tend to favour conformity and the emergence of stable norms of behaviour (Dupuy and Torre, p. 158).

Foray's (this volume) analysis of conventions of knowledge openness or disclosure in technological communities tends to confirm the conclusion that the forms of cooperation which promote positive learning externalities are unlikely to emerge spontaneously and may easily unravel in the presence of negative externalities associated with a positive pay-off to free-riding. Foray draws on Schelling's (1978) classic analysis of a multi-agent prisoners' dilemma to support this view. His analysis is richer, however, as he draws on a variety of historical and contemporary examples to show how in practice institutional devices come into play in the emergence and consolidation of both practices of knowledge disclosure and practices of secrecy and access restriction.

The Japanese patent system arguably illustrates how institutional devices can encourage knowledge disclosure. Foray argues that three critical features of the system promote knowledge openness and collective invention: early disclosure combined with relaxed novelty requirements and limited exclusion rights conferred by the patent. Quoting Ordover (1991), he explains how these features can have positive effects on the accumulation of knowledge: 'potential competitors who have 'reversed engineered' the invention during the laying-open and opposition phases can file their own patent application, thanks to the narrow scope of patent coverage and very relaxed novelty requirements'.

Recent tendencies in the US university system arguably illustrate the reverse situation where the interplay of changing behaviours and institutional devices promotes access restriction. Drawing on a variety of empirical studies, Foray suggests that increasing university participation in industrial research, by promoting various practices of access restriction, may be proving detrimental to the traditional university goal of 'open science'. Such restrictive practices may be institutionalised by the university's acceptance of formally imposed non-release of data requirements and restrictions on publishing as a condition for benefiting from industrial collaboration and finance. More generally, Foray (p. 176) observes, 'Emerging behaviours of access restriction and secrecy are followed and consolidated by the creation of an institutional system, which facilitates access restriction, strong protection of inventors and innovators, and the exclusion of others from using the new findings'.

Institutions and Trust

Foray's understanding of institutions is close to that developed by Coriat and Guennif (this volume), who argue that sustained cooperative behaviour among the members of a population is unthinkable in the absence of an institutional framework which reduces uncertainty and helps to stabilise individual expectations concerning how others will behave in recurrent situations. Coriat and Guennif (p. 56) are careful to point out, however, that there are limits to which institutions can ensure this risk reducing function: 'institutions ... never totally eliminate the fact that there are conflicting interpretations of the body of rules, which causes conflict to re-emerge and which creates ambiguity in human interactions'.

In our view, the limits of such institutionally grounded confidence to eliminate the problem of uncertainty is directly linked to the systemic or collective nature of the object of belief (see above). Since confidence, by definition, pertains to recurrent situations faced by a population of actors, the prescribed rule or behavioural regularity will necessarily have to be interpreted in adapting it to local circumstances which are specific to particular members. Such ambiguity in the meaning of institutionally grounded rules or norms inevitably leaves open the possibility of conflicting interpretations and hence some scope for opportunistic behaviour. When the costs of opportunistic behaviour are high, because the situation calls for significant relation-specific investments, confidence is unlikely to provide us with the assurances we need to commit our resources to a cooperative endeavour. In such circumstances we will want to complement confidence with a judgement concerning the trustworthiness of those with whom we propose to cooperate.[17]

Institutionally grounded confidence may prove enabling for the development of trust for at least two reasons raised by Coriat and Guennif. The first pertains to the idea that institutions have a contractual foundation and provide for various penalties or sanctions in response to the non-respect of specified commitments or obligations. By reducing the possibility of certain forms of opportunistic behaviour, institutions provide a foundation upon which trust may be established. Coriat and Guennif (p. 58) suggest that the lengthy procedures established to ensure quality inspection in the development of 'partnership' relations between a firm and its suppliers may be understood in this manner.

In addition to the idea of institutions as sanctioning mechanisms, Coriat and Guennif develop a notion of institutions as 'facilitators' which are more or less well adapted to promoting forms of cooperation that are trust-building. International comparisons are particularly well suited to substantiating this point. Sako's (1992) comparative study of supplier relations in Britain and Japan shows how specific features of the Japanese legal framework, financial system and pattern of employment relations tend to promote the build-up of trust. A similar conclusion may be drawn from Coriat's (1995) comparative study of work organisation and bargaining relations in the US, Japanese and German auto industries.

The chapter by Coriat and Guennif takes up more explicitly than most of the others in this volume the relation between structure and agency. Their discussion suggests that examining the links between institutions and trust should provide a useful means of addressing this classic tension in the social sciences. By exploring the limits of institutions to eliminate certain forms of uncertainty as well as the ways in which institutions can promote trust, it should be possible to develop an integrated view of economic cooperation, in which structure matters but is not all-determining.

TRUST AND ORGANISATIONAL LEARNING

We have argued above that trust can be understood as a judgement under uncertainty formed over time on the basis of direct interaction among individuals. This view leads naturally to the idea that learning within or between organisations depends upon a certain degree of trust. In order to persuade the reader of this, we start by presenting Marengo's (this volume) computational model of organisational learning. Although Marengo is largely concerned with the problem of establishing a common language within an organisation, his characterisation of an organisation in terms of condition/action rules leads naturally to an appreciation of the importance of trust.

Marengo argues that the sharing of a common base of knowledge is a precondition for the members of an organisation to communicate and to coordinate their actions effectively in an effort to solve the problems they confront. This problem can be modelled by treating each decision-maker as a set of condition–action rules which specify the execution of a certain action conditional upon the agent's perception of the present state of the world. A form of learning can then be analysed by assuming that the rules that perform better gain in strength relative to the others, and by allowing for change through the recombination of the elements of existing rules to generate new ones. The dynamics of collective learning can be explored under varying assumptions about the importance decision-makers attach to messages they receive from other organisational members situated at different levels of the organisational hierarchy.

Within this rule-based conception of organisational learning, questions of trust and power easily find their place (see Lazaric and Lorenz, pp. 2132–14). Organisational rules not only embody knowledge about what actions should be taken in specified circumstances, but also constitute political compromises which affect power relations and the distribution of organisational quasi-rents. Changes in the rule, the substance of organisational learning, become problematic because, given limited foresight and the possibility of opportunistic behaviour, agents will be uncertain whether the proposed changes are designed to bring about mutual gain or to benefit others at one's expense. Mistrust of the intentions of others can lead organisational members to resist even relatively simple changes that promise mutual advantage. In this sense, some degree of trust is a precondition for organisational learning.

As Lorenz and Lazaric (pp. 215–16) show, this rule-based framework can be adapted to the analysis of inter-firm learning. Both technological alliances and long-term partnerships between buyers and suppliers depend on the creation of a set of rules and procedures that allow firms to coordinate their decisions and to solve the technological and organisational problems they encounter. Elements of surprise and discovery will constitute critical conjunctures for technological partners because in such circumstances the incompleteness of the existing rules will call for the creation of new rules or the modification of the existing ones in adapting them to the new conditions. A certain degree of trust will be a necessary condition for individuals to risk such uncertain forms of cooperation. Given the bounds to human rationality, trust remains a tentative judgement, open to revision based on how one's partner adapts to contingencies which offer the possibility of opportunistic behaviour.

This suggests a conception of trust as a judgement which comes about over time as part of a virtuous circle of organisational learning, mutual gains and revised judgements concerning trustworthiness. Within this conception, two sorts of obstacle to organisational learning merit attention. First, there is no guarantee that the trust which favours organisational learning will come about, since mistrust and failed learning may also prove mutually reinforcing. On theoretical grounds there is little reason to preclude a vicious circle of mistrust and failed cooperation. Some of the case study evidence presented in this book suggests, however, that in practice the balance may be tipped in favour of positive learning by the careful crafting of the rules which guide response to the unanticipated. Sako (pp. 35–36), for example, based on her comparative study of subcontracting relations in Britain, Japan and the USA, suggests that the key to promoting successful learning is to put in place procedures which provide incentives for firms to make use of their available information not merely to monitor each other's behaviour, but rather to seek continuous improvements in products and processes.

Lorenz and Lazaric (pp. 219–22) develop a similar point based on their studies of inter-firm learning. Lazaric, for example, in her study of technological alliances among robot producers and automobile manufacturers describes some of the creative ways in which problems of intellectual property rights in innovative solutions are managed so as to avoid the conflicts which can breed mistrust. In the case of user-specific software for robots, a typical procedure is to separate the general methodology of the solution from the details of the user's application. The former may be transferred to other clients while the dissemination of the latter is delayed.

The second obstacle to organisational learning derives from the fact that the build-up of trust requires an initial leap of faith, since, as we have have argued above, the information about a potential partner which is publicly available inevitably leaves in place a degree of uncertainty. Edmondson and Moingeon (this volume) develop this point in arguing that in settings where trust is initially low or absent, its development is likely to require the intervention of an outside expert. This is linked to their adoption of Argyris and Schön's (1978) distinction between 'Model I' settings and 'Model II' settings. In Model I settings the organisational members' representations of the organisation and its environment (their 'theories-in-use') are counterproductive in that they not only lead to inefficient outcomes but systematically preclude learning about ways to escape these counterproductive effects. Information exchange is low and perceived threats can lead members to distort information flows. Model II involves going beyond incremental, self-reinforcing change to learning how one's current ways of thinking can be counterproductive. Model II involves learning new 'theories-in-use'.

The self-reinforcing properties of Model I mean that achieving such creative collective reflection typically requires the intervention of an expert:

> In sum, a low-level of trust within an organisation is an obstacle to learning. Lack of trust can create a self-sealing situation, because the existence of this lack of trust as an obstacle is not discussible ... Making the lack of trust discussible requires a high level of trust, which of course presents a dilemma. A skilled interventionist can make the issue discussible, allowing this obstacle to implementing an organisational learning process to be surmounted (Edmondson and Moingeon, p. x).

This solution to the problem of low trust raises a second-order trust problem, however, since there is nothing to ensure that the members of an organisation will trust the interventionist. A possibly more generic solution can be found in applying what Lazaric and Lorenz (p. 222) have termed the 'step-by-step' rule. This rule calls for potential partners to start out by making small commitments to each other and then to increase these commitments progressively depending on the quality of the exchange. In so far as the situation permits divisibility in the level of commitment over time, this rule has the nice property of not only minimising one's losses in the event that trust proves to be misplaced but, as Sako (p. 35) has stressed, of also being formative of trust since it calls for the sort of monitoring and information exchange that is likely to bring trust about. For this reason it may allow individuals to avoid another sort of potential pitfall discussed by Edmondson and Moingeon (p. 262), that of placing excessive trust in another and so promoting abusive use of power.

This discussion of possible errors of judgement and the 'step-by-step' rule brings us back to our point of departure in this introductory chapter: the inadequacy of the semantics of risk and of expected utility maximisation for analysing learning within or among organisations. The orthodox semantics is limited by the premise that agents will only take the first step towards cooperation if they share a complete description world and have well-defined priors over the possible states which allow them to calculate the expected returns from the entire sequence of future interactions. Starting from the premise of bounded rationality, we have argued that long-term contractual relations between organisations are often marked by a degree of incalculable risk associated with surprise and unanticipated discovery. This view is supported by the observation that firms tend to establish partnerships or alliances gradually, through a progressive build-up of their commitments. Such learning exercises are only intelligible in a world where foresight is limited and the success of cooperation cannot be guaranteed in advance.

In concluding this introductory chapter we point to two areas for future research. The first concerns the relation between trust, on the one hand, and contract and institutions on the other. More work of an empirical nature is needed to improve our understanding of which contractual forms and institutional arrangements are most likely to promote trust. Second, while we have argued that trust is a judgement under uncertainty, it remains to be seen whether criteria can be identified as founding this judgement in general.

Livet and Reynaud (p. 276) offer a positive response to this question, and propose a hierarchical set of criteria with a distinct axiomatic flavour. Sako's (p. 38) comparative analysis of supplier relations in Japan, Britain and the USA suggests that this exercise will have to be undertaken with considerable caution, since her evidence shows that the meaning of trust differs among nations and that behaviour which is seen as being consistent with trust in one nation may not be seen in this way in another.

Finally we would suggest that international or inter-regional comparisons provide a privileged means for addressing these issues. By comparing different institutional contexts with quite different legal and employment systems, it should be possible to advance our understanding of the conditions which favour trust and to determine whether such judgements have a national or regional specificity.

NOTES

1 See notably Coriat and Guennif (p. 54), Edmondson and Moingeon (p. 261), Lazaric and Lorenz (p. 218), Rivaud-Danset (p. 83), Sako (p. x), and Livet and Reynaud, (p. 274).
2 See Baudry (pp. 67–68), Coriat and Guennif (pp. 53–54), Lazaric and Lorenz (p. 216–17) and Rivaud-Danset (pp. 82–83).
3 Rivaud-Danset (p. 79) defines a 'state of confidence' as the generalised belief among the members of a population concerning the future state of the economy.
4 See also the comments in Sako (p. 29) on the distinction between interpersonal and interorganisational trust.
5 The definition of trust developed here is close in spirit to that proposed by Diego Gambetta (1988, p. 217).
6 See, however, Dupuy and Torre (this volume) who define trust as a behavioural pattern linked to underlying norms or conventions shared by the members of a community.
7 This point is developed extensively by Livet and Reynaud, who identify trust in organisational settings with an individual's judgement that the others with whom he is involved in some collective endeavour are implicitly committed to it.
8 This point is discussed at greater length in Lazaric and Lorenz (pp. 217–18).
9 More formally, this strategy combination constitutes a 'perfect equilibrium' in the sense that at any stage of the game, given the strategies of others, no player has an interest in deviating from his part of the equilibrium.
10 Corait and Guennif (pp. 57–59) make a similar point in the context of their discussion of the relation between institutions and trust.
11 For a general discussion of stochastic learning models with infinite populations and selfreinforcement, see Dosi and Kaniovski (1994).
12 See also Kirman (1993) and Topol (1991) for similar modelling approaches.
13 This follows the intuition of Keynes (1937, p. 214) who argued for the rationality of imitative behaviour in situations of ignorance. In his analysis of the behaviour of financial traders Keynes observed: 'Knowing that our own judgement is worthless, we endeavour to fall back on the judgement of the rest of the world which is perhaps better informed. That is, we endeavour to conform with the behaviour of the majority or the average'.

14 More formally, he shows that the dynamics of collective opinion define a Markov chain, where the transition probabilities are a function of a parameter measuring the degree of confidence individuals have in the collective opinion. For high degrees of this parameter, the limit distribution of the collective opinion becomes bimodal, with one peak corresponding to a 'bubble' where the majority choose incorrectly.

15 One can, of course, explain cooperation in the finitely repeated game by introducing incomplete information in the arbitrary form of an uninformed player who places a small positive probability on the event that an informed player is an 'irrational' cooperator. The revised equilibrium concept places an extraordinary cognitive load on the modeller, since it is necessary to specify how the players will revise their beliefs to all possible out-of-equilibrium actions to which they gave zero prior probability. How one assigns the out-of-equilibrium beliefs can make or break the equilibrium. (See Rasmusen (1989, chaptor 5) for an introductory discussion of dynamic games with incomplete information).

16 This is also a conclusion drawn by Boyer and Orléan (1995).

17 The distinction we are making here between institutionally based confidence and trust is similar to that made by Luhmann (1979) between 'system trust' and 'personal trust'. Luhmann, however, appears to argue that system trust replaces personal trust in advanced industrial societies, whereas we are arguing that confidence and trust are complementary. For a perspective close to our own which draws on Luhmann's categories, see Lane and Bachmann (1996).

BIBLIOGRAPHY

Argyris, C. and D.A. Schön (1978), *Organisational Learning: A Theory of Action Perspective*, Reading, MA: Addison-Wesley.

Arthur, W. B. (1989) 'Increasing returns, competing technologies and lock-in by historical small events: the dynamics of allocation under increasing returns to scale', *Economic Journal*, **99**, 116–31.

Axelrod, (1984), *The Evolution of Cooperation*, New York: Basic Books.

Boyer, R. and A. Orléan (1995), 'Stabilité de la coopération dans les jeux évolutionnistes stochastiques', *Revue Economique*, **46**, 797–806.

Coriat, B. (1995), 'Incentives, bargaining and trust: alternative scenarios for the future of work', *International Contributions to Labour Studies*, **5**, 131–51.

Dosi, G and Y. Kaniovski (1994), 'On "badly behaved" dynamics', *Journal of Evolutionary Economics*, **4**, 93–123.

Dosi, G., L. Marengo and G. Fagiolo (1996), '*Learning in evolutionary environments*', Working Paper, Department of Economics, University of Rome, August.

Foster, D. and Young, P. (1990), 'Stochastic evolutionary game dynamics', *Theoretical Population Biology*, **38**, 219–32.

Gambetta, D. (1988), *Trust: Making and Breaking Cooperative Relations*, Oxford: Basil Blackwell.

Keynes, J.M. (1937), 'The general theory of employment', *Quarterly Journal of Economics*, **51**, 209–23.

Kirman (1993), 'Ants, rationality and recruitment', *Quarterly Journal of Economics*, **108**, 137–56.

Kreps, D. (1990), 'Corporate culture and economic theory'; in J. Alt, and K. Shepsle (eds), *Perspectives on Political Economy*, New York: Cambridge University Press.

Lane, C. and R. Bachmann (1996), 'The social constitution of trust: supplier relations in Britain and Germany', *Organisational Studies*, **17**, 165–95.

Luhmann, N. (1979) *Trust; and, Power : Two Works by Niklas Luhmann*, Chichester: Wiley.
Maynard Smith, J. (1982), *Evolution and the Theory of Games*, Cambridge: Cambridge University Press.
Ordover, J. (1991), 'A patent system for both diffusion and exclusion', *Journal of Economic Perspectives*, **5**, 43-60.
Ramussen, E. (1989), *Games and Information*, Oxford: Basil Blackwell
Sako, M. (1992), *Prices, Quality and Trust: Interfirm Relations in Britain and Japan*, Cambridge: Cambridge University Press.
Schelling, T. (1978), *Micromotives and Macrobehaviors*, New York: Norton.
Shiller, R. J., (1989), *Market Volatility*, Cambridge, MA: MIT Press.
Topol, R. (1991) 'Bubbles and volatility of stock process: effects of mimetic contagion', *Economic Journal*, **101**, 786-800.

PART I

Notions of Trust in Economic Cooperation

1. The Information Requirements of Trust in Supplier Relations: Evidence from Japan, Europe and the United States

Mari Sako[1]

WHY STUDY TRUST NOW?

A recent wave of interest in trust has swept over the terrain of both inter-firm relations and intra-firm work organisation.[2] Particularly in the area of inter-firm relations, we have seen an upsurge in attempts at understanding the role of trust in two related settings, namely the Italian industrial districts (Piore and Sabel, 1984) and Japanese supplier relations (for example, Minato, 1988; Smitka, 1991; Sako, 1992).[3] What is common in both settings is the interpretation that trust is crucial in enhancing the dynamic efficiency of a region or a country. Specifically, trust enables a network of firms to adapt flexibly to unforeseen circumstances and to engage in continuous improvement and innovation, or what has become known fashionably as 'learning' (Senge, 1990; Sabel, 1992). Within organisations, it is argued that trust between management and labour has become increasingly important as Tayloristic bureaucracies are replaced by learning bureaucracies (Adler and Cole, 1993) that rely on decentralised decision-making.

Uncertain and unpredictable environments make it necessary to rely on trust, but it is also precisely in these circumstances that trust may be abused. In other words, a trust-based system is not free of problems, as the advantages of such a system are packaged with some pitfalls. One such pitfall is the danger of being taken advantage of due to vulnerabilities created by trusting behaviour. For example, a car manufacturer may trust a supplier to deliver daily on a just-in-time basis, but the resulting low inventory levels give the supplier the power to potentially stop the car manufacturer's production by intentionally withholding delivery. Thus a central question often posed in the study of trust is: what mechanisms are available to safeguard trusting actors from opportunists abusing their trust in a society inhabited by people who do not act in a trustworthy manner all the time (Gambetta, 1988)? This chapter argues that this question is misplaced, particularly if trust is valued as a basis for continuous improvement or learning. Safeguards against the abuse of trust – or opportunistic behaviour – are not the same as preconditions for enhancing trust.

Despite the attention paid to the role of trust in economic organisations, trust remains an elusive concept which means different things to different people. There is therefore a need to clarify the concept of trust and to operationalise it so that an appropriate methodology can be applied to empirical studies of trust. This chapter aims to address both the conceptual and methodological aspects of trust between organisations. The empirical work presented in the chapter is drawn from surveys of supplier relations in the automobile and electronics industries.

TRUST AS CULTURE OR AS A CALCULATIVE INVESTMENT? THE JAPANESE CONTEXT

My own exploration into the concept of trust dates back to the time when I was conducting an empirical inquiry into the nature of supplier relations in the electronics industry in Britain and Japan (Sako, 1992). My conceptual tool at the time was transaction cost economics, with opportunism as the central concept in understanding why coordination between production units was undertaken through vertical integration or relational contracting (Williamson, 1985). During the interviews with purchasing and sales managers in Japan, however, I did not come across much reference to opportunism but instead heard a lot about the importance of developing and maintaining trust in successfully executing design, production and delivery.

The centrality of trust in Japanese business was also revealed in a survey conducted by the Japanese Fair Trade Commission in 1987. In this survey, nearly half (47.7 per cent) of the 2241 large company respondents cited 'trust relations accompanying long-term trading' as a reason for engaging in long-term continuous trading (Keizai, 1990, pp. 198–201). This survey led me to believe that the Japanese valued trust relations in themselves, not as a means to an end. Many of my Japanese interviewees also believed that trust is a cultural predisposition of Japanese society – as Dore (1983) had found earlier – and that the economic benefits resulting from trust relations – such as the flexibility afforded in suppliers' involvement in design and development, suppliers' willingness to make suggestions for continuous improvement and cost reduction, and so on – were not plannned but fortuitous. In other words, trust exists in a state of nature and industrial competitiveness is its outcome. According to this view, trust is a cultural norm which can rarely be created intentionally because attempts at cultivating trust in a calculative manner would destroy the affective basis of trust.

Tempting though this assertion might be, and strong though the self-belief about the trusting inclination of the Japanese people, history tells its own story and at least in the area of industrial subcontracting, trust in cooperative behaviour was not the norm in pre-war Japan. For example, subcontracting relations in the machinery industry were fluid and unstable, organised in many cases through intermediary brokers, some of whom charged extortionate fees. Complaints about poor quality were said to be abundant. It was only after the Second World War that firms in electrical and automobile industries started to establish long-term committed relationships with their suppliers through the transfer of technical and management know-how such as Total Quality Control, Just-in-Time and Value Engineering. According to one interpretation, Japanese industry strove to achieve industrial competitiveness first and foremost, and trust was a by-product of an intensive interaction which was necessary to achieve this end.

The stark contrast between the two views – namely trust as a precondition and trust as an outcome of economic development – is rather simplistic, and the reality probably lies in between the two. But when Japanese business is studied with a view to extracting lessons for European or US business, it is tempting to have the cake and eat it. That is, it is argued that not only can we rely on trust to achieve competitive advantage (Barney and Hansen, 1994), but also that trust can be developed intentionally to achieve this end (Smitka, 1991). It would be of no use to those looking for policy prescriptions if the argument were merely that only some nations can benefit from the virtuous circle of high trust and industrial competitiveness while others are stuck in the vicious circle of low trust and industrial deterioration.

Prescriptions for breaking out of the vicious circle of low trust are offered in both a rational and a less rational mode. The recent popularity of game theory came to the rescue of the camp that argued that trust could be created intentionally. Axelrod (1984) argues that mutual expectations of repeated encounters over an infinite time horizon are sufficient to induce partners to act cooperatively, and trust may follow suit. However, trust is more than just cooperative behaviour, and cooperation may occur for reasons other than trust, such as a lack of alternatives or coercion. Moreover, in a finite time period, cooperation may never take root or may not be sustained. An alternative, less rational, prescription has been offered by Sabel who argues that all that is required for mistrust to turn into trust is for the actors to decide to explore the advantages of acting 'as if' they trusted each other (Sabel, 1992, p. 38). The 'as if' basis for acting must rest on the 'quintessential political skill' of individuals in experimenting, and possibly on the invention of traditions and the rewriting of history. This may be a rather tall order in pluralistic liberal democracies and market economies.

This chapter addresses the debate on whether trust is an unintended cultural norm or a calculative investment for economic growth, by focusing on the process of building trust between two business firms. Below, a taxonomy of three types of organisational trust is developed with a view to exploring how the development of one type may impact on the development of the others. This helps us in understanding the interplay between trust as a social norm and trust as a rational investment. The central focus of the taxonomy lies in the firm's ability to verify that the other partner firm has behaved in a trustworthy manner. Such ability depends on a process of intense mutual observation, which in turn depends on the firm's access to various types of relevant information and its capacity to signal its intention as to how the information will be used. Ultimately, the development and maintenance of trust relations require a fair amount of resources in frequent communication and information-sharing between organisations. This is therefore not necessarily economising on transaction costs. Moreover, if information is used to make continuous improvements rather than merely to monitor the other's behaviour, then trust relations would enhance dynamic efficiency. In this sense, the problem of trust in supplier relations is not so much a question of how to safeguard oneself against vulnerabilities and risk in a trading relationship, but more a matter of how to develop an effective incentive system for firms to make continuous improvements individually or jointly.

CONCEPTUAL FRAMEWORK: THREE TYPES OF TRUST

Trust may be defined as a mutual expectation that partners will not exploit the vulnerabilities created by cooperation. In this sense, the decision over whether to trust or not depends on the interpretation of the other party's intention and possible behaviour. The interpretation of whether vulnerabilities have been exploited or not – whether one has been taken advantage of – depends on one's understanding of what behaviour is acceptable. Mutual trust – that is, that each partner is considered both trusting and trustworthy by the other partner – is possible only if there is a shared sense of what is acceptable behaviour.

Trust is important and useful, particularly in facilitating cooperation in uncertain environments and unforeseen circumstances. If there were perfect information and foresight, trust would have no role to play in facilitating coordination between two actors. In uncertain environments, or in unforeseen circumstances, there is a wide range of possible behaviour by each party. What trust enables each actor to do is to narrow down the set of possible actions by the other actor by excluding those actions which are considered unacceptable. In this sense, the other actor's behaviour is more predictable in the presence of trust than in its absence. In other words, while environmental uncertainty is exogenous, the behavioural element of uncertainty is reduced in trust relations.

Predictability in behaviour of the other actor in this sense exists for different reasons, however, and this allows us to distinguish between three types of trust.

First, 'contractual trust' refers to the mutual expectation that promises made are kept. Promises may be written or oral, clearly spelt out in detail or left as tacit understanding. Contractual trust may be based on bilaterally agreed rules between trading partners or a more universal standard or law. For example, suppliers normally agree to produce and deliver ordered goods on the basis of written (or in some cases orally communicated) orders, in the expectation that they will be paid for work done within an agreed period of time after delivery. A payment period may be agreed bilaterally or may follow an industry norm, if one exists.

Second, 'competence trust' refers to a mutual expectation that the other party is capable of fulfilling his promises. Both technical and managerial competence is at stake here. In some cases, a buyer may entrust a supplier to carry out a task that the buyer himself has the ability to carry out. In other cases, he may entrust a specialist supplier to carry out tasks whose technicalities lie outside his comprehension. In either case, it has been conventional for the buyer to inspect components on delivery in order to ascertain whether they meet the stipulated quality standards or not; here the principle of *'caveat emptor'* applies so that the onus is on the buyer to monitor carefully, and sometimes penalize, the supplier for breach of competence trust. Increasingly, however, quality assurance by suppliers has enabled some buyers to do away with inspection on delivery, and to ask suppliers to deliver straight on to the buyer's production line. This indicates a higher degree of competence trust of such suppliers by the buyer. However, in most cases the buyer continues to get information from the suppliers about their quality assurance system and quality records.

Third, a more diffuse kind of trust, which I have come to call 'goodwill trust', is defined as a mutual expectation of open commitment to each other. A commitment is said to be open whenever an actor is willing to respond to a wide range of requests and to take initiatives whenever opportunities for mutual benefit are found. What distinguishes goodwill trust from contractual trust is the expectation in the former that trading partners are committed to take initiatives (or exercise discretion) to exploit new opportunities over and above what was promised. For example, withholding a vital piece of technological information which may determine the commercial success or failure of a risky joint product development project is a breach of goodwill trust but not a breach of contractual trust if the participants of this project are not contracted to supply such information.

This three-way classification of trust, based on reasons for trusting, is useful in furthering our understanding of the concept of trust in the following ways. First, different types of trust resolve to some extent the tension between the conceptualisations of trust as a social norm and trust as a calculative investment. Second, the informational requirement of maintaining trust relations increases as the level of trust is raised in a relationship. Consequently the ability to distinguish between different bases of trust is more important in high trust than in low trust relations. These arguments are developed in turn below.

One way of exploring the relationship between different types of trust is to typologise them in terms of a hierarchy of trust. In this formulation, contractual trust and competence trust may be considered basic prerequisites for two firms to engage in business over a period of time, while goodwill trust at a higher level of hierarchy is something that would give an extra edge to the quality of business relationship. This hierarchy may be thought of as a gradual bottom-up expansion in the congruence of beliefs and norms about what is acceptable as required in trust relations, with a minimum of congruence over the ethical code of keeping promises to a maximum of a shared understanding of joint goals and a shared sense of fairness in the distribution of the benefits and costs of the relationship.

The verification of whether a trading partner is worthy of trust is a matter of relying partly on its reputation before entering into a new relationship and partly on discovery through experience, waiting to see if the original expectation is fulfilled. Because contractual trust and competence trust are predicated on universalistic standards, it is possible to choose promise-keeping and competent companies as new trading by carefully collecting information on general market reputation (for example by checking a company's credit rating, by checking if it has obtained international quality standards such as ISO9000, and so on) as well as by carrying out factory audits. By contrast, goodwill trust is more contextual and therefore verifiable only in particular settings; a buyer and a supplier must start trading and see if they entertain a shared principle of fairness, for example. In this sense, the establishment of contractual and competent trust tends to precede the grounding of goodwill trust in new business relationships. Of course, it is quite plausible that in some societies, such as Japan where people assume a similar set of values and norms in other spheres of life besides business, the rate at which goodwill trust becomes established may be fast. But even in Japan, whenever new supplier relationships are found, as in the case of the relationships between Japanese 'transplants' overseas and their component suppliers, each potential supplier is chosen carefully after an elaborate process of audits and tests, and the relationship starts in a small way before a full-scale order is given. A cautious start is necessary, particularly if an investment is to be made to establish goodwill trust.

Thus it might appear that competence trust is more readily approximated to the calculative investment conceptualisation, and goodwill trust to the social norm conceptualisation, or that contractual trust or competence trust is predicated on universalistic standards while goodwill trust is more particularistic and contextual. However, goodwill trust is not something which just springs out of a national culture; it has to be cultivated in specific business relationships. This process of assessment of trustworthiness in specific contexts, though different from the calculation of expected costs and benefits in a situation of risk, applies to all three types of trust. For instance, contract law may safeguard business firms against breach of contract, but law in itself does not create trust. Contractual trust is ultimately established by actions which can be verified by the other party.

Another element of deliberation in the assessment process is introduced because our current concern is inter-organisational trust, not interpersonal trust. Conflating the two levels of analysis is appropriate only if we are happy with the neoclassical fiction of the firm as a sole proprietor. In the case of inter-organisational trust, the firm may behave in a trustworthy manner, but it is the individuals working for the firm who entertain trust as a belief. Moreover, individuals as a group are the basis of technical and managerial expertise, and these individuals move in and out of the firm with recruitment, quits and retirement. In order that the firm retains the trust of its trading partner, inter-organisational trust must be shielded from such individual movements. A sales manager may be head-hunted by a competitor firm, taking with him a whole set of personal contacts and orders from a valuable customer. The not-so-competent son of a founding owner-manager may take over as the managing director, which may lead its major customer to revise its views on the trustworthiness of this supplier. These are cases in which trust vested in specific people is not extended to trust in the organisation they work for. Inter-organisational trust requires that multiple channels of communication are established at various levels and functions of the two organisations – between managing directors, engineers and even shopfloor workers rather than just between a sales manager and a purchasing manager. Inter-firm trust also requires that much of what individuals have learned and accumulated as their own expertise is taught to others in the organisation. Only then would a firm be able to ensure that trust is institutionalised and long-lived at the inter-organisational level.

Next, the same behaviour may be caused by different factors and intentions, and may therefore be interpreted as trustworthy or untrustworthy. For example, let us suppose that a supplier fails to deliver on time. This failure may well be due to misplaced contractual trust, the supplier having taken on the work with the full knowledge that the capacity to complete the order on time was lacking. Alternatively, it may be an unanticipated machine breakdown due to a lack of experience on the supplier's part in operating the machine. The buyer may decide that the breach of contractual trust is unforgivable and unrectifiable – there is a note of moral opprobrium here – and may wish to terminate the trading relationship. By contrast, a one-time undermining of competence trust may be considered rectifiable with time and technical assistance from the buyer's engineering team. As another example, a buyer might cancel a substantial part of a large order at the last minute. The supplier may interpret this to be due to a general recession, the severity of which was not foreseen by anyone and was outside the buyer's control, or to be due to the buyer's managerial incompetence in not being able to forecast demand accurately. Alternatively the supplier may attribute the cancellation to pure opportunism on the part of the buyer who hoped to extract a low price for a large volume which it never intended to 'call off' in full.

What the above examples show is the importance of distinguishing between 'behaviour' and its possible causes, some of which are to do with 'intentions'. Trust is essentially a state of mind, a belief or an expectation held by one trading partner about another that the other will behave in a mutually acceptable manner. The source of what is acceptable may derive from an ethical code about keeping promises (contractual trust), a professional or technically competent standard of performance (competence trust), or a shared understanding of joint goals and a shared sense of fairness in the distribution of benefits and costs of the relationship (goodwill trust).

In an established relationship of high trust, the ability to distinguish among the three types of trust is important. As indicated above, when behaviour as manifested by one party does not appear to be trustworthy, the other party would attempt to identify the source of apparently untrustworthy behaviour, and to decide whether to continue trading depending on the reasons why the other party failed to behave in an acceptable manner. In most cases, such information is available to the relevant party because of the intense communication between trading partners which commonly accompanies trust relations in business. Thus a buyer facing a supplier with late delivery would be able to verify through a visit to the supplier that the late delivery was due to technical shortcomings which could be rectified in time. The buyer may respond by offering technical assistance to solve any teething problems with a newly installed piece of machinery which were the cause of late delivery. In some cases, however, the buyer may not be able to distinguish clearly among different types of trust immediately. In this case, the buyer is likely to continue trading (that is acting in a trusting manner) unless it is found out that the supplier was capable of, but unwilling to, deliver on time. In this way, the supplier is given the benefit of the doubt for a while.[4]

By contrast, in a state of mutual suspicion or low mutual trust, the trading parties' ability to distinguish between the three types of trust is minimal because the parties tend not to have the relevant information about each other's intentions and the specific circumstances surrounding each firm. Moreover, in this situation, the buyer may think it of no concern to find out if the supplier's late delivery is due to opportunism or to incompetence. The buyer is interested in maximising its own gain regardless of the supplier, and late delivery is late delivery with the same impact on its gain or loss whatever its cause. In this sense, firms in low trust relations are not capable of, and not interested in, distinguishing among different types of trust. This implies that breaking out of a low mutual trust equilibrium requires a willingness on the part of each actor to start to distinguish between different types of trust.

THREE TYPES OF TRUST IN THE AUTOMOBILE INDUSTRY

A large-scale survey of automotive parts suppliers, conducted with the sponsorship of the International Motor Vehicle Programme in 1993–94, was designed in part to further our understanding of the nature of trust in supplier relations. The survey is based on responses from 671 companies in the USA, 472 companies in Japan and 268 companies in Europe. For details on questionnaire design, the sampling framework and response rates, see Appendix A.[5]

Eight items which measure trust (or distrust) in the questionnaire are listed in Table 1.1. Each item is a five-point scale, ranging from 'strongly disagree' (1) to 'strongly agree' (5). The items were chosen to capture the notion of three types of trust. For example, the concept of contractual trust is operationalised by the statement: 'We prefer to have everything spelt out in detail in our contract'. The concept of competence distrust is operationalised by the statement: 'The advice our customer gives us is not always helpful'. Goodwill trust is operationalised by the statements: 'We can rely on our customer to help us in ways not required by our agreement with them' and 'We can depend on our customer always to treat us fairly'. Other items were included to capture the notion of opportunism ('Given the chance, our customer might try to take unfair advantage of our business unit'), the absence of which is a necessary but not a sufficient condition for establishing trust, and the notion of suspicion ('We feel that our customer often uses the information we give to check up on us rather than to solve problems').

oneside

Table 1.1 Trust in automotive supplier relation in Japan, Europe and the USA (per cent agreeing)

	Japan $n = 472$	Europe $n = 268$	USA $n = 671$	In USA Japanese Customers No	In USA Japanese Customers Yes	In USA Japanese – Owned No	In USA Japanese – Owned Yes
We feel that our customer often uses the information we give to check up on us rather than to solve problems	4.66	24.26	25.18	27.12	13.05***	26.00	18.67
The advice our customer gives us is not always helpful	11.41	29.85	23.40	24.53	16.31#	24.00	18.66
We prefer to have everything spelt out in detail in our contract	26.27	54.95	60.95	64.08	41.30***	62.75	46.67#
Given the chance, our customer might try to take unfair advantage of our business unit	5.08	28.73	32.94	36.10	13.04***	34.39	21.33***
In dealing with this customer, we spend a lot of time haggling unproductively over such issues as prices and responsibility for problems	5.93	29.11	28.47	31.09	11.96***	30.37	13.34***
We can rely on our customer to help us in ways not required by our agreement with them	38.77	48.88	36.52	31.78	66.30***	33.39	61.33***
Our business unit has a reputation for being more straightforward and open with our customer than are other suppliers	45.97	57.84	59.61	59.06	63.04	59.06	64.00
We can depend on our customer always to treat us fairly	67.37	46.40	41.88	36.79	73.91***	38.75	66.66***

Notes:
The figures show the percentages responding 4 or 5 on a five-point scale (5 = strongly agree; 4 = agree; 3 = neither agree or disagree; 2 = disagree; 1 = strongly disagree).
Pearson chi-square test on the five point scale is significant at: *** $p < 0.0001$; ** $p < 0.01$; * $p < 0.05$; # $p < 0.10$

When each item is examined separately, it is evident that Japanese suppliers entertain a significantly higher level of trust than US or European suppliers, except in their self-assessment of honesty and openness ('Our business unit has a reputation for being more straightforward and open with our customer than are other suppliers'). Beyond inter-country differences, intra-country variations are worthy of note. For instance, within Japan, suppliers to Toyota are somewhat more trusting of their customer according to a few of the items.[6] Within the USA, Japanese-owned suppliers and those which supply to Japanese customers tend to be more trusting of their customers.

In order to examine whether survey respondents differentiated between different types of trust, factor analysis was performed on the above items. Principal components analysis with Varimax (orthogonal) rotation was used throughout. Of the eight items listed in Table 1.1, one concerning contractual trust ('We prefer to have everything spelt out in detail in our contract') was dropped from the factor analysis because including it produced a factor loading of this item on all factors of below 0.2 in all three regions. Table 1.2, listing the analysis of the remaining seven items, shows that the results are substantially different in the USA, Europe and Japan. In the USA, only one main factor emerged, which combines six items with a Cronbach's alpha coefficient of 0.812. Only the suppliers' self-assessment of their trustworthiness emerged as a separate factor. In Japan, by contrast, three separate factors emerged: Factor 1 (combining four items with a Cronbach's alpha of 0.745) capturing the notion of opportunism and suspicion, Factor 2 (combining two items with a Cronbach's alpha of 0.601) capturing the notion of goodwill trust, and one separate item for competence trust. The European results are more similar to the Japanese than the US results; as in Japan, three separate factors emerged in Europe, capturing notions of opportunism/suspicion, goodwill trust and competence trust, respectively.

The above results lend support to the following conclusions. In Japan, where the level of trust was generally higher than in Europe or the USA, suppliers were discerning enough to be able to differentiate among different types of trust. The following section will examine to what extent this ability to distinguish between different types of trust is due to the suppliers having greater access to relevant information about customers' behaviour. In Europe, which appears to have a general level of trust intermediate between Japan and the USA, suppliers were also able to differentiate among different types of trust. By contrast, in the USA, suppliers conflated different reasons for trusting or distrusting their customers. This appears to be because, as argued earlier, distrust is self-perpetuating when the general level of trust is low; distrust in one area (for example, contractual) induces distrust in another area (for example, competence) due to the lack of information necessary to assess the source of misconduct.

Table 1.2 Factor analysis of trust scales in Japan, Europe and the USA

	USA ($n = 627$) Factor 1 Distrust	Factor 2 Goodwill trust	Japan ($n = 446$) Factor 1 Opportunism	Factor 2 Goodwill trust	Factor 3 Competence trust	Europe ($n = 268$) Factor 1 Opportunism	Factor 2 Goodwill trust	Factor 3 Competence trust
We feel that our customer often uses the information we give to check up on us rather than to solve problems	**0.60371**	0.17288	**0.37787**	-0.04711	0.31169	**0.46781**	-0.24457	0.21794
The advice our customer gives us is not always helpful	**0.39539**	0.02744	0.23630	-0.20161	**0.28703**	0.20302	0.04132	**0.29983**
Given the chance, our customer might try to take unfair advantage of our business unit	**0.82003**	0.03163	**0.71722**	-0.10273	0.07653	**0.73278**	-0.17679	0.00862
In dealing with this customer, we spend a lot of time haggling unproductively over such issues as prices and responsibility for problems	**0.68466**	0.08944	**0.71153**	-0.07332	0.06565	**0.70208**	-0.04962	0.05281
We can rely on our customer to help us in ways not required by our agreement with them	**-0.62093**	0.12872	-0.13262	**0.56388**	0.04762	-0.1668	**0.56309**	0.03289
Our business unit has a reputation for being more straightforward and open with our customer than are other suppliers	-0.15300	**0.18172**	-0.12683	**0.59591**	-0.11537	0.17425	**0.44499**	-0.09626
We can depend on our customer always to treat us fairly	**-0.74418**	0.14223	**-0.55921**	0.35628	-0.03974	-0.36687	**0.59851**	-0.02821
Cronbach's alpha coefficient	0.812		0.745	0.601		0.713	0.591	

THE LINK BETWEEN TRUST AND LEARNING

We turn to theory and evidence on how trust is sustained in supplier relations over time. A central point of argument developed in this section is that high trust goes hand in hand with intense communication and information exchange, and therefore there is no such thing as 'blind trust' in inter-firm relations. Evidence to illustrate this point is drawn from the automotive survey used earlier to measure different types of trust, and a survey of electronic component suppliers in Britain and Japan.

Mutual trust between business organisations can be developed and sustained through intensive observation of each other's behaviour and performance. Such vigilance through access to information about each other's performance, processes and technology is required in order to engage in continuous improvement. Successfully exploiting opportunities for improvement would in turn be interpreted as a manifestation of goodwill trust. This process of continuous improvement is similar to what Sabel (1994) calls 'learning by monitoring', in which monitoring is for the purpose of 'modifying joint tasks and goals' and 'for exploring new possibilities'. This form of monitoring is in contrast to the contractualist view of monitoring which is a mere periodic review of performance to see if the terms of the contract are met. This latter form of monitoring is often considered to be detrimental to the development of trust – monitoring is a sign of suspicion – to such an extent that trust is sometimes equated with the absence of monitoring.[7]

In inter-firm relations, as in personal relations, trust goes hand in hand with access to each other's information.[8] It is how such information is used which matters in developing trust or mistrust. For example, if the supplier believes that the buyer demands to see the supplier's internal quality records only to assign blame to the supplier for the latest delivery batch, then trust is not likely to develop. However, if the supplier expects the same information to be used by the customer to help it improve its quality assurance system, then the supplier is likely to come to trust its customer.

Thus trust does not consist in turning a blind eye to the state of a relationship, and it can occur with intense monitoring. It has even been asserted that, 'a slight amount of suspicion (however that is determined) – a kind of alert but not distracting guardedness – may be facilitative' (Kee and Knox, 1970, p. 358) in developing trust. Trust without monitoring may elicit compliance in a hierarchical command relationship, but not initiative-taking, which is required in learning. The latter requires access to information to evaluate the progress made in any relationship between a buyer and a supplier firm.

The above point concerning the informational requirement of trust and learning may be illustrated by the result of a short questionnaire survey conducted by the author in the electronics industry in 1989 (see Sako (1991, 1992) for details). In particular, the following hypothetical question was posed as part of a questionnaire to a small sample of 18 Japanese and 18 British electronic component suppliers. Following Williamson (1985), the questionnaire defined trust as the absence of opportunistic behaviour:

> When you are negotiating a new order, the customer talks about other favourable offers he is getting, implying that if you don't put the price down, he will switch to sourcing from your competitors instead of from you. By this time, you have become quite dependent on this customer for business, and agree to lower the price. Subsequently, you discover that the story of other offers was entirely fictitious. Is this acceptable? How likely is such a situation to arise? If unlikely, why?

Responses revealed a different code of business ethics between Britain and Japan (see Table 1.3). First, while this behaviour was not quite acceptable behaviour for the majority of respondents, a minority of British, but no Japanese companies, found it quite acceptable. Second, more Japanese than British suppliers responded that such a situation was unlikely to arise. The last question attempted to inquire whether customers' abstention from opportunistic behaviour as described was due to an internalised norm of ethical behaviour or the possibility of sanctions. Only a minority in both countries thought that they relied on the power to sanction alone. A significant number, in fact, thought that both customers' trustworthiness and their power to prevent such a situation from happening were equally important.

One interpretation of this result is as follows. In Japan, a common line of reasoning among those who cited both trust and power was that customers were generally trustworthy, but even if they acted otherwise, the suppliers could easily check who the other competing suppliers were, as they were most likely to be regular suppliers often organised in the same suppliers' association. Such an association facilitates lateral exchange of information between suppliers about their common customer (see Smitka, (1991) and Sako, (1995) for details). Thus access to relevant information is as much a basis for building and maintaining trust as for exercising checks and sanctions.

British suppliers held less information about their customers than Japanese suppliers on average. Some British firms reasoned that the opportunistic behaviour outlined above is not quite acceptable but forgivable as it confers a tactical advantage to the customer in price negotiations. In fact, they claimed

Table 1.3 Survey of electronic component suppliers in Japan and Britain

Question:
When you are negotiating a new order, the customer talks about other favourable offers he is getting, implying that if you don't put the price down, he will switch to sourcing from your competitors instead of from you. By this time, you have become quite dependent on this customer for business, and agree to lower the price. Subsequently, you discover that the story of other offers was entirely fictitious. Is this acceptable? How likely is such a situation to arise? If unlikely, why?

(a) The hypothetical scenario is:	BRITAIN	JAPAN
1. Quite acceptable	5	0
2. Not quite acceptable, but would continue dealing with the customer	10	12
3. Unacceptable, and would never wish to deal with the customer	3	6

(The British Japanese difference is significant at the 5 per cent level using Chi-square test)

(b) The hypothetical situation is encountered:	BRITAIN	JAPAN
1. Quite often	7	2
2. Occasionally from some customers; rarely from others	8	8
3. Hardly ever from any customer	3	8

(The British-Japanese difference is significant at the 10 per cent level)

(c) Of those which answered 2 or 3 to (b)	BRITAIN	JAPAN
Customers rarely behave as in the hypothetical situation because:		
1. Customers are trustworthy	3	8
2. We have the power to prevent it from happening	2	2
3. A combination of 1 and 2	6	6

(The British-Japanese difference is not significant)

to have kept their own suppliers of raw materials in the dark about alternative bids, which the suppliers had little means to verify.

The survey of automotive suppliers discussed in the previous section also lends support to the notion that high trust coexists with much information exchange. The survey asked suppliers what kind of information they received from their customers, and what kind of information they provided to their customers. Table 1.4 shows that in all three regions (Japan, Europe and the USA), the information flow from customers to suppliers has a positive impact on suppliers' trust of their customers, and in particular on goodwill trust. The flow of information from suppliers to customers has different links with trust depending on the type of trust. First, goodwill trust is associated with more information, perhaps indicating suppliers' willingness to disclose somewhat confidential information (for example, about the cost of each process step) to their customers once trust of this type is established. Second, suppliers' competence trust of their customers is associated with 'less' information provided by suppliers. Also, at least in Japan, contractual trust is associated with less supplier information. This negative correlation between trust and information flow indicates that suppliers' provision of information to customers on its own is associated with an increase in suppliers' mistrust of their customers. It appears that one-way flow of information from the supplier to the customer is regarded with suspicion by the supplier as a sign of increased control and monitoring.

Does the act of customers reciprocating with the provision of their own information to suppliers help to enhance trust? In order to gauge the extent to which reciprocity in information exchange is important in enhancing trust, the gap between the amount of information suppliers provide to customers and the amount suppliers receive from customers was measured. There is weak evidence that the smaller this gap – that is the more equally two-way the information flow – the higher the level of trust (see Table 1.4).

Next, the survey asked how often someone from the supplier company had a substantive discussion concerning issues such as design changes and quality problems with its customer. Frequency ranged from more than once a day to every six months or less often. The average frequency was weekly for all three regions in the case of face-to-face contact, and slightly more in the case of telephone and fax contacts. Interestingly, the frequency of communication was not significantly different between suppliers who entertained a high level of trust towards their customers and those with low trust of their customers. This was the case for all types of trust.

What makes a difference in the quality of the relationship is not the mere frequency of communication but how the contact time is used between the trading partners. In particular, the survey shows, as expected from the earlier discussion, that high trust, as compared with low trust, is associated with a

Table 1.4 Information exchange and trust in automotive supplier relations[9]

		Supplier information	Customer information	Information gap
Japan				
Contractual trust	H	3.70	1.43	2.27
	L	4.14*	1.57#	2.56#
Competence trust	H	3.83	1.49	2.34
	L	3.72	1.28*	2.44
Goodwill trust A	H	3.99	1.59	2.41
	L	3.71*	1.39**	2.31
Goodwill trust B	H	3.81	1.52	2.28
	L	3.84	1.36**	2.49
Opportunism	H	3.96	1.17	2.79
	L	3.81	1.49*	2.33
Europe				
Contractual trust	H	4.47	1.45	3.02
	L	4.76	1.54	3.22
Competence trust	H	4.49	1.49	3.01
	L	4.94#	1.53	3.41#
Goodwill trust A	H	4.74	1:69	3.05
	L	4.52	1.32**	3.20
Goodwill trust B	H	4.65	1.54	3.11
	L	4.61	1.47	3.14
Opportunism	H	4.42	1.38	3.04
	L	4.71	1.55#	3.16
USA				
Contractual trust	H	4.61	1.29	3.32
	L	4.73	1.33	3.40
Competence trust	H	4.59	1.30	3.29
	L	4.99**	1.37	3.62*
Goodwill trust A	H	4.97	1.49	3.47
	L	4.53**	1.22***	3.31
Goodwill trust B	H	4.66	1.40	3.26
	L	4.70	1.25**	3.45
Opportunism	H	4.62	1.19	3.42
	L	4.72	1.38**	3.34

Note: T-test is significant at: *** $p<0.0001$; ** $p<0.01$; * $p<0.05$; # $p<0.10$.

Table 1.5 Purposes of automotive suppliers' contacts with customers

Percentage of time spent for the purpose of:		Assigning blame rather than solving problems	Joint efforts to improve product or process
Japan			
Contractual trust	H	3.56	30.61
	L	3.03	32.31
Competence trust	H	3.08	31.21
	L	6.09**	29.80
Goodwill trust A	H	3.19	35.23
	L	3.57	28.39**
Goodwill trust B	H	2.85	33.81
	L	4.62**	25.35**
Opportunism	H	3.96	29.33
	L	3.40	31.14
Europe			
Contractual trust	H	6.38	30.62
	L	7.35	31.97
Competence trust	H	6.25	31.35
	L	8.45	31.38
Goodwill trust A	H	5.74	33.53
	L	8.02	29.28
Goodwill trust B	H	4.33	35.33
	L	8.95**	28.19*
Opportunism	H	12.62	24.87
	L	4.59***	33.97**
USA			
Contractual trust	H	5.98	27.33
	L	9.67**	34.21***
Competence trust	H	6.21	32.45
	L	14.82***	28.49
Goodwill trust A	H	3.97	37.12
	L	10.67***	28.31***
Goodwill trust B	H	3.74	37.00
	L	11.46***	27.58***
Opportunism	H	13.88	25.60
	L	5.45***	34.43***

Note: T-test is significant at: *** $p < 0.0001$; ** $p < 0.01$; * $p < 0.05$; # $p < 0.10$.

smaller proportion of the suppliers' contact time with their customer which is spent on 'assigning blame rather than solving problems' and a greater proportion of time which is spent on 'joint efforts to improve the product or process' (see Table 1.5). Thus frequent contacts in themselves are not conducive to the development of trust between a supplier and a buyer. The contacts must be perceived to be productive in continuous improvement and learning before a trading relationship is deemed to be based on high trust.

CONCLUDING REMARKS

The study of trust in supplier relations has become popular due to the increasing importance of coping with decentralised decision-making and initiative-taking in an uncertain business environment. Trust relations are considered important as a source of industrial competitiveness in Japan. This interest in Japan detracted from our understanding of the concept of trust by over-emphasizing the interpretation of trust as a cultural norm. However, a purely calculative mode of evaluating risk when all contingencies are known at the start is not a promising basis for understanding trust either (Williamson, 1993). This is because trust is most useful in a condition of uncertainty and bounded rationality, less so when risk calculations enable actors to assess expected costs and benefits of entering into, or sustaining, a relationship.

Although not a complete solution to this tension between trust in a purely calculative mode and trust in a non-calculative or affective mode, this chapter has outlined a typology of trust consisting of contractual trust, competence trust and goodwill trust. Partners in a high trust relationship would wish to, and can, distinguish among the three types of trust because of intense communication and information exchange which take place between them as a basis for engaging in continuous improvement. In contrast, parties in a low trust relationship would neither wish to nor are capable of distinguishing among the different types. The results of the large-scale survey of automotive suppliers lend support to this point.

Trust between organisations depends on mutual vigilance. It is the beliefs about how information is used which matters in maintaining a fine balance as between a trusting–learning relationship and a distrustful–monitoring relationship. Empirical evidence from both the automotive and electronics sectors supports this conceptual framework in which rich information flows and trust go hand in hand.

Some unresolved issues remain. In particular, conceptual disagreements persist over the usage of the term 'trust', with some wishing to use it broadly for all types of relationships in which one party depends on the other party for the execution of tasks, while others wish to restrict it to a non-calculative affective mode of relations at the personal level. Empirically, mutual trust is less well studied than trust from one side only. Moreover, the process of developing and sustaining trust may be better studied longitudinally rather than cross-sectionally. We need panel data to untangle the causal relationship between information exchange and trust. We have come a long way from being satisfied with laboratory experiments (Deutch, 1958; Axelrod, 1984), but our challenge is to attempt to draw generalisable conclusions from a study of the development of trust for which specific situations and sequences of events are likely to matter greatly.

APPENDIX A: QUESTIONNAIRE DEVELOPMENT AND COLLECTION OF DATA IN THE AUTOMOTIVE INDUSTRY

Data were collected by the author in collaboration with Professor Susan Helper at Case Western Reserve University during 1993 and 1994 from 671 first-tier automotive component suppliers in the USA, 472 suppliers in Japan and 268 suppliers in Europe according to the following procedure.

Questionnaire Design

A questionnaire was developed in English and Japanese in order to inquire into a broad range of issues concerning the nature of suppliers' relationships with their customers, the vehicle manufacturers. Because many companies supply their customers with several different types of product, and their relationships with their customers differ by product, respondents were asked to answer the questionnaire for their most important customer regarding one product which was typical of their company's output and with which they were familiar.

Many of the questions were taken from an earlier survey undertaken by Helper in North America in 1989 (Helper, 1991) and a short questionnaire on trust and opportunism administered by Sako in the electronics industry in Japan and Britain in 1988–89 (Sako, 1992). The measures of trust and opportunism were developed by surveying the academic literature in economics and psychology (for example, Anderson, 1988; Cook and Wall, 1980; Cook et al. 1981). The questionnaire was designed with the view more common in psychology than in economics that creating composite measures of trust would reduce measurement error, as compared with using a single measure. Thus the questionnaire adopted a number of items, each reflecting different types of trust.

Pilotting the Questionnaire

The draft questionnaire was sequentially piloted at a handful of supplier companies in the USA and Japan during 1992. As a result, improvements were made to the clarity of questions and the ease of answering them. Much attention was paid to the phrasing of questions in a vocabulary familiar to managers, and to the consistency of meaning in the English and Japanese languages. For instance, we asked several people to translate some questions from English to Japanese and others to translate them back from Japanese into English. The process of piloting and revision took around nine months.

Sampling Framework

The sample chosen for the North American questionnaire was every automotive supplier and auto maker component division named in the *Elm Guide to Automotive Sourcing* (available from Elm, Inc. in East Lansing, Michigan). This guide lists the major first-tier suppliers (both domestic and foreign-owned) to manufacturers of cars and light trucks in the United States and Canada.

In Japan, the sample consisted of all members of the Japan Auto Parts Industries Association (JAPIA), all automotive suppliers named in *Nihon no Jidosha Buhin Kogyo 1992/1993* (Japanese Automotive Parts Industry, published by Auto Trade Journal Co., Inc. and JAPIA, Tokyo, 1992), and the component divisions of vehicle manufacturers. This publication lists all the first-tier suppliers (both domestic and foreign-owned) to the manufacturers of cars and trucks in Japan.

In Europe, the sample was compiled from several sources, including trade associations (for example, the Society of Motor Manufacturers and Traders in the UK) and the major vehicle manufacturers in Europe. The combined list of companies is deemed to be comprehensive in its coverage of major automotive suppliers in Western Europe.

The target respondent in the USA was the divisional director of sales and marketing, and the divisional business manager or director of strategic planning in the case of components divisions of vehicle manufacturers. In Japan, the questionnaire was sent to the director of sales and marketing at independent firms. For member companies of JAPIA, the survey was sent to the main contacts named by JAPIA, many of whom were either chief executives or marketing directors. The Japan Auto Manufacturers Association took responsibility for identifing the respondents for auto maker components divisions. In Europe, the target respondent was the director of sales and marketing in each firm.

Response Rates

The questionnaires were sent out in spring 1993 in the USA, summer 1993 in Japan and spring 1994 in Europe. The responses were far above the norm for business surveys: 55 per cent in North America, 30 per cent in Japan (45 per cent among JAPIA members) and 17 per cent in Europe (25 per cent among UK-based suppliers), after taking into account those firms which were unreachable (mail sent to them was returned undelivered) and those which were not eligible to answer the survey (they were not first-tier automotive suppliers or they specialised in supplying for heavy trucks and buses). The respondents had a wealth of experience, and were thus able to answer all of our questions for the customer/product pair they chose. US respondents averaged more than 18 years in the automobile industry and more than 11 years with their company. Japanese respondents had worked for 22 years on average at their company. European respondents had an average of 16 years experience in the automotive industry and eight years' experience with their company.

NOTES

1 Reader in Industrial Relations, London School of Economics, Houghton Street, London WC2A 2AE. Tel. +44 171 955 7037; Fax +44 171 955 7424; E-mail: m.sako@lse.ac.uk.
2 It is noteworthy that before trust received recent attention, prominent economists had known for quite some time that the concept of trust is central in understanding industrial development and national competitiveness. Just over a century ago, J.S. Mill noted that, 'the advantage to mankind of being able to trust one another penetrates into every crevice and cranny of human life' (Mill, 1891, p. 68). A couple of decades ago, Arrow wrote in a similar vein: 'virtually every commercial transaction has within itself an element of trust, certainly any transaction conducted over a period of time. It can be plausibly argued that much of the economic backwardness in the world can be explained by the lack of mutual confidence' (Arrow, 1975, p. 24).
3 Lorenz's study of subcontracting in the French engineering industry (1988) and an ongoing study by Lane and Bachmann (1994) on supplier relations in the mining machinery industry and the kitchen furniture industry in Germany and Britain, are both valuable in diversifying the country context in which the role of trust is investigated.
4 This lagged relationship between trust as belief and trusting behaviour is emphasized by Kee and Knox (1970). They make a distinction between the observable behaviour which is of a dichotomous nature (one chooses either a trusting or a suspicious behaviour), and a subjective state of mind which is of a continuous nature. It is then assumed that a person must reach a threshold level of subjective trust before it becomes manifest as behavioural trust. Conversely, a person must feel that the other person is sufficiently untrustworthy before he switches to a suspicious behavioural option.
5 This section is based on the work I have conducted jointly with Susan Helper. See Appendix A and Sako and Helper, (1995), for details.

6 In particular, significant differences existed for competence trust (5.83 per cent of Toyota suppliers, as compared with 12.97 per cent of non-Toyota suppliers, agreed with the statement: 'The advice our customer gives us is not always helpful'), and for goodwill trust (76.70 per cent of Toyota suppliers, as compared with 64.87 per cent of non-Toyota suppliers, agreed with the statement: 'We can depend on our customer always to treat us fairly').

7 For example, Williamson (1993, p. 483) defines personal trust as a situation in which a person X: (1) consciously refuses to monitor person Y, (2) is predisposed to ascribe good intentions to Y when things go wrong, and (3) treats Y in a discrete structual way. Williamson appears to conflate the absence of a calculative mode to developing trust with the absence of monitoring. But even in high trust personal relations, such as in a marriage or true friendship, there is often periodic mutual vigilance, albeit not at all times and places.

8 Deutsch (1958) also emphasized the importance of communication in developing cooperative behaviour, which he interpreted to be a manifestation of trust. He applied a definition of a trusting choice as one in which the actor perceives that the occurrence of a beneficial event or a harmful event is contingent on the behaviour of another person, and that the expected harm is greater than the expected benefit, but still allows himself to be confronted with this risk. In Deutsch's experiments, it was shown that mutual trust, defined in this way, is most likely to occur when people are positively oriented to each other's welfare. However, mutual trust can occur even under circumstances where the people involved are overtly unconcerned with each other's welfare, provided some situations hold. One of these is the 'opportunity and ability to communicate fully a system for co-operation which defines mutual responsibilities and also specifies a procedure for handling violations and returning to a state of equilibrium with minimum disadvantage if a violation occurs' (Deutsch, 1958, p. 279).

9 Notes to Table 1.4:

Definition of trust items. Each item is on a 1–5 scale with 5 = strongly agree; 4 = agree; 3 = neither agree nor disagree; 2 = disagree; 1 = strongly disagree. In order to create dichotomous variables, the sample was divided into H (high trust) and L (low trust) according to each item. The scores for H follow.

Contractual trust: 1, 2 or 3 to 'We prefer to have everything spelt out in detail in our contract'.

Competence trust: 1, 2 or 3 to 'The advice our customer gives us is not always helpful'.

Goodwill trust A: 4 or 5 to 'We can rely on our customer to help us in ways not required by our agreement with them'.

Goodwill trust B: 4 or 5 to 'We can depend on our customer always to treat us fairly'.

Opportunism: 4 or 5 to 'Given the chance, our customer might try to take unfair advantage of our business unit'.

Definition of information exchange.

Supplier information: Information provided by the supplier to the customer about the process used to make the product. One point each for the following:

- Detailed breakdown of process steps;
- Cost of each process step;
- Financial information not publicly available;
- Production scheduling information;
- Type of equipment used;
- Your sources of supply;
- Detailed information regarding materials you use.

Customer information: Information the customer provides to the supplier. One point each for:

- Warranty or other data from final consumers;
- Financial information not publicly available;
- Information on how your product is used in their process.

Information gap: defined as (Supplier information) minus (Customer information).

BIBLIOGRAPHY

Adler, P.S. and R.E. Cole (1993), 'Designed for learning: a tale of two auto plants', *Sloan Management Review*, Spring, 85–94.

Anderson, E. (1988), 'Transaction costs as determinants of opportunism in integrated and independent sales force', *Journal of Economic Behaviour and Organization*, **9**, 247–64.

Axelrod, R. (1984), *Evolution of Cooperation*, New York: Basic Books.

Barney, J.B. and M.H. Hansen (1994), 'Trustworthiness as a source of competitive advantage', *Strategic Management Journal*, **7**, 175–90.

Cook, J. and T. Wall (1980), 'New work attitude measures of trust, organizational commitment and personal need non-fulfilment', *Journal of Occupational Psychology*, **53**, 39–52.

Cook, J.D. (1981), *The Experience of Work: A Compendium and Review of 249 Measures and Their Use*, Orlando: Academic Press.

Deutsch, M. (1958), 'Trust and suspicion', *Journal of Conflict Resolution*, **2** (4), 265–79.

Dore, R. (1983), 'Goodwill and the spirit of market capitalism', *British Journal of Industrial Relations*, **34**, 459–82.

Gambetta, D. (ed.) (1988), *Trust: Making and Breaking Cooperative Relations*, Oxford: Basil Blackwell.

Helper, S. (1991), 'How much has really changed between US automakers and their suppliers?', *Sloan Management Review*, Summer, 15-28.

Kee, H.W. and R.E. Knox (1970), 'Conceptual and methodological considerations in the study of trust and suspicion', *Journal of Conflict Resolution*, **14** (3), 357–66.

Keizai, K. (Economic Planning Agency) (1990), *Keizai Hakusho* (Economic White Paper), Tokyo: Okurasho.

Lane, C. and R. Bachmann (1994), *Risk, Trust and Power: The Social Constitution of Supplier Relations in Britain and Germany*, chapter prepared for the Work, Employment and Society conference, University of Kent, 12-14 September 1994.

Lorenz, E.H. (1988), 'Neither friends nor strangers: informal networks of subcontracting in French industry', in D. Gambetta (ed.), *Trust: Making and Breaking Cooperative Relations*, Oxford: Basil Blackwell.

Minato, T. (1988), 'Shitauke torihiki ni okeru ''shinrai'' zai no keisei katei' ('The formation of ''trust'' as an asset in subcontracting'), *Shoko Kinyu*, **10**, 7–10.

Piore, M. and C. Sabel (1984), *The Second Industrial Divide: Possibilities for Prosperity*, New York: Basic Books.

Sabel, C.F. (1992), 'Studied trust: building new forms of co-operation in a volatile economy', in F. Pyke and W. Sengenberger (eds), *Industrial Districts and Local Economic Regeneration*, Geneva: International Institute of Labour Studies.

Sabel, C.F. (1994), 'Learning by monitoring: the institutions of economic development', in N.J. Smelser and R. Swedberg (eds), *The Handbook of Economic Sociology*, Princeton, NJ: Princeton University Press.

Sako, M. (1991), 'The role of ''trust'' in Japanese buyer–supplier relationships', *Recherche Economique* **XLV** (2–3), 449–74.

Sako, M. (1992), *Prices, Quality and Trust: Inter-Firm Relations in Britain and Japan*, Cambridge: Cambridge University Press.

Sako, M. (1996), 'Suppliers Associations in the Japanese automobile industry: collective action for technology diffusion', *Cambridge Journal of Economics*, **20**, 651–72.

Sako, M. and S. Helper (1995), 'Determinants of trust in supplier relations: evidence from the automotive industry in Japan and the USA', London School of Economics mimeo, London.

Senge, P. (1990), *The Fifth Discipline: The Art and Practice of the Learning Organization*, New York: Doubleday.

Smitka, M. (1991), *Competitive Ties: Subcontracting in the Japanese Automotive Industry*, New York: Columbia University Press.

Williamson, O.E. (1985), *The Economic Institutions of Capitalism*, New York: Free Press.

Williamson, O.E. (1993), 'Calculativeness, trust and economic organisation', *Journal of Law and Economics,* **36**, 453–86.

2. Self-Interest, Trust and Institutions

Benjamin Coriat and Samira Guennif[1]

This chapter is a systematic attempt to assess the strengths and limitations of certain key contributions to the development of the emerging theory of trust. The ultimate aim of the authors is to highlight the key role played by institutional factors in the establishment and consolidation of mutual trust within an economic universe marked by conflicts of interest.

More specifically, the study has a threefold aim: first, to demonstrate how the need for a theory of trust has evolved; second, to contribute, within this framework, to the search for the appropriate definition of trust; and third, to clarify the role played by institutions in the creation of relations of mutual trust.

At this stage the authors only offer some preliminary observations which should contribute to an ongoing debate on this promising theme which requires further investigation.

THE NEED FOR A THEORY OF TRUST AND ITS APPEARANCE IN ECONOMIC THEORY

The first question to be addressed concerns the conditions which led to the development of a theory of trust. Its emergence in the field of economics might, *a priori*, seem surprising, given the standard assumptions of methodological individualism and utilitarian optimising.

Trust and Uncertainty

The reasons for the emergence of the concept of trust in economics are easy to formulate. It was developed as a response to the problem of uncertainty in the relationship between economic 'agents'. From a theoretical point of view, trust is, above all, a consequence of uncertainty.[2] In orthodox neoclassical modelling, with perfect rationality and complete information, there is no place for trust, or for anything closely resembling it. An auctioneer monitors the equilibrium between price and quantity in a market which functions perfectly. Admittedly, as Arrow (1976) postulates, trust is present as an 'invisible institutional factor'. But it simply facilitates trade, and within the framework of general equilibrium it is simply assumed in the sense that the market is automatically equipped with the institutions which guarantee its regulatory and optimising function. Within standard theory there is no clear conceptualisation of trust.

When economic agents act in circumstances of uncertainty, and when markets fail (that is, adjustments are not optimizing), the need for a theory of trust becomes more apparent, especially if the hypothesis of self-seeking agents is upheld. In a state of uncertainty, and with opportunistic agents, economic transactions cannot develop without there being extremely high transaction and contracting costs, since each agent seeks by way of ever more sophisticated contract specifications to protect himself from the opportunism of the other. Thus if something like trust is possible between economic agents, it should reduce the need for, and the cost of contracts. Consequently, trust becomes an efficient mode of economic coordination.

Trust, Uncertainty, Calculativeness

Nevertheless, a state of uncertainty does not justify in itself the need for an explicit hypothesis on the nature of trust. Even in conditions of uncertainty, some neoclassical theorists have made conceptual allowances which eliminate the need for such a hypothesis.

Two of these should be mentioned here.

First digression: two attempts to invalidate the need for trust within individualistic approaches: their inherent contradictions

Trust, incentives and control: agency theory If uncertainty is conceived within the framework of an agency relationship, and if the rationality of the agents is substantive but limited, incentives will be enough to reduce uncertainty. In this case, no hypothesis about trust is needed.

Nevertheless, this result cannot be obtained without making two 'heroic' assumptions. That they are implicit does not negate the fact that they are untenable. The first assumption is that the costs of monitoring and checking the controllers themselves (to temper the effects of moral hazard and adverse selection) are ignored, otherwise these costs may become prohibitive and cancel the savings which derive from the logical device which was set up to eliminate the need for a hypothesis concerning trust. The second assumption is that only a limited form of uncertainty is postulated, involving asymmetrical information.[3]

Oliver Williamson: authority and hierarchy The other major attempt to do away with explicit hypotheses on trust comes from the transactional approach, as formulated by Williamson (1985). Even if the agents are not fully rational (they 'satisfice' rather than maximise), two distinct arguments are proposed:

1. Under conditions of uncertainty, vertical integration and hierarchy, in so far as they establish a relation of authority, create a climate of confidence. Authority reduces the number of unknown factors and eliminates the need for trust.[4]
2. Alternatively, even without vertical integration, if the agents are calculating there is no need for trust to explain their behaviour. Behaviour which is supposed to fall within the ambit of trust should rather be interpreted as calculated behaviour – not of the first degree but of the 'nth' degree. As such, it cannot be classed as trust.

However, neither of these arguments is tenable. One depends on the other, which in turn only holds because of a very restrictive implicit assumption, thereby destroying the generality of the argument. Let us examine these assumptions again.

In response to one of Williamson's main arguments, it should be noted that vertical integration – and the authority relation – generate costs of coordination which *a priori* are impossible to limit. To assume that vertical integration reduces uncertainty by economising on the costs of transacting is an inadmissable shortcut. Nothing permits us in advance to assert that the costs of internal coordination will not be such that they make the hierarchy unworkable. And in this case, one has to take into account the behaviour of self-seeking agents active throughout the market (or some 'hybrid' version of market and hierarchy). This brings us directly to the second argument.

We are in agreement with Williamson when he states that in this 'no man's land', which ranges from a perfect market to hybrid forms, if behaviour is calculative in the strictest sense of the term (that is, if the future, including the effects of interactions, can be probabilised), then trust does not exist. Calculative trust is a contradiction in terms,' Williamson (1993, p. 471).[5]

If we assume conditions of radical uncertainty, and if the effects of the interaction are not predictable *a priori* because agents learn something from each interaction and modify their response,[6] then behaviour in accordance with the pursuit of self-interest will develop. These forms of behaviour are not strictly calculative, however, but constitute 'bets' or 'wagers' on the long-run effects of different forms of behaviour and interactions; 'wagers' which attempt to guide the evolution of the relation by a logic which cannot only be accounted for by calculation of future gains.

Are such situations conceivable? In the opinion of Williamson, they generally are not. He identifies two exceptional cases. On the one hand, these situations are confined to the special case of 'non-calculative' trust which applies to 'very special relations such as those between family, friends and lovers'. This 'personal trust' (Williamson,1993, p. 484) is too restricted to be integrated into the theory of exchange. On the other hand, if something approaching trust-based behaviour appears[7] (a form of 'non-calculative trust' but still within the domain of transactions between economic agents) it suffices to consider the general context within which this behaviour evolved. As soon as the limits imposed by institutions are taken into account, Williamson is led to interpret the forms of behaviour which typify 'trust' relations as, in fact, being ones of obligation (the case analysed by Williamson is that of mutual help between farmers, a case initially expounded by Coleman, 1982). It should be noted that for Williamson the inclusion of institutional factors transforms trust into obligation and prevents 'cooperative behaviour' from being construed as trust. But this amounts to the assumption that strategic behaviour in the presence of institutions is no longer possible. Obviously, this is untenable. Opportunism, like trust, can be manifested within the institutions in which the agents operate. We shall return to this key point later.

For the moment, we may merely note that in a universe where the future cannot be predicted with accuracy, even in the presence of institutions, something beyond the simple calculation of one's self-interest (by definition impossible to formulate) is possible, and this element may pertain to trust.[8]

Second digression: the concept of 'trust' in the theory of games and an impasse: probabilistic trust and the matrix of gains

The concept of trust which derives from game theory is pertinent in this respect. Consider the famous 'prisoners' dilemma' which arguably illustrates the need for a theory of trust in order to explain how agents can overcome the strong incentives to defect and so reap the benefits of mutual cooperation. In fact, all this shows is that cooperative behaviour is 'superior' to self-seeking behaviour as regards each player's gain.

Two cases may be envisaged. On the one hand, the economic agents do not start out knowing the matrix of gains, in which case if they pursue their own self-interest their behaviour is necessarily self-serving. Trust cannot arise in these circumstances. On the other hand, if agents do have the matrix of gains at their disposal, and they find it in their interest to cooperate, this is necessarily a calculative act which should not be taken for trust. Consider a game with an infinite number of moves, and in which information is more or less complete. However sophisticated the game may be, the simple fact that one refers to a matrix of gains implies that the future is predictable, and the probability of future events can be calculated. It is no longer a question of 'trust', but of self-interest calculated to optimise gains in period '*n*'. The calculation is inter-temporal but the results of the interaction are predictable. It is in this sense that game theory may postulate the equilibrium properties of cooperative behaviour (or of trust) between partners over purely opportunistic behaviour. However, it can only reach this conclusion by assuming that the matrix of gains is known in advance. The conventions of 'trust', which the theory demonstrates as being superior, are derived from inter-temporal optimising behaviour. They derive from calculativeness rather than trust.

INFERENCES: TRUST AND ITS CHARACTERISTIC FEATURES

There are several things that may be inferred from the features of trust outlined above, including the conditions under which it emerges.

The Attributes of Trust

First elements: a definition *a contrario*

Proceeding *a contrario,* we will now capitalise on these insights by formulating several behavioural propositions which the theories discussed above were unable to do.

It may first of all be asserted that trust only exists if economic agents operate in a universe where there is radical uncertainty rather than one in which the probability of future contingencies can be calculated. One decides to behave cooperatively towards the other despite the possibility that such behaviour is in neither his short nor his long term self-interest. Even if it were clearly evident that cooperative behaviour was in the immediate self-interest of the agent, he would have no guarantee that this behaviour would be optimal in the long term. (We have already stated that if the matrix of gains is known, behaviour termed 'cooperative ' cannot be taken as signalling trust but rather as optimising inter-temporal utility.)

Trust, interest, risk: towards a positive definition of trust

It may be deduced from the above that trust relations can only be considered as such if they carry an uncalculable risk for the agent who initiates them. Since the notion of trust is inseparable from that of self-interest, a trust-based relationship is one in which an agent gives his partner something which may prove in the future to have been in his interest to have kept for himself, and which he assumes will be in his partner's future interests as well. This form of behaviour is termed 'pure' trust.[9]

At this point, a distinction needs to be drawn between behaviour based on trust and 'altruistic' behaviour: the former is compatible with the pursuit of self-interest, while the latter is not. Having said this, behaviour based on 'pure' trust may be defined as an act whereby at least one of the partners refrains from opportunistic behaviour in the hope that this will produce a superior gain in the short or long term. In this way, even if trust means 'letting down one's defences' and making oneself vulnerable, it is not entirely a leap into the unknown, no more so than an act of faith. It is an act that is in one's interests, but one that inevitably carries a risk in a universe where the probability of future events cannot be calculated. The contribution by Lorenz (1988) analysing the relations between subcontractors and dealers in the Rhône-Alpes region is in keeping with this point. In the case studies presented by Lorenz, after establishing commercial relations, the entrepreneurs proceeded by progressive testing. If the risks are real, they are borne by progressive stages. There is no 'leap into the unknown', and trust grows with an increasing number of transactions.

In this spirit, if we do not wish to dissociate trust-based behaviour and the intentions surrounding and defining it from the pursuit of self-interest, one further step must be taken. Trust-based behaviour is favoured initially because it may be revoked at any moment. Risk-taking is only possible in a universe where self-interest is pursued if it is accompanied by the possibility of withdrawing trust. As a result, trust can only develop within the framework of a series of repeated actions, the intervals between which serve as periods of verification. These interactions, which facilitate periodic reassessment of reciprocal behaviour, offer the possibility of continuing or breaking off the trust relation. We will return later to the key issue of the 'reciprocal' nature of the trust relation and the role played by reciprocity in the construction of trust.

Interaction, Learning, Reputation

At this point, it is necessary to introduce the notions of learning and experience within the trust relationship. If trust evolves, it means that we are not dealing with interactions which are identical on each occasion within the series of exchanges, but with what may be termed 'meaningful' repetition: a term used here to describe the notion of interaction as opposed to 'simple' repetition. Defined in this way, an interaction is characterised by the fact that it provides additional information and meaning about the partners' behaviour. This qualification concerning the notion of interaction explicitly raises the question of the link between trust and information. We have already noted above that trust arises in conditions of uncertainty; *ipso facto* it is a means to reduce this uncertainty. It is in this sense that interaction amounts to 'meaningful' repetition. The additional information provided contributes to establishing a minimum of predictability in the behaviour of a partner. This is similar to Sako's perception of trust when she postulates that trust enables one, '...to increase the predictability of mutual behaviour by honouring commitments whilst at the same time facilitating the treatment of unexpected contingencies in a mutually acceptable way' (Sako,1992).

In our case, the interaction provides information about the partner's use of the trust placed in him. It is in this sense, as well, that a risk may be taken. It is not only because the added information provided periodically by each interaction enables the risk to be reduced. Furthermore, and this seems to us to be the final meaning of learning, each player is enriched by the information gained in all previous interactions and can modify his behaviour over time. Each new move can be played differently; the player may or may not renew existing trust, reinstate a more tentative trust relation, or place himself in a position which directly threatens his partner.

Information, reputation, experience.

It is at this point that the notion of 'reputation' (Shapiro, 1983) comes in. Granovetter sees reputation as the totality of a mass of vague pieces of information which may determine the agent's decision to trust his partner. Thus reputation may precede trust and encourage an agent's commitment. However, the relation of trust can only be maintained if the agent lives up to this reputation (that is, experience shows that trust has not been abused). So even in this case, it is experience which allows trust to take root. Trust always results from the agent's interpretation of his partner's use of the trust placed in him. Experience may precede trust or may stem directly from it, but in either case a trust-based relationship will only survive if it is supported by experience.

For any economic agent, the experience which derives from interaction is the only guarantee needed to assume the risk implied in placing his trust in another. In this sense, one can argue that experience is more fundamental than the information which constitutes an agent's 'reputation'. In any case, it is experience which allows one to interpret and validate the disparate pieces of information which make up a reputation.[10]

In this sense, the relation of trust, like that of reputation to which it is linked, results from a process and can be built upon, but we propose to show that whereas a reputation can be built by one agent independently, trust relations can only be based on reciprocity between agents.[11]

The reciprocal nature of the trust relationship.

If agents are motivated by self-interest and if they take risks, but these risks are periodically assessed thereby permitting behaviour to be modified, durable behaviour based on trust can only develop if it is reciprocated. In a relation based on repeated acts, with agents motived by self-interest, trust is either reciprocated or it does not emerge at all. Given that any one of the agents may, at any moment, cease to trust the other, the trust relation can only be self-reinforcing when, time after time, the players' actions confirm and consolidate the relations of trust. Any other situation would amount to a contradiction. Assume a relationship between one agent who repeatedly displays trusting behaviour towards another who responds with self-seeking behaviour. There are only two conceivable explanations for this:

1. On the one hand, he may pursue the trust relation because he has no other choice: he is in a situation where power is unequally distributed. By definition, this type of behaviour cannot be based on trust. Behaviour based on trust always presupposes that opportunism is an option but that it is non-opportunistic behaviour which is preferred.[12]
2. On the other hand, given the choice between opportunism and trust, he opts for the latter knowing full well that his partner will respond with opportunism. By thus refusing to pursue his own self-interest his behaviour becomes 'altruistic', which is radically different from trusting behaviour. Thus 'reciprocity' is at the heart of the relation of trust.

If we wish to examine the notion of 'reciprocity' more closely, two points need to be emphasized. Compare the notion of reciprocity with 'concession' and 'counter-concession' as introduced into the theory of exchange by Mauss (1995). Following Camener (1988), the concession/counter-concession relation, taken in its strictest sense, cannot in any way be considered as trust-building with a view to reducing uncertainty. Camener recalls that, for Mauss, one concession automatically calls forth another; a partner extracting a concession undertakes at the same time to grant a counter-concession. The relation is not based on trust, but rather expresses an 'obligation'. It is in this sense that Camener states that the behaviour is 'certain'.

The second point is linked to a distinction introduced by Dore (1987), who examines the nature of fully functioning reciprocity. According to him, only reciprocity in its wider sense attests to a verifiable relation based on trust (of the 'pure' trust type). Indeed, in reciprocity defined in the wider sense, the agents make a concession without in fact knowing whether this will call forth a counter-concession and whether it will be of equal value. Dore points out that in the context of this type of relation, a counter-concession may take a long time and be of a different value from the one to which it is intended to respond. Conversely, in an exchange based on 'narrow' reciprocity, the agents attempt to make concessions of equal value. We have here 'an exchange of friendly services', which should not be confused with a relation based on trust.

'Pure' and Actual Trust: the Key Role Played by Institutions

How do we pass from a state of 'pure' trust to trust as it is actually observed? In other words, can the purely theoretical situation we have just described really exist and, if so, under what conditions?

Uncertainty and institutions

As we have seen, there are some negative responses to the question: does trust-based behaviour exist and, if so, what legitimacy may be given to it? According to Williamson, such behaviour is unthinkable in economic exchange. For him, the existence of trust is confined to special cases (friendship, for example) and cannot usefully be considered in the theory of trade.

A more sophisticated argument incorporates the role of institutions to explain that what may have passed for trust is, in fact, obligation, or, alternately, that the inclusion of institutions transforms the nature of the relations which may, *a priori,* be interpreted as based on trust but in reality are based on obligation.

Williamson's analysis serves as a useful point of departure for a more general examination of the role played by institutions in the establishment of trust, the last important topic to be examined here. Williamson's argument on this point is entirely summed up in the fable concerning 'reciprocal aid between farmers', taken from Coleman (1982). It shows that if the field of observation is widened to include the 'informal organisation' within which the farmers operate, then, '...if accidents occur with stochastic regularity ... an informal reciprocal aid mechanism is one possible institutional response'.[13] In order to avoid the ever-present risk of opportunism, penalties are necessary, and from that moment onwards 'calculativeness' in the presence of possible penalties explains everything and 'trust aids for nothing'.

Two points are worth noting here. The first is linked to the implicit assumption by Williamson that no relation (in this case, Coleman's example of reciprocal aid between farmers) can be qualified without recourse to institutional mediation, that is, without first taking into account the institutional context. This argument is essential, since it underlines once again the fact that once the particular setting is characterised by uncertainty it is necessary to have recourse to explicit hypotheses about institutions in order to qualify and interpret behaviour. If the notion of an institution is taken in its widest sense to include norms, conventions, customs and the like, it must be noted that the designation of the degree and dimension of uncertainty is closely linked to the hypotheses made about the institutional framework. There is a close link between the concepts of uncertainty and institution, with one depending on the other (cf. the theme of 'embeddedness' as developed by

Granovetter (1985, 1994). It is to Williamson's credit to have stated this in the clearest possible way. As we shall see in a moment, this proposition, besides having solid theoretical foundations, has been borne out and clarified by applied studies on trust, more particularly those demonstrating how the institutional and contractual framework within which the agents operate gives rise to different forms of trust or opportunism (see below).

Parallel to this proposition, Williamson puts forward a second more controversial one. He states that via the existence of a 'penalty', uncertainty (probability cannot be attached to future events) is 'reduced' in such a way that the threat of a penalty transforms radical uncertainty into 'calculativeness'. This proposition is largely refuted by the large body of literature on the theory of contracts, of which Williamson was paradoxically one of the pioneers. For even if we accept that institutions reduce the risk factor – which is their primary function (see North, 1992) – they never totally eliminate the possibility of conflicting interpretations of the body of rules which would cause conflict to re-emerge and create ambiguity. Consequently, whatever the importance attached to these factors, differences of interest persist and give rise (via conflicts of interpretation) to opportunistic behaviour. In spite of his considerable insights into opportunism, Williamson does not take this proposition into account.

From Granovetter (1984, 1985) to North (1992), an important school of thought attempted to show how institutions play both a 'general' role in reducing risk, in the sense that they fix the limits within which the agents act, and the more specific role of providing a body of rules and contracts which contribute to the nature of the relations (of opportunism, trust and mistrust) arising from it. Fox (1974), for example, speaks of 'institutional trust', a term which he clarifies by observing that, '...trust, and mistrust, are perceived as being embedded in the rules, roles and relations which certain individuals impose or try to impose on others'.

The large number of applied economic studies in this field have clarified the often complex nature of the relations between trust and institutions. We shall attempt here to give the main conclusions from these studies. As we shall see, this digression into applied political economy, however brief, will enable us to confirm certain observations which have only been suggested so far, while at the same time allowing us to improve our understanding of the conditions under which such relations are established.

Contracts, opportunism and trust: some conclusions from applied economics

Despite the diversity of the contexts and the chosen fields of application, applied studies on inter-firm relations agree on several key points. We have chosen to focus our attention on four that bear a direct relation to the questions under review:

1. The first contribution of these studies is to confirm that the (*a priori*) non-specifiable nature of contracts is a given fact in inter-firm relations which opens the way to a wide range of behaviour, from opportunism in the strictest sense to variable degrees of trust. Consequently, even if trust in no way stems from uncertainty, it is nevertheless uncertainty that makes it possible and creates the need for it. Besides confirming that authority and hierarchy are in general unable to resolve the problems which arise from the unspecifiable nature of contracts, these studies show that inter-firm relations develop along a continuum which includes a complex group of specified and non-specified relations. Sako (1993), for example, is induced to postulate the existence of three forms of trust, entitled 'contractual', 'competent' and 'goodwill' trust. Basing her study on a comparison between Great Britain and Japan, she observes, in forms specific to each social context, the evolution and the strengthening of different forms and 'degrees' of trust.[14]
2. Another important contribution of these studies is to highlight the fact that 'institutions' and the specific contractual conditions from which they emanate, including various forms of penalty, constitute, in the final analysis, the factor which encourages the agents to risk renouncing their opportunistic behaviour. It is only with the institutional guarantee of risk reduction, which is always relative, that the agent will engage in trust-based behaviour. This seems to be the best explanation for the lengthy procedure involved in setting-up 'quality certification' with suppliers. This procedure ranges from inspections and tests to, finally, a ranking (from A to E), which is a prerequisite for 'partner relations' (Gorgeu and Mathieu, 1990; Lorenz, 1993), and which helps to set up trust-based relations. This clearly seems to show that the object of product quality – given the constraints of deadlines and cost penalties – is too important to be left to market forces. The visible hand of the institutional framework which acts as a common horizon is in this case preferred by both partners to the solutions offered by the free market (Coriat, 1995a). The institution, acting as a risk-reducer, appears to promote trust but cannot guarantee it.[15]
3. Another essential contribution of these applied studies has been to show how, in the face of all the hazards and unknowns inherent in the execution of a contract, significant 'contractual strategies' arise which influence the form of the contract. There are abundant examples showing how differences in contractual arrangements will have different effects on performance depending on the manner of dealing with unknowns. Consequently, if institutions are a necessary condition, all institutions are not equally effective in building and fostering trust (that is, they do not

do away with authority and incentives). Sako already reaches this conclusion, but it is more clearly expressed by Asanuma (1989), who, regarding what he calls 'relational rent', states that the conditions under which the rent is received are largely determined by the conditions which *a priori* determine how they will be shared. Asanuma goes on to say that these conditions are included in the contracts which make allowance for different arrangements for sharing the risk, and thereby also for sharing the relational rent (on this point, see also Aoki, 1991; Sako, 1991; Coriat, 1994). There is no better way than by using this small-scale example to prove the importance of institutions or contracts, right down to the details of the arrangements they generate.

4. A final conclusion of these studies is the fact that the establishment of a relationship based on trust is a complex process which is essentially revocable and which can only materialise if there is reciprocity. Lorenz, in particular, shows in his studies (1988, 1993) how, by stressing the two key elements of 'experience' and 'learning', trust can only develop over a series of interactions, the effects of which cannot *a priori* be predicted. In any process of trust-building, the very fact that it can only develop because it is revocable means that there is also a dimension of self-reinforcement.

Having reached the end of this overview, and having clarified the nature of the trust relation, a key question remains to be answered: in a universe of self-seeking agents motivated by self-interest, why should trust arise? Moreover, why should trust arise in preference to a relation based on opportunism? It is with this in mind that we wish to make some concluding remarks.

CONCLUDING REMARKS: TRUST, INSTITUTIONS AND INCENTIVES

The question of why trust is established was answered in part when it was pointed out that the moment it becomes reciprocal and an efficient means of coordination and problem-solving, it is in the interests of both parties.

Nevertheless, this answer alone is insufficient, for it fails to explain why the agents would take the risk of entering into a relationship based on trust 'before' reaping the gains that are to be had from it. Consequently further work is needed on this point.

This chapter suggests that future research on this question should be oriented towards the proposition that it is agents' view of certain characteristics of the institutional framework in which they function which determines whether or not they enter into a trust relation. In other words, it is asserted that, as risk-reducers, institutions are enabling factors in the building of trust; they allow agents to 'risk' a trust relation as opposed to one based on opportunism. Consequently, the building of trust feeds on institutions. Similarly, it is supposed that the trust relation cannot dispense with the use of authority and incentives. In the given institutional contexts, incentives are seen to be a determining factor in the decision to 'enter' into a trust relation.[16]

Likewise, the construction of trust – even in its 'pure' form as defined in this text – is linked in a subtle way to authority and incentives. Further study of the nature of the relations between institutions, authority and incentives as a means of understanding more clearly how confidence is established and consolidated, would be an important further research agenda.

NOTES

1 An earlier version of this paper was presented to the International Seminar on 'Trust, Learning and Economic Anticipation', held at the University of Technology of Compiègne, from 23 to 25 January 1995. The authors are both members of CREI (Centre for Research in Industrial Economics, University of Paris 13).

2 This point is clearly illustrated, for instance, by Akerloff, who by using a procedure which gives uncertainty a central place (cf. his well-known paper which appeared in 1970), stresses the role of trust as an efficient mode of coordination between agents (see also his 1982 article).

3 For an explanation of this dual critique of the agency theory, see Coriat and Weinstein (1995).

4 Note, however, that Williamson's assertion raises a delicate question: that of the status of trust vis à vis that of authority, a question which Kreps in particular has studied. According to Kreps, Williamson's position can be objected to on the following grounds: if trust is an 'exclusive' mode of coordination (that is, its use excludes the use of authority and incentives at the same time), then Williamson's argument holds. However, if we reject this idea and postulate that the use of trust may accompany that of authority, the question is to know whether trust and its construction are based on the use of authority (partly or fully) or whether the use of authority stems from trust. Kreps supports the latter proposition, showing that authority needs to rest on trust if it is to function efficiently. Kreps's analysis is interesting in that, like Williamson, he speaks of hierarchy, but this does not lead him to accept the idea of a strict dichotomy between authority and trust (Kreps, 1991, p. 97).

5 On this development, see the remarkable clarification undertaken by A. Orléan (1994a).

6 On this point see Lorenz's contributions (Lorenz, 1988, 1993) which will be cited again later in the text.

7 In this context, such behaviour is based neither on immediate interest (the agent renounces opportunistic behaviour), nor on his '*n*' ranked interest, the probability of which can by definition not be calculated.

8 Recall that the case presented by Coleman (1982) concerns a farmer who, as a result of not having his tractor at his disposal, is in danger of losing his entire crop because of rain. This is only avoided because another farmer, without posing any conditions or asking for anything in return, lends him his own tractor to enable him to harvest before the onset of the rain. Coleman sees in this situation an example of trust, a fact which Williamson contests.

9 Note, on this point, that from a neo-transactional perspective, Klein, Crawford and Alchian (1978) open the way to the possibility of opportunistic behaviour – even in a quasi-integrated universe – as regards the sharing of rents. On this discussion, see also Monteverde and Teece (1982).

10 Note that this definition of trust is close to the one proposed by Lorenz as far back as 1988.
11 In this sense, and as Lorenz asserts, even if reputation can play a role in the emergence of trust (conceived of here as 'pure trust'), it is experience which finally determines whether the trust relation is to be maintained or not.
12 Several of the contributions in Gambetta (1988) stress this point.
13 The 'informal reciprocal aid mechanism' considered here by Williamson is one which leads the farmers – because of custom – to help one another spontaneously when they are in difficulty, particularly when these difficulties (such as rain which threatens to destroy a crop) cannot be exactly forecast.
14 Of the three types of trust postulated by Sako, only the third, that of 'goodwill', has certain similarities to what we have designated 'pure trust'. But we may also observe that each of the other forms contains an element of 'risk' which cannot be directly evaluated, which transforms these relations into trust relations in the sense in which we have defined them. On this point, we may also observe that the notions of 'contractual' and 'competence' trust are included in Fox's (1973) notion of 'institutional' trust.
15 On this point, too, Kreps (1991) has a contribution to make. He recalls certain basic principles of company culture. Consequently, the setting up of institutions which govern the relations between individuals fosters trust, that is to say, respect for these institutions or trust in the person responsible for applying them.
16 Note that if we refer to the work of Sako (1992), the institution in this form permits us to build contractual and competence trust (or the institutional form of Fox, 1973). The assertion that the establishment of these forms of trust is only an enabling factor, and the elucidation of the conditions under which 'goodwill' trust or 'pure' trust arise, remains an open question. Lorenz (1993) begins to answer the question when he speaks of 'long relations' between individuals, which makes us think in terms of the 'neither friends – nor strangers' relations which are related to the process of learning and acquiring experience .

BIBLIOGRAPHY

Akerlof, G. (1970), 'The market for lemons: quality, uncertainty and the market mechanism', *The Quarterly Journal of Economics*, **84**, August, 488–500.

Akerlof, G. (1982), 'Labor contracts as partial gift exchange', *The Quarterly Journal of Economics*, **XCII** (4), 543–69.

Aoki, M. (1991), *L'Economie Japonaise, Information, Incitations et Marchandages*, Paris: Economica.

Arrow, K. (1976), *Les Limites de l'Organisation*, Paris: PUF.

Asanuma, B. (1989), 'Manufacturer–supplier relationships in Japan and the concept of relation-specific skill', *Journal of the Japanese and International Economies*, **3** (1), 1–30.

Baudry, B. (1992), 'Contrat, autorité et confiance: la relation de sous-traitance est-elle assimilable à la relation d'emploi', *Revue Economique*, **43** (5), 871–94.

Baudry, B. (1993), *Contrat, Autorité et Confiance: Une Etude des Mécanismes de Coordination dans la Relation de Sous-Traitance*, Doctoral thesis in economics, Université Pierre Mendès-France, Grenoble.

Camener, C. (1988), 'Gifts as economic signals and social symbols', *American Journal of Sociology*, **94**, 180–214.

Coleman, J. (1982), *The Asymmetrical Society*, NewYork: Syracuse University Press.

Coriat, B. (1994), *Penser à l'envers*, Paris: C. Bourgois, third edition.

Coriat, B. (1995a), 'Variety hierarchies and networks – the metamorphosis of the Fordist firms', *Industrial and Corporate Change*, **4** (1), 205–27.

Coriat, B. (1995b), 'Incentives, bargaining and trust: alternative scenarios for the future of work', *International Contributions to Labor Studies*, **4**, Winter 131–51.

Coriat, B. and O. Weinstein (1995), *Les Nouvelles Théories de l'Entreprise*, Paris: Hachette, Le Livre de Poche, Collection Références.

Dore, R. (1987), *Taking Japan Seriously*, Oxford: Stanford University Press.

Fox, A. (1974), *Beyond Contract: Work, Power and Trust Relations*, London: Society Today and Tomorrow.

Gambetta, D. (ed.) (1988), *Trust: Making and Breaking Cooperative Relations,* New York: Basil Blackwell.

Gorgeu, A. and R. Mathieu (1990), 'Partenariat ou sous-traitant? Qualité et ressources humaines chez les fournisseurs de l'automobile et de l'aéronautique', *Centre d'Etudes de l'Emploi, Research Dossier*, **31**, July.

Granovetter, M. (1985), 'Economic action and social structure: the problem of embeddedness', *American Journal of Sociology*, **91** (3), 481–510.

Granovetter, M. (1994), 'Les institutions économiques comme constructions sociales: un cadre d'analyse', in A. Orléan (ed.), *Analyse Economique des Conventions*, Paris, Economica, pp. 79–95.

Guennif, S. (1994), *Recherche sur une Théorie de la Confiance: Pluralité du Concept, Fondements Théoriques et Application de la Sous-traitance dans l'Industrie Automobile*, DEA dissertation, University of Paris 13.

Guerrien, B. (1992), *La Théorie des Jeux*, Economica, Paris.

Klein, B., R. Crawford and A. Alchian (1978), 'Vertical integration, appropriable rents and the competitive contracting process', *Journal of Law and Economics*, **21**, 297–326.

Kreps, D. (1991), 'Corporate culture and economic theory', in E. Alt and K.A. Shepsle (eds.), *Perspectives on Positive Political Economy,* Cambridge: Cambridge University Press, pp. 90–144.

Lorenz, E. (1988), 'Neither friends nor strangers: informal networks of subcontracting in the French industry', in D. Gambetta (ed.) (1988), *Trust: Making and Breaking Cooperative Relations,* New York: Basil Blackwell.

Lorenz, E. (1993), 'Flexible production systems and the construction of trust', *Politics and Society,* **21** (3), 304–22.

Mauss, M. (1995), *Sociologie et Anthropologie*, Paris: PUF, 6th edition.

Monteverde, K. and D. Teece (1982), 'Appropriable rents and quasi-integration', *Journal of Law and Economics,* **25**, 321–28.

North, D.C. (1992), 'Institutions', *Journal of Economic Perspective*, Winter, **5**, 97–112.

Orléan, A. (1994a), 'Sur le rôle respectif de la confiance et de l'intérêt dans la constitution de l'ordre marchand', *La Revue de Mauss,* **4**

Orléan, A. (1994b), *Analyse Economique des Conventions,* Paris: Economica.

Sabel, C. (1992), 'Elaborer la confiance: de nouvelles formes de coopération dans une économie volatile', in D. Foray and C. Freeman (eds.), *Technologies et Richesses des Nations, Paris: Economica,* pp. 419–50.

Sako, M. (1991), 'The role of trust in Japanese buyer–supplier relationships', *Recherche Economique*, **2–3**, April–September, 375–400.

Sako, M. (1992), *Prices, Quality and Trust, Inter-Firm Relations in Britain and Japan*, Cambridge: Cambridge University Press.

Shapiro, C. (1983), 'Premiums for quality products as return to reputation', *Quarterly Journal of Economics,* **98** (4), 552–79.

Williamson, O. (1975), *Markets and Hierarchies: Analysis and Anti-trust Implications*, New York: Free Press.

Williamson, O. (1985), *The Economic Institutions of Capitalism*, New York: Free Press.
Williamson, O. (1993), '*The Economic Analysis of Institutions and Organisation. In General Respect to Country Studies*', OECD Working Paper No. 133, Paris.

3. Trust in Inter-Firm Relations: Multiple Forms of Coordination

Bernard Baudry

INTRODUCTION

This chapter looks at the various forms of coordination that exist between firms in a quasi-integrated relationship. By forms of coordination we mean devices which allow the buyer to overcome the uncertainty that results from exchange involving complex products.

Our analysis of these forms of coordination tests two assumptions. First, although trust is a powerful form of coordination in a quasi-integration relationship, it does not stand alone; authority and incentives are also important. Second, devices to support trust are not the same for two distinct forms of quasi-integrated relationships, which we shall refer to as 'vertical' and 'oblique'.

The following section describes the different forms of quasi-integration between buyers and suppliers where there is significant informational asymmetry leading to the drawing up of incomplete contracts. In Section 3 we argue that trust is one possible response to an incomplete contract. In transaction cost economics and agency theory, trust (and distrust) influence the strategic behaviour of individuals, but in our analysis trust, supported by the social context and interpersonal relationships, is a form of coordination which reduces transactions costs. In Section 4 we show that trust is not the only form of coordination; it occurs in conjunction with authority or incentives depending on the type of quasi-integration.

QUASI-INTEGRATION AND LACK OF CONTRACTUAL COMPLETENESS

Figure 3.1 overleaf provides a diagrammatic representation of industrial organisation, where the vertical axis refers to the duration and the rigidity or flexibility of the buyer/supplier relationship. The horizontal axis reflects the supplier's degree of involvement in product design and production.

When quasi-integration is vertical, the buyer totally controls product design, and information transmission takes place vertically. This is equivalent to subcontracting where the subcontractor does not take any initiative. The duration of the relationship is short, often less than a year

Product design

Buyer ----------------------------> **Supplier**

Rigidity

Subcontractor/supplier

Oblique quasi-integration

Flexibility

Vertical quasi-integration

Figure 3.1 Different forms of quasi-integration.

Oblique quasi-integration occurs when product design is the result of collaboration between the two parties: the buyer provides the functional specifications for the product, leaving the design to the supplier (for example, automobile manufacturers). The duration of the relationship is at least medium term, and is often longer.

Thus there are two modes of buyer/supplier relationship: external flexibility associated with strict buyer control over supplier production, and external rigidity associated with the supplier's active participation in product design. Quasi-integration is the result of informational asymmetry between contracting parties. On the one hand there is *ex ante* uncertainty concerning the quality of the product offered by the supplier and his ability to fulfil the contract. On the other hand, there is *ex post* difficulty for the buyer in controlling the supplier's behaviour and in knowing if the supplier is minimizing production costs and disclosing them accurately.

In the face of informational asymmetry, when limited rationality and opportunism are assumed, it is impossible to draw up complete explicit contracts guaranteed by law (Williamson, 1985). What, then, are the forms of coordination that would facilitate an agreement between buyer and supplier?

TRUST

Trust is a possible response to uncertainty and could be said to be necessary whenever exchanges occur. To trust somebody *ex ante* assumes that the degree of risk associated with exchange is very low. In other words, in inter-firm relationships a client who trusts a supplier assumes that, independently of other forms of coordination, the contracting party will not default on his contractual obligations. The main questions will then be: what are the procedures which support this trust? Does trust constitute an independent form of coordination or does it combine with other forms? Before answering these questions, we briefly summarize, and criticize, the two approaches to trust which are taken by transaction cost economics and agency theory.

Trust and Contract

Trust and transaction cost economics

For the transaction cost economist, trust does not support transactions when they become risky. In the words of M. Granovetter, the firm is 'a functional substitute to trust' (1985, p. 489). Indeed, individual opportunism is an essential assumption. As Williamson sees it, opportunism represents a lack of honesty in exchange and involves 'self-interest seeking with guile' (1975, p. 26); it leads to manipulation of information or misrepresentation of intentions, in contrast to 'stewardship behaviour' which suggests that a promise can be considered an obligation. Strategic behaviour does not impede exchange so long as this assumption is not combined with an assumption of bounded rationality. In fact it is quite possible, as in agency theory, to establish a contingent claim contract which restrains opportunism. Neither does an assumption of bounded rationality without an assumption of opportunism create contractual difficulties; the contract is clearly incomplete but if unanticipated events occur, contractors using 'good faith' will find a way to adapt the contract to the new situation with minimal harm to both parties. In fact Williamson's analysis is more subtle than this: 'I do not insist that every individual is continuously or even largely given to opportunism. To the contrary, I merely assume that some individuals are opportunistic some of the time and that differential trustworthiness is rarely transparent *ex ante*' (1985, p. 64).

Opportunistic behaviour is thus a 'threat' which can impede exchange when specific assets are engaged in the transaction (the possibility of replacing a contractor then becoming costly). On the other hand, if the market is perfectly 'contestable', opportunism does not create contractual problems.

In a more recent text Williamson (1993) suggests a new interpretation of the concept of trust as 'calculative trust', which adds little to the understanding of inter-firm relationships. Non-calculative trust occurs when there is a decision not to monitor, when good intentions are assumed in the face of things going wrong, and the parties treat each other in a discrete structural way. Consequently it is only relevant to the analysis of 'very special relations between family, friends, and lovers'(Williamson, 1993, p. 483).

This analysis of the market can be compared with Hobbes's 'state of nature': how can the actions of individuals be coordinated when they have different interests, yet must cooperate to fulfil a contract? In other words, how to ensure cooperation in the absence of trust, when it is impossible to draw up a contract specifying duties and obligations to cover all contingencies. We know Hobbes's answer: individuals must renounce their liberty to an external authority which guarantees internal security to the group. Likewise, Williamson sees hierarchy, or the firm, as an institutional device which creates the authority to suppress bargaining and to impose rules of litigation.

This is an argument that is open to criticism. First, authority in the firm does not totally prevent strategic contractual behaviour when individual actions are not subject to observation. Although authority provides the means to exercise strict control on individuals, control does not solve the problem of effort measurement and it is costly to the organisation. Furthermore, this mechanism does not take into account the possible opportunism of auditors: who guards the guardians? Second, the market has its own norms and collective controls so that no actor, even an opportunist one, can manipulate it fully. This is an aspect that Williamson ignores. Third, we note A. Hirschman's (1986) analysis of the market which accepts that 'voice' is a powerful coordinating force and that contracting parties use promises to facilitate exchange.

Trust and agency theory

In incentive theory, and especially in agency theory, opportunism is not analysed as it is in transaction costs economics, from an *ex post* point of view but, because of the rationality hypothesis, it is more concerned with *ex ante* incentive alignment (that is, opportunism is constrained by incentive contractual safeguards). Nevertheless, and contrary to transaction cost theory, trust is not ignored but is analysed as an incentive mechanism; it represents a strategy which reduces agency costs. This strategy is supported by two incentive devices: reputation and relationship duration. Pratt and Zeckhauser (1984) indicate that, 'a large stock of value that could be lost through bad behaviour, such as reputation or assets subject to suit, is a strong incentive for good behaviour'. Reputation is thus assumed to be an incentive mechanism conducive to trust. The second mechanism is durability. For Pratt and Zeckhauser, 'long-term relationships, among other benefits, develop the stocks of value needed for enforcement and make limited monitoring more effective'.

The relationship between reputation and trust is analysed in a recent text of Kreps (1990). We can summarize it as follows. Two conditions are necessary to induce cooperation and generate trust: a game with an infinite tree, and reputation. In a repeated game between A and B, if B chooses not to cooperate on one occasion then A will break its relationship with B. Reputation is built by repeated cooperation. Individuals A_i, who have not previously exchanged with B, will have the confidence to do so because of the reputation that B has acquired. So reputation generates trust and such an arrangement is self-enforcing.

In fact, this is the game theory argument in which the probability of a continuing relationship allows a conflictual game to be transformed into a non-conflictual game; the durability of the relationship is comparable with an investment which is profitable. From one point of view individuals have an 'interest' in behaving honestly and in eluding opportunistic behaviour; in this sense trust is not really analysed; individuals are not electronic calculators.

This manner of conceiving trust is criticised by Williamson (1993). He argues that it is irrelevant to treat trust in terms of game theory as he sees only calculative trust and, 'calculative trust is a contradiction in terms'. This follows from Dasgupta (1988, p. 49): 'if the incentives are right, even a trustworthy person can be relied upon to be untrustworthy'. So when reasoning from the perspective of game theory, reputation is a sufficient concept, and reference to trust adds nothing. Finally, the use of trust by Kreps is merely 'incidental' because 'the intertemporal mechanism is the key' (Williamson, 1993, p. 474).

Neither transaction cost economics nor agency theory can explain trust as a coordination mechanism in inter-firm relations, so we propose an alternative explanation.

Trust and Social Norms

It is our contention that both interpersonal links and the social context in which a transaction takes place help to generate a reciprocal trust between firms. Analysis of industrial districts and localised industrial systems (Becattini, 1992) has stressed the importance of obligation and cooperation norms in the exchange process. Exchanges taking place between firms within the same industrial network lead to systems of preferential choice and, as a result of common beliefs and values, economic exchange is transformed into social exchange (Lorenz, 1993). For instance, the subcontractor or local supplier chosen is not always the most economically obvious one. Only by analyzing the social system within which these decisions are taken can such apparently irrational behaviour be understood.[1]

In inter-firm relationships the strength of one's obligation to conform to norms of cooperation depends on the geographical proximity of the contracting parties. The social context within which the transaction takes place becomes critical to understanding what, *a priori*, appears irrational. For instance, an important local buyer who generates a large volume of business may not always have a supplier selection strategy that follows economic principles.

In game theory, cooperation is the result of individual interests, but the anthropological and sociological approach emphasizes collective norms to support exchange. This debate concerning 'culture versus rationality' interprets the durability of relations in two contrasting ways: agency theory says that cooperation is created by a long-term contract between rational individuals, the sociological approach emphasizes norms.

Trust and interpersonal relationships.

Interpersonal relationships generate trust independently of other forms of coordination between contracting parties. For Granovetter (1985), it is not people's characteristics that are important, but the relationships that people establish among themselves. In contrast to neo-institutionalists, who see individuals as undersocialised, the 'embedding' argument stresses the role of strong personal relationships and of the structures of these relationships in producing trust and discouraging dishonesty.

Eymard-Duvernay and Favereau note that personal links may constitute a non-institutional means of enforcing exchange. Following Boltanksi and Thevenot (1987) they describe a 'domestic' model of the firm, highlighting the importance of actors' personal acquaintance and of link stability. Trust is supported by long-term relationships between individuals and objects that create 'domestic coordination'. French law takes this domestic logic into account by introducing the notion of *'intuitus personae'*. Exchange involving standardised goods in a spot market does not create *intuitus personae* because the seller is not responsible for the good's quality and price is the only variable factor.

In inter-firm relationships, the choice of supplier, and the eventual renewal of a contract, sometimes takes place within a context of relational exchange. Between small firms, supplier selection and contract renewal occur in a domestic exchange context because quality constraints are not as strong as between large and small firms, and because small firms do not have the resources to undertake stringent selection procedures. The choice of supplier thus becomes a network issue. Within industrial districts relationships are personalised and can be based on trust, thus reducing transaction costs.

In France subcontracting has a strong regional bias (INSEE, 1990) which is independent of technical and logistical considerations. Regional subcontractors are known and their reliability has been tested by other buyers. Numerous buyers establish relationships that involve real technical cooperation. If there is no formal, written contract, the age of the relationship can be important, but does not preclude temporary interruptions, for instance as a result of non-competitive pricing or as penalties for problems with poor quality or delivery dates.

In a well-known empirical study, Macaulay (1963) stressed the importance of personal relationships in buyer/supplier interactions. He noticed that the implicit component of the contract is large in comparison with the explicit component. In addition, a frequently invoked reason for not needing written contracts is that the parties had been dealing together for many years.

A study by Palay (1985) on trucking companies and shippers showed that the contracting parties generally make deals verbally, but the continuation of these agreements depends on the people who created them remaining in the firms. Should one of them leave, there is a risk of litigation, and a renegotiation of the deal becomes necessary. This relational behaviour is the opposite of purely incentive behaviour. Indeed, one incentive mechanism described earlier relies on explicit contracts of specified duration which continue regardless of changing personnel.

Trust and reciprocity

Finally, interpersonal relationships lead to a reciprocal system between firms which is not explicitly written into the contract. Social exchange involves engagements between individuals built on trust, in contrast to economic exchanges in which obligations are completely specified in advance (contingent claims contract). This lack of completeness gives rise to reciprocity during the transaction: the *ex ante* contract relies in part on promises implicity written into the contract which has yet to be signed. Accordingly, trust provides a means of handling exogenous and endogenous events which were not anticipated at the start of the long-term relationship. Suppose that an unexpected decrease in final demand takes place during the contract period. The buyer can react opportunistically by withdrawing production to his own manufacturing facilities, a negative effect for the supplier. In practice, buyers will try to maintain some purchases from their suppliers in order to ensure that the suppliers depreciate their equipment (Gorgeu and Mathieu, 1991), and in return the buyer will expect the supplier to take steps to reduce costs, and hence prices. Similarly, for endogenous events, a supplier who is experiencing temporary technical difficulties will eventually be helped by the buyer in exchange for a reduction of his costs. In this manner reciprocity sustains organisational learning in long-term relationships.

In sum, market rationality is inadequate for explaining the complexities of economic behaviour, but various forms of coordination based on rationality go a long way towards explaining quasi-integration relationships. In the next section we will elucidate this position and show that there does exist a plurality of forms of coordination.

TRUST, AUTHORITY AND INCENTIVE: THE LOGIC OF QUASI-INTEGRATION

Authority

Authority within a system of vertical quasi-integration (subcontracting) constitutes a powerful mechanism of coordination; it allows the client to manage the physical organisation of production and decreases the uncertainty of the transaction. Although this works well for the buyer, it is questionable whether it stimulates vendors to maximum effort.

As far as market products are concerned, there could not exist, *a priori*, an authority relation between contracting parties, as they are legally independent agents. However, when firms are in vertical quasi-integration the situation is rather different: the contract affects a constrained transfer of decision-making power from supplier to buyer as a result of bias in the relationship. In most situations of vertical quasi-integration, it is possible to show evidence of an inter-firm dependency that results in an authority relation, albeit in a different form from that legally written into the labour contract. Dependency results from three concurrent criteria: concentration of exchange,[2] technical subordination, and the difference in the size of contracting firms.[3] The situation of economic dependency establishes an authority relationship viewed as a forced transfer of decision-making power from the subcontractor to the client.[4] Three main mechanisms form the basis of authority for the buyer: short contract duration, ownership of specific physical assets, and controls. By these devices, authority gives the client partial internal certainty and an ability, *a priori*, to coordinate plans with the subcontractors.[5] It also favours litigation-solving, as the bias in the relationship allows the client to impose his solution.

However, authority is limited by three important factors. First, it generates relatively high surveillance and control costs. Second, the client cannot totally take over the supplier's portion of the work. Authority alone cannot prevent the subcontractor from delivering the products late, from cheating on quality or from minimizing his effort. Ultimately authority only ensures partial coordination. Third, it can generate pernicious effects, notably insufficient innovation and investment by the subcontractor, who has no guarantee of a continuing relationship.

Incentive

Incentive is the second form of coordination and it corresponds to the type of industrial organisation described as oblique quasi-integration or partnership. In this type of relationship, the buyer attempts to get maximum effort from the supplier by encouraging his participation in the organisation of production and in product design.

Partnership can be analysed as an ensemble of reciprocal components with the buyer establishing an incentive structure as a way of coping with internal uncertainty.[6] In dealing with moral hazard (how to ensure that the supplier produces a maximum effort), the buyer establishes the following incentive procedures. First, a medium-term contract (and its renewal), most commonly explicit but which can also be implicit, which increases the duration of the inter-firm relationship. Second, an incentive to innovate through a price-bargaining mechanism (which affects a trade-off between risk-sharing and individual incentives to innovate. This may be explicitly or implicitly written into the partnership contract).

In order to deal with adverse selection risk (how to obtain supplier information on product quality), the buyer incites the supplier to send a signal which testifies for product dependability. This signal takes the form of processes covering quality-insurance.

Inter-firm partnership contract and its renewal

The inter-firm partnership contract can effectively be analysed as a reciprocal arrangement between firms; it is a warranty of duration for the supplier and in return the buyer expects better economic performance, notably through a reduction of production costs. This process allows the supplier to take more risk by favouring a policy of medium- to long-term investment, and gives the buyer the benefit of experience. Indeed when only one or two major suppliers are involved in the manufacturing of an important volume of components, the buyer legitimately expects lower costs and prices as a result of economies of scale (Lyons, Krachenberg and Henke, 1990).

In the framework of agency theory, it is clear that the medium-term contract, conceived as an incentive procedure, enables the actors to overcome the disastrous situation of non-cooperation (prisoners' dilemma). For the supplier, an explicit contract provides security for a set period, and the prospect of contract renewal is an incentive to fulfil obligations satisfactorily. The supplier is thereby encouraged to modernize, to improve product quality and to be loyal.

Incentives for innovation.

Duration does not appear to be either necessary, or sufficient, to maintain cooperative behaviour: it must be in each participant's interest to pursue the relationship. This requires that the relational quasi-rent (Aoki, 1988) be distributed in such a way that each firm benefits, a condition which in turn encourages a continuation of the cooperation.

If the contract provides incentives to cooperate, it also reflects the trade-off between risk-sharing and innovation incentives. Analysis of these mechanisms is necessary to calculate the degree of interest that the relationship holds for each party. It can be argued that there are incentives for the contractors to share the productivity gains that result from cooperation. Empirical studies (Baudry, 1993) show that the split is about 50/50 (that is, the buyer permits the supplier to keep a good part of the benefits of his innovation). Since the buyer gains experience and also keeps a share of the rent due to innovation, a virtuous circle of inter-firm cooperation can be triggered.

Adverse selection and insurance-quality procedures.

In the case of moral hazard, the principal must find an incentive procedure to ensure that the agent makes an optimal decision. To solve the problem of adverse selection, the principal must establish a procedure to obtain information on the intrinsic quality of the product. An authority relationship relies on controls being imposed by the buyer at every stage of the contractual relationship, although this is a costly process. Moreover, in view of new production techniques (just-in-time), product failure cannot be tolerated as it results in heavy monetary penalties. The technique of *ex post* control is therefore being progressively replaced by an *ex ante* mechanism of a signal directed at inciting the supplier to reveal the true quality of his products, and thus to decrease the risk associated with the contract. This signal comes from increasingly generalised quality-insurance procedures. Quality-insurance is clearly a signal designed to reduce the uncertainty of exchanges and, therefore, belongs to the incentive framework.

INTER-FIRM RELATIONSHIPS AND PLURALITY OF COORDINATION FORMS

We have shown three forms of coordination support exchange in quasi-integration relationships: authority, incentives and trust. Unlike Powell (1990), we do not see trust operating independently of authority and incentives, but in combination with these mechanisms. What, then, is the logic behind this plurality?

Considering the forms of coordination within oblique quasi-integration, it is apparent that incentives are essential. Indeed, the procedures relying on authority alone are extremely weak. The only mechanism is the functional specifications imposed by the main firm, and the norms of obligation and cooperation – the social context – are of limited importance. Supplier selection relies mainly on industrial procedures such as the type of equipment, personal qualifications, and the degree of technological expertise, which do not depend on the social context. Furthermore, it should be noted that explicit contracts signed between buyers and suppliers are relatively detailed, since as product design is shared, it is important that the obligations of the contracting parties are clearly delineated. On the other hand, personal relations are important; shared product design, value analysis and information exchange all generate a specificity of human assets. Daily scientific and technical collaboration creates routines specific to people working together, thus establishing reciprocity between firms. Figure 3.2 summarises this analysis.

Incentives

- explicitly renewable
- middle-term contract
- innovation incentive
- quality-insurance procedures

Authority

- functional specifications

Trust

- social norms: weak
- reciprocity during the long-term relationship
- personal relations: technical collaboration, information exchange

Figure 3.2 Forms and mechanisms of coordination in oblique quasi-integration.

Vertical quasi-integration exhibits quite different coordination forms. First, the authority issue is very important, as subcontractors are in a dependent state *vis-à-vis* the buyers: product specifications are very strict and there is no notion of a basic contract but rather one of repeated orders. Firms are systematically placed in a bidding position. However, and this is no contradiction, the trust issue is also very strong.

As we underlined above, inter-firm relationships evolve from a relational logic. Personal relations play an important role, notably when selecting a contracting party and in resolving disputes when the contract is running. Mainly because of this, legal rules are less important than those occurring in an oblique quasi-integration.

The age of the relationship becomes important despite temporary interruptions. For example, the regular subcontractor will be assisted in keeping his prices competitive. Trust and authority are then combined. However, even when trust supports the exchange, authority is capable of taking over at any time and of sending the parties back to the market test. The market test will reappear as soon as the smallest doubt overtakes the client. Even a long-term relationship will be interrupted if the supplier defaults his contractual obligations or is no longer competitive. On the other hand, incentive only relies on the traditional market game: the buyer regularly tests the market to maintain competition. Figure 3.3 summarises this plurality of coordination forms.

Incentives

- competition for each order

Authority

- technical instructions: strict
- controls: important
- penalties

Trust

- importance of social context: obligation and cooperation norms
- reciprocity: weak due to short-term explicit relationship
- personal relations: supplier selection, litigation-solving

Figure 3.3 Forms and mechanisms of coordination in vertical quasi-integration.

CONCLUSION

In this chapter we have argued that trust is a device which supports exchange, but have shown that it is not the only form of coordination regulating inter-firm relationships. Thus we disagree with Powell who makes trust the 'critical component' of inter-firm relationships. On the contrary, we saw that even when trust supports exchange, authority is able to emerge when the supplier is no longer competitive or fails in his duties. Our position is intermediate between Williamson's 'non-calculative trust' and Kreps's view of trust in terms of reputation.

Finally we think that trust must be a powerful means of coordination when firms are not in a situation of quasi-integration. For example, in some localised industrial districts, firms which do the same job are in a situation of 'co-traitance' (that is, the output of one firm is not simply the input of another, rather they share production). In this case authority and incentives cannot be forms of coordination for regulating transactions. Thus firms rely on devices mainly supported by trust and, in particular, by interpersonal relationships.

NOTES

1 See E. Lorenz (1993, p. 308): 'Embedding the firms in a community promotes cooperation among them because in communities relations are many-sided as opposed to specialised. The violation of a norm in the economic sphere has ramifications in other spheres of activity and affects the entire social order'.
2 Moreover, management studies specify that when a subcontractor receives more than 25 per cent of the sales from a single source, he runs the risk of losing his independence. This is in fact the case in many sectors (INSEE, 1990).
3 It has been estimated that in France two-thirds of industrial firms which permanently practise subcontracting (excluding craftsmen) have less than 50 employees (Altershon, 1992).
4 Dependency can exhibit varying degrees of intensity in different situations: in vertical quasi-integration, dependency is at a maximum. Under oblique quasi-integration, dependency is much weaker and incentives are more important than authority.
5 See Baudry (1995) for further explanations.
6 See Baudry (1993) for more details.

BIBLIOGRAPHY

Altershon, C. (1992), *De la Sous-Traitance au Partenariat Industriel*, Paris: L'Harmattan.

Aoki, M. (1988), *Information, Incentives, and Bargaining in the Japanese Economy*, New York: Cambridge University Press.

Baudry, B. (1993), 'Partenariat et sous-traitance: une approche par la théorie des incitations', *Revue d'Economie Industrielle*, **66** (4), 51–68.

Baudry, B. (1995), *L'Economie des Relations Interentreprises*, Paris: La Découverte, Coll. Repères.

Becattini, G. (1992), 'Le district marshallien: une notion socio–économique', in G. Benko and A. Lipietz (eds), *Les Régions qui Gagnent*, Paris: PUF, pp. 35–55.

Boltanski, L. and L. Thevenot (1987), *Les Economies de la Grandeur*, Paris: PUF.

Dasgupta, P. (1988), 'Trust as a commodity', in D. Gambetta (ed.), *Trust: Making and Breaking Cooperative Relations*, Oxford, Basil Blackwell, pp. 49-72.

Eccles, R. (1981), 'The quasi-firm in the construction industry', *Journal of Economic Behavior and Organization*, **2**, 335–67.

Eymard-Duvernay, F. and O. Favereau (1990), 'Marché interne, modèle de l'entreprise et convention de qualité', Paper presented at the University of Quebec, Montreal.

Gorgeu, A. and R. Mathieu (1991), 'Les pratiques de livraison en juste à temps en France entre fournisseurs et constructeurs automobiles', *Dossier de Recherche du Centre d'Etudes de l'Emploi*, **41**, Paris.

Granovetter, M. (1985), 'Economic action and social structure: the problem of

embeddedness', *American Journal of Sociology*, **91,** November, 481–510.
Hirschman, A. (1986), *Vers une Economie Politique Elargie*, Paris: Editions de Minuit.
INSEE (1990), 'L'industrie carrefour d'échanges', Special Number of the *Economie Lorraine*, **93,** November.
Kreps, D. (1990), 'Corporate culture and economc theory', in J. Alt and K. Shepsle (eds), *Perpectives on Political Economy*, New York: Cambridge University Press.
Lorenz, E. (1993), 'Flexible production systems and the construction of trust', *Politics and Society*, **21**, September, 304–21.
Lyons, J.F., A. Krachenberg and J. Henke (1990), 'Mixed motive marriages: what's next for buyer supplier relations', *Sloan Management Review*, **31**, Summer, 29–36.
Macaulay, S. (1963), 'Non–contractual relations in business: a preliminary study', *American Sociological Review*, **6**, 55–66.
McMillan, J. (1990), 'Managing suppliers: incentive systems in Japan and the US', *California Management Review*, **32**, Summer, 38–55.
Palay, T. (1985), 'Avoiding regulatory constraints: contracting safeguards and the role of informal agreements', *Journal of Law, Economics and Organization*, **1**, Fall, 155–75.
Powell, W. (1987), 'Hybrid organizational arrangements: new forms or transitional development?', *California Management Review*, **XXX** (1–Fall), 67–89.
Powell, W. (1990), 'Neither market nor hierarchy: network forms of organization', *Research in Organizational Behavior*, **12**, 295–336.
Pratt, J. and R. Zeckhauser (eds) (1984), *Principals and Agents: The Structure of Business*, Cambridge, Ma.:Harvard Business School Press.
Williamson, O. (1975), *Markets and Hierarchies*, New York: Free Press.
Williamson, O. (1985), *The Economic Institutions of Capitalism*, New York: Free Press.
Williamson, O. (1993), 'Calculativeness, trust, and economic organization', *Journal of Law and Economics*, **XXXVI**, 453-86.

4. Trust and Collective Action in Financial Markets

Dorothée Rivaud-Danset

> Le crédit ou la confiance est évidemment une cause d'augmentation des moyens d'action de l'homme sur la nature lorsque cette confiance existe chez celui qui possède en faveur de celui qui agit. (Enfantin, *Le Producteur*, 1825 quoted in Gille, 1970, p. 118)

Economists are showing a renewed interest in the phenomenon of trust. This non-tradable resource which enables agents to coordinate their actions is often taken as given in capitalist societies, particularly in the domain of innovation. Because there are diverse approaches to analysing trust, and because of its similarity to other modes of coordination (in particular reputation), the first task is to settle on a definition capable of bringing out its specific qualities. The second part of this chapter deals, via the theory of implicit contracts, with the efficiency of trust and with the nature of routine behaviour. The broader aim of this chapter is to show how, under certain conditions, trust enables economic agents to formulate the judgements necessary for rational decision-making. At the same time, we aim to clarify some of the practical questions raised by credit relations which, like industrial relations, are often repetitive.

TRUST AND UNCERTAINTY

Trust can be conceived as an ethical, *a priori* resource. Arrow judges trust to be a consequence of economic agents' general moral disposition.[1] He compares it with altruism, an exogenous resource given by nature: 'There is an element of trust in every transaction' (Arrow, 1984, p. 145). This externality, which reduces the costs of economic exchange and increases the efficiency of the economic system, is a good which cannot be negotiated on the market. 'Trust is an important lubricant of a social system' (Arrow, 1974, p. 23).

The existence of trust illustrates the limits of the market. In a similar vein, it can be defined as a scarce resource that is a by-product of the social norms which define a community and, therefore, is threatened by the globalisation of markets (Greenwald and Stiglitz, 1992).[2]

If the non-tradable character of trust is beyond dispute, its origin is controversial.[3] It can be considered not so much a by-product of social norms, but a personal resource which is intentionally constructed to help agents anticipate each others' behaviour (see Dasgupta, 1988; Gambetta, 1988; Good, 1988; Lorenz, 1988), which means it can be accumulated in the same way as reputation or skill. This viewpoint presupposes that actors take a long-term perspective when forming relationships, and it is this position which will be developed further in this chapter.

While the French language possesses only one term to express both collective confidence in a 'state of affairs' and personal trust in another's behaviour, Anglo-Saxon economists use the term 'confidence' in the first case and 'trust' in the second.[4]

Confidence, or more precisely a 'state of confidence', sometimes denotes a generalised belief concerning the future state of the economy. At other times it is used to refer to shared beliefs concerning those institutions in commercial societies which are characterised by a certain opacity, such as the institution of money. This generalised or 'meta' confidence facilitates the smooth operation of market exchange and affects the overall level of economic activity. Thus in 1930 Keynes deplored business leaders' lack of confidence in the future level of business activity, a lack of confidence which led them to postpone investment decisions. Following Keynes, it is common to argue that these anticipations have an arbitrary character, emerging through the cumulative effects of such phenomena as imitation or contagion, where the rationality of anticipations can be deduced from their self-fulfilling character.

Trust refers to situations of strategic uncertainty. It is concerned with personal beliefs about the other's character and his likely actions. This personal belief is constructed within the framework of an on-going interaction between two people, between a person and an organisation (for example, a borrower and his bank), or between a person and a social group (for example, employer and employees). Here the opinion formulated by each about the possible behaviour of the other is specific to the relationship and cannot be generalized outside it.

The difference between these two phenomena can be illustrated as follows. Take the case of an agent, A, who is both a depositor and a borrower with bank B. As depositor, the confidence of A in B depends upon the collective or average opinion held by depositors on the strength of banking institutions, an opinion which can be modified by public information. On the other hand, as a potential borrower wishing to renew a contract with B, the trust which A has in his ability to borrow in the future depends on private information which is not relevant to the beliefs of other borrowers. Similarly, the behaviour of bank B can be viewed from two different perspectives. The bank can treat depositor A as an anonymous agent whose behaviour is subject to various responses (for example, panic) or it can formulate a personal judgement as to the trustworthiness of A in order to anticipate his individual behaviour. In the latter case, trust, or the lack of it, enables the bank to formulate a judgement concerning his likely behaviour. It is this latter notion of trust which concerns us here.

RISK-ANALYSIS AND JUDGEMENT

In order to clarify this concept we shall begin by questioning its necessity. If generalised confidence in institutions is necessary for the working of a capitalist society, there are numerous instances where interpersonal confidence or trust is not a prerequisite for successful coordination. For example, granting consumer credit merely requires a more or less generalised hypothesis of morality.

The book on trust edited by Diego Gambetta (1988) uses the strong version of the hypothesis whereby trust is necessary once the assumptions of perfect information and anonymity underlying the operation of perfectly competitive markets are relaxed. The weaker version which we are proposing here is that trust is only necessary once the principles or forces which normally restrict an agent's behaviour, and permit us to anticipate his actions, are no longer valid. In the case of credit relations, these principles include:

- statistical estimation enabling the demand for credit to be dealt with by classifying borrowers under standard categories with known distributions of risk;
- the rational interest an agent may show in building-up and maintaining a good reputation;[5]
- the force of routine or customary behaviour;
- contractual obligations enforced by a third party such as the legal system.[6]

When the borrower is perceived as a unique case which cannot be easily classified, his actions cannot be predicted on the basis of observed empirical regularities. Similarly, when the incentive effects of maintaining one's reputation are weak, or recourse to the justice system proves impracticable, or the force of custom and habit cannot be counted upon, B will find it difficult to formulate correct hypotheses about the actions of A. Under such conditions, the decision to lend involves an exercise of pure judgement which depends upon trust. Here trust is being defined as a cognitive device which helps individuals to predict each other's behaviour and to coordinate their actions independently of any external constraint upon their liberty (Dasgupta, 1988; Gambetta, 1988).

Our basic argument, then, is that in a bilateral exchange relationship the influence exercised by trust depends upon the importance that the actors attach to other principles for resolving uncertainties. In the case of credit relations the importance attached to statistical methods is often the key factor, though international comparisons show that trust occupies a different position in different countries. Thus in the larger American banks, the decision to extend credit rests upon an 'arm's length' relation, as personal knowledge of the other is held to induce perverse effects and to be a source of distortions from the ideal of anonymous competitive markets. In French banks, on the other hand, the study of individual applications is generally completed by a personal interview. Codified knowledge is not thought to be capable of replacing *'savoir-faire'*.

Consider the possibility of accounting for banking practice in terms of Knight's (1921) conception of uncertainty. Knight makes a distinction between the actuarial treatment of uncertainty, where 'the objects or merely ''things'' manifesting constant modes of behaviour' (p.204) (including people) can be grouped and classified in terms of statistical measures of risk (mean, standard deviation, and so on), and the treatment of uncertainty through judgement where such techniques are not applicable. In fact, bankers tend to use both approaches when evaluating their clients. Their treatment of risk depends in part on standard forms of information which allow them to put each demand for credit in a particular risk category. It also requires an exercise in judgement based on clues and non-standard information.

According to Knight, such an exercise in judgement takes a form analogous to a type of probability that is distinct from an *a priori* probability (as in a game of dice) or from a frequentist probability inferred from data (as in insurance).[7] The judgement constitutes both an estimation based on opinion or intuition: 'I estimate that A will succeed and pay off the debt', and because the estimation is subject to error: 'In nine cases out of ten I am right'. As Knight stated: 'The action which follows upon an opinion depends as much upon the amount of confidence in that opinion as it does upon the favourableness of the opinion itself' (Knight, 1921, p. 277).

It is in the course of this double cognitive exercise leading to a judgement that trust intervenes. It intervenes both in the estimation of A's chances and in B's evaluation of his own predictive power.

TRUST AND REPUTATION

The two methods which Knight identifies in the treatment of uncertainty may be complementary when dealing with credit relations, but their relative importance depends on the distance of the borrower from the seat of decision-making. The role of judgement diminishes as the client's dossier finds itself at ever higher levels of the bank hierarchy, as intimate personal knowledge of the client is increasingly replaced by statistical risk-analysis. The need for judgement also depends upon the practicality of statistical methods. In Knight's terminology, 'the radically new' excludes all reference to predefined classes of risk. But this is clearly an extreme situation, since the expert can always establish analogies with earlier cases. In practice, bankers' judgement is especially necessary when the borrower fits into an average category for which the objective analysis of risk does not provide the sort of information that can dispel doubt and discriminate between high or low risks. On the other hand, when statistical analysis is able to classify credit demand by risk level, personal judgement is unnecessary.

Defining trust as a resource deployed within an interpersonal relationship when the statistical treatment of uncertainty is inefficient or impossible, raises the subject of reputation. The association of trust with reputation generally leads to the former either being derived from, or confused with, the latter (Kreps, 1990a), even though their principles of construction differ.

If agent A is anxious to maintain his reputation, his range of possible actions will be limited. This will make it easier for agent B_i to anticipate his behaviour. This principle is applicable even in novel situations and where there is uncertainty about the underlying honesty of A. Reputation has the quality of a public good that is constructed by, and maintained in, the interests of A in order to reassure others (B_j,...B_n) about his likely behaviour. This facilitates cooperation between them. It can even be argued that the acquired reputation is comparable with accumulated capital and is capable of being transferred by the market from one generation of managers to the next (Kreps, 1990a). The theory of repeated games, in which the character and strategy of each player is unknown to the other, attempts to show that reputation favours the emergence of cooperative behaviour. The maintenance of reputation 'capital' explains why agent A's behaviour is sometimes at odds with his immediate interest. Thus the debtor will honour his debts in order to maintain his social capital and his creditworthiness.

From an economic point of view, interpersonal trust and reputation share certain characteristics. Like reputation or 'the state of business confidence', trust in the behaviour of the other has an incentive effect. Thus B, in according his credit (or trust) to A, motivates the latter to behave in conformity with B's expectations and to respect the contract. Trust is liable to modify the character of the actors, their degree of honesty and also their customary rules of behaviour and routines. Trust, like reputation, permits the prediction of the behaviour of the other via the formulation of a judgement which can take the form of a non-frequentist probability in the sense of Knight (1921).

Let us now turn to the differences between reputation and trust. Unlike reputation, trust is based on private evaluation and:

- is not focused solely upon the problem of whether an agent will respect his explicit commitments but encompasses a wider field of strategic uncertainty;[8]
- does not presuppose respect for a rigid rule of conduct;[9]
- is thought of as 'capital' that cannot be detached from the individual concerned;
- is not a collective resource.

To some extent trust or distrust can be rendered public, but the signal is really more of a 'rumour' of uncertain reliability. Resort to collective judgement, that is to say, to reputation, as a foundation of trust between two contracting parties, implies that defection can be translated into publicly recognisable actions. For social sanctions to operate there must be general agreement over what constitutes 'good' behaviour.

The definition of trust retained here does not imply that the actors remain isolated from all exterior influence. Trust in a partner intuitively presupposes confidence in the institution to which the latter belongs. To be sure, trust can result to some extent from the shared values held by members of a community and be reinforced by conventional social objects. On the other hand, empirical studies of a major bank's credit relationships (Lindgren, 1990) or of subcontracting relations (Lorenz, 1988, 1993) have established that trust cannot be reduced to an unintentional by-product derived from reputation or from customary behaviour, but is something intentionally sought because of the inevitable incompleteness of contractual relationships.

Trust is a resource that is constructed within a relationship between two people or between two social groups. The specificity of trust is deduced from the fact that it is needed in precisely those situations where neither the existence of an arbitrator to a conflict, nor the judgement of a community, nor the threat of losing one's reputation, nor any other external sanction hanging over the participants can offer sufficient incentives to ensure that the behaviour of A responds to the expectations of B. In this sense trust is a resource which is independent of institutional constraints. This conception is akin to that of implicit contracts in the distribution of risks, where information is shared between two parties and ignored where there is no third party capable of enforcing a legal or explicit contract.

IMPLICIT CONTRACTS AND THE EFFICIENCY OF TRUST

The theory of implicit contracts provides a heuristic conceptual framework for the study of trust. In contrast to the agency theory approach or to the work of Williamson (1985), which is centred upon the minimisation of coordination costs, it attempts to emphasize the gains of cooperation.

Let us briefly recall the basics of the theory of contracts. Standard economic theory admits that the ideal contract is the complete contract which, because it anticipates *ex ante* all the future states of the world relevant to the decision, constrains parties' *ex post* freedom of action. On the other hand, the incomplete nature of implicit contracts, and the agent's corresponding freedom of action, can lead to sub-optimal outcomes. The expression 'implicit contract' is ambiguous, as it is not meant to be contrasted with explicit contracts. Contracts are implicit in the sense that:

- even if they are written and defined *ex ante* their fulfilment does not depend upon third-party enforcement but upon anticipated future gains;
- the contracting parties agree on a rule of conduct which determines how risk will be shared and how an uncertain stream of quasi-rents will be distributed between them;[10]
- they coordinate their actions without recourse to authority or to the exclusive use of the competitive market mechanism.

Nineteenth-century economists, more preoccupied by adaptation to short-term fluctuations than with their anticipation, and little preoccupied by the opportunistic behaviour studied by contemporary economists, refer to trust as a resource enabling contracting parties to conserve their freedom of action.[11] Thus Marshall, in his preface to a book which proposes the institution of arbitration commissions in industrial relations and the establishment of the principle of the sliding scale to regulate earnings, observes that these mechanisms cannot solve all the problems raised by profit-sharing. He underlines the need to establish trust in order to achieve flexibility in wage-setting. Profit-sharing agreements are desirable because they improve the situation of everyone, but they are difficult to manage and cannot be based on the competence of an outside commission:

> Profit-sharing arrangements when well managed are a gain to all concerned: but it is difficult to make them, and more difficult to keep them up. They require a good deal of mutual knowledge and confidence on the part of employers and employed;

> they are essentially matters for individual dealing, and not as a rule suitable for management by boards of conciliation, which often have to deal with very wide areas. ... If there is any change in the circumstances of trade, its details may be handled with great freedom. ... the meetings are frequent, and managed with frankness and kindliness, the future though unknown, may cause no anxiety; it is nearly as good for either side to know that a fair concession wil! be made by the other whenever circumstances require it, as to know what that change will be. And the elasticity of this plan gives it great advantages over the rival plan of a sliding scale .... (Marshall, 1887, pp. xviii–xix)

In other words, the latitude accorded to the two parties in the fixing of wages facilitates the adoption of the best possible strategy, given that trust and negotiating relations are established. In the absence of opportunism, sequential adaptations to fluctuations allow the two parties to reach an optimal agreement. Recourse to an incomplete contract – one which can be revised by the actors in the light of the actual situation – can be more advantageous than the negotiation of rigid, impersonal rules of conduct or a complete, and therefore rigid, *ex ante* contract.

Contemporary economists, particularly those concerned with the theory of non-cooperative games, emphasise the lack of respect for contractual commitments by *homo oeconomicus*. We know that the contracting parties can avoid the problem of opportunism, in the sense of contract evasion, when the agreement is self-enforcing. This self-enforcing character of the implicit contract derives from a threat of foreclosure sufficient to ensure that contractual obligations are met, that is, if the net present value of future gains (or penalties) exceeds the immediate advantages of breach of contract. The efficiency of this calculation presupposes that the sequence of transactions is open-ended (to avoid the problems of backward induction) or, at the very least, that the probability that the two parties will renegotiate is not zero. It also presupposes that the rate of discount is very low. If these two conditions are fulfilled, the *ex ante* calculation enables one to judge the credibility of an implicit agreement.[12]

However, the efficiency of an *ex ante* calculation poses a problem which is rarely raised and which, indeed, cannot be raised if the agents are supposed to have perfect foresight. Here we suppose that the implicit gains from a long-term contractual relationship are not entirely known in the first period, and that the rate of discount is not constant. In such conditions of uncertainty, trust becomes important because it serves to reinforce the advantages and weight of the future. To demonstrate this, assume that B grants credit to A for a period t_l Trust in A enables B to conjecture that A will honour his commitment and reimburse the debt in t_l with a subjective probability of ∂ per cent. In other words, B has trust of degree ∂ in A. The loan (L) is granted at a rate of $i_l(A)$, with $i_l\ (A) < i$ where i is the rate of interest on the competitive market. Trust is a resource for A with a gross immediate value

$g_1 = L_1 \{i - i_1 (A)\}$ inciting A to honour his contract. This incentive increases if the contract is renewed in t_2.

Now we introduce apprenticeship in the sense that B accumulates information which allows him to have a degree of trust $> \partial$. In this case B will offer A a more advantageous rate of interest in t_2 $\{i_2 (A) < i_1 (A) < i\}$, so that the present value of the expected gain, g_2, increases as the discount factor $1/1+r$ approaches the value of 1 with $r = r\{i(A)\}$. The development of trust diminishes A's preference for the present. Given that the present value of future gains $[g_2{=}L_2\{i{-}i_2(A)\}/(1{+}r)]$ exceeds the present advantages of cheating, the calculation eliminates the risk of opportunism on the part of A.[13]

This example presents trust as a necessary ingredient for initiating or for 'completing' an implicit, risk-sharing contract. Confirmation of the first period trust leads to an estimation of the net present value of second period cost–benefits which, in turn, lends credibility to a commitment initially founded upon a wager on trust. When the future has sufficient weight, it constrains short-term behaviour and encourages the parties to cooperate, thus making the contract self-enforcing.

This example is not intended to support an instrumentalist vision of standard economic theory where individuals are modelled as pure calculators of maximum utility with their actions entirely subordinated to *ex ante* calculations founded on subjective or objective statistical measures of outcome so that, in the first case, trust is reducible to circulation and, in the second one, trust has no place. On the contrary, we intend to show that trust and calculation are not conflicting principles. Our position contrasts with that defended by Williamson.[14]

For Williamson, 'trust merely muddies the (clear) waters of calculativeness' (Williamson, 1993, p. 471). The banker is a conscious calculator but often the waters of calculativeness are far from being sufficiently clear for calculation to be pertinent. The comparison between future and immediate gains cannot always form the basis of an evaluation – even ordinal – with meaning and weight. Interpersonal trust, as defined here, renders doubt tolerable to B and it can influence the acts accomplished by A. Reference to trust adds something to the understanding of reality as soon as reality (competencies, acts and outcomes) is not conceptualised as predetermined. The reduction of all the determinants of behaviour to the unique category of 'calculation', as Williamson proposes, does not shed the light we need. Calculation is by no means an unambiguous category. Thus, as Knight underlines, evaluation of the validity of an opinion takes the form of a ratio on the lines of a statistical probability – but the two probabilities are not of the same type. The cognitive operations which lead to the elaboration of statistical or frequentist probabilities and to non-frequentist probabilities are not of the same nature.

In our chosen example, the lender has accumulated private knowledge of the borrower which reduces the lender's risk and improves the borrower's loan conditions. The value of this knowledge cannot be salvaged if the contract is broken and, in this sense, the two parties are 'locked-in' to the relation. Neither of them has an interest in breaking their long-term relationship from the moment when *ex ante* calculation leads them to cooperate. On the other hand, this example simplifies the problem of calculating the net present value of the future flow of gains; the range of implicit gains from a credit relationship founded upon trust cannot be reduced to the offer of a privileged rate of interest. Theoretical literature and empirical work demonstrate the scale of implicit gains in the long-term credit relationship. For Okun, the client relationship insures the borrower against the price variations of the market-place (Okun, 1981). This 'umbrella against bad weather' associated with periods of money scarcity gives faithful clients priority on the waiting list, banks implicitly promising them access to credit at a lower rate than the equilibrium market rate. Other approaches suggest that an implicit contract increases the likelihood of credit being supplied to firms in situations of non-anticipated growth, for example, unanticipated innovation. Trust facilitates easy adaptation to the other party's actions, and the credit relationship becomes flexible.[15]

Trust plays a particularly important role when firms are threatened with bankruptcy. Without it the firm would be in the situation described by the agency theory of debt contract, that is, pushed towards bankruptcy and definitively placed under bank control. In practice, the existence of trust encourages the main creditor to seek alternative solutions involving implicit risk-sharing (for example, the rescheduling of debt). A comparative case study undertaken by Reich of Toyo Kogyo and AEG-Telefunken shows how, in Japan and Germany, respectively, the existence of privileged long-term links allows the main bank to salvage a client threatened by failure (Reich, 1985). Research undertaken by Lindgren on the relations between the Swedish bank Stockholms Enskilda Bank (SEB) and its clients, highlights their interest in constructing a long-term, risk-sharing relationship based on mutual confidence (Lindgren, 1990).[16] The series of interviews we have undertaken in France demonstrate that such a relationship motivates the banker to offer more favourable conditions of credit to a client in temporary difficulty than those which could be expected, given the level of risk. This facilitates the client's recovery.

INEFFICIENCIES: ROUTINE AND ERRORS OF JUDGEMENT

Marshall's intuition that the adaptive treatment of uncertainty is preferable to a rigid rule approach has resurfaced in the theoretical work on cooperation. Coordination based upon an informal exchange of information between independent actors, trust, duration and reciprocity can be superior both to a competitive market with incomplete price information and to authority based on inflexible, codified behaviour (Dulbecco, 1994, p. 533). It could be argued that this approach is too idealised; if trust is conscious and intentional, its establishment leads to specific habits and routines. Trust can promote the emergence of initially effective new practices which develop into monopoly rents, inertia and irreversibilities of a sub-optimal character. This is the problem conceptualised by 'path dependency'.

Confidence also permits one party to anticipate new products and future markets constructed by the other – but these anticipations may prove unconfirmed independently of the possible opportunism of other actors. In the years following the First World War, the confidence of English bankers in the traditional industrial sectors led them to expect a renewed conquest of the world market. In particular, in the Lancashire cotton industry, abundant credit was granted in the traditional form of short-term advances. However, these anticipations proved to be unjustified, particularly at the lower end of the market where an unforeseen competitor in the shape of Japanese industry appeared. The decline of the cotton industry, which started in the 1920s, prevented British industrialists from paying off their short-term debt within the expected time period, thereby imposing difficulties on the creditor banks.

What does this example prove? That confidence or trust in the other is a useful ingredient which allows one to treat uncertainty in a way which suits the actors but which can turn out to be erroneous. The example suggests that the evaluation of future returns from cooperation is more complex than that conceived in the theory of repeated games centred on defection. Can we treat this case in terms of sub-optimal choice, inefficient capital allocation and inefficiency of the organisation? Can we consider that the lack of rationality of banking organisations leads them to make bad choices by preferring traditional industries to new ones?

Posing the question in these terms assumes that banks are in a position to allocate credit between two categories of borrower, that they can access into two possible worlds, that of traditional clients and that of new firms. But the problem cannot be posed in these terms; it is an *a posteriori* reconstruction in terms of alternatives. This presupposes that banks face a range of choices and that there is an optimal reference point from which they are distanced by the weight of routine. If, on the other hand, one situates the actors in their context, bankers had no reason to turn away from traditional export industries in favour of new industries, all the more so given that the latter were largely self-financing. Their behaviour can be analysed as an error of judgement which only emerges as such *ex post* and not as the *ex ante* irrationality of the banking organisation.

CONCLUSION

Following Knight's conception of uncertainty, trust has been analysed as a resource which permits one agent to formulate a judgement and thereby to predict the actions of another (a wider but vaguer definition describes it as a resource which resolves the problem of uncertainty concerning the actions of an agent). Trust is constructed and maintained by contracting agents; it is a form of capital for one agent which cannot be separated from his person, and a resource for the other agent, necessary for handling uncertainty in certain situations. A consequence of this definition is that trust 'links' the agents and promotes the emergence of mutual gains rendering credible implicit contracts. Here we have attempted to conceptualise trust as a category which is neither opposed to that of calculation nor reducible to it. Like economic calculation, it can be a guide to action. The introduction of trust allows us to relax, indeed to abandon, the hypothesis of omniscient actors who, despite their lack of past experience with each other, are assumed to be able in any situation to operate according to the principle of substantive rationality. When it is not possible to act on the basis of statistical knowledge founded upon a frequentist calculation of probability inferred from observations, the actor can formulate a judgement. What we have here is the rationality of the 'practical man' in behaviour which might seem like mere routine. The personal treatment of uncertainty, including the degree of conviction of each in his own predictions and in the value of his judgement, is important when the methodological cognitive procedures which permit the statistical prediction of outcomes are not sufficient. A specific competence, the capacity to formulate judgements, is necessary to deal with singular situations and to produce a rule of action. In this kind of situation, trust lifts the doubt which inhibits action and contributes to the making of a credible future.

NOTES

1 This is the thesis of 'gentle commerce' according to which, 'commerce is communication and based upon narrow and close contacts between contracting parties who use promises, have confidence in each other and frequently exchange complaints and condolences'

(Hirschman, 1986, p. 69). For Granovetter (1985), the implicit hypothesis of generalised morality is necessary if the market is to be the foundation of the social order. On the other hand, the market conceptualised by O. Williamson (1985) is the atomised, anonymous market of neoclassical economics but without the discipline of competition and the implicit hypothesis of 'generalised morality.'

2 For Greenwald and Stiglitz, confidence and reputation are the two principles which ensure the respect of (financial) contracts in the absence of an efficient system of justice. With economic development and the weakening of community links, confidence has lost its efficacy as a discipline device (Greenwald and Stiglitz, 1992).

3 Altruism has been the object of a similar debate (Hausman and McPherson, 1993).

4 See also Luhmann's (1979) distinction between 'institutional trust' and 'personal trust'.

5 We shall argue below that trust and reputation, though often linked, are distinct beliefs depending on different types of information.

6 Agency theory aims to show how the standard debt contract can resolve the problem of 'moral hazard' in an optimal manner. The creditor, B, can undertake to contract with A even though their interests diverge, they have not signed a complete contingent contract and the *ex post* actions of A are not observable by B. By specifying a general rule of behaviour for responding to contingencies which is observable by the parties and which can be enforced by the court system, the contract can be considered as complete for all intents.

7 The definition retained here of non-frequentist probability is differentiated from the subjective probability defined by Fisher (or Savage's personal probability) where each individual can allocate to each state of the world a distribution of probability founded upon his beliefs and not upon objective estimates, even when the latter exist.

8 M. Sako distinguishes three levels: contractual trust, competence trust and goodwill trust (Sako, 1992).

9 Kreps attempts to show that reputation is a commodity like any other, by arguing that the maintenance of trust depends on respect for unambiguous implicit rules of conduct (Kreps, 1990, p. 128).

10 In the classic implicit contract one of the parties (the employer) bears the fluctuation and the other (the employee) is assured of a fixed income (but not employment). The classic implicit contract considers that only one of the parties displays aversion to risk.

11 For Le Play, a pioneering French sociologist in the 19th century, the confidence which is implicitly presumed constitutes an abundant resource which would be ruined by regulation (See Baudin, 1947). For the French Social Catholics, on the other hand, excessive competition destabilises confidence, which needs regulation to be established. (The author would like to thank C. Didry for these remarks.)

12 The overlap between the theory of repeated games and that of contracts permits us to specify the advantages of implicit contracts relative to explicit contracts. To be sure, implicit contracts are advantageous when the contracting parties share the information that they cannot use in an explicit contract. But even when explicit contracts can be executed, in certain circumstances implicit agreements are just as good (when the conditions for the 'folk theorem' are brought together, if the discounting factor approaches one, self-enforcing agreements reach nearly all the outcomes which can be realised rationally and individually) (Pierce, 1992, pp. 160–61).

13 Diamond proposes a model of the acquisition of reputation on the market for credit where the incentive effect of reputation is delayed (Diamond, 1989). In this model, reputation incites agents to choose projects without risk, but its effect is not acquired in the first period during which the incentive effect on the borrowing group of firms which can choose between risky and non-risk projects is very weak. Those who choose risky projects and succeed unintentionally acquire a good reputation. They find themselves offered a lower rate of interest in the second period and fall into the group of firms which undertake projects with a definite profit. Their factor of discount (supposed to be determined only by the rate of interest) increases and the advantages of respect for reputation, initially very weak, are sufficiently re-evaluated for reputation to exercise, in the second period, an incentive effect.

14 With Williamson, everything turns around a more or less intentional calculation. In the case where coordination is supposed to bring about the intervention of trust, the latter only

constitutes a fallacious or useless argument, behaviours which explain human variables (outside those within the family) including norms and social sanctions can all be interpreted in terms of calculation (Williamson, 1993).

15 Despite its importance, the question of flexibility is not central to the theoretical literature on credit. Here the dominant figure of the borrower is that of an entrepreneur perfectly capable, at the time of signing the contract, of estimating his financial requirements.

16 Thus Lindgren (1990) studies the relation established in the first half of this century, between the Swedish bank SEB and small client firms independent of the bank. Being creditworthy and cooperative by accepting the control of the bank in one's own business the firm in practice acquires the assurance of being aided by SEB both in situations of growth and crisis (Lindgren, 1990, p. 275). This research demonstrates that : (1) trust is a source of personal initiatives. It emerges from regular encounters during which a bank examines accounts and constructs its information about the firm; (2) the borrower is insured against the risk of credit-rationing when he undergoes fluctuations specific to him; (3) conflicts between the managers and SEB were regulated by negotiations and compromises preferential to the latter's directives; and (4) written contracts were considered as 'gentlemen's agreements' based on confidence.

BIBLIOGRAPHY

Arrow, K. (1974), *The Limits of Organization*, New York: Norton.

Arrow, K.J. (1984), *The Economics of Information*, Coll. papers IV, Oxford: Basil Blackwell.

Baudin, L. (1947), *Le Play: Textes Choisis*, Paris: Dalloz

Baudry, B. (1992), 'Contrat, autorité et confiance', *Revue Economique*, **5**, September, 871–94.

Brousseau, E. (1993), *L'Economie des Contrats, Technologies de l'Information et Coordination Interentreprises*, Paris: PUF.

Charreaux, G. (1990), 'La théorie des transactions informelles: une synthèse', *Economies et Sociétés*, série Sciences de gestion, **15**, May, 137–61.

Dasgupta, P. (1988), 'Trust as a commodity', in D. Gambetta (ed.), *Trust: Making and Breaking Cooperative Relations*, Oxford: Basil Blackwell, pp. 49–72.

Diamond, D. (1989), 'Reputation acquisition in debt markets', *Journal of Political Economy*, **97**, 828–62.

Dulbecco, P. (1994), 'La coopération comme mécanisme de coordination intertemporelle', *Revue d'Economie Politique*, **104,** July-August, 518–37.

Fudenberg, D. (1992), 'Explaining cooperation and commitment in repeated games', in J.J. Laffont (ed.), *Advances in Economic Theory, Sixth World Congress, I,* Cambridge: Cambridge University Press, pp. 89–131.

Gambetta, D. (ed.)(1988), 'Can we trust trust?', in D. Gambetta (ed.), *Trust: Making and Breaking Cooperative Relations*, Oxford: Basil Blackwell, pp. 213–38.

Gille, B. (1970), *La Banque en France au XIXème Siècle*, Genève: Droz.

Good, D. (1988), 'Individuals, interpersonal relations, and trust', in D. Gambetta (ed.), *Trust: Making and Breaking Cooperative Relations*, pp. 31–48.

Granovetter, M. (1985), 'Economic action and social structure: the problem of embeddedness', *American Journal of Sociology*, **91,** November, 481-510.

Greenwald, B. and J.E. Stiglitz (1992), 'Information, finance and markets: the architecture of allocative mechanisms', in V. Zamagni (ed.), *Finance and the Enterprise*, London: Academic Press, pp. 11–36.

Hart, O. and B. Holmström (1987), 'The theory of contracts', in T. Bewley (ed.),

Advances in Economic Theory, Fifth World Congress, Cambridge, MA: Cambridge University Press, pp. 70–155.
Hausman, D.M. and M.S. McPherson (1993), 'Taking ethics seriously: economics and contemporary moral philosophy', *Journal of Economic Literature*, **XXXI,** June, 671–731.
Hirschman, A. (1986), *Vers une Economie Politique Elargie*, Paris: Les Editions de Minuit.
Holmström, B.R. and J. Tirole (1989), 'The theory of the firm', in R. Schmalensee and R.D. Willig (eds), *Handbook of Industrial Organization, I,* Amsterdam: North-Holland, pp. 61–133.
Keynes, J.M. (1973 [1921]), 'A Treatise on probability' in *The Collected Writings of J.M. Keynes*, Vol. 8, London: Macmillian.
Knight, F.H. (1921]), *Risk, Uncertainty and Profit*, Boston and New-York: Houghton Mifflin Company.
Kreps, D.M. (1990), 'Corporate culture and economic theory', in J.E. Alt and K.A. Shepsle (eds), *Perspectives on Positive Political Economy*, Cambridge:: Cambridge University Press, pp. 90–143.
Kreps, D.M. (1990), *Game Theory and Economic Modelling*, Oxford: Clarendon Press.
Kreps, D.M. and R. Wilson (1982), 'Reputation and imperfect information', *Journal of Economical Theory*, **27** August, 253–79.
Lewis, D. (1986), *On the Plurality of Worlds*, Oxford: Basil Blackwell.
Lindgren, H. (1990), 'Long-term contracts in financial markets: bank–industry connections in Sweden, illustrated by the operations of Stockholm's Enskilda Bank, 1900–70', in M. Aoki, B. Gustafsson and O. Williamson (eds), *The Firm as a Nexus of Treaties*, London: Sage Publications, pp. 263–88.
Lorenz, E. (1988), 'Neither friends nor strangers: informal networkers of subcontracting in French Industry', in D. Gambetta *(ed.)*, *Trust: Making and Breaking Cooperative Relations,* pp. 194–210.
Lorenz, E. (1993), 'Flexible production systems and the social construction of trust', *Politics and Society*, **21** (3), 304–22.
Luhmann, N. (1979), *Trust and Power*, Chichester, Wiley.
Marshall, A. (1887), 'Preface' to L.L. Price, *Industrial Peace: Its Advantages, Methods, and Difficulties*, London: Toynbee Trustees, pp. v–xxvi.
Okun, A. (1981), *Prices and Quantities: A Macroeconomic Analysis*, Washington: The Brookings Institution.
Orléan, A. (1994), 'Sur le rôle respectif de la confiance et de l'intérêt dans la constitution de l'ordre marchand', *Revue du Mauss*, **4,** 17–35.
Pearce, D.G. (1992), 'Repeated games: cooperation and rationality', in J.J. Laffont (ed.), *Advances in Economic Theory, Sixth World Congress, I,* Cambridge: Cambridge University Press, pp. 132–74.
Reich, R.B. (1985), 'Bailout: a comparative study in law and industrial structure', *Yale Journal of Regulation*, **2** (2), 163–224.
Rivaud-Danset, D. (1995), 'Le rationnement du crédit et l'incertitude', *Revue d'Economie Politique*, **2**, 223–47.
Rivaud-Danset, D. (1996), 'Les contrats de crédit dans une relation de long terme. De la main invisible à la poignée de main visible', *Revue Economique*, **47** (4), 937–62.
Sako, M. (1992), *Prices, Quality and Trust. Inter-Firm Relations in Britain and Japan*, Cambridge: Cambridge University Press.
Salanié, B. (1994), *Théorie des Contrats*, Paris: Economica.
Telser, L. (1980), 'A theory of self-enforcing agrements', *Journal of Business*, **53**,

27–44.

Williamson, O. (1985), *The Economic Institutions of Capitalism*, New York: Free Press.

Williamson, O. (1993), 'Calculativeness, trust and economic organisation', *Journal of Law and Economics*, **XXXVI,** April, 453–502.

PART II

Collective Learning Dynamics

5. The Formation of Beliefs on Financial Markets: Representativeness and Prototypes

Hélène Tordjman[1]

INTRODUCTION

As rational expectations and, more recently, rational learning, have become the usual way to embody the formation and evolution of individual beliefs in economic models, empirical evidence gathered from market surveys and experiments is accumulating which shows systematic departures from the rationality hypothesis. These departures are especially salient to financial markets, where numerous studies (for example, Frankel and Froot, 1987; Shiller, 1989; De Bondt and Thaler, 1990) have highlighted systematic biases in the formation of agents' beliefs.[2]

This kind of bias has long been studied in different settings by cognitive psychologists (see Kahneman, Slovic and Tversky, 1982). Their pervasiveness and their similarity across domains (that is, their robustness) suggest that agents do not behave in a rational fashion in constructing their judgements and expectations, whether in financial markets or elsewhere. More specifically, the way they revise their beliefs in the face of new information is not Bayesian: they tend to be insensitive to prior knowledge and to sample size (Kahneman, Slovic and Tversky, 1982; Camerer, 1987) and to be overconfident in their judgements relative to the available evidence (Kahneman, Slovic and Tversky, 1982; Shiller, 1989; Griffin and Tversky, 1992). Hence from a descriptive point of view, the evolution of individual beliefs does not seem to be adequately modelled by a rational learning process which postulates, among others things, Bayesian revision and convergence of beliefs towards a unique 'true' model of the world.[3]

As put forward by Kahneman and Tversky, the fact that these judgements are systematically biased in the same direction shows that we do not use probabilistic updating to form our judgements, but resort to simpler procedures, such as rules of thumb and heuristics, some of which have been identified and studied extensively, such as representativeness, availability and anchoring (see Kahneman, Slovic and Tversky, 1982).

This chapter is about the representativeness heuristic which can loosely be defined as assessment of closeness to, and/or familiarity with a typical case (a more precise definition will be given below). The discussion will be restricted to representativeness and its consequences on the formation of beliefs, but further investigation should show that other heuristics, such as availability, anchoring and simulation also play a role in markets.

The purpose of this chapter is centred around the following question raised by Kenneth Arrow (1982): is the representativeness heuristic at work in financial markets and, if so, could it help to explain some of the apparent irrationality of these markets? In other words, is it possible that phenomena such as overreaction to new information, cumulative deviations and bubbles are generated by agents using representativeness instead of Bayes's rule in constructing their judgements? The findings of this study tend to favour positive answers to these questions: heuristics matter.

The theoretical implications of these 'appreciative' results[4] are not trivial. If economic agents do use a heuristic such as representativeness to form and revise their beliefs, the Bayesian learning approach no longer offers an adequate framework for representing individual knowledge and its evolution. Thus one needs another representation of learning processes which would at least be compatible with empirical evidence, and account for the fact that individuals mainly, but not exclusively, use heuristics rather than probability theory in constructing their beliefs. Some recent theoretical developments in cognitive psychology and artificial intelligence could shed light on the cognitive mechanisms generating behaviours such as judgement by representativeness. These approaches are not unified, but they share some basic concepts, such as prototypical categories and mental models (see, for instance, Johnson-Laird, 1983; Holland *et al.,* 1986), and can give some theoretical foundations as to why individuals use heuristics in forming and revising their beliefs.

The chapter is organised as follows. Section 2 presents some empirical evidence about the representativeness heuristic. The consequences of the use of this heuristic on financial behaviours and asset price dynamics are discussed in section 3. Section 4 introduces theoretical issues concerning representativeness and processes of categorisation. Section 5 concludes and highlights perspectives for future research.

EMPIRICAL EVIDENCE ABOUT REPRESENTATIVENESS

Definition

Before presenting some empirical results on the use of the representativeness heuristic in belief formation, it is necessary to provide a precise definition of the term. Tversky and Kahneman (1982c) distinguish two different meanings. First, representativeness refers to a sample and its quality: 'how representative of the population under study is the sample on which I base my judgement?'. It has been shown that judgements of the representativeness of a sample are generally wrong, giving rise to biases such as the gambler fallacy, and to what Tversky and Kahneman (1982b, chap. 2) have labelled 'the law of small numbers'.

Failures in judgements *of* representativeness can certainly be spotted in economic behaviour, but that is not the concern of this chapter. Instead, I wish to explore the consequences of a second version of representativeness which is less 'statistical' and more 'cognitive'. In this second sense, representativeness is a method or heuristic by which individuals construct subjective probability judgements, and we will talk about judgements *by* representativeness. More precisely, the probability of an event constructed in this way is evaluated:

> ... by the degree to which [this event] is: (i) similar in essential properties to its parent population; and (ii) reflects the salient features of the process by which it is generated. ... In many situations, an event A is judged more probable than an event B whenever A appears more representative than B. (Kahneman and Tversky, 1982a, P. 33)

For instance, if one has to evaluate the probability that a given animal is a dog, the more the encountered animal resembles a typical dog, the higher the evaluated probability that it is a dog. Thus similarity is essential in the way individuals form beliefs about which object, A, belongs to which class, X. Representativeness is also present in attributing causality, in evaluating the probability that an event, A, is caused by a process, X. Let us take a description of a manager and try to predict if his firm makes high profits. If the manager is described in terms such as 'young, ambitious and well educated', the probability that his firm makes high profits will be judged higher than if the manager is 'old, conservative and has not been to college', because the stereotype of a successful firm usually includes, in our times, a representation of a young and dynamic manager. It should be noted that these stereotypes often have a strong social dimension. The stereotypical successful manager is not the same in France and in Japan, and these representations are different now from what they were in the 19th century. In other words, cognition – at least some part of it – is 'embedded' (Granovetter, 1985) or 'embodied' (Lakoff, 1987) in more global social structures such as institutions, norms and collective representations (Durkheim, 1896). How such stereotypical categories are constructed, and how they evolve, is an issue of great importance involving different theoretical questions, some of which will be evoked in section 4.

Empirical Evidence

Experiments on the representativeness of belief formation are numerous, and many frequently observed systematic biases seem to be generated by the use of this heuristic. (see Tversky and Kahneman, (1982a) for a brief introduction). Their results show that the Bayesian model of belief revision is not descriptively correct. In particular, it is well established that people tend: (1) to ignore prior information, and (2) to underestimate the importance of the 'quality' of the evidence (they misjudge the representativeness of the sample and are prone to small sample bias, and so on). At the same time, they often give too much weight to the 'strength' of the evidence (that is, to the semantic content of information) which can lead to an overestimation of probability judgements and to behaviours of overconfidence.[5]

Neglect of base rates information

A well-known experiment performed by Kahneman and Tversky (1982b) demonstrates that, contrary to the predictions of Bayes's rule, there is a tendency to be insensitive to prior information. Two groups of subjects[6] were given identical descriptions of some persons (age, family status, tastes and hobbies). They were told that people could be of two 'types': engineers and lawyers. In addition, they were given the prior probabilities attached to the two groups, lawyers and engineers, but the first group was told that 30 per cent were lawyers and 70 per cent engineers while the second group was told the reverse, that 70 per cent were lawyers and 30 per cent engineers. They were then asked to evaluate the probability of the person described belonging to the group of engineers. Altogether, subjects were presented with descriptions of five persons, and the results were identical in all cases: prior information concerning the relative frequency of engineers in the population was not deemed relevant. One such description was the following:

> Jack is a 45-year-old man. He is married and has four children. He is generally conservative, careful and ambitious. He shows no interest in political and social issues and spends most of his free time on his many hobbies, which include home carpentry, sailing and mathematical puzzles (Tversky and Kahneman, 1982b, p. 54).

Given the configuration of the priors in the two groups of subjects, the prediction of Bayesian theory would be that the first group would give a higher probability to the fact that Jack is an engineer and the second group would estimate it to be less probable. The results obtained by Kahneman and Tversky do not exhibit such a pattern. Indeed, the two groups gave more or less the same estimation of the probability of Jack being an engineer, revealing that they were not taking their prior information into account.[7]

Different criticisms have been addressed to this kind of experiment. For instance, it is often argued that such verbal descriptions are not randomly drawn from the population, and this could explain the observed biases. Moreover, there is room for interpretation, and framing effects could explain deviations from Bayes's rule. Another criticism often made by economists concerns the monetary incentives individuals have in making the right choice. Economists usually claim that on real markets, people are experienced and must make the correct choice if they are to survive. Otherwise they are selected out of the market,[8] a constraint which is not overwhelming in experiments.[9]

Other experiments about representativeness and the neglect of priors have been designed to avoid these problems (see, for example, Grether (1980) and Camerer (1987)). In order to compare the relative descriptive adequacy of Bayes's rule versus, representativeness in evaluating subjective probabilities, Grether carried out the following experiment. He used three 'bingo cages' (that is, urns) each containing six balls. The first cage, X, contained six balls numbered 1 to 6. The second cage, A, contained four balls marked with an 'N' and two balls marked with a 'G', whereas in the third cage, B, there were three 'N' balls and three 'G' balls. The first urn, X, was used as a prior: a ball was drawn from X, and if it was numbered 1 to 4, urn A would be chosen; when the ball was numbered 5 or 6, urn B would be used. Then, six balls were drawn, with replacement, from the chosen urn. The subjects knew how the whole procedure functioned, and the content of the three cages, but they were just observing the final draw of six balls ('Ns' and 'Gs') without knowing from which urn, A or B, they had been drawn. For each sample of six balls, they were asked to estimate the probability that the sample had been drawn from A. As they also knew the content of X and the rule determining the choice between A and B, they knew the prior probability that the sample was coming from A (this prior could be modified from one draw to another, but the people were immediately notified of such a change).[10] In order to evaluate the incidence of monetary incentives, the subjects were divided into two groups: the first group was guaranteed a reward at the end of the experiment; in the second group, payment would depend on the correctness of their answers.

The results obtained by Grether are not as clear-cut as the ones from the lawyers/engineers experiment. First, in most experiments, prior information is taken into account by the subjects, although its importance is generally underweighted; but even if they are not pure Bayesians, they do use base rate information in estimating probabilities. However, there is a systematic bias in the formation of beliefs which is generated by something like the representativeness heuristic. For instance, whenever the final outcome (a draw of six balls) was exactly representative of urn A (four 'Ns' and two 'Gs') or urn B (three 'Ns' and three 'Gs'), the priors were almost ignored and the probability that the sample was drawn from urn A (respectively urn B) was very high, whatever the priors.[11] Second, a rather puzzling result of Grether's experiment, at least for economists, is that monetary incentives do not seem to be of much importance: the general patterns were the same in the two groups, whether there was an incentive to make the correct choice or not.

Kahneman and Tversky's results call for a more 'radical' rejection of the Bayesian hypothesis than the ones obtained by Grether (1980) and Camerer (1981). But these results are less contradictory than may appear at first glance. Indeed, when the problems are set up in terms of urns, as in Grether and in Camerer, it is easier to build a 'good' representation of the problem because all the data are given and well defined, and the necessary knowledge to solve the problem is contained in the data. The evidence at hand does not really ask for interpretation: the randomness only derives from the fact that the draws can be made from two different urns. In the engineer experiment, the knowledge mobilised and processed to solve the problem is much more complex, and involves one's model of what an engineer looks like, which in turn comes from our particular past experience – encounters with specific engineers – and the collective images entailed by social structures and 'culture' at large. Thus it may be possible to be almost Bayesian in well-defined, 'close-worlds' problems, but the more complicated the environment becomes, the richer the necessary knowledge and the higher the probability of using simplifying heuristics instead of sophisticated mathematical constructions to form our beliefs.

Overconfidence

Another frequent type of behaviour at odds with Bayes's rule is overconfidence (Griffin and Tversky, 1992). For instance, some studies about how people judge their own ability to drive a car show that a great majority of people, when asked where they rate themselves in relation to other drivers, answer that they are above the average driver. This anecdote is about overconfidence in one's skills, but many experiments about the formation of beliefs exhibit the same feature: people tend to overestimate their ability to form the 'right' beliefs. Economic behaviour is not an exception: for instance, managers of small businesses often show overoptimism about their chances of success (Kahneman and Lovallo, 1993) and financial operators frequently underestimate the risk they are taking. It is possible to explain such behaviour in terms of motivational factors such as 'wishful thinking', and this is certainly part of the story, but 'purely' cognitive procedures such as representativeness can generate overconfidence as well.

In probability theory, and more generally in issues on the formation of beliefs and opinions, it is usual to distinguish between the weight of the evidence (its 'quality' or 'precision') and its strength (the semantic content of the evidence). In the engineer/lawyer problem, when people were presented with a stereotypical description of a lawyer ('ambitious, politically conservative, rather unscrupulous'), they would pay a lot of attention to the extreme characteristics in the description (strength), without taking into account the accuracy of the description or the credibility of the person who wrote it (weight). At the extreme, the more caricatural the description, the higher the estimation: real stereotypes generated probabilities of 0.05 and 0.95, values which are close to certainty. Such confidence in judgement was produced by close correspondence between the description and the stereotype. Neither the base rates nor the weight of the evidence influenced beliefs.

An example of the combination of weight and strength of the evidence in a simple and well-defined setting is given by the heads and tails game, where weight is sample size and strength is sample proportion. Even in such a simple setting, Griffin and Tversky (1992) showed that people tended to be overconfident when strength was high and weight was low. People were presented with a series of heads and tails resulting from spinning a coin. The subjects were told, 'unlike tossing, which (on average) yields an equal number of heads and tails, spinning a coin leads to a bias favouring one side or the other because of slight imperfections on the rim of the coin'. People were given the value of the bias – the coin fell on one side three times out of five – but they did not know if the favoured side was heads or tails. They were then presented with 12 different samples of heads and tails, with varying sizes (from three to 33) and numbers of heads (from two to 19). All samples favoured heads. The subjects were asked to estimate the probability for each sample that the bias was in favour of heads. The results of this experiment highlight the way judgement by representativeness can induce overconfidence: each time the sample was small (from three to five) and the relative proportion of heads high, people's estimates were above their Bayesian values. Thus overconfidence can be associated with insufficient attention being given to sample size (weight of the evidence) and too much attention to the sample proportion (strength of the evidence). But the reverse is also true: when the sample was larger and the proportion of heads relatively smaller, people exhibited underconfidence (that is, their estimates always lay below the Bayesian values).

Representativeness in a complicated and evolving environment is much more difficult to define precisely than in pure games of chance where the similarity criterion is unique and well-defined, and it is thus possible to talk about 'exact representativeness' (for example, Camerer, 1987). In the real world, it is impossible to define *a priori,* 'the factors that make particular task and problem characteristics the salient ones with respect to which representativeness is judged' (Olson as quoted by Bar-Hillel, 1982, p. 73). In experiments with two possible criteria of similarity people would order them differently and arrive at different conclusions despite following the same heuristic and the problem being well defined. Some studies have been done to make people 'reveal' their representativeness criteria by estimating similarities instead of probabilities (see Bar-Hillel, 1982). But it seems that this approach is bound to fail because of the infinity of possible criteria. Typical categories are context-dependent and history-dependent and, if there is agreement about some features of some basic categories – and without this communication would be impossible – the extent to which such agreement exists is very difficult to evaluate. I will come back to these issues in section 4. Another way to approach the problem could be to try to identify, in a given domain, some representations that seem to be commonly shared (that is, some stereotypes) and to analyse the formation of individual beliefs that are not randomly chosen, but share similar concerns (as has been done, for instance, by Kahneman and Lovallo (1993) on small businesses). The next section about representativeness on financial markets is a preliminary effort in this direction.

REPRESENTATIVENESS AND FINANCIAL INSTABILITY

The history of financial markets abounds in illustrations of judgemental biases (that is, departures from the predictions of the Bayesian approach to belief formation). Accounts of speculative crises all emphasize the strangeness, from a purely economical point of view, of the evidential basis on which individuals construct their beliefs during such episodes. During the tulip mania which took place in Holland at the beginning of the 17th century, people would sell acres of land and all their possessions in order to buy one single tulip bulb. As Mackay (1841 [1980], p. 90) reports: 'In 1634, the rage among the Dutch to possess them was so great that the ordinary industry of the country was neglected, and the population ... embarked in the tulip trade'.

'Rage', 'euphoria', 'mania', 'insanity', 'fever' and other similar terms expressing some kind of irrationality are found in all descriptions of financial upheavals, from tulip mania and the 1929 crash to the events of October 1987, the Mexican crisis in the winter of 1994/95 and the recurring attacks on EMS currencies.

Beyond the collective aspect of these episodes – often analysed in terms of mimetic contagion and herd behaviour (see, for instance, Orléan (1990) and Kirman (1993)), it is also possible to identify specific biases in the formation of individual beliefs, biases which could explain particular features of the functioning of financial markets. For instance, it seems that most financial assets are characterised by excessive volatility or price movements not warranted by changes in the fundamental variables supposed to determine them (see, for instance, Shiller (1989)). Another related pathology is the speculative bubble, which is a persistent and cumulative deviation of the price from its fundamental value. These empirical traits of financial dynamics are at odds with the standard rational view of markets as exemplified by the rational expectations and market efficiency hypotheses. Up to now, economic theory mainly oscillates between two extreme standpoints: these phenomena are either considered as totally irrational, and therefore cannot be studied, or they are 'reframed' in order to be compatible with rational behaviour. In the latter view, market instability is produced by wars, inadequate policies and other exogenous factors, and in any case is only transitory: the market is endowed with automatic regulatory mechanisms which push prices back to their equilibrium level (for example, Friedman, 1953).

However, a minority stream of research, which can be traced back at least to Keynes, develops another view of market functioning where people are neither perfectly rational nor totally irrational. They have cognitive limitations and drawbacks but are generally more or less reasonable: their behaviour is intentional and they have a certain idea of the adequacy between means and ends. Moreover, they are able to modify their representation of the world when experience has repeatedly proved the latter to be 'wrong', that is, they can learn from their experience. They may nonetheless be prone to euphoria and panic, and more generally to different kinds of influence which may be either 'environmental' (for example, the influence of colleagues, friends, so-called experts and newspapers) or 'historical' (for example, their own past experience and collective representations of historical events).

More precisely, as claimed by Arrow (1982), Camerer (1987) and others, heuristics such as representativeness can play a role in market functioning. For reasons evoked earlier, it seems that rigorous and formal studies of representativeness in real-life situations are at the moment impossible; categories are too complex and similarity criteria are too numerous and variable across individuals to be listed in a systematic way. It is nonetheless possible to exploit the empirical literature on speculative episodes; to begin to identify the representations that financial operators seem to have and the specific biases they display.

This empirical literature mainly takes two forms: historical studies of 'great bubbles' (Mackay, 1841; Kindleberger, 1978; Galbraith, 1990) and analyses of market surveys and questionnaires designed to understand how financial operators form expectations (Frankel and Froot, 1987; Shiller, 1989; De Bondt and Thaler, 1990). These studies provide evidence consistent with the view that representativeness can be at the origin of financial 'anomalies' such as bubbles and overreaction. First, the tendency to judge by similarity without taking into account prior information produces more extreme judgements than would be the case if individuals were perfect Bayesians: thus agents very often overreact to new information. Second, the overconfidence generated by an overweighting of the strength of the evidence relative to its quality can explain both the unrealistic optimism which is characteristic of the growth of a bubble (the euphoric phase) and the crash (the explosion of the bubble).

Overreaction and Volatility

One frequently expressed explanation for the extreme volatility of asset prices is in terms of 'news'. In this view, price volatility is provoked by the process of information aggregation taking place on the market: new information is rationally interpreted, producing a modification of previous expectations, and price dynamics should thus follow a similar process. As there is no reason to think that the arrival of new information is not random, asset prices should follow a random walk and the price dynamics should not exhibit regularities such as 'weekend effects' and 'January effects'. Unfortunately, this is not the case (LeRoy, 1989). An alternative explanation of the high volatility experienced by financial prices is that individuals overreact to this new information: the way they revise their beliefs to take this information into account is too drastic. In other words, by according too much importance to new information, people do not behave in a Bayesian fashion.

For a number of years, some public and private institutions have been periodically recording traders' and/or analysts' expectations of the evolution of stock prices, exchange rates and other financial prices. We thus start to have at our disposal some databases of individual forecasts that can be exploited to test alternative hypotheses about expectations formation on financial markets.

De Bondt and Thaler (1990) studied one database of one-year and two-year forecast changes in earnings-per-share made by security analysts. As data for actual returns are available, it is possible to test the accuracy of these predictions. One of the reasons why they chose security analysts' forecasts was that, as they put it: '... the precision of analysts' expectations represents a natural upper bound to the quality of the earnings forecasts of less sophisticated agents' (p. 52).

If the predictions of so-called experts are biased, it is reasonable to think that it will be even more so for 'standard' operators.

Their results can be summarised as follows. First, compared with the rational expectations predictions, they found evidence of a systematic bias in forecasts. Regressions of actual changes of earnings-per-share on forecasted changes shed light on the regularity of expectational errors. De Bondt and Thaler found that forecast errors can be predicted from forecasted changes in earnings: although the forecasts are in the right direction, they are too extreme. In other words, security analysts seem to overreact to information and to judge the probability of 'big events' higher than proves to be warranted *ex post*. Second, De Bondt and Thaler wanted to know if this phenomenon of overreaction was correlated with uncertainty about the future, and they compared the results obtained with one-year and two-year forecasts, as uncertainty increases with length of forecast period. They found that the two-year forecasts were more extreme than the one-year ones (that is, overreaction seems to be more pronounced when uncertainty is higher). As noted by Arrow (1982, p. 5), representativeness entails a 'tendency to underestimate uncertainties', which is at the base of the general phenomenon of excessive reaction to information.

This feature of overreaction has been found in other databases. For instance, Frankel and Froot (1987) and Froot and Frankel (1989) have extensively analysed predictions (one month, three month, six months and one year) of traders on foreign exchange markets. Frankel and Froot (1987) did not look for overreaction, but found that expectations about future exchange rates were systematically biased, although they could not find a simple alternative model of expectations (for example, adaptive, extrapolative or regressive) that fitted the data. They concluded by emphasising the complexity of the process that generates the predictions. Froot and Frankel (1989) used the same database to study the relation between the spot exchange rate and the forward rate, that is, the well-known 'forward bias' problem. They first decomposed the bias into a time-varying risk premium and an expectational error, and showed that the bias essentially stemmed from a failure of rational expectations. They then looked for overreaction (they labelled it 'excessive speculation') and regressed the expectational error on the expected depreciation of the exchange rate. Their results are similar to the ones obtained by De Bondt and Thaler (1990) with earnings predictions: the expectational error is positively correlated with the expected depreciation, and forecasted changes are again too extreme. As for the security analysts, there is evidence that the Forex traders are also prone to overreaction.

The link between this overreaction behaviour and the representativeness heuristic is quite straightforward. To overreact to new information implies giving more weight to this information in the construction of a probability judgement than would be justified by Bayes's rule. Its corollary is insensitivity to prior information: the posterior judgement mainly reflects the latest information, as if no summary data on the phenomenon were available.

As we saw in section 2, such a neglect of prior information is often a result of constructing judgements by representativeness. For instance, the security analysts from the De Bondt and Thaler study displayed overreaction in letting their predictions of future earnings be overly influenced by recent and maybe irrelevant information, whereas earnings dynamics were also determined by structural factors which could be known through a fundamental analysis. Even with total ignorance of these fundamentals, a professional analyst would, if economic theory is to be believed, know something about the distribution of earnings across the population of firms, and use these known frequencies in the construction of his or her belief. Instead, they seem to take each new piece of information at face value, and construct their expectations by extrapolating the content of this information. This seems to be quite similar to the engineer/lawyer story: if the received signal is part of a more general picture of a successful firm (a young and dynamic manager, a new high-tech product, a restructuration plan and so on), the predicted future earnings will be high and, as shown by De Bondt and Thaler, higher than the actual ones. Hence overreaction and high volatility can be generated by the fact that individuals acting in the market use a heuristic akin to representativeness.

Overconfidence and Positive Feedback Trading

Overreaction, as expressed in extreme judgements, often entails unrealistic optimism or pessimism (De Bondt and Thaler, 1990). But there is more to unrealistic optimism, and to overconfidence in general, than a neglect of prior information. Studies of overconfidence, such as the ones mentioned above, show that it is produced by a simultaneous underestimation of the weight of the evidence and an overestimation of its strength. This pervasive bias is part of the mechanism by which a speculative bubble both appears and bursts.

Let us briefly recall what a bubble is. For most economic historians and practitioners, a speculative bubble is the cumulative deviation of an asset price from its believed 'normal' or equilibrium value; it is characterised by a slow but accelerating price rise followed by a crash. In this view, psychological factors such as euphoria, crowd behaviour and contagion are emphasised. As Kindleberger has observed, a bubble is usually initiated by a 'displacement' or, 'some outside event that changes horizons, expectations, profit opportunities' and induces confidence (Kindleberger, 1978, p. 41). Then:

> ...optimism sets in. Confident expectations of a steady stream of prosperity, and of gross profits, make portfolio plunging more appealing. Financial institutions accept liability structures that decrease liquidity, and that in a more sober climate they would have rejected. The rise is under way, and may feed on itself until it constitutes a mania. (Kindleberger, 1978, pp. 29–30)

A speculative 'mania' or 'euphoria' has positive feedback dynamics: the more confidence people have in the value of an asset, the more they buy and the more its price increases, thus justifying their optimism. At this point, whatever the information, agents interpret it in a way which is consistent with their expectations. Examples of such cognitive dissonance are numerous (see the changing interpretations of exchange rate movements witnessed by financial newspapers). But cognitive dissonance is not the whole story; I will try to show how representativeness can also be invoked to give an account of speculative euphoria.

As shown by historical accounts and expectations surveys, traders and other market practitioners are well aware that price dynamics are mainly generated by the collective opinion that they, as a group, have on the future evolution of the price. The main activity of a speculator is to guess what the average opinion will be. Hence, the specific representations and models that agents have of the world are of primary importance in financial price dynamics, and the way these models are formed and evolve strongly determine these dynamics.

Market surveys, especially the one made by Shiller (1989) just after the October 1987 crash, teach us a lot about the kind of representations agents seem to use and the way they use them. If, as is claimed here, people mainly construct their judgements by representativeness, the specificity of these models can give some insights into the typical categories and similarity criteria shared by financial operators which condition their beliefs.[12]

During the year 1986, Shiller sent questionnaires to private and institutional investors each time there was a sharp move in the Dow Jones. Answers were sometimes difficult to interpret, but slowly Shiller modified the formulation of the questions, and in October 1987 he was ready with a questionnaire which he sent to about 2000 investors – private and institutional – on Tuesday the 20th, the day after the Dow Jones had a drop of 508 points or 22.6 per cent. Among the many questions that were asked, some pertained to the beliefs, intuitions and 'visions of the world' those investors had on this day and the week before the crash, and what they expected for the near future. The answers to this survey may, for our purpose, be separated into two groups: the first concerns the general representations agents have about the functioning of the market and the mechanisms underlying speculative crisis, and the second has to do with the way individuals judge the evidence at hand and how they are prone to overconfidence.

General representations of market functioning

The difference between practitioners' and theorists' view of the functioning of financial markets is quite striking. The broad picture which appears from Shiller's survey makes clear that, for traders and other operators, market psychology is central to the determination of price dynamics. One of the questions asked on the 20 October was: 'Which of the following better describes your theory about the declines: a theory about investor psychology or a theory about fundamentals such as profits or interest rates?' (Shiller, 1989, p. 394).

A large majority of private and institutional investors (around 65 per cent) chose the 'market psychology' explanation. One of the main features of this 'psychology' is the tendency to be affected by the behaviours of the others; however, this phenomenon of mutual influences and imitation is not completely irrational: as people know that their collective behaviour is at the origin of price movements, what the others are thinking and doing is of the first importance. During the October 1987 crisis, investors reported having talked to others about what was going on 'very many times' or 'continuously'. Interpersonal communication was high: 'Moreover, 23% of the individual investors and 40.2% of the institutional investors reported experiencing a contagion of fear from other investors' (Shiller, 1989, p. 388). Hence people seem to be well aware of the positive feedback process characterising price dynamics.

Another quite striking feature of many answers is the frequent reference to the 1929 crisis, showing that the memory of this crash was still vivid half a century later, although of course today's investors have not experienced it personally. Both crashes happened on a Monday, 'after a preceding week of great market turmoil' and many people reported having symptoms of anxiety building up over the week end (Shiller, 1989, pp. 388, 393). Thus on Monday morning, the possibility of a 1929-type crash was judged high and, in such a context of defiance, any small event or unimportant news could produce a panic. As Shiller puts it:

> Investors had expectations before the 1987 crash that something like a 1929 crash was a possibility, and comparisons with 1929 were an integral part of the phenomenon. It would be wrong to think that the crash could be understood without reference to the expectations engendered by this historical comparison. In a sense, many people were playing out an event again that they knew well. (1989, p. 399)

The 1929 crash appears to be, at least in troubled times, the typical representation of a financial crisis, the model of reference by which agents construct their judgements. As noted by Shiller, in 1987 agents compared the situation they were going through with the 1929 crisis, and the more they felt it was similar, the higher the probability judgement they formed about the eventuality of a crash, whatever the low priors of such a dramatic event and the weight of the evidence (often being rumours, second- or third-hand information, and so on). These pessimistic beliefs were self-fulfilling because many people started to sell, and the crash happened.

Of course, it is impossible to be sure that this story exactly describes what happened in October 1987. We do not have enough data on the general representations individuals have concerning market functioning and speculative phenomena. Moreover, if the notion of representativeness is precisely defined from a theoretical point of view, its empirical manifestations in real-life situations are much more complicated to track down. In fact, we do not know if similarity criteria are identical, and it may well be that different individuals, having different cultural and educational backgrounds and different sources of information, also have different models of what a financial crisis is and what 1929 was about.[13] From the little data we have it seems, nonetheless, that some basic features of the representation of market functioning, namely the role of market psychology and of positive feedback trading, are shared by the majority of financial operators. (Historical accounts of speculation tell us the same kind of story, see, for instance, Mackay, 1841; Kindleberger, 1978 and Galbraith, 1990). Because agents use heuristics such as representativeness to construct their beliefs, the peculiarities of these representations and models could shape financial dynamics.

The role of overconfidence in speculative euphoria and crashes

After having discussed some general background representations, let us now turn to the mechanisms by which judgement by representativeness may produce euphoria and crashes. Note that these mechanisms are very similar: bubbles and crashes share the same feedback processes which develop because people share the view that asset price dynamics is mainly determined by the so-called market psychology.

In section 2, we saw that overconfidence may be an outcome of judgement by representativeness. By focusing mostly on the magnitude of events, with little attention to the quality of evidence, people generally overweight some salient traits of events, whereas they do not take into account 'statistical' data. This appears very clearly in the answers to Shiller's questionnaire. As long as the price is rising, such a rise is interpreted as a sign that markets are optimistic or bullish, even though some agents may think that the asset is overvalued. Either people believe that such an increase is justified by fundamentals (they seem to be more numerous at the beginning of the euphoria than just before the crash), or they know that the asset is overvalued but they follow the herd because they understand the role of market psychology. In both cases, investors display some kind of overconfidence: in the first case because they interpret information at face value, without taking into account prior information; in the second case because they are sure they can predict the turning point and 'beat the market'.[14] To the question: 'Did you have a sense just before the crash (around 12 October 1987) that the market was overpriced relative to fundamental value? (Try hard to remember what you thought then)' (Shiller, 1989, p. 391), 71.7 per cent of the private investors and 84.3 per cent of the institutional ones answered 'yes'. At the same time, between 12 September and 12 October, among the net buyers, 68.1 per cent of the private investors and 93.1 per cent of the institutional investors recognised that the market was overpriced (Shiller, 1989, p. 392). Thus agents were following the trend, which implies that they were confident in their ability to 'time the crash', that is, to go out of the market before the others. The discrepancy between private and institutional investors' evaluations can be interpreted in the same way: institutional investors were more overconfident than the private ones, because they felt that they, as 'experts', could not be wrong (on this point, see Griffin and Tversky, 1992).

This feature is also apparent in the behaviour of foreign exchange traders analysed by Frankel and Froot (1987) during the bubble on the dollar in the mid 1980s: they had short-term 'extrapolative' expectations, they followed the trend but judged the dollar overpriced in a long-term, fundamentalist view. As for October 1987, it seems that people knew the market was overvalued, but the rise of the dollar continued nonetheless for more than two years (until February 1985), even though all fundamental information would, if it had been taken into account, have pushed the dollar down.

The kind of overconfident behaviour just described is impossible to disentangle from positive feedback trading. It is because each individual believes he is more intelligent than his colleagues that he follows the trend, confident that he will be able to 'jump off the train' before the crash. When generalised, this behaviour engenders a self-referential functioning of the market in which any judgement can be validated *ex post* if enough people share it. Contagion is thus another important part of the story, but this goes beyond the scope of this chapter (see Orléan Chapter 6, this volume).

As just shown, positive feedback trading may produce euphoria, but it also plays an important part in crashes and their timing. Indeed, one of the standing puzzles in financial economics concerns the causes of the market's turning points. In other words, why does the price, after a long and steady rise, collapse dramatically? As is usual in finance, in the absence of a more compelling explanation, 'news' is deemed to be the stimulus. When the overvaluation is patent and everyone is more or less aware of it, confidence in the future vanishes, it is now believed that it has been 'too long too far' for the price not to go back to its equilibrium level. In such a situation, any news that can be interpreted as a sign that 'markets become normal again' may produce the crash.

The answers to Shiller's questionnaire cast some doubt about this news theory. He explicitly asked investors to rate different news items in order of the importance they had for them on 19 October (on this precise day only, not after the crash). Among these news items there was, for instance, 'trade deficit figures announced Wednesday, October, 14, 1987', 'producer price index figures announced Friday, October 16, 1987' and 'the 200 points drop in the Dow the morning of Monday, October 19' (Shiller, 1989, p. 384). What is striking in the answers is that news about exogenous events was not deemed to be very important, the most important news was the price movements themselves. The 200 points drop in the Dow Jones came in first position, followed by the price drops of the week before. The major news that provoked the decline of stock prices was the fall of prices itself. Hence it seems that the most important information for prediction is contained in price changes.

The fact that agents are assigning great importance to the magnitude of some events (here, the percentage of price decline), as opposed to the quality of the evidence (for example, the priors: 'how many times such a decline provoked a crash?' or the source of the information and its credibility: 'is it a rumour or was it published by the *Wall Street Journal*?') is inherent in positive feedback trading. The more the price changes, the more it is expected to change (because of the overestimation due to the strength of the evidence), and the more this judgement is made with confidence (when the strength of the argument is high, people judge by similarity and forget the weight or precision of their information). Thus overconfidence and, more generally, representativeness seem important on speculative markets.

REPRESENTATIVENESS AND CATEGORISATION

The preceding sections have highlighted the role of the representativeness heuristic on financial, speculative markets. The supposed anomalies of these markets are not, in the perspective developed here, anomalies, but clues that individual decision-making does not proceed as postulated by the rational/Bayesian approach. Indeed, representativeness is not a pathology, but a learning heuristic which helps individuals to form beliefs about the occurrence of uncertain events in a non-transparent and always changing environment. When problems are ill-defined, it is easier to assess a 'probability' by comparing the closeness of the possible event with a typical case than to use Bayes's rule to revise a probability judgement. Of course, beliefs obtained by judging closeness and similarity have no reason to follow axioms of probability theory. From the point of view of Bayesian theory, they are systematically biased. In real-life situations, however, they seem to be quite intuitive and robust procedures in forming beliefs in varying and ill-defined contexts. As such, representativeness can be considered as a 'metaheuristic' or a 'rule on how to generate rules' (Einhorn in KST, 1982;

see also Johnson-Laird, 1983). Moreover, representativeness suggests a stable procedure of how to construct beliefs in uncertain and complex environments: the 'probability' of the occurrence of an event depends on the similarity of this event to a stereotypical event which is part of the knowledge base of the agent. The study of representativeness thus becomes a study of what kinds of stereotype are used by individuals and how these stereotypical categories are formed.

There are basically two opposing views of categories and concepts (Lakoff, 1987). In the first approach, categories are defined by a list of their qualities which form a set of necessary and sufficient conditions: 'a dog is hairy, has four legs, sweet eyes, moves its tail each time it is happy, and so on'. An encounter with an aggressive dog or with a Mexican hairless dog contradicts the whole category of dog, and the 'object' is impossible to identify. One of the main problems with this 'objectivist view' is that it cannot cope with the variety of the real world: either the object exactly corresponds to the known category, or it is discarded as unknown. In this perspective, similarity between two objects or events is a notion that does not exist: either it is a dog, with all the well-known properties of dogs, or it is something else. There is no possible measure of resemblance, of some fuzziness of the basic category which would allow for diversity; it is either all or nothing.

Following the work of Rosch (1975), another approach to categorisation has been developed. In this perspective, categories are formed by a stereotype or prototype (the distinction is defined below), accepting some variations or defaults. For instance, every individual forms a prototype of what a dog looks like (it is generally hairy and has sweet eyes, and so on..), but hairless dogs, aggressive dogs, and so on, also exist. In other words, a category is defined by a prototype of a set of assorted defaults (that is, exceptions which do not contradict the category of a dog). The procedure of categorisation here is the same as in the lawyer/engineer experiment described in section 2: each individual seems to have a model of lawyer and engineer which are representative of these classes of 'object', and membership of a class, namely categorisation, is judged by closeness to, and similarity between, the object and the representative instance of the class. As lawyers are different from one another, and in general there is variation within classes, categorisation must allow for some diversity while preserving the basic or essential features which define the specificity of the class. This flexibility is obtained by the defaults that are judged acceptable, namely the characteristics of the object or the event, which can vary without questioning the standing classification. These defaults are usually organised in a pyramidal or hierarchical way. For instance, the category 'dog' is first defined by some basic features (hairy mammal, sweet eyes...) and progressively refined because of encounters with hairless, aggressive, big or small, yellow or brown ... dogs. These operations of specification consist in adding defaults to the prototype in a hierarchical way: first, dogs are hairy mammals (but some hairless dogs exist); then, if they are hairy, they can be either yellow or brown, and so on. Theoretically, there is no limit to this kind of specification procedure. This organisation of defaults is labelled a 'default hierarchy', and allow individuals to form and test hypotheses about the environment.[15]

Such a method of categorisation is more flexible and more global than the one built upon necessary and sufficient conditions; individuals can form categories of varied, changing and possibly ill-defined objects and events. Experiments on children's ability to acquire concepts tend to confirm that they use something like prototypes to classify objects. This could explain their ability to recognize objects very early, even though they do not know all the necessary and sufficient conditions (see Johnson-Laird, 1983, pp. 121–30). This approach to categorisation also helps us to understand why we usually consider that New York and Timbuktu belong to the same category 'city', although they do not share many objective features.

In order to be precise about the relations between the representativeness heuristic and prototypical categorisation, as well as some theoretical implications of these relations, let us briefly make some remarks about the nature of stereotypes and prototypes, and some of their properties.

The Nature of Prototypes: Typical Features and Family Resemblance

The prototypical approach to categories emphasizes their fuzziness, the fact that, 'they have no clear-cut boundaries...[but] blurred edges' (Johnson-Laird, 1983, p. 189). This is why they can accommodate diversity. Hence prototypes are not defined by their essence, but by, 'schemata of their most characteristic members' (Johnson-Laird, 1983, p. 190). In Johnson-Laird's terminology, a schema is 'a model that underlies the ability to form an image'; thus a category can be represented by a, 'schema that specifies, not a set of necessary and sufficient conditions, but the typical or default characteristics of the items it subsumes' (Johnson-Laird, 1983, p. 190). In other words, a prototype, as defined here, is a model of an object or an event that embodies their more typical features. For instance, saying that 1929 is a prototype of a financial crisis refers to a model embodying typical features such as a collapse in asset prices after a long period of euphoria, individuals and institutions ruined in two days, banks and firms going bankrupt, and popular images such as a panicking crowd at the New York Stock Exchange, queues of people at the doors of banks and, a bit later, a pervasive misery.

The difficulty that immediately comes to mind concerns the way of defining 'the more typical features' of an object and 'the most characteristic members' of a class. As we saw in section 2, this is quite feasible in pure chance settings such as the heads and tails game, where the typical features of, say, a fair draw, are determined by probability theory. In these cases, exact representativeness has a precise meaning. However, the task becomes much more complicated in real-life situations where the most simple objects we have to deal with are dogs, houses and cities. Here representativeness cannot be exact (that is, there is not one single way to define what is typical). Indeed, typical features are by definition different from necessary and sufficient conditions: they are sufficient but not necessary. For instance, most birds have feathers and fly. Hence feathers and the ability to fly can be considered as typical attributes of birds, even though some birds do not fly and some non-birds do. In the standard approach to prototypical categorisation, typical attributes will be chosen by what is labelled their 'cue validity' or their degree of predictability. An attribute such as feathers has a high cue validity because it is very frequent in birds and almost absent in all other categories. On the contrary, the feature 'having legs' does not help much in categorizing an animal because a lot of different animals have legs: such an attribute has a low cue validity, it is not a typical feature.[16] A prototype (or a stereotype, those two terms often being used as synonyms) is thus a 'best example' of a given category. It contains more typical attributes than any other object of the class (for example, a sparrow is often considered as a prototype of a bird, whereas this is never the case for a penguin). In this view, judgement by representativeness is a judgement of the degree of prototypicality of the object considered.

The definition of similarity as closeness to a prototype goes back to Wittgenstein and his notion of family resemblance, that is, 'the idea that members of a category may be related to one another without all members having any properties in common that define the category' (Lakoff, 1987, p. 12). Trying to identify what kind of commonality may ground the definition of a concept, Wittgenstein notes: '... we see a complicated network of similarities overlapping and criss-crossing: sometimes overall similarities, sometimes similarities of detail' (quoted by Johnson-Laird, 1983, p. 189) .

Hence, as hinted at by the results of the experiments discussed in section 2, similarity occurs at different levels and has multiple meanings, and it seems impossible to define one single criterion of similarity that would allow us to comprehend representativeness, at a theroretical level as well as in its empirical manifestations.

Properties of Prototypical Categories: Embeddedness and Path-Dependence.

There are many debates about the possible origin of the criteria on which concepts are built. The nature of concepts and of meaning is related to the origin of these criteria, and the many questions underlying this issue are recurrent in the history of philosophy. They certainly lie outside the scope of this chapter, but let us, for our purpose here, briefly recall the general terms of the debate. A long tradition in philosophy, from Plato to Frege, claims that concepts exist outside the human mind, and that, to put it grossly, they can be defined by a set of objective, necessary and sufficient conditions. The criteria by which to judge a dog are well defined and reflect the intrinsic properties of dogs, something like their essence. Of course, humans can only have a subjective idea, a partial knowledge, about dogs, but the concept of a dog exists nonetheless outside individuals. This realist approach (to which the objectivist view of categories evoked earlier corresponds) is in opposition with the psychological view of concepts and meaning emphasizing the fact that criteria are social constructs, conventions in the terminology of Wittgenstein, and depend, among others, on the structure of the mind. These conventions are wide societal agreements allowing individuals to communicate, to be sure that when they say 'dog', they mean the same hairy animal which has the ability to bark and moves its tail when happy.[17] Certainly, as these fundamental similarity criteria do not completly describe a dog, many defaults and exceptions will slowly be added to the prototype by inductive mechanisms, and the concept will become richer with every encounter with a dog, that is, with experience (for a more detailed account of this debate, see Johnson-Laird, 1983, Chapter 9).

In this perspective, criteria are images and models that are embedded in collective, social representations and, as such, are contingent to the specific society and epoch in which they emerge. Let us go back to the answers given by Shiller's traders when they evoked 1929 as a reference they were using in making their predictions about what would happen next. Even if at a theoretical level it is possible to define a financial crisis as a set of necessary and sufficient conditions (indeed, it is our task as scientists), 'intuitive' predictions do not seem to be built on such conditions. Instead, the traders and analysts interrogated by Shiller showed that they were using a typical case of a financial crisis, namely 1929, to construct their judgements: they were judging the actual situation by its similarity to what they knew about this typical case. In turn, their state of knowledge about financial crisis was mainly determined by what they learned at college, the books they read about the subject, stories of friends and of friends of friends concerning 1929 and other dramatic speculative episodes, and so on. Similarity criteria appear to have been shaped by the specific social history people have collectively lived through, and by 'culture' at large – with some marginal variations stemming from particular individual experiences. Because prototypes, at the heart of the processes of categorisation, are mainly social constructs, it seems that it is possible to talk about an 'embodied cognition' (for example, Lakoff, 1987).

This notion of an embodied cognition is quite close to the one of 'embeddedness' which has been developed by Granovetter (1985) concerning the embeddedness of economic behaviours in social structures and culture.

A second property of prototypical categorisation, related quite closely to the one of embeddedness, is path-dependence: categories at an instant depend on what they were before, (that is, on their history). In fact, a distinction has to be made here. As just seen, fundamental criteria on which categories are built are mainly determined by something akin to social conventions and, as such, they depend on history because they are social constructions: the typical characteristics of an engineer today are different from what they were during Da Vinci's time. This dependence on history comes from the embodiment of cognition in social structures and in what is usually denominated as 'culture'. The process of prototypical categorisation is path-dependent in a different way: it depends on history because its mechanisms are mainly inductive ones, and induction is a path-dependent process (for example, Holland *et al.*, 1986; Johnson-Laird, 1991; and for a discussion in economics, Arthur, 1992). Remember that a prototypical category is composed of similarity criteria plus a default hierarchy, that is, a complicated but nonetheless organised network of exceptions which do not contradict the category. Similarity criteria are taught by parents, learned at school or through television at an early age, and, as has just been said, they depend on history because they are embedded. But, at the level of one's individual experience, they are more or less given. Default hierarchies are path-dependent in a more direct way, because, as they are slowly built through experience, the precise manner in which they will evolve, their semantic content, is an outcome of the specific history of the individual, something like a summary of his or her individual history. My default hierarchy may include a default for Mexican hairless dogs because I have encountered few of them, but other people may have totally different default hierarchies, depending on the kinds of dog they have encountered and the experience they have had with them.

The aim of this section was to highlight the basic cognitive mechanisms which are behind the use of the representativeness heuristic. To summarize, one can say that similarity and family resemblance are at the heart of such mechanisms of categorisation; hence judgements by representativeness are easily understandable and do not imply that individuals are irrational. Moreover, one could draw general properties from the process of categorisation and, as representativeness stems from prototypical categorisation, conjecture that judgement by representativeness has the same properties of embeddedness and path-dependence.

CONCLUSION

This chapter has tried to highlight the role of the representativeness heuristic on financial markets. As this alternative way of constructing judgements in complicated and evolving environments is much less demanding in terms of computational and cognitive abilities than Bayes's rule, it is not surprising that it should be pervasively used by agents, especially in environments such as financial markets. Let us summarize the main findings of this preliminary study:

- If individuals primarily use representativeness in forming their expectations on speculative markets, overreaction to new information and bubbles need no longer be considered as 'anomalies'. These phenomena are the aggregate results of the interaction of agents following the 'rules' of prototypical categorisation.
- At a more micro level, representativeness is a clue that learning does not proceed as stated by Bayes's rule; instead it hints at a radically different vision of learning and microbehaviours. If, as it seems, representativeness is a learning heuristic – 'a rule of how to learn new rules' – prototypical categorisation becomes a central learning mechanism and its properties could be considered as more general learning properties. We saw that embeddedness and path-dependence of cognition typify the inductive process of building categories and models. It follows that learning dynamics depend on the specific social structures the agent is embedded in, and the particular history he or she has gone through. Such properties of learning processes may greatly affect price dynamics on financial markets, as the latter are basically 'markets for representations'.[18]
- Finally, many theoretical questions about categorisation and inductive learning processes are still unsolved. For instance, how are similarity criteria formed? They are conventions and, as such, social constructs, but how do these conventions emerge? They may evolve through learning and collective experience, and possibly through individual experience as well. But what are the precise mechanisms of their evolution? What are the links between individual and collective learning dynamics? Another related set of questions concerns the characterisation of the dynamics of inductive learning. Categories are composed of a prototype and hierarchy defaults, and organised to form mental or cognitive models. As we have seen, the evolution of these models is embedded and path-dependent. How can one define learning in such a context? Is it only an evolution of representations and models, whatever the 'direction'? The notion of learning is usually impossible to dissociate from that of amelioration, but when one abandons the reference to a 'true' model of the world, the very definition of amelioration becomes problematic.

NOTES

1 CREA, Ecole Polytechnique, and CREI, University of Paris XIII.

2 The focus here is on individual beliefs; for studies of the formation of collective beliefs from individual interactions, see, for instance, Orléan (1990) and Chapter 6 in this volume. These two issues are nonetheless linked, and individual biases which are observed at the agent's level certainly have some impact at the collective level, although this has not yet been studied at length.

3 The literature on rational learning is immense; for a good overview, see Frydman and Phelps (1983).

4 The terminology follows Nelson's 'appreciative theorizing'. See Nelson (1995).

5 Let us briefly recall Bayes's rule. Let H_A and H_B be two independent hypotheses such that $H_A \cap H_B = \varnothing$ and $H_A \cup H_B = \Omega$. Let C be an event one can observe (that is, information). $P(H_A)$ is the prior probability of having hypothesis A true; $P(H_A|C)$ is the posterior probability of having hypothesis A verified when the event C is observed; $P(C|H_A)$ is the conditional probability of observing the event C when hypothesis H_A is true, and $P(C)$ is the unconditional probability of the event C. If we know $P(H_A)$ – it can be whatever subjective assessment – $P(C)$ and $P(C|H_A)$, then Bayes's rule allows us to calculate the posterior probability of hypothesis A knowing C (the same holds, of course, for H_B):

$$P(C) = \sum_{i=1}^{n} P(C/H_i)\, P(H_i)$$

where

$$P(C) = \sum_{i=1}^{n} P(C/H_i)\, P(H_i)$$

and $H_i = 1...n$, that is n mutually exclusive and collectively exhaustive hypotheses (here, $n = 2$, H_A and H_B). Let us just remark that, if the calculus is very simple, it is nonetheless difficult to perform because the prerequisites in terms of knowledge are quite high. In order to calculate $P(H_i|C)$, the individual has to know $P(C)$ and $P(C|H_i)$, which may not be obvious.

6 The term 'subject' is, as Hey remarks, rather unfortunate, but 'it is now part of the experimental folklore' (Hey, 1991, p. 4).

7 As emphasised by Grether (1980) commenting on this experiment, for another proposed description, the median estimate of the probability that the person was an engineer was close to 0.05, and still for another one it was roughly 0.95, and this, for both groups of subjects. The fact that the two groups made nearly identical estimates clearly shows that prior information was, if not ignored, at least grossly underweighted. A closely related argument is that the extremeness of these estimates (0.05 for one description and 0.95 for another) is in itself favourable to the representativeness hypothesis: these descriptions were stereotypes of lawyers and engineers, and the estimates were mainly determined by the closeness of the description with the stereotype, that is, the strength of the evidence, whatever the base rates.

8 This is the well-known 'as if' argument that Friedman (1953) uses to show that speculation is stabilizing.

9 For a discussion of the methodological issues attached to experimental economics, see, for instance, Hey (1991).

10 The same results have been obtained by Camerer (1987) in a similar setting; priors are underweighted but not ignored, and there is evidence of what Camerer calls, 'exact representativeness' (that is, a neglect of priors when there is a perfect adequacy between the outcome of the draw and the content of the urn).

11 In this type of setting, there is no room for interpretation, and the only randomness

individuals have to face is intrinsic to the game: the criticism that biases are due to interpretation of verbal descriptions cannot hold here.

12 As just said, speculative dynamics are positive feedback dynamics where the dominant models or collective representations (in the sense of Durkheim) coordinate and 'anchor' individual beliefs. The identification of such collective models is thus central to the comprehension of the particular processes of judgement formation which characterize financial markets.

13 This issue of a possible heterogeneity of beliefs, which contradicts rational expectations and its 'true' model of the world, is at the core of an important debate in financial economics, namely, the 'no trade' paradox. The question is about why so much speculative trade occurs on financial markets if people are rational and have consistent beliefs in equilibrium. Seminal contributions are Milgrom and Stokey (1982) and Tirole (1982). Note that if beliefs are mainly formed by following heuristics such as representativeness, as beliefs come from categories and mental models, and in turn the formation and evolution of these models are engendered by contextual and path-dependent processes, it is easy to give an account of heterogeneity (see section 4).

14 Galbraith (1990) notes that investors, especially at the beginning of the mania, are inclined to speculative euphoria because, first, they become rich or richer, and second, they believe their increased wealth is the sign of a 'superior intelligence', a common belief on financial markets and elsewhere. This bias in attributing causality is labelled by psychologists the 'fundamental attribution error', which consists underestimating, 'the impact of situational factors and (in overestimating) the role of dispositional factors in controlling behaviour' (Ross and Anderson,1982, ch. 9, p. 135).

15 For more details on default hierarchies, see Johnson-Laird (1983) and Holland *et al.* (1986).

16 There are many debates about this issue in linguistics and cognitive psychology, and it is not clear that cue validity is the best way to define typical traits (see, for instance, Lakoff, 1987). The 'standard approach' just mentioned refersto the work of Rosch and her followers in the 1970s.

17 The study of the mechanisms by which such norms and conventions appear and perpetuate is outside the scope of this chapter (see Lewis (1969) and Orléan (1994

18 The consequences of these general properties of learning processes on financial dynamics have been studied elsewhere (see Marengo and Tordjman, 1995).

BIBLIOGRAPHY

Arthur, W.B. (1992), 'On Learning and Adaptation in the Economy', Santa Fe Institute Working Paper No. 92-07-038.

Arrow, K.J. (1982), 'Risk perception in psychology and economics', *Economic Inquiry*, **20** (1), 1–9.

Bar-Hillel, M. (1982), 'Studies of representativeness', in D. Kahneman, P. Slovic and A. Tversky (eds), *Judgement under Uncertainty: Heuristics and Biases*, Cambridge, UK: Cambridge University Press, Chapter 5, pp. 68–83.

Blanchard, O.J. and M.W. Watson (1982), 'Bubbles, rational expectations and financial markets', in P. Watchel (ed.), *Crisis in the Economic and Financial Structure*, Lexington, Mass: D.C. Heath .

Camerer, C.F. (1987), 'Do biases in probability judgement matter in markets? Experimental evidence', *American Economic Review*, **77** (5), 981–97.

Camerer, C. (1989), 'Bubbles and fads in asset prices', *Journal of Economic Surveys*, **3** (1), 3–41.

Clapp, J.M. and D. Tirtiroglu (1994), 'Positive feedback trading and diffusion of asset price changes: evidence from housing transaction', *Journal of Economic Behavior and Organization*, **24** (3), 337–55.

De Bondt, W.F.M. and R.H. Thaler (1990), 'Do security analysts overreact?', *American Economic Review*, **80** (2), 52–7.

Durkheim, E. (1896), *Formes Elémentaires de la Vie Religieuse*, Paris: Presses Universitaires de France.

Einhorn, H.J. (1980), 'Learning from experience and suboptimal rules in decision making', in D. Kahneman, P. Slovic and A. Tversky (eds), *Judgement under Uncertainty: Heuristics and Biases*, Cambridge, UK: Cambridge University Press, Chapter 19, pp. 268–83.

Frankel, J.A. and K.A. Froot (1987), 'Using survey data to test standard propositions regarding exchange rate expectations', *American Economic Review*, **77** (1), 133–53.

Friedman, M. (1953), *Essays in Positive Economics*, Chicago: The University of Chicago Press.

Froot, K.A and J.A. Frankel (1989), 'Forward discount bias: is it an exchange risk premium?', *Quarterly Journal of Economics*, **104** (1), 139–62.

Frydman, R. and E.S. Phelps (eds) (1983), *Individual Forecasting and Aggregate Outcomes. 'Rational Expectations' Examined*, Cambridge, UK: Cambridge University Press.

Galbraith, J.K. (1990), *A Short History of Financial Euphoria*, Paris: Editions du Seuil (French translation, 1992).

Granovetter, M. (1985), 'Economic action and social structure: the problem of embeddedness', *American Journal of Sociology*, **91** (3), 481–510.

Grether, D.M. (1980), 'Bayes' rule as a descriptive model: the representativeness heuristic', *Quarterly Journal of Economics*, **95** (4), 537–57.

Griffin, D. and A. Tversky (1992), 'The weighing of evidence and the determinants of confidence', *Cognitive Psychology*, **24** (3), 411–35.

Hey, J.D. (1991), *Experiments in Economics*, Oxford: Basil Blackwell.

Holland, J.H., K.J. Holyoak, R.E. Nisbett and P.R. Thagard (1986), *Induction Processes of Inference, Learning, and Discovery*, Cambridge, MA: The MIT Press.

Johnson-Laird, P.N. (1983), *Mental Models*, Cambridge, MA: Harvard University Press.

Johnson-Laird, P.N. (1991), 'A model theory of induction', *Journal of Technology and Social Studies on Society and Technology.*

Kahneman, D. and D. Lovallo (1993), 'Timid choice and bold forecast: a cognitive perspective on risk taking', *Management Science*, **39** (1).

Kahneman, D. and A. Tversky (1982a), 'Subjective probability: a judgement by representativeness', in D. Kahneman, P. Slovic and A. Tversky (eds), *Judgement under Uncertainty: Heuristics and Biases*, Cambridge: Cambridge University Press, Chapter 3, pp. 32–47.

Kahneman D. and A. Tversky (1982b), 'On the psychology of prediction', in D. Kahneman, P. Slovic and A. Tversky (eds), *Judgement under Uncertainty: Heuristics and Biases*, Cambridge, UK: Cambridge University Press, Chapter 4, pp. 48–68.

Kahneman, D., P. Slovic and A. Tversky (eds) (1982), *Judgement under Uncertainty: Heuristics and Biases*, Cambridge, UK: Cambridge University Press.

Keynes, J.M. (1936), *A General Theory of Employment, Interest, and Money*, Paris: Payot, (second French edition, 1969).

Kindleberger, C.P. (1978), *Manias, Panics and Crashes*, New York: Basic Books.

Kleiber, G. (1990), *La Sémantique du Prototype*, Paris: Presses Universitaires de France.

Lakoff, G. (1987), *Women, Fire, and Dangerous Things. What Categories Reveal about the Mind*, Chicago: The University of Chicago Press.

Lane, D.A. (1993), 'Artificial worlds and economics', *Journal of Evolutionary Economics*, **3**, 89-117..

Langton, C.G., C. Taylor, J.D. Farmer and S. Rasmussen (eds) (1991), *Artificial Life II*, Redwood City, CA: Addison-Wesley.

LeRoy, S.F. (1989), 'Efficient capital markets and martingales', *Journal of Economic Literature*, **27** (4), 1583–1621.

Lewis, D. (1969), *Convention. A Philosophical Study*, Cambridge, MA: Harvard University Press.

Mackay, C. (1841), *Extraordinary Popular Delusions and the Madness of Crowds*, NewYork: Harmony Books (second edition, 1980).

Marengo, L. and H. Tordjman (1995) 'Speculation, heterogeneity and learning: a model of exchange rates dynamics', *IIASA* Working Paper No. 95-17.

Merton, R.K. (1936), 'The self-fulfilling prophecy', *Social Theory and Social Structure*, New York: The Free Press (second edition, 1968), pp.475–90.

Milgrom, P. and N. Stokey (1982), 'Information, trade and common knowledge', *Journal of Economic Theory*, **26** (1), 17–27.

Nelson, R.R. (1995), 'Recent evolutionary theorizing about economic change', *Journal of Economic Literature*, **33** (1), 48–90.

Orléan, A. (1990), 'Contagion mimétique et bulles spéculatives', in J. Cartelier (ed.), *La Formation des Grandeurs Economiques*, Paris: Presses Universitaires de France, pp. 285–321.

Orléan, A. (ed.) (1994), *Analyse Economique des Conventions*, Paris: Presses Universitaires de France.

Palmer, R.G., W.B. Arthur, J.H. Holland, B. Le Baron and P. Tayler (1994), 'Artificial economic life: a simple model of a stockmarket', *Physica D*, **75**, 264–74.

Rosch, E. (1975), 'Cognitive representation of semantic categories', *Journal of Experimental Psychology*, **104**, 192–233.

Ross, L. and C.A. Anderson (1977), 'Shortcomings in the attribution process: on the origins and maintenance of erroneous social assessments', in D. Kahneman, P. Slovic and A. Tversky (eds) (1982), *Judgement under Uncertainty: Heuristics and Biases*, Cambridge, UK: Cambridge University Press, Chapter 9, pp. 129–52.

Shiller, R.J. (1989), *Market Volatility*, Cambridge, MA: MIT Press, (third edition, 1991).

Tirole, J. (1982), 'On the possibility of speculation under rational expectations', *Econometrica*, **50** (5), 1163–81.

Tversky, A. and D. Kahneman (1982a), 'Judgement under uncertainty: heuristics and biases', in D. Kahneman, P. Slovic and A. Tversky (eds) (1982), *Judgement under Uncertainty: Heuristics and Biases*, Cambridge, UK: Cambridge University Press, Chapter 1, pp. 3–20.

Tversky, A. and D. Kahneman (1982b), 'Belief in the law of small numbers', in D. Kahneman, P. Slovic and A. Tversky (eds) (1982), *Judgement under Uncertainty: Heuristics and Biases*, Cambridge, UK: Cambridge University Press, Chapter 2, pp. 23–31.

Tversky, A. and D. Kahneman (1982c), 'Judgements of and by representativeness', in D. Kahneman, P. Slovic and A. Tversky (eds), *Judgement under Uncertainty: Heuristics and Biases*, Cambridge, UK: Cambridge University Press, Chapter 6, pp. 84–98.

6. The Ambivalent Role of Imitation in Decentralised Collective Learning

André Orléan

INTRODUCTION

In order to understand how a group of agents collectively reacts to changes in its environment, many variables have to be taken into account, such as conflicts of interest, incentive compatibility, beliefs and information. The present chapter will focus on the cognitive dimension of collective learning. More precisely, the purpose of this chapter is to study the aggregation problem: how information initially dispersed among atomised agents is made available to the group. This question is of great importance for markets as well as for organisations. For example, M. Aoki (1984) has emphasised the importance of cognitive issues in the theory of the firm. He has shown that the ability of a firm to deal with the random events affecting its optimal production schedules depends crucially on its internal informational structure. He has compared the efficiency of two types of coordination: vertical (managerial hierarchy) and horizontal (decentralised learning at the level of each shop). Aoki's results clearly show that, in order to understand how a group learns, we have to take into account not only the accuracy of the private information possessed by each individual, but also the way each agent of the group is linked to the others. This last point is at the core of the present work. In order to be more precise, a few notations will be introduced.

We consider a group of N agents named i, with $i \in \{1,2,..., N\}$. Each individual i controls an action, say $a_i \in A_i$. $\mathbf{a} = (a_1, ..., a_N)$ is the group action and we will note $\mathbf{a}_{-i} = (a_j)_{j \neq i}$. $\boldsymbol{a}$ belongs to $A = A_1 \times ... \times A_N$. Let us denote the state of the environment, $\theta \in \Theta$. It is determined exogenously according to a certain probability distribution $\mu(\theta)$ on the set Θ of possible states. Before choosing an action, each group member receives an information signal, σ_i. σ_i is the private information possessed by the agent i about the state θ. The value of the signal σ_i will lead the agent to revise his prior belief μ_i about the value of θ. If the signal is sufficiently precise, the agent will be able to guess the true value of the state of the world. Nevertheless, in most cases his private information is insufficient, and agent i will have to seek additional information to improve his estimate. The determination of this complementary information will depend on the structure in which collective action takes place. We will note by ω_i agent i's information, that is σ_i plus what agent i knows about the information possessed by others. ω_i is a random variable depending on θ. The N–tuple $\omega = (\omega_1, ..., \omega_N)$ will be called the information structure of the group. The central question is to what extent the information structure is able fully to reveal to each member all the information possessed by the group, $\sigma = (\sigma_1, ..., \sigma_N)$.

In most of the situations studied by economic theory, individual agents cannot observe directly the information held by others; they can only access it indirectly through observing their actions (or a function of their actions). Such an information structure will be called 'decentralised'. Markets provide an example: their information structure is given by $\omega_i = (\sigma_i, P)$ with $P = P(a_1, ..., a_N)$ being the price. A great deal of work has been devoted to the analysis of this particular information structure: among others, the theory of signalling (Spence, 1973), the debate on the informational efficiency of competitive stock markets (Grossman, 1976; Grossman and Stiglitz, 1980), and the discussion about the informational merits of alternative resource-allocating schemes for economies (Hurwicz, 1960; Marschak, 1986).

To evaluate the efficiency of an information structure, we have to analyse the way ω affects the determination of **a**. Let us first consider agent i's action. It can be written:

$$a_i = f(\mathbf{a}_{-i}, \omega_i, \mu_i) \qquad (6.\ 1)$$

Equation (6.1) is the result of agent i's expected utility maximisation given ω_i. From the modeller's point of view, recalling that ω_i is a random variable, it follows from equation (6.1) that agent i will choose action a_i with probability:

$$\pi_i\,(a_i \mid \Phi\,(\mathbf{a}_{-i}))\ \forall a_i \in A_i \qquad (6.2)$$

It should be emphasized that $\mathbf{a}_{-i}$ affects the determination of agent i's action through two different effects because agent i's utility depends on the actions of others and because these actions are part of the information structure. This double role is at the core of the analysis of the informational efficiency of prices that stresses the 'dual role of price, affecting demand through the budget constraint and through expectations' (Gennotte and Leland, 1990, p. 1000). The set of probability laws $\{\pi_i\}_{i=1,...,N}$ is called a random field if $\pi_i\,(a_i \mid \Phi\,(\mathbf{a}_{-i}))$ is positive, $\forall a_i \in A_i$. It generates a global probability Pr over the space A. In other words, $Pr(\mathbf{a})$ gives the probability of observing the collective decision **a** when the individual decisions are taken simultaneously according to the set of local probabilities $\{\pi_i\}_i$. This general formalisation has been introduced by Föllmer (1974) to describe random economies composed of many interacting agents. It is very well suited to the analysis of complex structures and has been used by S. Durlauf (1993) and A. Kirman (1993) to study spatially localised interactions.

In what follows, we will only consider decentralised information structures. ω_i is equal to $\omega_i = (\sigma_i, X)$ with $X = X(a_1,...,a_N)$. X will be called the collective opinion of the group. The market information structure is a particular case where X is equal to P, the price. In assessing the probability of the state θ, each agent uses both his private information and the group opinion expressed by X. A central rule of probabilistic calculus is that the relative weight assigned to private information and to collective opinion is controlled by the expected accuracy of X. This is a consequence of Bayes's rule. We will denote by s the expected accuracy of X. s is a measure of the group's confidence in the relevance of the collective opinion. For small values of s, individual estimations are close to the ones that would be formed on the sole basis of their private information, σ_i. When s increases, the relative weight individuals assign to the opinion of others increases. This constitutes a form of imitative behaviour. Thus s can be considered as a measure of the role played by imitation in the formation of individual expectations. The purpose of this chapter is to analyse the way s affects the efficiency of a decentralised information structure.

Our main result is to show that the role played by s is ambivalent. When s is too small, individuals rely mainly on their private information. In such circumstances, an increase in s can generate better estimations. Hence imitation improves collective learning within decentralised structures because it allows σ, the information of the group, to be taken into account by individual agents. However, when s reaches the critical threshold s_c, the group opinion, X, is given too much weight relative to private information. This introduces a self-reinforcing dynamic which becomes disconnected from the group's information, σ, and leads to strong biases in the individual and collective estimations. By analogy with financial dynamics, these self-reinforcing processes will be called 'bubbles'. This ambivalence of s is a direct consequence of the intrinsic ambivalence of imitation: it is efficient for me to imitate others as long as they are really better informed; it becomes inefficient if they are also imitators. This result is partly negative because it shows that, within a decentralised information structure, the information possessed by the group as a whole cannot be completely revealed to each individual. The collective action, X, can reflect σ only partially. This result can be interpreted as a new formulation of Grossman and Stiglitz's paradox about the impossibility of informationally efficient markets (Orléan, 1998). This negative result provides an argument for some degree of centralisation of information structures.

This result is demonstrated in the context of a dynamic model. At each period, t, the way agents use both sources of information, their private signal, σ_i, and $X(t-1)$, in revising their beliefs, is modelled as a stochastic process, the asymptotic properties of which are studied. Our model is close to the one proposed by Bikhchandani, Hirshleifer and Welch (1992). As in their model, the dynamics of imitative decision processes result from entirely rational behaviour. The main distinction between their model and the model presented here lies in the sequence of individual decisions. In Bikhchandani *et al.*, individuals enter the market one by one, and each agent takes a unique and irreversible decision on the basis of the decisions of all those who have entered ahead of him. Here we study the behaviour of agents who are interacting simultaneously with one other and who modify their actions at each period in the light of new information.

Section 2 presents the basic model. Section 3 shows that, because agents cannot directly observe the information obtained by the others but have to infer it from their actions, it is rational for them to be partly imitative. Section 4 demonstrates that two kinds of imitative dynamic must be distinguished: one which is efficiency-improving and another which gives rise to self-validating opinions. A final section concludes.

THE BASIC MODEL

Let us assume that the group is composed of N agents named i, $i \in \{1,2,...,N\}$ and that their environment, θ, is either in state {H} or in state {L} with equal probability. The agents cannot observe directly the state of the environment; they only have access to a signal, σ, which is defined as follows: σ is either {+} or {–} and its value is linked to the value of θ through the following conditional probabilities:

$$\begin{cases} P(\sigma = + \mid \theta = H) = P(\sigma = - \mid \theta = L) = p > 0.5 \\ P(\sigma = - \mid \theta = H) = P(\sigma = + \mid \theta = L) = 1 - p < 0.5 \end{cases} \tag{6.3}$$

The closer p is to 1, the more precise is the signal. Agent i's private information, σ_i, is defined as an independent observation of the signal σ.

The decision a_i that each agent i has to make is to determine whether the state of nature is {H} or {L}: he has to guess what the true state is. Then the collective opinion of the group a will be completely defined by n, the number of agents having chosen {H}, or by $f = n/N$, the proportion of such agents. We will consider an information structure such that $\omega_i = (\sigma_i, f)$.

Let us begin by analysing the situation where each agent makes his choice on the sole basis of his private information: $\omega_i = \sigma_i$. To determine his choice, agent i will calculate $P(H \mid \sigma_i)$ and $P(L \mid \sigma_i)$ by applying Bayes's rule:

$$P(H \mid \sigma = +) = P(H \mid +) = \frac{P(+ \mid H) \cdot P(H)}{P(+)} \tag{6.4}$$

with:

$$P(+) = P(+ \mid H) \cdot P(H) + P(+ \mid L) \cdot P(L)$$

Knowing that each state is equi-probable, agent i obtains:

$$P(H \mid +) = p_i \quad \text{and} \quad P(H \mid -) = 1 - p_i \tag{6.5}$$

With p_i, the evaluation made by agent i of $p = P(+ \mid H)$. Agent i will choose the state corresponding to the highest probability. It follows that agent *i's* choice will depend upon his prior belief about the value of p. If i has observed {+}, he will choose {H} if his estimation of p_i is greater than 0.5, and {L} if p_i is less than 0.5. Let us assume that each agent has the same probability of correctly interpreting the signal σ:

$$P\{p_i > 0.5\} = q\,(+) \tag{6.6}$$

$q\,(+)$ will be supposed greater than 0.5. Agents who correctly interpret σ will be called type A agents, while agents who misinterpret the signal will be called type B agents. An agent's type is not determined ex ante. It changes at each time, t, according to the probability $q\,(+)$. $\{q\,(+) = 1\}$ corresponds to the case where each agent makes the right inference (i.e. $p_i > 0.5\ \forall i$). Then the probability $q_0(\sigma_i)$ to choose {H}, when private information is σ_i, is given by the following formula:

$$q_0\,(+) = q\,(+) \quad \text{and} \quad q_0\,(-) = q\,(-) = 1 - q\,(+)$$

The probability of choosing {H} depends on q (+) and on the probability $\alpha(\theta)$ of observing (+). It is equal to:

$$P(\theta) = \alpha(\theta) \cdot q(+) + [1 - \alpha(\theta)] \cdot [1 - q(+)] \tag{6.7}$$

This probability depends on the value of θ through the variable $\alpha(\theta)$ equal to:

$$\alpha(H) = p \quad \text{and} \quad \alpha(L) = 1 - p \tag{6.8}$$

Then $f = n/N$ is a random variable that follows a binomial law, called $\tilde{f}$, whose parameter is equal to $P(\theta)$ (equation 6.7). We obtain:

$$\begin{cases} E(\tilde{f} \mid \theta) = P(\theta) \\ Var(\tilde{f} \mid \theta) = \dfrac{P(\theta) \cdot (1 - P(\theta))}{N} \end{cases}$$

It follows that when the information structure does not promote interaction among the agents, the collective frequency of making the right choice is, on average, equal to the individual probability of making the right choice. This result clearly shows that the information structure under consideration does not allow for the dissemination of the global information, σ. If we measure the efficiency of the information structure by the expected proportion of agents having made the wrong choice, we find:

$$E(e \mid \theta) = p \cdot (1 - q(+)) + (1 - p) \cdot q(+) \quad \forall \theta \in \Theta = \{H, L\} \qquad (6.9)$$

With e being the error defined as follows:

$$\begin{cases} \text{if } \theta = \{H\}, & e = 1 - f \\ \text{if } \theta = \{L\}, & e = f \end{cases}$$

The average error is at a minimum for $q = 1$; then its value is equal to $(1 - p)$. Obviously the rule q_0 is not very efficient. Because f reveals some part of the global information, σ, possessed by the group, it should be useful to try to take advantage of this variable which is made publicly available by the information structure. We will now analyse decision rules that take f into account.

THE ROLE PLAYED BY RATIONAL IMITATION IN INDIVIDUAL DECISIONS

Let us consider an agent of type A. When he observes (+) and $\{f > 0.5\}$, the two signals are consistent, thus he will choose {H}. When he observes {+} and $\{f < 0.5\}$, he faces two contradictory pieces of information. He can decide either to follow the majority side of the group (that is, to be imitative) or to follow his private information. His decision will depend on the relative confidence he has in these two pieces of information. An agent's confidence is a function of his prior beliefs about the way that the group forms its opinion, σ_i. Before analysing the general case, let us consider the following example of such prior beliefs.

Suppose that agent i believes that the other agents' behave such that their probability of making the right choice is equal to u_i. Let us also suppose that agent i believes that other agents are making their choices independently, according to the probability u_i. In this case, for agent i, the number of agents having made the right choice follows a binomial law of parameter u_i. u_i is agent i's estimation of the precision of the collective opinion $f = n / N$. It has to be compared with p_i, agent i's estimation of the precision of his own private signal, σ_i. Applying Bayes's rule, agent i can calculate:

$$P(H \mid f,+) = \frac{P(f,+ \mid H) \cdot P(H)}{P(f,+ \mid H) \cdot P(H) + P(f,+ \mid L) \cdot P(L)}$$

with:

$$\begin{cases} P(f,+|H)=P(f|H)\cdot P(+|H)=\binom{N}{n}u_i^n(1-u_i)^{N-n}\cdot p_i \\ P(f,+|L)=P(f|L)\cdot P(+|L)=\binom{N}{n}(1-u_i)^n u_i^{N-n}\cdot(1-p_i) \end{cases}$$

Agent i will choose {H} if and only if $P(H\,|\,f,+)>0.5$, which can be expressed as:

$$\left(\frac{u_i}{1-u_i}\right)^{2n-N}\left(\frac{p_i}{1-p_i}\right)>1$$

or as:

$$2N(f-½)\,k_i+h_i>0 \tag{6.10}$$

with:

$$\begin{cases} k_i=g(u_i) \text{ and } h_i=g(p_i) \\ \text{with}: \; g(x)=log\left(\frac{x}{1-x}\right) \end{cases}$$

$g(x)$ is a strictly increasing function that is negative when x is inferior to 0.5, positive when x is superior to 0.5 and equal to 0 when x is equal to 0.5. k_i and h_i measure the precision of f and σ_i respectively. If $p_i>0.5$ and if $u_i>0.5$, k_i and h_i are strictly positive. Then, when $\{f>0.5\}$, the condition (6.10) is always verified. This result is quite evident: an agent of type A who draws (+) and observes $\{f>0.5\}$ will always choose {H}. However, when the agent observes $\{f<0.5\}$, the decision is more problematic because the two signals are conveying contradictory information. In that case, which signal will be favoured? It follows from equation (6.10), that the agent will choose {L} if:

$$\frac{k_i}{h_i}>\frac{1}{2N}\cdot\frac{1}{\frac{1}{2}-f}=v(f) \tag{6.11}$$

This condition can be interpreted in the following way: the favoured signal will be the one that has the higher relative precision in the sense of equation (6.11). To study how our agents will behave, we thus have to know their prior beliefs about the relative precision of the two sources of information. We will characterise agents' prior beliefs by the distribution $\mu(k\,/\,h)$. This could be interpreted in two manners. One possibility is that each agent is characterised by a particular u_i and p_i, and μ is the distribution of k_i / h_i over the whole population. Alternatively, each agent is characterised by the distribution μ of k_i / h_i, and each time an agent makes a choice it is based on a random draw according to the distribution μ. While these two hypotheses give rise to the same mathematical formulation, the latter interpretation is developed in this text.

It follows from these considerations that, for an individual of type A who has observed (+), the probability of choosing {H} for $f \in [0, ½[$ is:

$$P\left(\frac{k}{h} < v(f)\right) = \int_0^{v(f)} d\mu \tag{6.12}$$

It appears that the probability of choosing {H} is an increasing function of f. This result can easily be generalised to the cases of an agent of type A having observed (–), or of an agent of type B. We will now make a comparative study of populations of agents when μ is allowed to change. To do this we will consider a family of $\mu(k / h, s)$ indexed by the parameter s such that: when $s_1 > s_2$, $\mu(s_1)$ stochastically dominates $\mu(s_2)$, $\forall s \in [0, +\infty]$, that is:

$$\int_{-\infty}^{x} d\mu\left(\frac{k}{h}, s_1\right) < \int_{-\infty}^{x} d\mu\left(\frac{k}{h}, s_2\right) \forall x \in R \tag{6.13}$$

In other words, the population $\mu(s_1)$ attributes a greater precision to the signal f than does the population $\mu(s_2)$. The higher s, the more important the role of imitation in the construction of the individual estimations. Hence the probability of choosing {H} for an agent of type A having observed (+) and $\{f < 0.5\}$ is smaller for the population $\mu(s_1)$ than for the population $\mu(s_2)$. This follows directly from equations (6.12) and (6.13). The explication is simple: the population $\mu(s_1)$ is more sensitive to the information conveyed by f than the population $\mu(s_2)$.

These properties have been established when agents' prior beliefs about the way that the collective opinion f is formed follows a binomial distribution of parameter ui. Let us now consider the general case by denoting by $q(f, \sigma_i, s)$ the probability of choosing {H} when agent i's information is (σ_i, f) and when his confidence in f is measured by s. The properties of $q(f, \sigma_i, s)$ are then considered as a generalisation of what has been obtained in the previous case.

For $s = 0$, we have the rule q_0. The agents are not imitative at all. When making their choices, they ignore the decisions of others. When s increases, the importance of imitation increases. This means that the probability of following the majority opinion will increase. In other words:

$$\begin{cases} \text{if } f \in \left[0, \frac{1}{2}\right[& q(f, \sigma_i, s) \text{ is a decreasing function of } s \\ \text{if } f \in \left]\frac{1}{2}, 1\right] & q(f, \sigma_i, s) \text{ is an increasing function of } s \end{cases} \quad (6.14)$$

When $s = +\infty$, agent i completely relies on others' decisions. He is totally imitative. The rule q_∞ verifies the following constraints:

$$\begin{cases} \text{if } f \in \left[0, \frac{1}{2}\right[& q_\infty(f,+) = q_\infty(f,-) = q_\infty(f) = 0 \\ \text{if } f \in \left]\frac{1}{2}, 1\right] & q_\infty(f,+) = q_\infty(f,-) = q_\infty(f) = 1 \end{cases} \quad (6.15)$$

Thus the family of rules $q(f,\sigma_i, s)$ indexed by s will verify:

$$\begin{cases} q(f,\sigma_i,s) \text{ satisfies the condition (6.14)} \\ q(f,\sigma_i,s) \text{ is an increasing function in } f \\ q(f,\sigma_i,0) = q_0(\sigma_i) \\ q(f,\sigma_i,\infty) = q_\infty(f) \\ q(f,-,s) = 1 - q[(1-f),+,s] \quad \text{(symmetry)} \end{cases}$$

$q(f, \sigma_i, s)$ corresponds to equation (6.2) within our model. To analyse the way collective action is linked to the parameter s, we have to find the global probability $P(f, s)$ that is generated by the individual probabilities $q(f, \sigma_i, s)$. To do so, we will introduce a particular family of decision rules verifying conditions (6.15), that is the logistic functions determined by:

$$q(f,\sigma_i,s) = \frac{q(\sigma_i)}{q(\sigma_i) + [1 - q(\sigma_i)]e^{-m(f-0.5)}} = q_s(f,\sigma_i) \quad (6.16)$$

where $m = m(s)$ is a strictly increasing function such that $m(0) = 0$ and $m(\infty) = \infty$. In the rest of the chapter, we will simply assume that $m(s) = s$. Figure (6.1) corresponds to the case $q(+) = 0.8$ and $s = 0.5$. We verify that $q_{0.5}(f, +)$ is very close to $q_0(f, +)$, a constant function equal to $q(+)$. Figure (6.3) corresponds to $s = 15$. We verify that $q(f, +, 15)$ is close to $q_\infty(f)$ (that is, a step function).

THE DYNAMICS OF IMITATIVE DECISIONS

To understand how the collective opinion is formed when individuals follow the rule $q(f, \sigma_i, s)$, we will consider the following dynamic process. At time $(t = 0)$, the state θ is drawn randomly and held constant. The collective opinion $f(0)$ is arbitrarily determined. At time $(t + 1)$, an individual[1] is randomly drawn within the whole population. He makes an observation, σ_i, of the signal, σ. On the basis of σ_i and $f(t)$, the collective opinion publicly announced at the end of period t, this agent revises his last opinion according to the rule $q(f, \sigma_i, s)$. His probability of choosing {H} at $t + 1$ is equal to:

$$J(f, s, \alpha(\theta)) = \alpha(\theta) \cdot q(f, +, s) + (1 - \alpha(\theta)) \cdot q(f, -, s)$$

with $\alpha(\theta)$ given by the equation (6.8). For the sake of simplicity, we will write α in place of $\alpha(\theta)$. Let us emphasise that the value of θ affects the calculation through the value of α. If, at date t, $n(t) = n$, then at time $(t + 1)$, $n(t + 1)$ can be equal either to $n - 1$, or to n, or to $n + 1$. The transition probabilities are given by:

$$\begin{cases} P(n \to n+1) = (1-f) \cdot J(f,s,\alpha) = W_+(f,s,\alpha) \\ P(n \to n-1) = f \cdot [1 - J(f,s,\alpha)] = W_-(f,s,\alpha) \end{cases} \tag{6.17}$$

Let us call $P(f;t)$ the probability law which the random variable $f(t)$ follows. It verifies the following master equation:

$$\frac{dP(f;t)}{dt} = P(f - \frac{1}{N};t) \cdot W_+(f - \frac{1}{N}) + P(f + \frac{1}{N};t) \cdot W_-(f + \frac{1}{N}) - P(f;t) \cdot [W_+(f) + W_-(f)] \tag{6.18}$$

A good approximation of equation (6.18) is the following Fokker-Planck equation in one dimension:

$$\frac{\partial P(f;t)}{\partial t} = -\frac{\partial}{\partial f}[K(f)P(f;t)] + \frac{\varepsilon}{2} \cdot \frac{\partial^2}{\partial f^2}[Q(f)P(f;t)] \tag{6.19}$$

with:

$$\begin{cases} K(f,s,\alpha) = W_+(f,s,\alpha) - W_-(f,s,\alpha) \\ Q(f,s,\alpha) = W_+(f,s,\alpha) + W_-(f,s,\alpha) \\ \varepsilon = \dfrac{1}{N} \end{cases} \tag{6.20}$$

The stationary distribution will be noted $P_{st}(f, s, \alpha)$ or $P_{st}(f)$. For $s \in [0, +\infty[$, it can be shown that the process is ergodic: $lim_{t\to+\infty} P(f;t) = P_{st}(f)$, $\forall f(0)$. For $s = +\infty$, the process is no longer ergodic. There exist two stationary distributions: δ_0 and δ_1, the Dirac distributions in $\{f = 0\}$ and $\{f = 1\}$.

To get an intuitive idea about this stochastic dynamics, one can note that, when $W_+(f)$ is greater (resp. smaller) than $W_-(f)$, f will on average increase (resp. decrease) equation (6.17). Therefore, it can be shown (Weidlich and Haag, 1983) that, if the fluctuations are neglected, f will follow the deterministic path given by:

$$\frac{df}{dt} = K(f,s) \tag{6.21}$$

The fixed points of this deterministic process will be the extrema of the stationary distribution. The stable fixed points are maxima; the unstable ones are minima. From equation (6.17), it follows that:

$$K(f, s, \alpha) = -f + J(f, s, \alpha) \tag{6.22}$$

It follows that the extrema of the stationary distribution are given by:

$$J(f, s, \alpha) = \alpha \cdot q(f, +, s) + (1 - \alpha) \cdot q(f, -, s) = f \tag{6.23}$$

Because $K(0, s, \alpha) = J(0, s, \alpha) > 0$ and $K(1, s, \alpha) = -1 + J(1, s, \alpha) < 0$, it follows that there always exists at least one interior maximum. Figures (6.4–6.6) show the transformation of $K(f, s, \alpha)$ when s varies, for $\theta = \{H\}$ and $\alpha = p = 0.7$. To present our results, we will suppose that $\theta = \{H\}$, which is equivalent to $\alpha = p$. Then f, the proportion of individuals having chosen {H}, is a direct measure of the efficiency of the information structure. Because of the symmetry condition of $q(f, \sigma_i, s)$ it is easy to deduce the results when the state is {L} from what is obtained when the state is {H} because f is transformed in $(1 - f)$.

It can then be shown that there exists a value s_c which verifies the following properties. For $s \in [0, s_c]$, the stationary distribution is unimodal (Figure 6.7). Its maximum is noted $f_1(s, p)$. For large N, its variance is very low and $f(t)$ will remain in a small neighbourhood around f_1. Then it is easy to measure the efficiency of the information structure: the closer f_I is to 1, the more efficient is the way the information structure reveals the collective information.

For $s = 0$, $f_I(0, \alpha) = P(\theta)$ (equation 6.7). When s increases, $f_I(s, p)$ increases. Thus, it appears that being imitative improves collective performance. The observation of f allows unlucky individuals, for instance type A agents who have observed (–), to correct their initial choice and to change it to the correct decision. Because imitation is the specific decentralised manner through which collective information is disseminated, collective efficiency is improved.

However, when s becomes greater than s_C, the stationary distribution is qualitatively modified: it becomes bimodal (Figure 6.8). A new peak appears, which will be noted $f_M(s, p)$. $f_M(s, p)$ is always smaller than 0.5. Thus it corresponds to a collective configuration where the majority of agents make the wrong choice even if the proportion of agents having observed (+) is approximately equal to $p > 0.5$. The collective opinion is determined in contradiction to the information possessed by the majority of its individual members. This situation corresponds to a self-validating process that will be called a 'bubble'. The first peak f_I remains present. It should be emphasised that the transition time for collective opinion to change from one peak to the other is extremely long, approximately λe^N. So if we observe the group during a plausible finite time, no 'phase transition' will be observed: the collective opinion will remain in the neighbourhood of one of the two peaks. The probability of reaching one peak or the other depends on the initial state, $f(0)$.

When s increases from s_C to $+\infty$, $f_M(s, p)$ decreases from $f_M(s_C, p)$ to 0. The higher the weight given to collective opinion, the stronger the bias generated by the bubble. For very large values of s, one can observe a quasi-unanimity on the wrong choice {L}. Simultaneously, when s increases from s_C to $+\infty, f_I(s, p)$ tends towards 1. There can be a quasi-unanimity on the right choice, even if a substantial proportion of agents have observed (–) or is of type B.

CONCLUSION

This chapter has shown that imitation can generate two kinds of very different dynamic. The first one, expressed by $f_I(s, p)$, is efficiency-improving. Through behaviour relying partly on imitation, agents incorporate in their estimations a part of the global information. Imitation can then be viewed as the specific manner through which decentralised information structures disseminate their information: because people cannot directly observe the information of others, they infer it indirectly from collective action through imitation. When s increases, $f_I(s,p)$ tends towards 1.[2] The second kind of dynamic, expressed by $f_M(s,p)$, is quite different. There, imitation gives rise to a self-reinforcing process that disconnects the collective opinion from the information possessed by the group. When s increases, the magnitude of the bubble increases: $f_M(s,p)$ tends towards 0.

Because private information in decentralised information structures is revealed by the very same dynamic process that produces self-validating beliefs, namely imitation, the collective information can only be partially revealed. A totally decentralised information structure becomes inefficient when the threshold s_C is reached. The best performance of the group is equal to $f_I(s_C)$. This negative result has been demonstrated on the basis of a particular family of decision rules (equation 6.16). It can be shown that, as soon as we consider a family of rules that verifies:

$$\exists \varepsilon \text{ such that } \forall f \in [0,\varepsilon[, \quad \lim_{s \to +\infty} q(f,\sigma_i,s) = 0$$

this result holds. The ambivalent role of inter-individual interactions can help us to understand why financial markets can suddenly evolve from a partially efficient regime to a bubble, even if the qualitative features of individual behaviour remain the same. The emergence of a bubble is not the consequence of sudden irrationality on the part of the investors. Rather, it results from a slight modification in the individual's level of confidence in the group opinion.

Figure 6.1 : q(f, s, +) with q(+) = 0.8 and s = 0.5

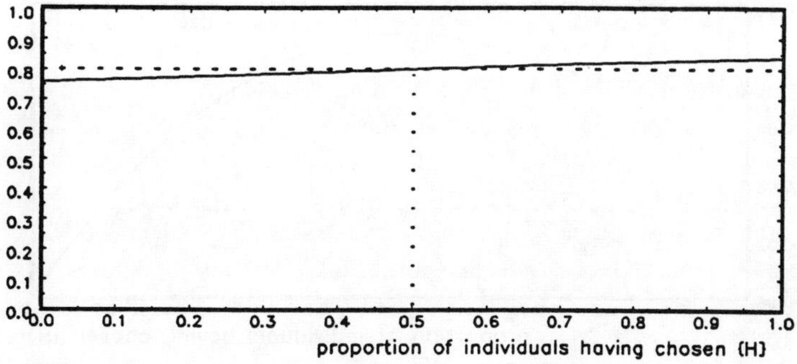

Figure 6.2 : q(f, s, +) with q(+) = 0.8 and s = 6

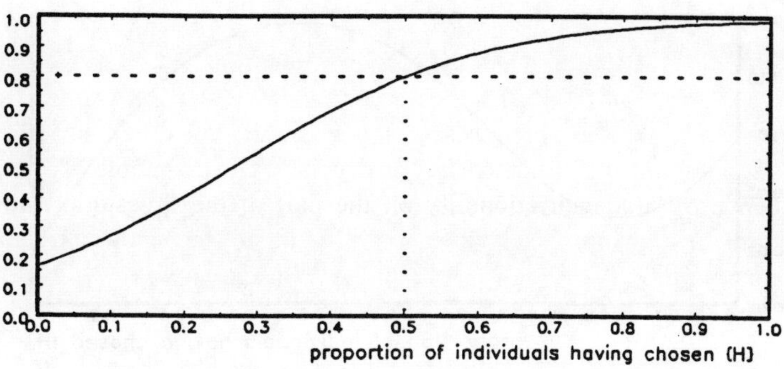

Figure 6.3 : q(f, s, +) with q(+) = 0.8 and s = 15

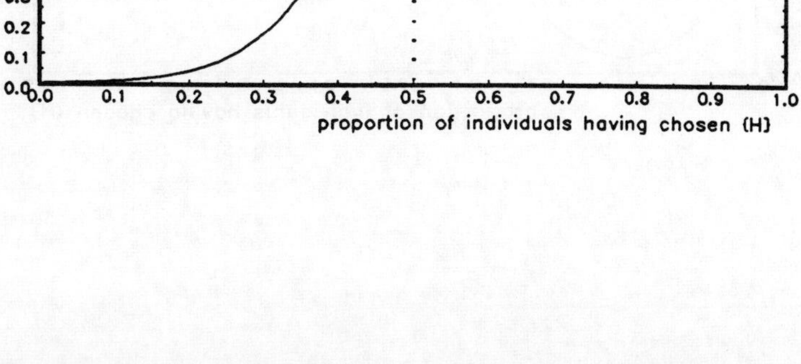

Figure 6.4 : K(f,s) with q(+) = 0.8 and s = 6

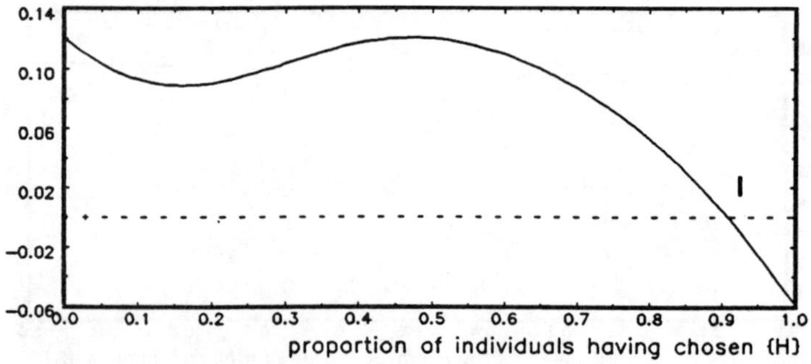

Figure 6.5 : K(f, s) with q(+) = 0.8 and s = 7.79

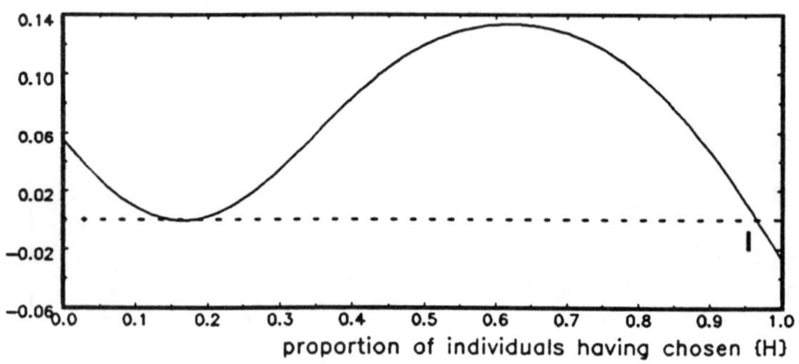

Figure 6.6 : K(f, s) with q(+) = 0.8 and s = 9

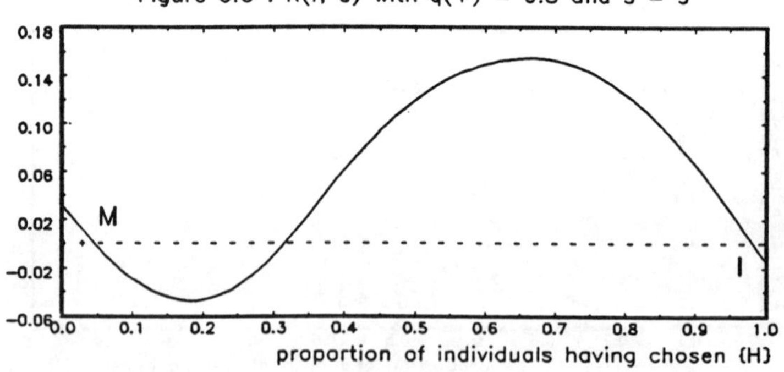

Figure 6.7: Pst(f, s=5, 0.7)

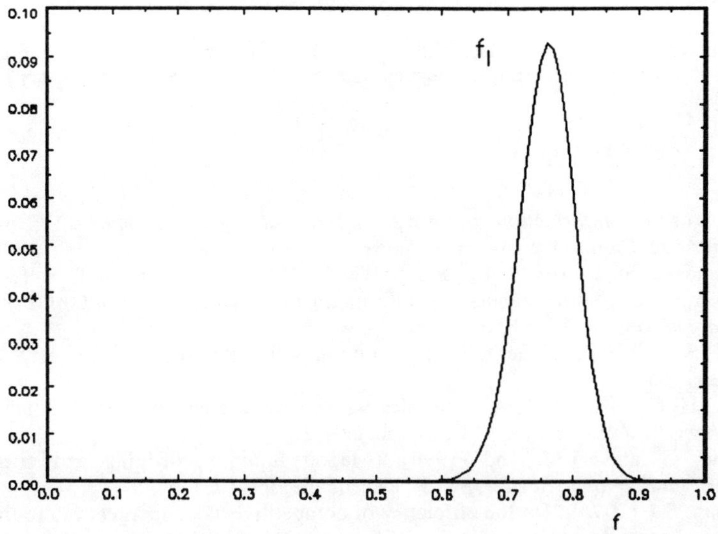

Figure 6.8: Pst(f, s=9, 0.7)

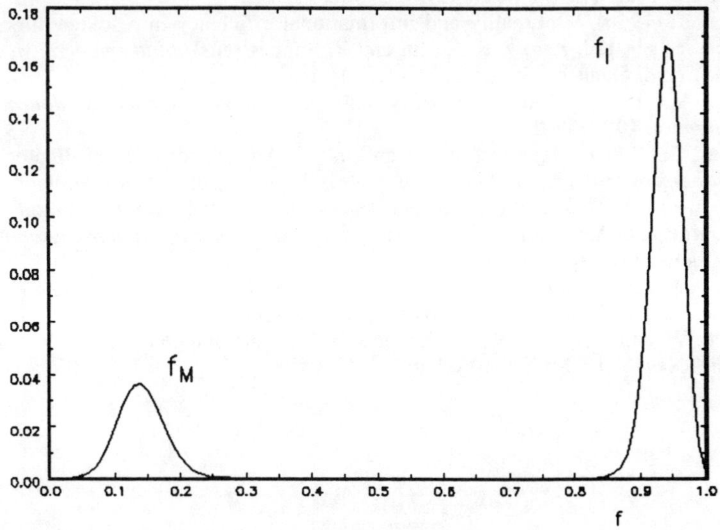

NOTES

1 One could have drawn L individuals with L ≪ N, without qualitatively modifying our results.
2 Recall that we are considering a situation such that {θ = *H*}. For {θ = L}, f_I (*s,p*) tends towards 0.

BIBLIOGRAPHY

Aoki, M. (1984), *Information, Incentives and Bargaining in the Japanese Economy*, Cambridge: Cambridge University Press.

Bikhchandani, S., D. Hirshleifer and I. Welch (1992), 'A theory of fads, fashion, custom, and cultural change as informational cascades', *Journal of Political Economy*, **100** (5), 992–1026.

Durlauf, S.N. (1993), 'Nonergodic economic growth', *Review of Economic Studies*, **60**, 349–66.

Föllmer, H. (1974), 'Random economies with many interacting agents', *Journal of Mathematical Economics*, **1** (1), March, 51–62.

Gennotte, G. and H. Leland (1990), 'Market liquidity, hedging and crashes', *American Economic Review*, **80** (5), December, 999–1021.

Grossman, S.J. (1976), 'On the efficiency of competitive stock markets where traders have diverse information', *Journal of Finance*, **31**, May, 573–85.

Grossman, S.J. and J.E. Stiglitz (1980), 'On the impossibility of informationally efficient markets', *American Economic Review*, **70** (3), June, 393–408.

Harris, M. and A. Raviv (1993), 'Differences of opinion make a horse race', *The Review of Financial Studies*, **6** (3), 473–506.

Hurwicz, L. (1960), 'Optimality and informational efficiency in resource allocation processes', in K.J. Arrow, S. Karlin and P. Suppes (eds), *Mathematical Methods in the Social Sciences*, Stanford: Stanford University Press.

Kirman, A. (1993), 'Ants, rationality and recruitment', *Quarterly Journal of Economics*, **108**, 137–56.

Marschak, T. (1986), 'Organization design', in K.J. Arrow and M.D. Intriligator (eds) *Handbook of Mathematical Economics*, Vol. III, Amsterdam: North-Holland.

Orléan, A. (1998) 'Informational influences and the ambivalence of imitation', in J. Lesourne and A. Orléan (eds), *Self-Organisation and Evolutionary Economics: New Developments*, Paris: Economica.

Spence, A.M. (1973), *Market Signalling: Information Transfer in Hiring and Related Processes*, Cambridge, MA: Harvard University Press.

Weidlich, W. and G. Haag (1983), *Concepts and Models of a Quantitative Sociology*, Berlin; New York: Springer-Verlag.

7. Cooperation and Trust in Spatially Clustered Firms

Jean-Claude Dupuy and André Torre[1]

INTRODUCTION

A considerable amount of research has recently been undertaken at the frontier between industrial and spatial economics, especially around the theme of proximity in the dynamics of the locally clustered firms.[2] A particularly interesting aspect of this debate relates to the possible advantages firms derive from being located on the same site, and more generally to the causes of the spatial concentration of firms. The notion of 'proximity' lies at the heart of much of this recent work, and in particular, stress has been laid on the importance of proximity for the emergence of cooperative relations among groups of firms.

Trust is often seen as a necessary ingredient for establishing and maintaining cooperative patterns of behaviour among spatially concentrated firms. Trust relations are seen as protecting the local system against the risks of destabilisation and collapse. Placing trust at the centre of the analysis of local agglomeration of firms, raises the question of whether new entrants may have a destabilising impact on established patterns of cooperation. This is an important issue to raise, since it can be argued that new entrants are in a superior position to offer new skills and to promote innovation within the local cluster of firms (Elliasson, 1991; Jayet and Torre, 1995). The increasing recognition of the importance of a local dimension in the renewal of productive resources (Feldman, 1994) suggests the need for a more systematic analysis of this issue.

In what follows we take up a series of questions related to the possible tension between the need for openness and the need for restrictions on entry in a local system of firms. How can the stability of the local system be made compatible with the competitive entry process? Is it possible to sustain bonds of trust while simultaneously allowing for new entrants? In section 3 we address these questions by developing an evolutionary game theoretic model of local learning inspired in part by Axelrod's (1984) computer simulations of the repeated prisoners' dilemma. Before doing this, we develop in section 2 the basic principles underlying the local clustering of firms and the relation of this process to trust.

TRUST RELATED TO PROXIMITY LINKS

Following Krugman (1991a), local relations among firms can be analysed along two dimensions: in terms of the weight of past events on current behaviour; and in terms of the convergence of expectations towards a shared future. As regards the convergence of expectations, which is what principally interests us here, two ways of envisaging the construction of a common future can be identified, according to whether stress is laid on the behaviour of the actors or on the social origins of their shared representations. In the case of shared representations, emphasis is often placed on the way given cultural norms or values can sustain cooperative patterns of behaviour among a local cluster of firms. The basic idea is that the violation of a prescribed norm by any individual member of the community will entail a penalty in the form of the loss of the trust formerly placed by other local agents. Of course it may be necessary to go beyond a purely cultural approach and to take into account the way institutions and local policy can reinforce collective rules of behaviour.

When emphasis is laid on the individual, the most interesting case is where individual behaviour proves self-reinforcing because of some positive feedback mechanism between individual belief and choice and the collective outcome. By analogy one can think of the way mimetic behaviour on financial markets can reinforce the optimism of individual traders through its impact on share prices. An important question to raise is the role played by trust in such self-fulfilling processes.

Regardless of whether one begins the analysis at the level of individual behaviour and beliefs or at the level of shared representations, it can be claimed that trust is the key to the stability of cooperative patterns of behaviour among locally clustered firms. However attractive this proposition may seem, it requires careful scrutiny, if only because the meanings of the terms 'trust' and 'shared representation' are far from clear. For example, it might seem that trust is a purely informal dimension of inter-firm relations. However, it can be argued that an element of trust will be present in any contractual relation given the difficulty of observing all the characteristics of a product or a service which is exchanged. A related point is that inter-firm relations may combine elements of trust and cooperation with elements of competition (Rullière and Torre, 1995). For example, cooperation over some aspects of technological development does not preclude competition in the final product market. Finally, as is implicit in this latter observation, cooperation is inevitably linked to trust. This is a rather hasty conclusion that requires further examination.

Arrow's (1971) remark that, 'trust cannot be purchased in the marketplace' is a useful starting point for investigating the concept. First, it is noteworthy that the problem of trust is raised under conditions of uncertainty associated with imperfect or incomplete information. In particular, trust pertains to the problem of an individual's inability to predict fully the future behaviour of competitors or partners. It is right at this starting point, however, that analytical difficulties appear. Even if trust exists *ex ante* in a relationship, it is necessary to give some account of its origins. If one argues that the initial build-up of trust was based on a form of economic calculation which aims to eliminate uncertainty from the exchange relation, one faces the problem that such calculative modes of reasoning tend to raise doubts in the minds of one's partners about one's intentions. Making the economic calculation is fundamentally a mistrustful move, a fact which justifies applying the expression 'trust paradox' to this situation (Rullière, 1994).

This point was raised by Williamson (1993) in his attack on the improper use of the term 'trust' in economic literature. For Williamson (1993, p. 463), 'calculative trust' is a contradiction in terms, and it is not appropriate to talk of trust where calculation is involved, since, as Orléan (1994) points out, in this case the standard theory of risk would be perfectly applicable. To back up his point, Williamson produces a series of convincing examples in which the terms 'risk' and 'trust' are interchangeable.

One way of transcending this dilemma while simultaneously relating it to the question of spatial proximity is to follow Sabel (1992) in distinguishing two ways in which trust can be produced: 'firstly, when there are many exchanges ...; and secondly, on account of reasons that can be explained in terms of a common historical background – the same religion, the same political convictions, or a common cultural or ethnic inheritance ...'.

Thus, it is possible to identify alongside interpersonal trust based on repeated interactions, a second approach which can be called 'shared' or 'absolute' trust based on the diffusion of a cultural norm within a localised innovation and production system (LIPS). These two dimensions will now be examined and situated in their spatial context.

Interpersonal Trust and Cooperation

Interpersonal trust and the role it plays in perpetuating LIPSs can be tackled by analysing the term 'commitment'. In committing themselves, actors are responding to two concerns (Rullière, 1994). First, by providing advance indications of how they will react to certain changes in their environment, they restrict their liberty of action. Second, by circulating information about their future decisions, they seek to reduce uncertainty regarding the likely behaviour of others. The public character of the action of making a commitment thus contributes to simplifying the matter of anticipating how other agents will behave. This is particularly important in the constitution of LIPSs.

It is necessary to look at the role trust plays in this process, as commitment can be openly cooperative or, alternatively, it may represent a credible threat. In both cases it can contribute to the construction of a cooperative process. This is illustrated by the fact that a credible threat is a way of informing partners of one's actual preferences and dispositions, something which can often lead to cooperation rather than conflict. The fact that a threat can lead to cooperation shows that trust and cooperation should be clearly distinguished.

One way of exploring the mechanisms leading to the establishment of relations of trust between actors in a context artificially shorn of its cultural attributes is to consider the 'tit-for-tat' strategy discussed by Axelrod (1984). In the repeated prisoners' dilemma, cooperative behaviour may be sustained through the mutual adoption of the strategy of tit-for-tat, which consists in starting out by cooperating and then in subsequent moves adopting the choice your opponent adopted in the previous move. Axelrod's approach is not without its critics. Le Cardinal and Guyonnet (1994) propose a 'confidence strategy' method for resolving conflicts, while Delahaye (1992) claims that no account is taken of the nature of incomes in Axelrod's experiment nor of the stability of trust itself, nor indeed of the possibility of learning during the course of the game itself. For these reasons, a tit-for-tat strategy cannot take into account the strategy of the 'swindler', who hides his intentions until his final move when he brutally betrays the other player (Le Cardinal and Guyonnet, 1994). This latter strategy is founded on the increasing trust created by the effect of reputation and the positive experience derived from repeated moves. But here again the frontier between trust and cooperation is treated in an ambiguous manner, giving rise to the doubt that there is any real autonomy between the terms.

The assimilation of cooperation and trust is understandable. Both concepts require cooperative strategies and the reciprocity of good behaviour. Nevertheless, important differences appear. These can be illustrated by comparing tit-for-tat strategies with a strategy of 'generalised' or 'absolute' trust. Tit-for-tat is by nature essentially based on suspicion, since the initial action of cooperation is followed by observing the partner's actions. Generalised trust, on the other hand, finds its justification in the prevailing atmosphere of a community of actors, as in the Marshallian approach. The very idea of punishment is foreign to this setting.

The difference between trust and cooperation is also evident if we compare

Kreps's (1990) analysis of trust with Axelrod's analysis of tit-for-tat. For Kreps, trust is irremediably sullied at the first sign of defection. This is not so in the case of tit-for-tat or 'cooperative TFT' (where punishment ensues after the second defection), since it is possible to win back the trust of one's partner after a shortcoming by adopting a cooperative attitude and entering a new phase of the game. This proves not only that trust in the strong sense of the term is not a necessary condition for cooperation, but that distrust (a way of testing the opponent's reactions, not to be confused with defiance, which leads to systematic defection) is often more capable of producing better results. Trust, in the absolute sense of the term, is an ingredient which may combine with a cooperation strategy, without being absolutely necessary to its survival.

We agree with Rivaud-Danset's view (1995) that the object of trust is to reinforce the weight of the future and to lessen the agent's preference for the present in those situations where the gains from an inter-temporal relation are not known. Correspondingly, as Sako (1995) remarks, trust can be defined as the mutual expectation that partners will not take advantage of areas of vulnerability opened up by the relation of cooperation. The major interest of trust, in face-to-face relations, lies in the inadequacies of explicit (and even implicit) contractual relations. Indeed, its association with informal modes of coordination in which contracts are not fully specified leads to the view that trust can have a distinctive 'domestic' quality, often seen as typical of relations marked by geographic proximity. This result is in line with the suggestions made by Dupuy and Gilly (1995), Torre (1995) and Servet (1994), for whom trust enjoys a dialectical relationship with proximity. It leads to the general question of whether relations of geographical proximity between actors foster the establishment of a bond of trust which contributes to the stability of a dynamic process.

A further point to remember is that the existence of a trust relation in no way guarantees the absence of future difficulties, if only because the establishment of harmonious relations does not preclude errors of anticipation. Agents' expectations are rarely rational. It is hard for them to foresee the way in which the system will evolve, especially when it comes to externally produced mutations, such as those associated with the arrival of new actors in the local system. Finally, trust in no way precludes sub-optimal outcomes. One can even argue that trust can give rise to inertia where local actors simply reproduce existing routines and patterns of interaction.

Shared Trust

It is difficult to reduce the notion of trust to that of an interpersonal relation, at least for those situations which are of interest to us. The characteristic

LIPS organisation of the production of goods and technical objects resembles the construction of a local order, in Friedberg's (1993) sense of the term. In other words, it is the result of a social construction involving multiple actors who find themselves entangled in collective processes. Extending the analysis beyond the dimension of bilateral inter-firm relations leads to a conception of a network of individual interests or, to use Granovetter's (1985) phrase, of local actors embedded in a network of relations.

The local order thus created is subject to permanent modification. Far from being in equilibrium, it is ceaselessly being challenged and perhaps even threatened. This is shown by the problems currently being encountered by the industrial districts of the 'third Italy' or by the way certain rural zones have been abandoned. An example is given by Courlet and Dimou (1995) in their comparison of the productive systems of Castres and Mazamet. The permanent process of change can lead either to reinforcement or to the risk of disintegration.

A first clue to the role of 'absolute' trust in the dynamics of a local system is to be found in the idea of 'domestic' or 'community' exchange in which the element of monetary equivalence is not paramount (de Sainte Marie, Casablanca and Poggi, 1994). This type of exchange is often associated with the strength of ethnic or religious ties among the members of the group, who because of their common culture are able to communicate easily and diffuse certain behavioural standards or conventions (David, 1994). The cultural homogeneity the group displays ensures that relations of trust are maintained. This is all the more true for networks that are small and that do not overlap with others (Granovetter, 1994). This type of trust may actually be a brake on economic expansion on account of its excessively localised character and due to the fact that it is limited to a small number of participants. The dynamic process of locking out new entrants can result in lower standards being sustained and in the relative decline of the local system.

Trust, in this strong sense of the term, is linked to the diffusion and acceptance of common cultural norms within a system. It goes back to Hobbes's reply to the question about individual coordination when agents have diverging interests yet must cooperate. The solution lies in renouncing their liberty in exchange for an external authority. Being the product of a shared historical background within a social group, trust is immediately granted and cannot be seen as being based on a succession of actions designed to establish a reputation.

Furthermore, if we assume that trust is freely given, a setback does not constitute a challenge to the overall stability of the system, at least in so far as it is not repeated systematically. It is more akin, if we stretch the meaning of the term slightly, to a notion of 'interpersonal' trust which is restricted to a family or a close set of neighbours. What is distinctive about this absolute trust is that it is very difficult to create it intentionally. furthermore, as with all situations involving trust, it can cause negative effects due to irreversibilities and the persistence of sub-optimal routines, as stressed above. It may even be responsible for the granting of exorbitant privileges to members of the same community. This indicates how very difficult it is to incorporate external elements into a LIPS – external elements which may carry a potential threat of disorder if they do not conform to shared rules and standards.

If group members are sufficiently similar, they will be able to communicate, both within their own community and to those outside it, certain easily recognisable social conventions and standards of behaviour. The similarity does not need to be perfect, but it does require anchor points, conveyed by social communication. It can be seen that such a system, provided it does not break down, promotes cultural homogeneity through the efficiency of established information networks. This is the bedrock on which relations of trust, with the stamp of a feeling of common identity, are founded. As information circulates, it supplies the basis for general recognition among individuals.

The individual in such settings is never entirely anonymous. A certain number of community 'qualities' are attributed to him, so that a minimum amount of knowledge can be said to exist between those involved, even in the absence of interpersonal experience. It is this which enables trust to be formed and maintained. As Orléan (1994) observes: 'The question of trust is closely linked to the fact that protagonists belong to certain communities. When X seeks to evaluate whether or not he can trust Y, what he analyses is Y's relation with a certain community and its rules. Can Y be said to be a reliable member of that community?'.

A certain anonymity may be introduced into such a community as soon as the relationship transcends its established communal bounds. This is what often occurs when certain communities are forced to acquiesce to new 'rules of the game'. Opening the door to new behaviour patterns or to new enterprises and, therefore, simultaneously to alternative cultural schemes, leads to a contradiction between the maintenance of identity and the necessary renewal of the industrial tissue. We will postulate here that geographical proximity can constitute a factor of cohesion and diffusion of information, and that it fosters the creation of relations of cooperation and helps to render them durable.

FROM TRUST TO COOPERATION : CAN LOCALISED INDUSTRIAL PRODUCTION SYSTEMS (LIPS) BE DESTABILISED?

If the argument developed above is valid, the question of trust is found to be at the centre of the contemporary debate about territorial dynamics. In what follows we shall attempt to address two related questions. First, is the maintenance of a situation of absolute trust (that is, the existence of relations of systematic trust between LIPS actors) compatible with the opening-up of the system to external influences? In other words, is a trust-based LIPS able to assimilate the external forces it needs for its renewal? After a period of upheaval, will it be able to reach a new equilibrium?

Second, does the proximity enjoyed by local actors favour the establishment and maintenance of mutual relations of trust? Is it the cement which maintains relations of cooperation, specially designed to maintain LIPS and renders them durable, as is often claimed in the literature?

A first approach used to address these questions is to take the simple framework of a closed community of individuals (a LIPS) governed by strict rules accepted by all. This encourages generalised trust, which has at least two conditions attached to it: legitimacy of the rules and a certain degree of transparency. The repercussions due to the introduction into such a system of new players, who do not necessarily share the same rules and penalties bound up with these rules, will be examined. These new actors will not necessarily use the same strategies as the original actors. For the model of these relations and their evolution, we shall use the evolutionary game (Dupuy and Luga, 1995) that has been inspired, by and developed out of, Maynard Smith's work in biology (Maynard Smith and Parker, 1976; Maynard Smith, 1982), and which was later popularised by Axelrod (1980, 1984).

The central notion in this approach is that of the evolutionary stable strategy (denoted ESS) which was pioneered by Maynard Smith. The ESS excludes the existence of would-be competing strategies. Its properties are such that any new strategy that appears will be incapable of invading the population of actors, with the (almost) unanimous adoption of the original strategy being re-established. A strategy is said to be dominant if, and only if: (1) it is generally adopted by most members of the population under consideration; and (2) small deviant groups are less successful than ESS actors.

The case of mutations that may affect LIPS is illustrated by means of the following model. A game with n players is considered to have two possible strategies: i and j. The proportion of players choosing i, at the time period t, is called $p(t)$, and the proportion choosing j is denoted $(1 - p(t))$. It is postulated that, at each stage in a game, a player is confronted with only one competitor, who may or may not have adopted an identical strategy, so that the players' expected gain can be written as follows:

for a player choosing i: $E(i,p) = p(t)\, U(i/i) + (1 - p(t))\, U(i/j)$
for a player choosing j: $E(j,p) = p(t)\, U(j/i) + (1 - p(t))\, U(j/j)$

with $U(i/j)$ the utility a player gets from the adoption of strategy i when his opponent has chosen the strategy j.

If strategy i is evolutionary stable, in other words if $E(i,p) > E(j,p)$, the number of players adopting it will grow in the population under consideration. This can be expressed in the following form :

$$dp(t)/dt = F\{E(i/p) - E(j,p)\}$$

If the function F grows and keeps its sign, it is considered to be collectively stable (Maynard Smith, 1982). As Crawford remarks (1992), 'this definition is founded on the intuition that if all members of a population play an ESS, the mutants appearing among the population will replicate more slowly than those using an ESS. Thus, the relative frequency of mutants will tend to zero over time' if $E(i,p) > E(j,p)$. Consequently, if p tends to 1, i invades j if, and only if:

$$U((i/i) >= U(j/i)$$

or

$$U(i/j) = U(j/i) \text{ and } U(i/j) > U(j/j)$$

The interest of the notion of stability lies in its evolutionary character. This makes it possible to analyse the way in which agents behave inside a given system. A strategy will remain stable, then, as long as no mutant strategy appears, or as long as the mutant strategy does not expand enough to challenge the dominant strategy. This might be by chance, by rational decision or simply by trial and error. It is now possible to introduce a dynamic element into the analysis.

The basic mathematical model for analysing evolutionary and selection phenomena, known as a dynamic replicator, is based on the hypothesis that individuals interact in pairs, in the form of a finite and symmetrical game for two players. The pairs of individuals are distributed at random and the gains from the game represent the extent to which the player has adapted to the environment, each player being programmed always to use a constant strategy. An extensive mathematical treatment of the properties of these equations is given by Hofbauer and Sigmund (1988) and Weibul (1993).

With a view to testing LIPS stability, we shall assume that the behaviour of each player is defined by the variable, *Vi*. This variable can have two values, either +1 (cooperate) or -1 (defect). Two possible evolutions of the game, stemming from different methods of introducing mutations, are compared. The starting-point is a population of players composed initially entirely of individuals who trust each other systematically – a situation of absolute trust. At each time period, a certain number of mutants, corresponding to external agents, are introduced. These mutants represent the system's openness to external influences. These mutants may have the same strategy of absolute trust as the original players, or they may have new strategy, drawn at random from the following eight categories, as defined by Axelrod (1984):

- *Absolute trust* (you always cooperate);
- *Defiance* (you always betray);
- *Cooperative/mistrustful* (you cooperate initially, and then you play the same move as your counterpart did in the preceding one. This is known as 'tit-for-tat', as popularised by Axelrod (1984). It is a fundamentally cooperative strategy);
- *Spiteful* (you cooperate but as soon as your opponent begins to betray, then you betray at all future moves);
- *Unpredictable* (you betray every second move in a random fashion);
- *Periodically mean* (you betray, betray, cooperate... continuously);
- *Periodically cooperative* (you cooperate, cooperate, betray ... continuously);
- *Mean/mistrustful* (in the first game, you betray, and then you play the move chosen by your opponent in the preceding period).

In order to ascertain how much change is required to destabilise the LIPS and jeopardise the strategy of absolute trust, successively greater quantities of mutations are introduced, in a constant manner with respect to time (that is to say, 1 per cent, then 5 per cent, 10 per cent, 15 per cent ...). These random mutations are used to maintain diversity in the population and to test the stability of absolute trust or of any other strategy that could take its place.

On this basis two types of population dynamics are tested. The first has agents interacting in a random manner. This means that, at each period, each player interacts with eight other randomly drawn actors. He is then able, in the light of the results of these interactions, to modify his own strategy after comparing his accumulated gains with those of his opponent. The second has the actors interacting in the context of a neighbourhood. This makes it possible to test the effects of proximity on the emergence and durability of ESS. Each player's game is structured in such a way that he can only play with neighbouring players so that LIPS stability, and the consequences of introducing a spatial dimension into actor relations, can be studied. The closest neighbour solution on the cellular automaton grid is opted for here: the player is restricted to playing on a lattice with his eight neighbours, following Elliasson (1993).

As is often the case in the analysis of evolutionary stable games, a prisoners' dilemma is tested. If this does not favour cooperative behaviour patterns, it may nevertheless, after much repetition, lead to the appearance of cooperative strategies, as actors are in a position to ascertain the gains to be obtained from different types of strategy at earlier stages in the game.

Mutations in a System Bereft of Proximity

In an attempt to understand how a system dominated by relations of absolute trust can evolve as a function of the mutations to which it is subjected, we start with a proximity-free game. The mutants can be new actors or existing ones who under the influence of new environmental constraints, modify their rules for action. Even if the results are more complex than those obtained by Axelrod, they are nevertheless similar to his in the sense that the tit-for-tat strategy is often the winner. However, it is only victorious if the volume of mutations is sufficiently great (that is, if the system itself is sufficiently open), without being so great that it leads to a destabilisation of the system. This introduces serious constraints compared with the traditional evolutionary game scheme. Next, the simulations show that absolute trust (or loyalty) is not an ESS. It is very quickly challenged by other strategies. This result confirms a certain number of intuitions (see Jaisson, 1993): a system founded on absolute trust is easily undermined by the appearance of actors who 'do not play the game'. It quickly finds itself being invaded by other strategies from new players or from existing ones confronted with repeated failure and who, therefore, change their strategy. Overall, it is established that the stability and durability of a system founded on absolute trust are jeopardised by the introduction of exogenous mutations.

If, to give a precise example, 1 per cent mutations are introduced into the system (Figure 7.1), it can be seen that the absolute trust norm is rapidly undermined and quickly replaced by an ESS, that is to say a strategy of defiance. This result reveals how very difficult it is to ensure the permanence of relations of trust in a system which is open (in however small a degree) to the outside world, given the speed with which it has problems when actors with new rules of action make their presence felt. Despite the fact that the system possesses the alternative strategy of tit-for-tat (see Boyer and Orléan, 1995), it is clear that this alternative does not emerge on account of the system's lack of openness .

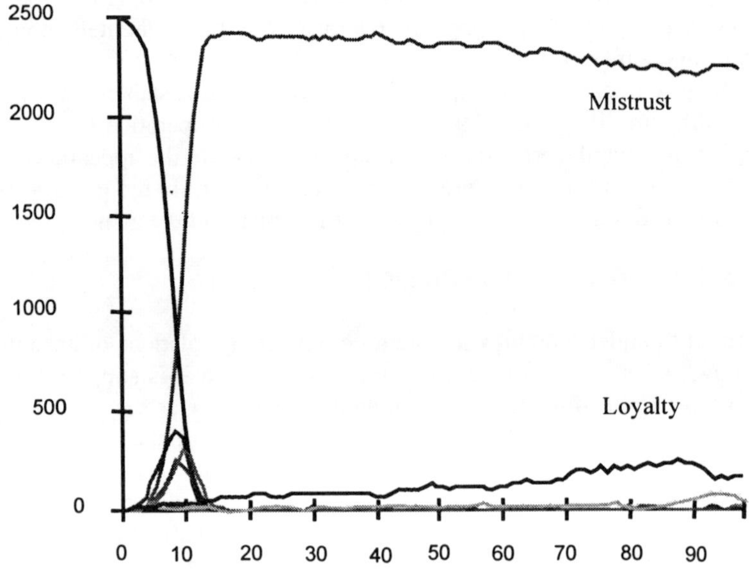

Figure 7.1 The prisoners' dilemma: 1 per cent mutations, 2500 individuals, no proximity

The situation is radically different in the case of simulations with initially 5 per cent and then 10 per cent mutations (Figures 7.2 and 7.3). In both cases, absolute trust is again quickly undermined by the appearance of exogenous mutations. The process that ensues is relatively complex. At first, there emerges, as with the previous case, a strategy of defiance. However, it is subsequently challenged by tit-for-tat, which wins the day to become an ESS. It is to be noted that the period of time which needs to elapse before tit-for-tat emerges is a relatively lengthy one. This is because it is a strategy that learns from, or at least makes allowances for, results achieved during preceding periods.

If Axelrod's results are largely confirmed in the above two situations, the same does not apply in the case where 15 per cent mutations are introduced in each period (Graph 4). Indeed, the higher degree of openness of the system makes the emergence of a tit-for-tat type norm much more delicate, and leads to the coexistence of a variety of strategies (that is, defiance, cooperative/mistrustful and periodically cooperative), without any ESS necessarily being able to gain the upper hand.

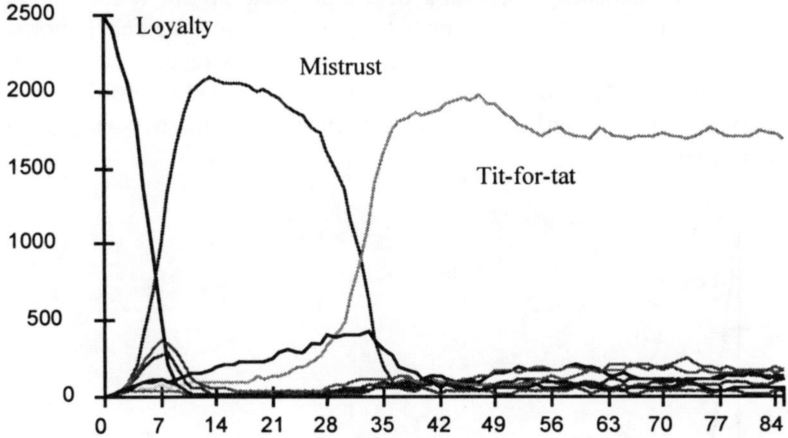

Figure 7.2 The prisoners' dilemma: 5 per cent mutations, 2500 individuals, no proximity

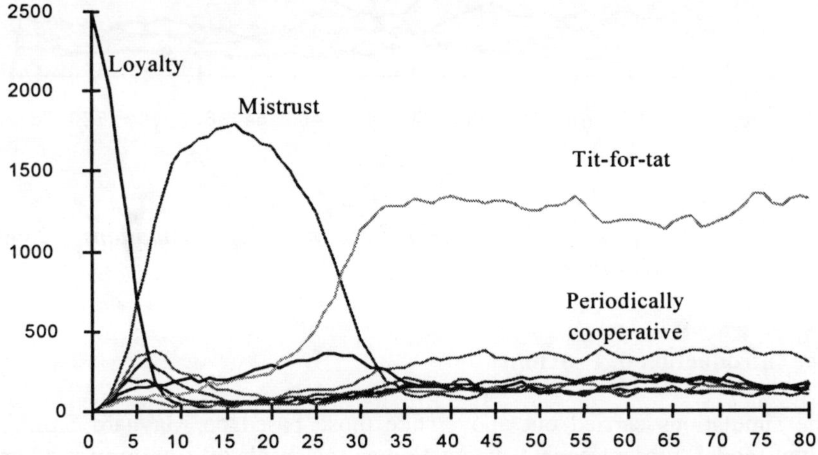

Figure 7.3 The prisoners dilemma: 10 per cent de mutations, 2500 individuals, no proximity

In sum, the spontaneous emergence of cooperation in the bosom of an anonymous population, which is interacting in a random manner, is not so certain as Axelrod's work would have us believe. This result is also to be found in Boyer and Orléan (1995). This suggests that neither absolute trust nor tit-for-tat can be an ESS in a system that undergoes large-scale endogenous mutations.

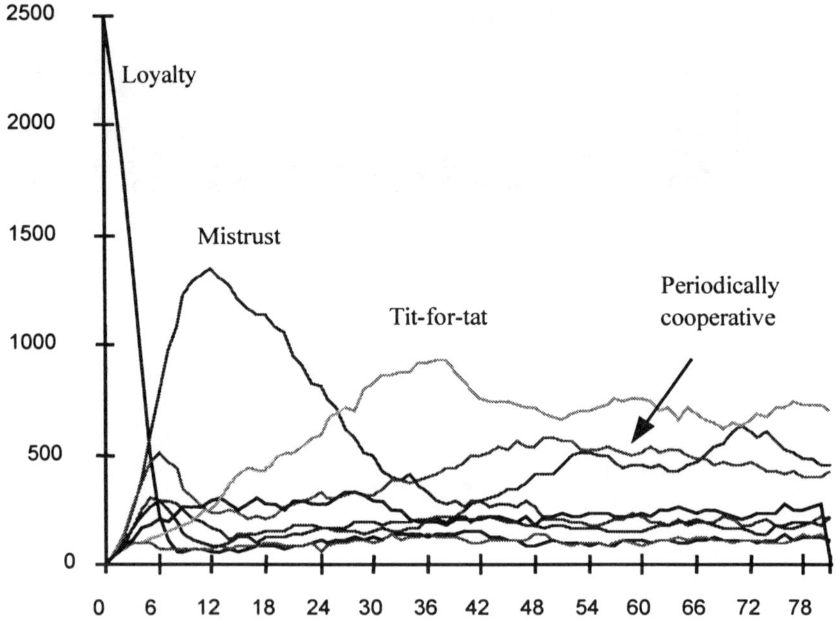

Figure 7.4 The prisoners' dilemma: 15 per cent mutations, 2500 individuals, no proximity

The Introduction of Proximity

The simulations carried out above, like those based on Maynard Smith's initial model, present agents' interaction as the result of a uniform random draw in a given population. They ignore proximity. In the case that interests us, it is postulated that actor proximity is important, and can lead to stronger relations of trust and cooperation. In other words, the question relates to the degree of stability of a LIPS, or to its capacity to undergo large changes. For this reason, we ask ourselves at this point if the proximity that exists between local actors favours the establishment and maintenance of mutual relations of trust, or whether, on the contrary, it brings no modification compared with a non-spatial world. The intuition, suggested by Axelrod (1984) and then taken up again by Boyer and Orléan (1994), that neighbourhood interactions could constitute a vector for the diffusion of new strategies in a territory through the phenomenon of imitation or colonisation of ideas, places the agent in a spatial framework. In our simulation, we follow one of the cases highlighted by Elliasson (1993). Each agent is limited to playing with his immediate neighbours, of whom there are eight in all, on a lattice (see Figure 7.4). It is clear that the proximity here is plural, and that it cannot be interpreted solely in geographical terms.

The results obtained by the simulation are very clear. They show that proximity constitutes a factor of cohesion and that it helps the diffusion of information liable to contribute to the establishment and perpetuation of relations of cooperation in a LIPS. Indeed, in marked contrast to the proximity-free simulations, the tit-for-tat strategy emerges in every case envisaged, and it is always an ESS. On the other hand, in conformity with the preceding example, the absolute trust norm quickly loses out, in every case, to other strategies (defiance or tit-for-tat). This indicates nicely that it is chronically incapable of constituting an ESS when the system is open, in however minor a way, to the outside world. It draws attention to the danger of confusing absolute trust, which is an ineffective strategy here, and cooperation (the sole game–ESS tested). It is established that the effect of local interaction encourages each actor to conform to the choice made by his neighbours. It engenders a simple behaviour selection process which tends to favour the emergence of a norm. This construction of a 'social' norm is, by its very nature, dynamic, as it transcends simple individual behaviour. In fact, it is the spatial character of the relation that favours the early establishment of the tit-for-tat strategy in small 'islands' of population. From this base, it goes on to colonise the remaining opinions. It goes without saying that, in the absence of proximity links, the appearance of clusters of players adopting tit-for-tat takes a great deal longer to emerge, on account of the fact that actors won over to it are dispersed throughout the population. Thus proximity accelerates the rhythm of change and favours the adoption of tit-for-tat strategies. There is, indeed, a geometry of altruism.

A more detailed examination of the simulation results confirms these elements. In the 1 per cent mutation with proximity prisoners' dilemma (Figure 7.5), absolute trust is swiftly undermined, losing out initially to defiance and then subsequently to tit-for-tat, which emerges here for the first time. The results are very similar when 5 per cent or 10 per cent mutations are introduced (Figure 7.6 and 7.7): the only difference is the slower rate of emergence of tit-for-tat strategies. Finally, the 15 per cent mutation test

(Figure 7.8) has a quite different form compared with the earlier proximity-free graphs. Whereas previously several strategies were able to live under the same roof, now there emerges an ESS (tit-for-tat, yet again). This shows, first, how robust this strategy is and, second, that the existence of relations of proximity serve to boost its presence. Despite strong mutations, LIPS stability remains strong and is little influenced by the degree of openness. The risks here, whether from new firms or mutant behaviour, are limited by the spatialisation of relations.

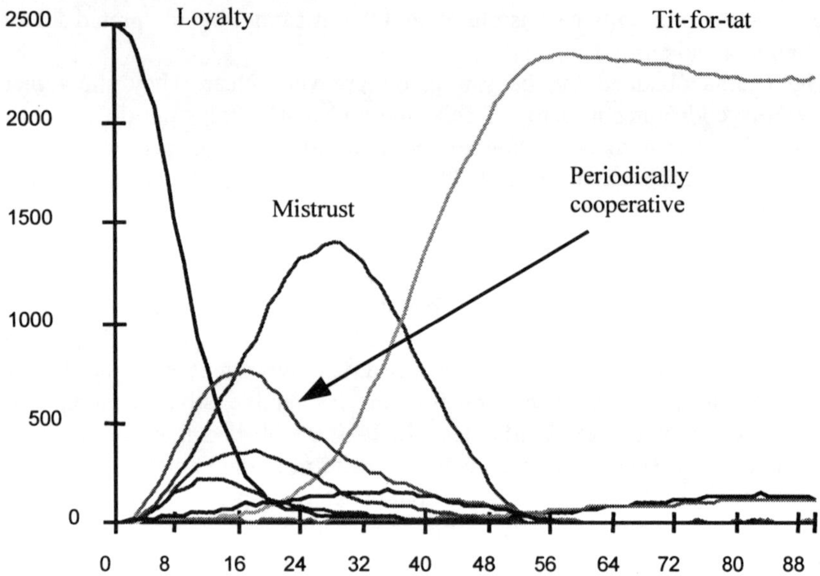

Figure 7.5 The prisoners' dilemma: 1 per cent mutations, 2500 individuals, proximity

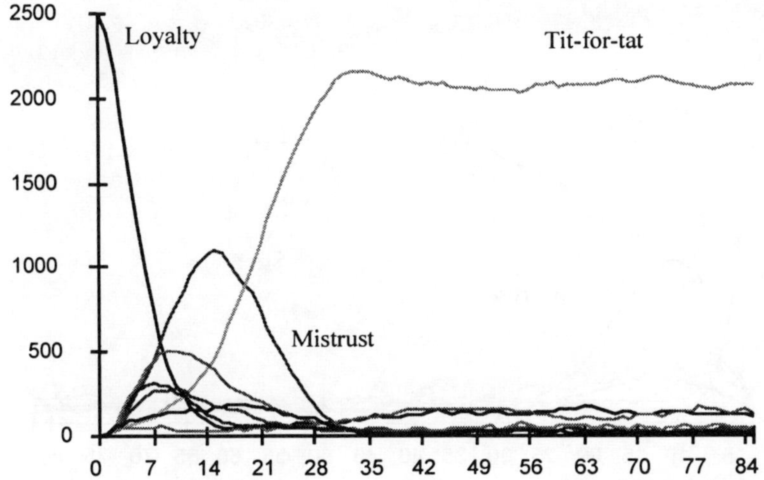

Figure 7.6 *The prisoners' dilemma: 5 per cent mutations, 2500 individuals, proximity*

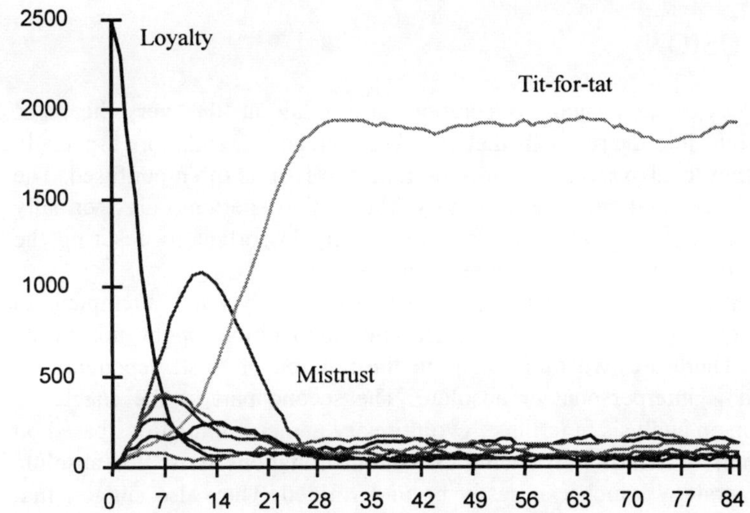

Figure 7.7 *The prisoners' dilemma: 10 per cent mutations, 2500 individuals, proximity*

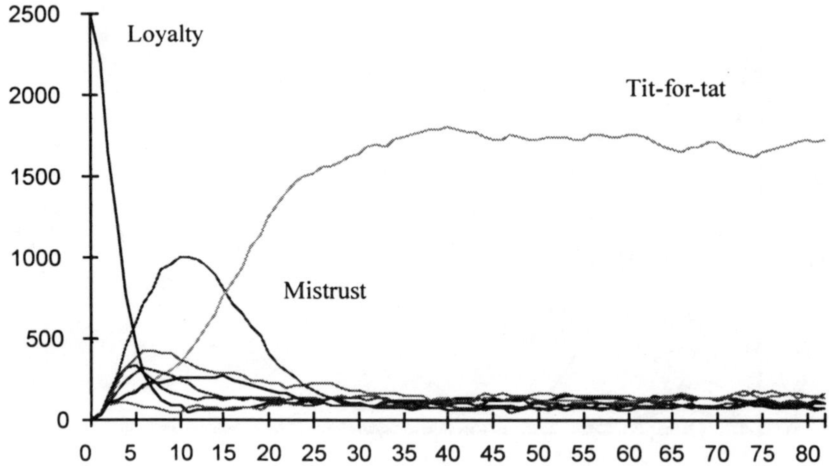

Figure 7.8 The prisoners' dilemma: 15 per cent mutations, 2500 individuals, proximity

CONCLUSION

The themes of trust and cooperation are today at the very heart of investigations into the relations that exist between actors, and more especially firms, within local systems. The discussion, however, is often confused. The impression is sometimes given that these two notions are virtually interchangeable, and that they are both equally important in ensuring the stability and perpetuation of local relations.

Our chapter aims to clarify the debate. Initially, we attempted to demonstrate that the notions of trust and cooperation ought not to be confused. There are two dimensions in the relation of trust, depending on whether it is interpersonal or absolute. The second part of the chapter is founded on an analysis in terms of evolutionary games. Simulations based on the prisoners' dilemma introducing exogenous mutations show that absolute trust is a strategy which can easily be undermined. They also suggest that Axelrod's findings on tit-for-tat strategies require some modification. Tit-for-tats do not always appear. Their emergence is facilitated by the existence of proximity relations between actors. It can be deduced from this that the spatialisation of economic relations really does favour the stability and perpetuation of localised industrial production systems.

NOTES

1 The simulations in this chapter were developed by C. Dupuy and H. Luga (Institut de Recherche en Informatique de Toulouse). The computer programming was carried out by H. Luga in the course of his research into virtual reality. C. Dupuy, Institut d'Economie Regionale (LEREP), Université des Sciences Sociales de Toulouse, 21 allées de Brienne, 31046 Toulouse Cedex; e-mail: cdupuy@cict.fr .
2 See Rallet and Torre (1995) for an overview.

BIBLIOGRAPHY

Arrow, K. (1971), 'Political and economic evaluation of social effects and externalities', in M. Intriligator (ed.), *Frontiers of Quantitative Economics*, Amsterdam: North-Holland.

Axelrod, R. (1980), 'Effective choice in the prisoner's dilemma', *Journal of Conflict Resolution*, no. 24.

Axelrod, R. (1984), *The Evolution of Cooperation*, New York: Basic Books, 1992.

Boyer, R. and A. Orléan (1994), 'Persistence et changement des conventions: deux modèles simples et quelques illustrations', in A. Orléan (ed.), *Analyse Economique des Conventions*, Paris: PUF.

Boyer, R. and A. Orléan (1995), 'Stabilité de la coopération dans les jeux évolutionnistes stochastiques', *Revue Economique*, **46**(3), 797–806.

Courlet, C. and M. Dimou (1995), 'Les systèmes localisés de production: une approche de la dynamique longue', in A. Rallet and A. Torre (eds), *Economie Industrielle et Economie Spatiale*, Paris: Economica.

Crawford, V.P. (1992), 'Nash equilibrium and evolutionnary stability in large and finite populations', *Annales d'Economie et de Statistique*, no. 25/26, 299–313.

David, P.A. (1994), 'Les standards des technologies de l'information, leurs normes de communication et l'Etat: un problème de biens publics', in A. Orléan (ed.), *Analyse Economique des Conventions*, Paris: PUF.

Delahaye, J.P. (1992), 'L'altruisme recomposé?', *Pour la Science*, **181**.

Dupuy, C. and J.P. Gilly (1995), 'Collective learning and territorial dynamics: a new approach to the relations between industrial groups and territories', *Environment and Planning*.

Dupuy, C. and H. Luga (1995), 'Les paradoxes de l'évolution: l'importance de la proximité dans le développement de la coopération', Colloque de l'ADSLRF, Toulouse, September.

Elliasson, G. (1991), 'Modelling the experimentally organized economy: complex dynamics in an empirical micro-macro model of endogenous economic growth', *Journal of Economic Behavior and Organization*, **16**(1-2), 153–82.

Elliasson, G. (1993), 'Learning, local interaction, and coordination', *Econometrica*, **61**, 1047–71.

Feldman, M.P. (1994), *The Geography of Innovation*, Boston: Kluwer Academic Press.

Friedber, G.E. (1993), *Le Pouvoir et la Règle*, Paris: Seuil.

Granovetter, M. (1985), 'Economic action and social structure: the problem of embeddedness', *American Journal of Sociology*, **91**, 481–510.

Granovetter, M. (1994), 'Les institutions économiques comme constructions sociales: un cadre d'analyse', in A. Orléan (ed.), *Analyse Economique des Conventions*,

Paris: PUF.
Hofbauer, J. and K. Sigmund (1988), *The Theory of Evolution and Dynamical Systems*, Cambridge: Cambridge University Press.
Jaisson, P. (1993), *La Fourmi et le Sociobiologiste*, Paris: Odile Jacob,.
Jayet, H. and A. Torre (1995), 'Vie et mort des entreprises: quelles analyses?', *Problèmes Economiques*, **2423**, 15–23.
Karpik, L. (1989), 'L'économie de la qualité', *Revue française de Sociologie*, *XXX*, 187–210.
Kreps, D.M. (1990), 'Corporate culture and economic theory', in J.E. Alt and K. Shepsle (eds), *Perspectives on Positive Political Economy*, Cambridge: Cambridge University Press, 90–143.
Krugman, P. (1991a), *Geography and Trade*, Leuven and Cambridge, MA: Leuven University Press and MIT Press.
Krugman, P. (1991b), 'History versus expectations', *Quarterly Journal of Economics*, **106**, 651–67.
Le Cardinal and J.F. Guyonnet (1994), 'Comparaison de trois approches stratégiques de la coopération', *Revue Internationale de Systémique*, **8**, 105–21.
Maynard Smith, J. (1982), *Evolution and the Theory of Games*, Cambridge: Cambridge University Press.
Maynard Smith, J. and G. Parker (1976), 'The logic of asymmetric contest', *Animal Behavior*, **24**, 159–75.
Orléan, A. (1994), 'Sur le rôle respectif de la confiance et de l'intérêt dans la construction de l'ordre marchand', *Revue du Mauss*, **4**, 17–36.
Rallet, A. and A. Torre (1995), *Economie Industrielle et Economie Spatiale*, Paris: Economica.
Rivaud-Danset, D. (1995), *La confiance, l'Action Collective et les Mondes Possibles : le Cas Contrat de Crédit*, Communication au Séminaire interdisciplinaire 'Confiance, apprentissage et anticipation économique', Université de Technologie de Compiègne, January.
Rullière, J.L. (1994), *Modéliser la Confiance: Usage et Limite du Calcul Economique*, Communication au Séminaire 'Nouvel institutionnalisme: la confiance', MRASH, Lyon: March.
Rullière, J.L. and A. Torre (1995), 'Les formes de la coopération inter-entreprises', *Revue d'Economie Industrielle*, no. exceptionnel 'Développements théoriques récents en Economie Industrielle'.
Sabel, C. (1992), 'Elaborer la confiance: de nouvelles formes de coopération dans une économie volatile', in D. Foray and C. Freeman (eds), *Technologie et Richesse des Nations*, Paris: Economica.
de Sainte Marie, C., F. Casablanca and M. Poggi (1994), 'Des difficultés de la transition entre économie souterraine et économie formelle', Colloque 'La Corsica i sola problema traEuropeo e Mediterraneo', Salerno, April.
Sako, M. (1995), 'The informational requirement of trust in supplier relations: evidence from Japan, the UK and the USA', Communication au Séminaire interdisciplinaire 'Confiance, apprentissage et anticipation économique', Université de Technologie de Compiègne, January.
Servet, J.M. (1994), 'Paroles données: le lien de confiance', *Revue du Mauss*, **4**, 37–56.
Storper, M. (1995), 'La géographie des conventions: proximité territoriale, interdépendances non marchandes et développement économique', in A. Rallet and A. Torre. (eds), *Economie Industrielle et Economie Spatiale*, Paris: Economica.

Torre, A. (1993), 'Proximité géographique et dynamiques industrielles', *Revue d'Economie Régionale et Urbaine*, **3**, 431–448.

Torre, A. (1995), 'La construction de la confiance dans les relations de proximité géographique', Communication au Séminaire interdisciplinaire 'Confiance, apprentissage et anticipation économique', Université de Technologie de Compiègne, January.

Weibul, J.W. (1993), 'The as if approach to game theory: 3. positive results and 4. obstacles', paper presented at The European Economic Association, Helsinki, August.

Williamson, O.E. (1993), 'Calculativeness, trust, and economic organization', *Journal of Law and Economics*, **36**(1), 453–86.

Young, H.P. and D. Foster (1991), 'Cooperation in the short and in the long run', *Games and Economic Behavior*, **3**, 145–56.

8. The Economics of Knowledge Openness: Emergence, Persistence and Change of Conventions in the Knowledge Systems

Dominique Foray[1]

INTRODUCTION

In the realm of science and technology, a 'knowledge system' is a network of agents and entities which assume specific functions in the process of generating, transforming, transmitting and storing knowledge. Examples of knowledge systems include industrial districts, the world-wide community of scientists, national industry and any other kinds of highly cohesive sub-group. The critical degree of cohesiveness necessary to form a knowledge system is simply defined by parameters describing the frequency of knowledge interactions. This definition of a knowledge system has, therefore, a great deal of suppleness and flexibility.

A knowledge system includes economic agents (or learning entities) as well as the institutions which operate as remedies to overcome the deficiency of the market for the production and distribution of knowledge.[2] The learning entities, however, do not exist in isolation. Each entity needs to draw upon pre-existing knowledge generated in some other part of the system; consequently, the extent to which knowledge is exchanged, and the conditions of exchange, are important features of the system.

Economic Properties of Knowledge Openness

Two properties of knowledge as an economic good are relevant to an explanation of why it is economically efficient to improve the distribution of existing scientific and engineering knowledge, and to increase access to the latest additions to the knowledge stock. First, knowledge is usually described as a non-rival good, that is, a good which is infinitely expansible without being diminished in quality; it can be possessed and used concurrently by as many as care to do so.[3] Such an economic good cannot be treated as if its transfer were a zero-sum proposition. Second, the process of knowledge generation is cumulative and integrative. Knowledge is not only an output of the innovative process, it is also the main input. Cumulative forms of knowledge are those in which today's advances lay the foundation for tomorrow's progress. Synthetic knowledge is generated through the convergence or collateral integration of previously independent pieces of knowledge.

Due to these properties, the process of knowledge generation produces 'positive externalities'. As Machlup (1983) puts it, 'the more that is invented the easier it becomes to invent still more', assuming wide distribution and timely, inexpensive access to new findings.

Thus openness is vital for the efficient use of costly research resources in creating reliable knowledge. Open access that distributes knowledge widely and rapidly serves a number of purposes: first, it facilitates independent replication of findings; second, it promotes swift generalization of results; third, it avoids excessive duplication of research; and fourth, it increases the probability of creating useful new products, processes and ideas arising from novel and unanticipated combinations, thus raising the social value of knowledge by lowering the chance that it will reside with persons and groups which lack the resources and ability to exploit it.

Instability of Knowledge Openness

However, the conditions for the efficient distribution and utilization of knowledge cannot be expected to arise automatically from an interplay of market forces. Various obstacles impede knowledge distribution. These include the creation of intellectual property rights, designed to allow agents to capture rents from their innovative efforts; and the presence of institutional incompatibilities among organisations, such as distinctive rules of disclosure, institutional goals and reward structures.

The activity of diffusing economically relevant knowledge is not itself a natural one. Rather, it is socially constructed through the creation of appropriate institutions and conventions, such as open science or (some kinds of) intellectual property rights. Improving what David and Foray (1995a, b) termed, 'the distribution power of the system of innovation' has often been portrayed as a desirable objective that has to be sacrificed to provide stronger market incentives for private investment in organized R&D, since copyright, patent and trade secrecy laws create obstacles to access and restrict the commercial utilization of knowledge. There is, therefore, a persistent tendency for increasing penetration of market-driven rivalry (generating secrecy and access-restriction practices) into domains of knowledge production which previously operated under the non-commercial norms of openness and cooperation.

Precis of the Argument

In sum, knowledge openness is a critical efficiency factor at the system level. For a knowledge system as a whole, the pace of innovation may be speeded up if competitors are able to build on one other's innovative advances. To use a concept developed by Klein (1988), knowledge openness generates positive-sum games; there will be winners and losers during every round of the game, but owing to the economic properties of openness, the gains will exceed the losses. However, the norms of openness and free access are very fragile as a positive-sum game does not preclude the possibility that at each period in the game any given agent may be a loser. In the final analysis, this means that the stability of openness as a norm of behaviour requires the future (that is, the long term where each entity is a winner) to be sufficiently significant with respect to the present (the short term where there are both winners and losers).

In this chapter, we propose to treat knowledge openness as a social convention imposing itself within a given (regional, sectoral) space through the operation of certain social mechanisms (such as the formation of structures of mutually consistent expectations). We explore how such a convention can emerge and persist over time, the reasons for its degradation, and the factors forcing a system to move rapidly between conventions of disclosure and openness behaviour. The chapter is structured as follows: in the next section we describe some historical knowledge systems based on a particular convention of knowledge openness and we derive from each description the efficiency properties of the system. In sections 3 and 4, we address the problem of the emergence of knowledge openness as a social convention, exploring the reasons why it persists or why it degrades to restricted access and control. Section 5 concludes.

HISTORICAL FIGURES AND HISTORICAL CHANGES OF THE CONVENTION OF KNOWLEDGE OPENNESS

A system of knowledge can be characterised with reference to a particular convention of openness. We will describe some of these in this section and will try to derive from each description the efficiency properties of the system under consideration.

Alchemist

The knowledge system of the alchemist is based on secrecy and enigma ('I am revealing my secrets to you figuratively, speaking with enigmatic examples and signs').[4] For various reasons (alchemy is a 'divine science' rather than a purely natural one), knowledge is kept secret. Alchemy is codified but the codes are not shared (alchemical writers used obscure symbols, paradoxes, allegories and secret names). The esoteric language of alchemy was never intended to be understood literally, but was deliberately used to protect divine secrets and to guarantee their possession by a small circle of initiates. Here knowledge is either not disclosed or put into very idiosyncratic codes. As a result, the efficiency properties of the knowledge system are very weak. The potential for cumulative progress is not exploited: 'L'alchimie est une science qui ne progresse pas. On doit refaire tout seul le chemin qui a été fait par d'autres au cours des siècles. C'est une démarche personnelle, une initiation sans intitiateur' (Fulcanelli, 1927).

Craftsmen and Engineers in the Middle Ages

In the Middle Ages, the knowledge system of craftsmen was also based on secrecy. Disclosure of craft techniques threatened to undermine the monopoly of craftsmen with specialized skills. Engineers and inventors were also reluctant to publish their discoveries for fear of losing public recognition for their inventions. Leonardo da Vinci adopted the practice of mirror-writing in his notebooks to make casual copying difficult, in order to maintain property rights over his inventions. Giovanni da Fontana, another famous engineer, composed several treatises on technology, all written in cipher to prevent them from being read![5] Here again, the efficiency property of the system is very low.

Towards New Conventions

In the XVIIth century, Bacon claimed that knowledge is progressive. More and more people realised that secrecy and access-restriction resulted in the stagnation of knowledge rather than the protection of valuable secrets. They realised that technical knowledge is a cumulative store that is built up by successive individual contributions. Each individual takes over what has been accumulated by his predecessors, adds his contribution and passes the augmented store on to his successors who, in turn, are expected to make further contributions. Newton himself acknowledged the role of cumulativeness: 'If I have seen far, it is by standing on the shoulders of giants'.

Intellectual Property Rights and the Disclosure of Technical Knowledge

This position led quite naturally to the creation of intellectual property rights as a response to growing awareness that scientific knowledge could be put to practical use. In 1421 when an Italian engineer, Brunelleschi, designed a new type of ship he wrote (referring to himself in the third person):

> He refuses to make such a machine available to the public in order that the fruit of his genius and skill may not be reaped by another without his will and consent, and that, if he enjoyed some prerogative concerning this, he would open up what he is hiding and would disclose it all. (quoted in David, 1993a)

Thus a necessary prerequisite for the exploitation of invention is for society to grant intellectual property rights to private producers for their discoveries, and permit them to charge (possibly differential) fees for their use by others. This creates private markets for knowledge and gives rise to 'private knowledge-products'. Patents and copyrights are means of defining and protecting intellectual property rights. Patents confer a monopoly right over a device or a method, awarded on the basis of novelty, originality and non-obviousness, in exchange for public disclosure of codified knowledge. Thus a new convention of openness emerged based on the 'paradoxes of patenting' (MacLeod, 1991): the patent, as a device to prevent the free use of new ideas and methods, is also a means by which codified information is disclosed. Historically, the disclosure provisions were an essential and natural aspect of the effort to induce foreign artisans 'to reveal a mystery', and to train domestic craftsmen in its pursuit (David, 1993b). However, this enforced disclosure was also viewed by inventors as a major failing of the system, and the issue was endlessly debated throughout the 19th century (Machlup and Penrose, 1950).

At the root of the debate was the assumption that the patent was a form of reward (that is, protection for one party and exclusion of all others). For instance, the first superintendent of the US patent office considered that, ideally, the specifications of an invention should remain confidential until the patent had expired, otherwise inventors might decide not to risk patenting and their inventions would never become available to the public (MacLeod, 1991, p. 898). There are many historical examples of inventions being hindered by patent systems that ignore the need to disseminate knowledge. Renouard's 'Treatise on Patents' (1844), for example, has the following words to say about the property rights granted to Watt for his invention of the steam engine:

> When, in 1775, Parliament renewed the patent that he had been given in 1769 for a period of 25 years, it gave great power to a man whose thinking had long since

> stultified. Watt refused to license his invention; he discouraged Murdoch from experimenting with locomotives; he was hostile to the use of high-pressure steam; and the authority he enjoyed was such that he held back the development of the metalworking industry for over a generation. Had his monopoly expired in 1783, England would have had railways much sooner.

However, it slowly appeared that what seemed to be a deficiency of the system is, in fact, one of its strong points. The patent system requires patentees to disclose certain items of information in exchange for monopoly rights. Although the patent only reveals the codified information needed to make use of the innovation, it provides an invaluable indication of the potential success or 'practicability' of a particular line of research. It gives information on the 'state of the art', and thus allows rival firms to allocate their research resources more efficiently (Kitch, 1977). Compared with the system of trade secrets, therefore, patents actually increase the output of resources allocated to technological innovation. Thus, what was initially considered to be a serious failing in the patent system – the patent as an open book – is here viewed as a major asset that points the way to future improvements: 'The development of improved systems of information retrieval and promulgation in order to promote more effective use of the new knowledge created by patent application' (Massel, 1991, p. 290).

Firms must therefore be encouraged to use patents as their main mechanism for appropriating knowledge.

Here the efficiency of the knowledge system is dependent on the institutional design of the patent system which may vary widely in ways that affect both incentives to engage in research and the extent of access afforded to the information that is disclosed (see below, the Japanese case). In particular, the patent scope decision can strongly influence cumulativeness and the development of a technology (Merges and Nelson, 1994). For instance, it is possible to make the innovations of patentees available for others to use at reasonably modest costs. This goal can be achieved by restricting the scope of the patent grant, and the degree of novelty required of the typical patentable innovation. Narrow patents and patents involving low degrees of novelty tend to favour knowledge recombination because they promote 'pooling' and cross-licensing of innovations. However, manipulation of the parameter of scope raises the problem of how to optimize the allocation of property rights between the initial and subsequent inventors (Scotchmer, 1991).

The Invisible College and Open Science

One important result of the Baconian vision was to encourage informal associations of individual interests for promoting experimental science, and to cultivate informal channels of communication through which the results of their research could be disseminated. This institution of the 'invisible college' describes a new convention of openness based on informal networks of communications restricted to small circles of personal contacts. One essential factor at the origin of those circles was a common scientific approach; the experimental method introduced by Galileo and Bacon: 'The general acceptance of the experimental method made it possible for hundreds even thousands of specialists to build the results of their individual research into a single store of information, usable across all sciences' (Rosenberg and Birdzell, 1986).

The world of 'open science', as described by Merton (1973) and his students, expresses the ideas of free pursuit and open disclosure of knowledge accompanied by a reputational reward and resource allocation system based on validated claims to priority in discovery or invention (David, 1991). The Mertonian 'norms' represent, of course, idealizations having little correspondence in the real world.[6] The rule of priority plays a key role in the organisation of the system: first, it established a context of a race for scientific discoveries; second, it is a mechanism to accelerate the public disclosure of new findings. As demonstrated by Dasgupta and David (1994), it is a remarkable social innovation in its ability to separate 'moral property' and 'physical possession' by making incentives to researchers ('winning the race') compatible with the organisation of quick and broad dissemination of the new findings. Universities have always been the key institutional components of the open science system. In the history of Western democracies, they have been concerned with the preservation, interpretation and transmission of knowledge. Furthermore, the traditions of cooperative, disinterested scholarship that the academies support, along with the institutional norms of open science communities to which university regulations have been adapted, make these institutions, in their generic form, particularly well suited to the task of integrating internationally distributed sources of knowledge, and of training people in how to locate and use it.

Collective Invention

An interesting convention of openness characterised some local knowledge systems in the 19th century. These systems are described as involving an institutionalised process of 'collective invention'. An essential feature of 'collective invention' is the free exchange of information about new techniques and plant designs among actual and potential competitors. Allen (1983) described one such system in the case of the iron industry:

> If a firm constructed a new plant of novel design and that plant proved to have lower costs than other plants, these facts were made available to other firms in the

> industry and to potential entrants. The next firm constructing a new plant could build on the experience of the first by introducing and extending the design change that had proved profitable. The operating characteristics of this second plant would then also be made available to potential investors. In this way fruitful lines of technical advance were identified and pursued. (Allen, 1983, p. 2)

It is this behaviour which allows cumulative While this pattern of knowledge-sharing described innovative behaviour in some British industrial areas between 1850 and 1875, it is not irrelevant to the Japanese knowledge system as a particular institutionalised form of collective invention.

Knowledge Openness in Japan

Indicators of innovative activity organisation would suggest that Japan's policies and institutions are oriented towards the intensive use of existing scientific and technical knowledge for the purpose of generating technological innovations (Foray, 1994). One measure that indicates the importance of patenting activities is the measurement of the ratio of intellectual property rights to total R&D. This feature, which runs counter to one of the main findings of recent Western innovation surveys, can be explained by the absence of any legislation relating to trade secrets and by a combination of the following three features of Japan's patent regime: low cost of filing; the priority given to the first to file (as opposed to the first to invent); and the freedom given to applicants to make changes to a proposed patent for a limited period of time after the initial application has been filed. These features encourage innovators to file patents as quickly as possible. However, the high rate of patenting should be interpreted in this case as the 'victory of a method of coordination' rather than the 'triumph of a mode of exclusion'. All parties are aware that by making their own knowledge available through licensing they will very rapidly be able to benefit from reciprocal arrangements to gain access to the knowledge of others. It is essential to stress the role played by the combination of limited exclusion rights, relaxed novelty requirements and early disclosure (pre-grant disclosure). Early disclosure (prior to the granting of a property right) is a highly effective means of disseminating information and has some dynamic effects on the accumulation of knowledge since the scope of property right is limited and the requirements of novelty relatively undermining. Indeed, Ordover (1991) notes that: 'Potential competitors who have "reverse engineered" the invention during the laying-open and opposition phases can file their own patent applications, thanks to the narrow scope of patent coverage and very relaxed novelty requirements'.

Early disclosure, combined with the limited exclusion rights conferred by the patent, lies at the heart of collective invention.

The Destruction of the Convention of Openness

Progress from the medieval attitude against openness and disclosure to the 'open Japanese model' has not been without setbacks. As already suggested, the norms of openness and free access are very fragile. Policy measures that make the knowledge stock more socially useful will frequently conflict with measures designed to enhance its value to the individual owner. There is, therefore, a persistent market-driven pressure towards reducing openness by altering the norms, incentive mechanisms and property rights systems in a direction that encourages non-cooperative modes of pursuing and transmitting scientific and technological knowledge.

Access Restriction in the University System

The traditional world of 'open science' described above is now being undermined. In a recent paper, David, Mowery and Steinmueller (1994) have analysed the sources of inherent conflict between university and industry research institutions resulting from their contrasting reward systems:[7]

> As a consequence, university participation in industrial research involves a series of restrictions aimed at balancing, regulating, and containing these conflicts, including guarantees of (eventual) disclosure of research after predetermined delays, negotiation of intellectual property rights deriving from research outcomes, and scrutinity of potential personal conflicts of interest in faculty research activities.

Many empirical studies deal with particular facets of that problem. Henderson, Jaffe and Tratjenberg (1994) document the extension of university patenting and research contracts activities and their implications for the organisation of research. Cohen, Florida and Goe (1994) provide evidence on increasing industrial influence on, and control of, the research agenda of university laboratories through the extension of University–Industry Research Centres. Hilgartner and Brandt-Rauf (1994) document the adoption of access restriction practices regarding 'research-related information' – information that cannot be published in journals, such as experimental materials and innovative instruments, locally produced software, data sets and novel research techniques. The new practices include: (1) non-release of data, which are held privately in labs while production proceeds; (2) delayed access, for example maintaining a significant gap between that which is provided and that which is locally available; and (3) data isolation that allows access only to isolated portions of the data stream which cannot be readily used or reassembled by other laboratories. Dasgupta and David (1994) point to the increasing frequency of scientific publications with insufficient disclosure of relevant findings to permit replication by other scientists (for example, reduced ratio of publications of molecular structures whose coordinates are disclosed to total published structures; and reduced disclosure of algorithms used in mass spectographic analysis).

These diverse indicators are particularly worrying, since universities are logical candidates for an enhancement rather than a curtailment of their functionality as 'open nodes' in global scientific and technological information networks. As observed by David, Mowery and Steinmueller (1994), the interactions between universities and industries that are likely to prove most dysfunctional tend to arise when companies have succeeded in persuading universities to internalize the norms of highly proprietary research (that is, research that is closely linked to the strategic aims of the firm, or when universities adopt practices designed to enhance their own financial interest).

Openness Limitation in the Software Industry

Early protection of intellectual property in the software industry was governed by copyright law; a system which prohibits the users of a software program from making copies of it without permission.[8] This prevents one company from appropriating another's work and selling it as its own, but the existence of a copyright does not prevent other programmers from using algorithms or techniques contained in the program in their own work. A single software technique can be implemented in different ways to do totally different jobs. Thus the institutional system of the software industry was 'diffusion-oriented', encouraging information dissemination and facilitating coordination among innovative projects. Under this regime, it was normal for computer scientists in the commercial, as well as the academic world, to publish their discoveries. Secrecy about techniques was not a significant problem, and universities played a critical role by developing software and distributing it free of charge.[9] Within the last few years, however, software developers have been surprised to learn that hundreds, even thousands, of patents have been awarded for programming processes ranging from sequences of machine instructions to features of the user interface. Many of the patents cover processes that seem conventional or obvious, and developers now fear that any of the thousands of individual processes in their programs may be subject to patent-infringement claims.

This new game leads to a radical disruption of networks of cooperation. The expansion of software patents could mean the end of software being developed at universities and freely distributed. Patents could also mean an end to public-domain software which has played an important part in making computers affordable to schools. Software patents would pose a special danger to small companies, which often form the basic structure of software development but which cannot afford the cost of patent searches for litigation. Last but not least, software patents introduce a major timing problem in a system where the product cycles are very short with respect to the patent application time, which is, on average, 32 months.

Thus a crucial issue arising from this story is whether or not the industry is evolving towards a cross-licensing system where firms secure narrow patents enabling them to trade for the right to other patents, thereby sustaining the existing cooperative networks. Given the characteristics of the product (a modern software package may contain thousands of separately patentable processes, each of which adds to the risk of infringing patents that are already in the pipeline), it is hard to see how the patent system could become a coordinating factor in this industry.[10]

Institutional Changes to Restore Openness: Weakening Property Rights

Unlike the Japanese patent system described above, the patent system of Western economies provides strong protection for innovators but impedes the rapid disclosure of information. It places greater emphasis on novelty and on monopoly rights while loosening the constraints of disclosure. However, such a system need not necessarily hamper the diffusion of knowledge. Indeed, under certain circumstances it may even prove to be an efficient mechanism which allows both goals to be met simultaneously.

First, a strongly protectionist system has the advantage of dissuading firms from maintaining trade secrets, a practice which could be even less favourable to the diffusion of knowledge. As a result, the legislation on trade secrets in the United States ('Uniform Trade Secrets Act') makes it necessary, to some extent, to introduce a stringent property rights regime. Second, a strong patent regime lowers the risks involved in commercial exploitation and thereby encourages certain forms of diffusion. Third, the expanding use of compulsory licensing systems, whereby applications for a licence to produce and market variant versions of a given innovation cannot be refused, offers one way to restore some balance between the functions of diffusion and protection within the patent–system. In the case of biotechnology, a system of paid free access, based on the system of dependent compulsory licensing (Hermitte and Joly, 1992), demonstrates that it is possible to offer protection to an innovator while upholding the principle of free access for research use. Compulsory licensing systems may be organised by industrial sector. Bes (1993) describes, for example the European Space Agency's (ESA's) practice with regard to intellectual property. Contractors employed by the ESA can apply for patents and obtain property rights for applications in the space sector.[11] They are, however, obliged to grant licences requested by nationals of ESA member countries in sectors other than space.

Compulsory licensing systems can also offer a favourable solution to intellectual property rights problems posed by the design and use of technical compatibility standards. Networking effects clearly enhance the advantage afforded an innovator by intellectual property rights. In the case of compatibility standards, there is a mismatch between the aim of the legal system (that is, the award of monopoly rights limited in duration and scope) and the dynamic advantage that the owner of the intellectual property rights can profitably exploit (Farrell, 1989, 1992). To avoid these effects, some standardisation committees require that innovators relinquish or grant licences at a 'reasonable' fee as a precondition for incorporating private technology into the official. The compulsory licensing system thus offers a significant alternative incentive and coordination scheme which might make it possible to strike a balance between protection and diffusion within existing intellectual property rights systems.

Institutional Changes to Restore Openness: Building High-Tech Consortia

Another strategy to minimize secrecy practices is to promote collective forms of 'pre-competitive' R&D (high-tech consortia, industrial collective research) and inter-firm cooperation in the development of anticipatory technical standards. A research consortium creates a local convention of knowledge openness that facilitates access to research results at lower costs and reduces duplication among the research activities of competitor firms (Grindley, Mowery and Silverman, 1994). The elaboration of specific rules of knowledge-sharing among the participants is a very important *ex ante* prerequisite of cooperation. Cassier (1995) shows how it is possible to design procedures among the participants to favour the free circulation of knowledge at the same time as encouraging industrial protection. Thus, as suggested by Lundvall (1995): 'Hybrid forms of knowledge that are neither completely private nor completely public become increasingly important. More and more strategic know-how and competence is developed interactively and shared within subgroups and networks'.

Thus the proliferation of consortia is conducive to new forms of knowledge which have characteristics of both private and public goods (Arrow, 1994). Moreover, empirical evidence on tacit toleration of secret sharing and know-how trading through informal coordination among engineers attests to the existence of institutions and norms of behaviour which warrant sole local convention of knowledge openness within a general context of private appropriation and control for competitive advantage (Von Hippel, 1988).

THE DYNAMICS OF THE CONVENTION

This long sequence of short stories attests to the richness of the institutional devices for allowing the system to maintain or restore the convention of knowledge openness in the face of continual threats from the natural forces of the market. All these cases, describing either the stability or the instability of the convention, and always revealing its fragility, raise the problem of how the convention emerges and why it persists or degrades over time.

How a System can get Locked-In to a Dominant Convention of Openness

Let us briefly review the problem of the emergence of a dominant convention of openness in a given domain of research (either scientific or commercial). This is a coordination problem that can be solved by the creation of common knowledge about mutual disclosure behaviour. Three mechanisms will be briefly reviewed.

Emergence

We define a convention as a way of aligning individual expectations. What matters above all is that the players possess the same, consistent expectations about the ruling convention, and that they must be mutually aware of this fact. As argued in David (1994), 'to be effective, which is to say ''to have force'', a convention must attain the status of being 'common knowledge'' . Each player must know that other players will promptly disclose knowledge once discovered in a well-documented form. This argument raises the question of how do such commonly held expectations become established? Where does such knowledge come from if not from shared history and fine institutional mechanisms elaborated in a given historical context? Thus precedence emerges as an important factor in allowing the players to align their individual expectations. As demonstrated by David (1994), the reinforcement of mutual expectations may cause 'accidents of history' to acquire a status of surprising durability. The first mechanism therefore entails the historical emergence of structures of mutually consistent expectations, resulting in the creation of a 'common knowledge' which shapes the cooperative/competitive strategies of agents. As Long (1991, p. 353) puts it in discussing the 16th-century authors who decided to disclose their knowledge in clear and well-diffused articles:

> Despite their diversity, these authors shared the context provided by the capitalist expansion of mining. As a result, they elaborated a group of seemingly unrelated attitudes from a remarkably consistent point of view. Their affirmation that knowledge should be transmitted openly was closely associated with beliefs related to early modern mine and metallurgical capitalism: wealth is a positive

good; investment in mining should be encouraged and would pay off in riches; clear technical language and understandable discussions of technical processes, careful measurement, honest and precise assaying, and practical skill all are necessary to high productivity. They criticized alchemy not on the basis of whether transmutation occurred, but in terms of the criteria of clarity, honesty, and productivity.

Consolidation

The second mechanism is based on the complex interplay between the perception of a positive-sum game associated with knowledge openness and the policy response in terms of institutional setting (intellectual property rights, subsidies for cooperative research, and so on) that will consolidate the perception, and thus produce self-reinforcing effects. Under a system which is perceived as rich in positive learning externalities, it is pro-innovative to reduce the obstacles to information dissemination due to intellectual property rights and appropriation by secrecy, replacing them with devices for coordinating the actions of innovative agents. For instance, the knowledge system of the software industry was initially perceived as generating positive-sum games; norms of cooperative behaviour and the formal institution of copyright were self-reinforcing mechanisms that locked the system into a dominant convention of openness and disclosure. The policy response confirms the perception by strengthening the positive feedback elements already present in the system.

Persistence

Finally, there are strong aspects of complementarity between features of the institutional landscape within any society which increase institutional stability, forcing successful institutional innovation to take an incremental form. Of course this could not occur if the society, or the organisation, as a whole were disrupted or absorbed by one that was differently structured. Institutions generally are less plastic and less malleable than material technologies, and the inter-relatedness among their constituent parts, like their mutual interlocking dependence within a given societal context, only makes it more difficult to introduce radical changes into any one part of the structure. Therefore the feasible space for institutional innovations in a given society is likely to be tightly constrained by its history (that is, its institutional structure is path-dependent) (David, 1994; David and Foray, 1995a).

How a System can get Locked-In to a Dominant Convention of Access Restriction

Our view of the emergence of a convention of openness also applies when a convention of secrecy develops. Emerging behaviours of access restriction and secrecy are followed and consolidated by the creation of an institutional system which facilitates access restriction, strong protection of inventors and innovators and the exclusion of others from using the new findings. In such a system, some institution types have been created to provide stronger market incentives for private investment in organized R&D. These institutions are likely to include: strong intellectual property rights (in terms of patent scope); high reliance on mechanisms of appropriability (such as trade secrecy which does not imply any disclosure constraints); low incentives to codify knowledge (codification facilitates diffusion); and some modes of cooperative arrangements designed as forms of (minimum yield) insurance.[12] This view of the world – one that requires inducements to entrepreneurs to invest by offering them extra-normal profit in compensatiom for risk-taking – leads to institutional adaptations that reinforce negative externalities. Stronger property rights in knowledge reduce the possibilities of self-reinforcing expansion of knowledge based on technical progress. Monopolists curtail access to knowledge by others, as well as underinvesting in capacity to exploit new knowledge, both because they exercise their monopoly power, and because they avoid destroying old lines of business within their control.

MICROMOTIVES AND THE MACRODYNAMICS OF THE CONVENTION

This section explores the relation between individual and aggregate behaviour characteristics. Schelling's approach to the collective behaviour faced by individuals with binary choice in the presence of externalities, provides an elegant device for understanding the nature of the process of emergence and destruction of knowledge openness conventions. Two patterns of collective behaviour will be analysed: a tipping pattern describing a transition mechanism between two conventions; and a splitting pattern describing a system which splits into two different conventions.

Tipping Behaviour: Construction and Destruction of the Convention of Knowledge Openness

Let us assume a predominantly open system of innovation. Any deviation from this convention will be treated as a defection in cooperation and will, therefore, generate a chain of reprisals so that the system can very rapidly switch towards one characterised by a restricted access convention. As argued above, the policy response to the perception of such a system can lead eventually to a redesign of its institutions (by creating stronger intellectual property rights, writing laws to protect commercial secrecy, and so on). The same is not true, however, in regard to the 'reverse' process.

Consider a system of innovation characterised by secrecy, access restriction and the associated formal institutions. Any 'deviation' (cooperative behaviour) from this norm occurs when one player decides to disclose his new knowledge. The rationale for such action may be, for instance, the existence of redistributive pecuniary effects. I disclose my knowledge because I have invested in complementary assets, the value of which will be likely to increase once the knowledge is diffused (see Hirshleifer, 1971). Such an instance of individual cooperative behaviour will not automatically lead the system to switch towards a convention of openness. On the contrary, the individual deviant will reinforce, at least in the short term, the non-cooperative behaviour of the other player, as suggested by the standard results of a classic prisoners' dilemma.

This example demonstrates that the process of switching from one system to another will confront a set of problems that depend upon the direction of the switch. While a convention of secrecy and access restriction can diffuse spontaneously, a convention of openness and cooperation has to be constructed. Cooperation is impossible without communication. One player must signal to the other his willingness to cooperate (and even tolerate some defections) for the other to determine that it is better not to free-ride. In contrast, no signal is needed for free-riding. The cooperative, altruistic strategy seeks 'reciprocity', whereas the egocentric, individualist strategy does not.

The diffusion of the convention of openness: a coalition-building problem

When a system moves to a convention of openness, the problem is in the form of a 'uniform multi prisoners' dilemma' (UMPD) as described by Schelling (1978). A UMPD can be defined as a situation in which:

1. There are *n* people, each with the same binary choice – O (for openness) or R (for restriction of access) – and the same pay-offs.
2. Each has a preferred choice whatever the others do, and the same choice is preferred by everybody. In our case, the preferred choice is R. Thus there is a natural tendency towards the norm of non-cooperation.
3. Whatever choice a player makes, the greater the number of those who choose their unpreferred alternative (O) the better off he is. Thus all players have an interest in the commitment of a majority of others to the norms of disclosure (O choice), but for everybody it is more profitable to stay out (R), since the fruits of the O option have a public good nature. As a result, there is a strong probability that the system can be trapped in a

situation of non-cooperation.

4. There is, however, a specific solution to the coordination problem in the case of a UMPD (unlike a two-agent prisoners' dilemma). There is some number, *k*, greater than 1, such that if *k* or more individuals choose their unpreferred alternative, they are better off than if they had chosen their preferred alternative.

Following Schelling, *k* represents the minimum size of any coalition that can gain by abstaining from the preferred choice. It is the smallest disciplined group that, though resentful of the free-riders, can be profitable for those who do join (though more profitable for those who stay out). A simple graphical device has been applied by Schelling as a way of making this framework easy to understand. On a horizontal axis measured from zero to *n*, two pay-off curves are drawn. One curve corresponds to the preferred choice (R); its left end is arbitrarily taken as zero, and it rises to the right, perhaps levelling off but not declining. Below it we draw the curve for the unpreferred choice (O). This begins below zero, rises and crosses the axis at some point denoted by *k*. The number choosing O is denoted by the distance of any point rightward from the left end. Figure 8.1 shows a first configuration that meets this definition. The only constraints on these curves are that the four extremities of the two curves must be in the vertical order shown and that the curves rise to the right and do not cross, which means that in every case it is more profitable to choose R.

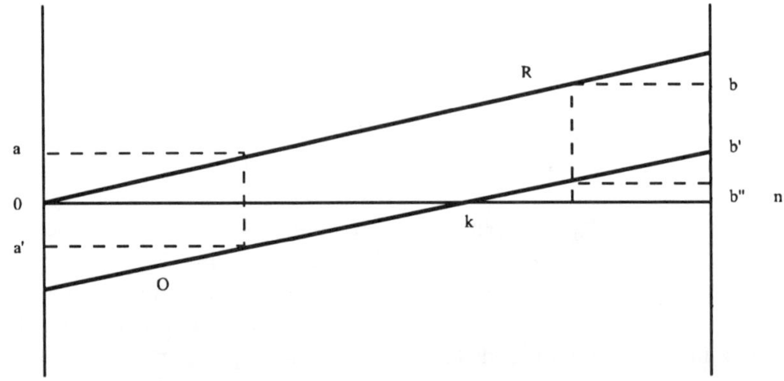

Figure 8.1 The basic representation of a UMPD[13] *(adapted from Schelling, 1978)*

As a result, the construction of a convention of openness: 'Calls for some effort at social organisation, some way to collectivise the choice or to strike an enforceable bargain or otherwise to restructure incentives so that people will do the opposite of what they naturally would have done' (Schelling, 1978).

However, it is possible that in the course of the coalition-forming process, the openness (O) alternative becomes the unconditionally preferred choice. Beyond a number *k'*, the coalition becomes large enough to generate positive feedbacks based on the effects of synergetic cooperation, informational learning and the efficient use of new knowledge among coalition members – these factors being reinforced by some institutional adaptations as well as the adoption of standardised procedures (infratechnologies, measurement) which increase the efficiency of the coordination among the actions of innovative agents. As a result, members of the coalition will derive a net profit from their commitments. On the other hand, the agents choosing to stay out do not enjoy these positive externalities based on the adoption of common standards of collective works.

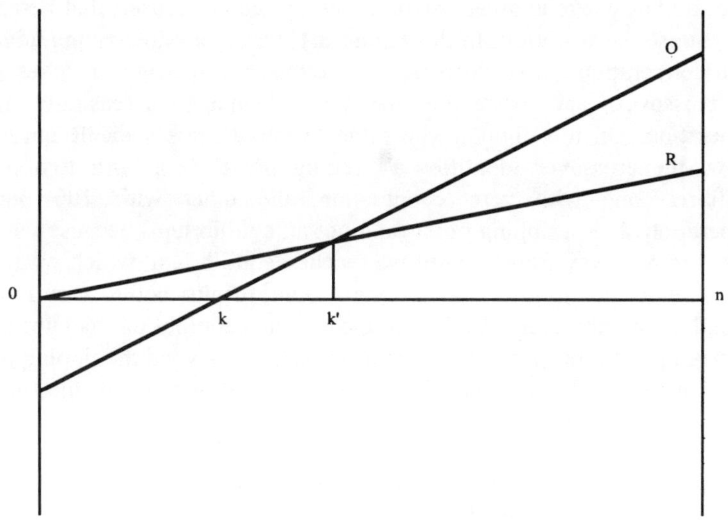

Figure 8.2 Pay-off curves in the intersecting case (adapted from Schelling, 1978)

Figure 8.2 shows intersecting curves, both rising to the right. The O choice is preferred at the right and the R choice is preferred at the left. Two equilibria thus become possible: an all-O choice and an all–R choice. The O equilibrium, enjoying positive externalities, is better. But if everybody chooses not to participate, no one individual has a motive for participating.

These two figures determine the various degrees of fragility of the convention. In the former, the restricted access alternative is the unconditionally preferred choice. In this case the convention is very fragile and can be spontaneously degraded by some causal chains of defections and reprisals. In the latter, openness may become the unconditionally preferred choice in the course of the process. Beyond *k'* the probability of persistence of the convention of openness is very high.

In a recent paper, H. Margolis (1991) showed how path-dependent properties can be derived from the diagrams described above. Starting with Figure 8.2, the R curve lies above the O curve and so is at the extreme left where no-one is cooperating. As we move across the horizontal axis, each person at some point becomes the marginal chooser and, whatever we might assume about the prevailing level of O agents, that marginal chooser always does better by free-riding. Consequently, the prevailing level would move a bit to the left where another person is the marginal chooser; that person will also choose the R option. In the Figure 8.1, the strong free-riding advantage when cooperation is low decreases as we move to the right, reaches zero at the crossover, and thereafter the net advantage increasingly favours cooperation. On this figure, where the O curve crosses the R curve from below, the crossover identifies a 'tipping point' (*k'*), with two possible equilibria, one with zero cooperation, the other with 100 per cent cooperation. *k'* is a tipping point (and not an equilibrium) because we would always move away from *k'* until we reached equilibrium, which would be at the extreme possibilities. Accordingly, the results could vary radically depending on how events leading to the eventual equilibrium had unfolded. It is thus important to shift the system to some point beyond the tipping point in order to place the process in the field of attraction of the preferred equilibrium.

The spontaneous diffusion of the convention of access restriction: the example of the software industry

A transition towards a convention of access restriction can be studied by employing various applications of the theory of 'Markov random fields' (see David and Foray, 1993a, 1994). It is obviously a percolation problem: to what extent can the new (non-cooperative) behaviour contaminate the entire space of the system? The collective behaviour of the system, which is a non-ergodic stochastic physical system that may have only a small finite number of additively interacting particles, is capable of exhibiting long-run dynamic transformations that feature recurrent spontaneous 'phase transitions' or endogeneous fluctuations (David and Foray, 1993b). Thus the only way to stop the contamination of the system is to isolate the deviants by degrading the mixed-percolation probabilities (David and Foray, 1994).

Take, for example, the current story of the migration of the software industry away from one intellectual property regime to another (see above). There are two features in this 'phase transition': (1) it is a process which exhibits the main characteristics of a spontaneous mode of diffusion; and (2) the process is one conducive to a dramatic disruption of the cooperative research networks that sustained the dissemination of information and the coordination of activities among innovators.

The spontaneity of the process is caused by chains of reprisal encouraging a new form of behaviour and turning it into a norm (as suggested above, this process can be formally analysed as a process of additive interdependent Markov chains). Thus although very few programmers and entrepreneurs believe that patents are necessary for improving the social organisation of R&D, there is a proliferation of patents. This paradox is due to the fact that most patenting by companies is done in order to have something to trade or as a defence against other patent-infringement suits. As a result, a new game, with new rules and new norms of behaviour is emerging spontaneously and rapidly.

On the size of the system

It is useful to ask whether the size of the system is an important factor in shaping transition dynamics. It is clear that the probability of a norm of openness and learning coordination emerging, is greater among a small group of interacting decision agents, since the frequency of the direct interactions is high (Axelrod, 1984).

On the other hand, the qualitative macrobehaviour of a small group of interacting decision agents can move extremely rapidly towards the 'wrong' norm. These systems will be most prone to exhibiting the working of history in its strongest form: convergence to an indefinitely persisting equilibrium characterized by perfectly correlated individual policy choices. Moreover, the prevailing collective policy, or behavioural norm, will have been 'selected' adventitiously as a result of some particular concatenation of small events on the historical path. In as much as the policy thus settled upon may well be one that is globally inefficient – indeed, collectively disastrous – this may be a reason why small systems of economic interaction appear historically to have a greater tendency to become extinct or absorbed into larger systems (David, 1992; David and Foray, 1994).

Rationales for policy in the presence of a range of transition processes

In contrast to the process of transition towards a collective norm of access restriction, there are no spontaneous 'phase transitions' towards openness. Thus in the latter case, a single, deviant decision (towards disclosure and cooperation) is probably less common in generating a movement towards a new norm than in the former case.

With respect to the normative proposition on the importance of knowledge openness, as mentioned in the introduction, the policy problem raised by asymmetry in transition processes is complex. The policy option will depend upon the determinant character of an individual action on the frame of reference in which agents operate (Franck, 1991). This determinant character, in turn, is affected by three parameters: the state of the system – O, R or somewhere in between; the nature of the action (is it a deviation from the dominant convention?); and the size of the system. For instance, an individual action which is the first deviation from openness convention in the context of a small size system will be considered as highly determinant.

If the transition is towards secrecy and access restriction (the system is close to O), it is important to intervene very early in the process of spontaneous diffusion. The main difficulty with policy actions to prevent self-reinforcing processes from leading to undesirable outcomes is that the time period for low–cost and successful intervention tends to be relatively brief and to occur early in the development of the emergent convention, well before a tipping point is reached (David, 1992).

By contrast, the transition towards the institutions of openness (the system is close to R) requires an active policy of building new forms of cooperation and some efforts to construct 'collaboratories' (Hilgartner and Brandt-Rauf, 1994), in order to tip the balance in favour of coordination among individual innovative projects (Sabel, 1992).

Splitting Behaviour: the Survival of the Convention of Knowledge Openness through Complementarity Relationships

A system can split into two (or more) coexisting systems, each characterized by different conventions as in the case of the open science system. Section 2.9 describes how university research is experiencing a degradation of its openness convention as a result of increasing market-driven rivalry. New behaviours and strategies for knowledge disclosure and sharing are emerging (patenting activities, delayed access, non-release of data, and so on). Thus two systems are coexisting: one still based on complete openness and the other characterised by the internalisation of some of the norms of proprietary research. However, these two systems are strongly inter-related since the same agents and entities can operate within both systems. As Callon (1994) suggests, 'in the morning the mathematician drafts an article on equations of partial derivatives, and in the afternoon he sells an algorithm to Dassault or the Aerospatiale'.

We again face a problem of binary choice with externalities: each agent must decide whether he wants to work in a completely open science system (O) or in a system characterised by a compromise between openness and some norms of proprietary research (O–R). However, the problem here is rather different from the problem where there was a preferred choice favoured by everybody. In this context, the problem is to maintain the two systems in a dynamic balance since they involve complementary research activities. The system O–R needs the maintenance of the system O for three reasons (Dasgupta and David, 1994). First the system O generates public knowledge which can be used free of charge by the system O–R. This pool of knowledge is an essential input for the research activities carried out in O–R. The important economic pay-offs to O–R from research undertaken in O come in the form of higher rates of return on expenditures allocated to applied research in O–R (David, Mowery and Steinmueller, 1992). Second, the system O is an institution providing training mechanisms. The availability of scientific training institutions is particularly valuable for O–R agents when the rate of growth of scientific knowledge is rapid with a high risk of obsolescence of existing knowledge. Third, the system O generates screening externalities. System O involves an incentive system (priority rule, prizes) which allows the researcher to generate a clear signal about his talents, and this typically affects the conditions of a researcher's future employment, including the option of finding employment in O–R.

Thus, O–R agents need the maintenance of a strong O system. The opposite is also true. A strong O–R system is required to warrant the viability of the O system. The latter is not a self-contained system – and, indeed, could not survive as such.

We are thus facing a new problem of choice addressed by Schelling (1978): things are better if the agents distribute themselves between O and O–R. Although everyone prefers that the world demonstrates a mixture of alternatives, he himself may prefer to be part of the majority, part of the minority or may have an unconditional preference. Thus an agent could have any one of three preferences:

- First, there might be a uniform preference, everybody wanting to enter into the O-system or into the O–R system independently of the choice ratio in the population of researchers, while badly wanting that researcher-population ratio close to fifty–fifty.
- Second, everybody might prefer to be in the minority. Working in the minority group might be advantageous.
- Third, the dominant choice might have a majority advantage outweighing 'scarcity value'; and researchers might deplore a preponderance of O or O–R while selecting the convention of the preponderant system.

In the first case there is a happy equilibrium, in the second case there are two unhappy equilibria, and in the third case there is a single unhappy equilibrium (Figure 8.3).

BY WAY OF CONCLUSION

In this chapter we have studied the processes of emergence, persistence and degradation of the convention of knowledge openness within the realms of science and technology. The efficiency properties of this convention have been explored and some historical framework has been presented.

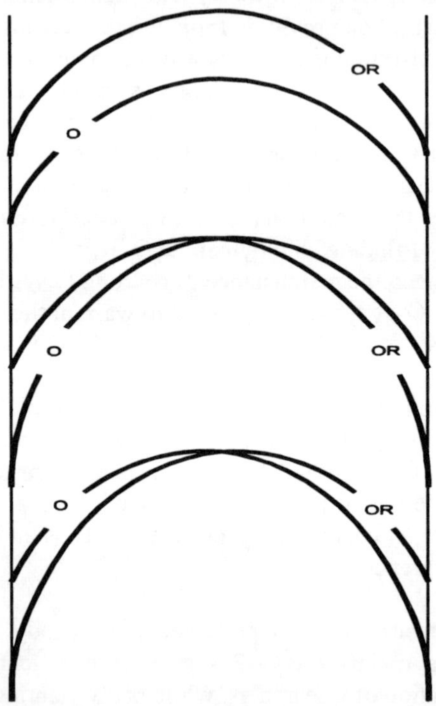

Figure 8.3 Pay-off U-shaped curves with three variants (adapted from Schelling, 1978)

Defining a social convention as a way of aligning individual expectations, we have explained that the emergence of the convention of knowledge openness is caused by some 'shared history' that allows such jointly held expectations to become established. Consolidation of the convention is based on a collective perception of the mutual benefits associated with knowledge openness and on policy response in terms of institutional setting. Finally, its persistence is caused by the path-dependent nature of the institutional system.

The emergence of this convention is not a spontaneous process. It requires the building of a 'coalition', which is a minimum group of agents who may be resentful of free-riders but, nevertheless, find it profitable to join. On the other hand, the convention can very rapidly be degraded through dynamic allocation processes which exhibit the properties of spontaneous order. There is here a fundamental asymmetry: while a convention of secrecy can diffuse spontaneously, a convention of openness has to be constructed. Finally, a convention of openness can also survive through complementary relationships with a system characterised by a more moderate convention (involving some access restriction features).

NOTES

1 Paul David has been responsible for shaping my view about most of the issues treated here. This chapter draws upon my collaborative work with him in the context of the OECD project on National Systems of Innovation (see David and Foray, 1995a,b). All remaining errors remain, of course, my responsibility.

2 The market mechanism has a tendency to discourage the production of public goods (or of goods which have some aspects of public good) because of an inability on the part of producers to appropriate fully the value of the fruits of their efforts.

3 The expression 'infinitely expansible' is proposed by Paul David (1993a) as a substitute for the notion of 'non-rival', which comes from the public finance literature. Callon (1994) offers a discussion of non-rival goods from a sociological point of view. We agree with him that the exploitation of the property of 'infinite expansibility' requires investments, competences and infrastructures; all elements forming the 'absorbtive capacity' for the knowledge considered. This means that the economic value of non-rivalry depends upon those investments: a very sophisticated mathematical statement, which cannot be understood by more than two mathematicians in the world, is, of course, a non-rival good, but this non-rivalry characteristic has a very low economic value.

4 Extract of the *Secretum secretorum*, quoted by Eamon (1985, p. 324).

5 All examples are from Eamon (1985, p. 327).

6 See Latour and Woolgar (1979). Let us be clear. Latour (1987) has come to portray the Mertonian 'norms' as apologetic ideology, self-serving 'myths' about cooperative, disinterested science. In David (1991), it is argued that the norms are prescriptive, and that beliefs that are instilled in scientists as part of the 'culture of science' have an effect on their behaviour – making it easier to form cooperative networks where it is in their mutual interests (and that of society at large) to organize research cooperatively.

7 By contrast to open science, achieving commercial gain from knowledge requires a reward and resource allocation system based on the 'appropriation' and control of knowledge for competitive advantage.

8 This section draws upon Kahin (1990), Garfinkel, Stallman and Kapor (1991) and Merges (1995).

9 The place where trade secrecy is used extensively in software is the 'source code' for programs.

10 On the opportunity of creating a new kind of intellectual property for computer programs, see

Samuelson (1985) and Schmidt (1985).

11 Article 37.1 of the ESA's standard contract for contractors states that the contractor, subject to the provisions of his or her national legislation, has ownership rights to inventions and technical data arising or resulting from work carried out in performance of the said contract. The contractor is therefore entitled to protect such inventions and technical data by means of a patent or any other similar form of protection.

12 Where an individual's search capabilities are limited and the location of opportunities is uncertain and transitory, information pooling becomes an attractive form of insurance.

13 It is possible that the incentive to choose C increases or decreases with the size of the coalition. It can increase in the presence of indivisibilities: the cost of participating in the coalition will decrease as more join the coalition. A phenomenon of increasing returns to free-ride is also possible (the example proposed by Schelling is the capture of whales: the more the rest of you restrict your whaling, the more whales I catch by staying out of the coalition).

BIBLIOGRAPHY

Allen, R.C. (1983), 'Collective invention', *Journal of Economic Behavior and Economic Organization*, **4**, 1–24.

Arrow, K. (1962), 'Economic welfare and the allocation of resources to invention', in R. Nelson (ed.) *The Rate and Direction of Inventive Activity: Economic and Social Factors*, Princeton: NBER.

Arrow, K. (1994), 'Methodological individualism and social knowledge', *American Economic Review*, Papers and Proceedings, May, pp.1–9.

Axelrod, R. (1984), *The Evolution of Cooperation*, New York: Basic Books.

Bes, M.P. (1993), 'Regards à l'intérieur de la boîte noire des satellites: tâches de conception et modalités d'apprentissage des technologies spatiales', *Revue d'Economie Industrielle*, **64**, 61–81.

Besen, S. and L. Raskind (1991), 'An introduction to the law and economics of intellectual property', *Journal of Economic Perspectives*, **5** (1), 3–27.

Callon, M. (1994), 'Is science a public good? Fifth Mullins Lecture', *Science, Technology and Human Value*, 19(4), pp.395–423.

Cassier, M.(1995), 'Les Règles de bonne Conduite du Projet Bridge: Appropriation et Partage des Connaissances Technologiques dans un Réseau Coopératif', IRIS Université de Paris Dauphine.

Cohen, W., R. Florida and W. Goe (1994), 'University–Industry Research Centers in the United States', CEPR/AAAS conference 'University goals, institutional mechanisms and the 'industrial transferability' of research', Stanford University.

Dasgupta, P. (1987), 'The economic theory of technology policy: an introduction', in P. Dasgupta and P. Stoneman (eds), *Economic Policy and Technological Performance*, New York: Cambridge University Press.

Dasgupta, P. and P.A. David (1987), 'Information disclosure and the economics of science and technology', in G. Feiwel (ed.), *Arrow and the Ascent of Modern Economic Theory*, New York: New York University Press.

Dasgupta, P. and P.A. David (1994), 'Toward a new economics of science', *Research Policy*, **23** (5).

Dasgupta, P. and J. Stiglitz (1980), 'Industrial structure and the nature of inventive activity', *The Economic Journal*, **90**, pp.266–93.

David, P.A. (1991), 'Reputation and Agency in the Historical Emergence of the Institutions of 'Open Science', CEPR Discussion Paper, no. **261**, Stanford

University (reissued in revised version as MERIT Memorandum (2) 94–006, January 1994).

David, P.A. (1992), 'Path-dependence in economic processes: implications for policy analysis in dynamical system contexts', to be published as the theme-essay for a special issue of the *International Journal of Industrial Organization*, forthcoming.

David, P.A. (1993a), 'Knowledge, property and the system dynamics of technological change', in M. Wallerstein, M. Mogee, R. Schoen (eds), *Proceeding of the 1992 World Bank Annual Conference on Development Economics*, Washington, DC.

David, P.A. (1993b), 'Intellectual property institutions and the panda's thumb', in *Global Dimensions of Intellectual Property Rights in Science and Technology*, National Research Council, National Academy Press.

David, P.A. (1994), 'Why are institutions the 'carriers' of history?: path dependence and the evolution of conventions, organizations and institutions', *Structural Change and Economics*, **5** (2).

David, P.A. and D. Foray (1993), 'Markov random fields, percolation structure and the economics of diffusion of document standard', in G. Pogorel (ed.), *Global Telecommunications Strategies and Technological Changes*, Amsterdam: Elsevier Publishers.

David, P.A. and D. Foray (1994), 'Dynamics of technology diffusion through local network structures', in L. Leydersdorff (ed.), *Evolutionary Economics and Chaos Theory: New Developments in Technology Studies*, London: Pinter.

David, P.A. and D. Foray (1995a), 'Accessing and expanding the science and technology knowledge-base', *STI Review*, **16**, pp.13–68.

David, P.A. and D. Foray (1995b), 'Information distribution and the growth of economically valuable knowledge: a rationale for technological infrastructure policies', in M. Teubal, D. Foray, M. Justman and E. Zuscovitch (eds), *Technological Infrastructure Policies: An International Perspective,* forthcoming, Dordrecht: Kluwer Publishers.

David, P.A., D. Mowery and W.E. Steinmueller (1992), 'Analyzing the economics pay off of basic research', *Economics of Innovation and New Technology,* vol.2, **1**, pp.73–90.

David, P.A., D. Mowery and W.E. Steinmueller (1994), 'University–Industry Research Collaborations: Managing Missions in Conflict', CEPR/AAAS conference 'University Goals, Institutional Mechanisms and the 'Industrial Transferability' of Research', Stanford University.

Ehrnberg, E. and S. Jacobsson (1997), 'Technological discontinuities and incumbents' performance', in Edquist C. (ed.) *Systems of Innovation*, Pinter

Farrell, J. (1989), 'Standardization and Intellectual Property', *Jurimetrics*, **30** (1), 35–50.

Farrell, J. (1992), 'Some Arguments for Weaker Intellectual Property Protection in Network Industries', mimeo, Department of Economics, Berkeley.

Foray, D. (1991), 'Industrial cooperation and the organisational dynamics of the innovative firm', *Research Policy*, **20**(5), pp.393–404

Foray, D. (1994), 'Production and distribution of knowledge in the new systems of innovation: the role of intellectual property rights', *STI Review*, **14**, OECD.

Foray, D. and C. Freeman (eds) (1992), *Technology and the Wealth of Nations*, London: Pinter.

Frank, R. (1991), 'Positional externalities', in R. Zeckhauser (ed.), *Strategy and Choice*, Cambridge MA: The MIT Press.

Fulcanelli, S. (1924), *Le Mystère des Cathédrales*, Paris: Schemit

Garfinkel, S., R. Stallman and M. Kapor (1991), 'Why patents are bad for software',

Issues in Science and Technology, fall, pp.50–55.
Grindley, P., D.C. Mowery and B. Silvermann (1994), *The Design of High-Technology Consortia: Lessons from SEMATECH*, Center for Research in Management, University of Berkeley.
Henderson, R., A. Jaffe and M. Tratjenberg (1994), 'Numbers up, quality down? trends in university patenting 1965–1992', CEPR/AAAS conference 'University Goals, Institutional Mechanisms and the 'Industrial Transferability' of Research', March 18–20, Stanford University.
Hermitte, M.A. and P.B. Joly (1992), 'Plant biotechnology and patents in Europe: an economic analysis of alternative models of intellectual property rights', *International Journal for Technology Management*, pp.76–94
Hilgartner, S. and S. Brandt-Rauf (1994), 'Controlling data and resources: access strategies in molecular genetics', CEPR/AAAS conference 'University Goals, Institutional Mechanisms and the 'Industrial Transferability' of Research', Stanford University.
Hirshleifer, J. (1971), 'The private and social value of information and the reward to inventive activity', *American Economic Review*, **61**, pp.561–74.
Kahin, B. (1990), 'The software patent crisis', *Technology Review*, April, pp.50–58.
Klein, B.H. (1988), 'Luck, necessity and dynamic flexibility', in H. Hanusch (ed.) *Evolutionary Economics*, New York: Cambridge University Press.
Kitch, E. (1977), 'The nature and function of the patent system', *Journal of Law and Economics*, **20**, pp.265–90.
Latour, B. (1987), *Science in Action: How to Follow Scientists and Engineers through Society*, Cambridge MA: Harvard University Press.
Latour, B. and S. Woolgar (1979), *Laboratory Life*, Beverly Hills, CA: Sage Publications.
Long, P. (1991), 'The openness of knowledge: an ideal and its context in 16th century writings on mining and metallurgy', *Technology and Culture*, **32**(3), pp.318–55.
Lundvall, B.A. (1995), *The Social Dimension of the Learning Economy*, Inaugural Lecture, Aalborg University.
Machlup, F. (1983), 'What do we mean by the optimum utilization of knowledge', in K. Boulding and L. Senesh (eds), *The Optimum Utilization of Knowledge*, Boulder Colorado: Westview Press.
Machlup, F. and E. Penrose (1950), 'The patent controversy in the nineteenth century', *The Journal of Economic History*, **X** (1), pp.1–29.
Macleod, C. (1988), *Inventing the Industrial Revolution: The English Patent System 1660–1800*, New York: Cambridge University Press.
Margolis, H. (1991), 'Free-riding versus cooperation', in R. Zeckhauser (ed), *Strategy and Choice*, Cambridge MA: The MIT Press.
Massel, M. (1991), 'Antitrust and patent law: effects on innovation', *American Economic Review*, pp.289–92.
Merges, R. (1995), 'A comparative look at property and the software industry', in D.C. Mowery (ed.), *The International Computer Software Industry*, Oxford: Oxford University Press.
Merges, R. and R. Nelson (1994), 'On limiting or encouraging rivalry in technical progress: the effect of patent scope decisions', *Journal of Economic Behaviour and Organizations*, **25**, pp.1–24.
Merton, R.K. (1973), 'The sociology of science: theoretical and empirical investigations', in N.W. Storer (ed.) *Science in Context*, Chicago: The University of Chicago Press.
Metcalfe, S. (1992), *Competition and Collaboration in the Innovation Process*,

University of Manchester, Discussion Paper 79.
Nelson, R. (1959), 'The simple economics of basic scientific research', *Journal of Political Economy*, **67**, pp.297–306.
Nelson, R. (1992), 'What is 'commercial' and what is 'public' about technology, and what should be?', in R. Landau, D.C. Mowery and N. Rosenberg (eds), *Technology and the Wealth of Nations*, Stanford: Stanford University Press.
Ordover, J. (1991), 'A patent system for both diffusion and exclusion', *Journal of Economic Perspective*, **5** (1), pp.43–60.
Perez, L.H. (1991), 'Invention and the state in 18th century France', *Technology and Culture*, **32** (4), 911–31.
Renouard, A.C. (1844), *Traité des Brevets d'Invention*, 1987, reissued by CNAM, Paris.
Richardson, G.B. (1990), *Information and Investment*, Clarendon Press.
Rosenberg, N. and L.E. Birdzell (1991), 'Science, technology and the western miracle', *Scientific American*, **263**(5), pp.19–25.
Sabel, C. (1992), 'Studied trust: building new forms of cooperation in a volatile economy', in D. Foray and C. Freeman (eds), *Technology and the Wealth of Nations*, London: Pinter.
Samuelson, P. (1985), 'Creating a new kind of intellectual property: applying the lessons of the chip law to computer programs', *Minnesota Law Review*, **70**, 471.
Schelling, T. (1978), *Micromotives and Macrobehaviors*, New York: Norton.
Schmid, A. (1985), 'Intellectual property rights in bio-technology and computer technology', *Journal of Institutional and Theoretical Economics*, **141**(1), pp.127–141.
Scotchmer, S. (1991), 'On the shoulders of giants: cumulative research and the patent law', *Journal of Economic Perspectives*, **5** (1), 24–41.
Simon, H. (1982), 'The economics of information processing', Part VI, in H. Simon (ed.) *Behavioral Economics and Business Organization*, Cambridge MA: The MIT Press.
Steinmueller, E. (1992), 'The economics of production and distribution of user–specific information via digital networks', in C. Antonelli (ed.), *The Economics of Information Networks*, Amsterdam: North-Holland.
US Congress, Office of Technology Assessment (1992), *Finding a Balance: Computer Software, Intellectual Property, and the Challenge of Technological Change*, OTA–TCT–527.
Von Hippel, E. (1988), 'Trading trade secrets', *Technology Review*, February–March, 58–64.

9. Technological Evolution, Self-Organisation and Knowledge

Pier Paolo Saviotti[1] and G.S. Mani[2]

INTRODUCTION

Studies of technological change have pointed out that technological evolution is characterised both by discontinuities and by long periods of stable, incremental development. Examples of discontinuities leading to the highest degree of qualitative change are the transitions between different dominant designs (Abernathy and Utterback, 1975, 1978), technological regimes (Nelson and Winter, 1977), technological guideposts (Sahal, 1981) and technological paradigms (Dosi, 1982). The existence of such discontinuities and their role in economic development was well understood by Schumpeter (1942), who identified them simply with radical innovations.

The existence of dominant designs, technological regimes and so on, has been inferred from the results of innovation studies. In this chapter we attempt to find a theoretical justification for their existence. Such a justification is related both to the mechanisms of knowledge generation and diffusion, and it constitutes an important part of the process of self-organisation of the economic system. Self-organisation is characterised by the invariance of a number of entities and relationships constituting the economic system in the presence of forces which can in theory lead to changes in these same entities and relationships. In particular, since the transition between different paradigms and the direction of movement forwards within each paradigm depends on knowledge accumulation, self-regulation depends also on the characteristics and dynamics of technological knowledge. Such dynamics are fundamentally related to learning. In particular, this chapter considers only learning effects obtained by means of search . These learning effects have two properties of interest: first, they are obtained by allocating resources/investment, as opposed, for example, to learning by doing; and second, they are a way of 'learning by not doing'.

The following section introduces some general considerations about search activities, learning and knowledge. In the following sections of the chapter the setting of search efforts and their time-dependence are treated by means of nucleation theory. This theory predicts the existence of barriers to the transitions between two different technologies. The relationship between such barriers and the general features of knowledge and search introduced in section 2 are then analysed. It is argued that the existence of such barriers justifies the discontinuities occuring at the transition between two different paradigms/regimes, and so on. Furthermore, the variables which could influence the size and the time evolution of the barriers are discussed.

This chapter does not provide a fully worked out model of the transition between two technologies. It points out that, given the general features of knowledge and of technological populations, nucleation theory is capable of describing the transition between different technological populations. Furthermore, based on the structure of nucleation theory, we can expect that the transition will involve overcoming a barrier, and that this barrier is responsible for the discontinuity. In turn, the nature and the height of the barrier can be interpreted in terms of the knowledge base of the new and of the old technology.

SEARCH ACTIVITIES, LEARNING AND KNOWLEDGE: SOME GENERAL CONSIDERATIONS

Firms and other organisations need knowledge in order to create innovations. Such knowledge is generated in a number of ways. New knowledge is generated by means of R&D. However, R&D is also useful to retrieve knowledge already possessed by other organisations. That is, R&D increases the absorptive capacity of firms (Cohen and Levinthal, 1989, 1990). R&D strictly defined is only one, although perhaps the most important, of the class of search activities (Nelson and Winter, 1982). These are activities which scan the external environment looking for alternatives to the firm's present routines. Search activities can include activities in the field of design and marketing or simply those activities in the sphere of production which are exploratory in nature. In general, search activities are ways of learning by not doing. This chapter is concerned with search activities and not only with R&D.

A distinction must be made here between knowledge and information. Information is to be interpreted as factual (Saviotti, 1988, 1991a). Knowledge, on the other hand, establishes generalisations and correlations between variables. Knowledge is, therefore, a 'correlational structure'. The extent of such correlation is not infinite. Each piece of knowledge (for example a theory) establishes correlations over some variables and over particular ranges of their values. In other words, knowledge has a 'local character', a concept introduced in a more limited way by Nelson and Winter (1982). The degree of such local character can be measured by the 'span' of a given piece of knowledge, that is, by the number of variables and the amplitude of the range over which correlation is provided. General theories will have a greater span than a very specific piece of applied knowledge. The local character is a concept applicable to scientific, technological and organisational knowledge. Particular pieces of information can be understood only in the context of a given type of knowledge. New knowledge, for example relative to a radical innovation, creates new information. However, this information can only be understood and used by those who possess the new knowledge. In other words, knowledge also has a 'retrieval/interpretative' function. In summary, knowledge is a correlational and a retrieval/interpretative structure, and it has a local character (Saviotti 1994, 1995).

Knowledge is also cumulative, tacit or codified and it has a limited appropriability (Teece, 1981; Nelson and Winter, 1982). The cumulative character of knowledge implies path-dependence and the creation of barriers, as established participants in given technologies accumulate a differential advantage with respect to potential entrants. Furthermore, 'tacit' and 'codified' do not represent two discrete situations, but the extremes of a range of possible situations. A given piece of knowledge has a certain degree of codification.

Knowledge in firms and organisations is collective in character. It is not simply the sum of the pieces of knowledge 'owned' by the individual members of the organisation. In this sense we can define the knowledge base (KB) of a firm (or organisation) as the collective knowledge that the firm uses for its productive purposes. A firm's KB is used to produce its output or revealed technological performance (RTP). The development of KB has to precede that of RTP, or equivalently, RTP lags behind KB. KB can be increased by means of search activities or by the retrieval of the knowledge already existing in other organisations. As previously pointed out, search activities improve the absorptive capacity of a firm, but they are not the only possible means of retrieval of existing knowledge. However, in this chapter attention is focused exclusively on search activities.

Search activities are a more general analogue of R&D, including all the activities aimed at exploring alternatives to existing routines, even if they are not classified formally as R&D. Search efforts represent the amount of resources allocated to search activities. Different types of search effort can be described by means of: (1) the range, and (2) the probability of success (Figure 9.1).

For example, we may think that a very basic type of research over an unexplored field is likely to scan a very wide range, but will have a limited probability of success. We can imagine representing this situation as a very flat distribution of the probability of success over a very wide range. On the other hand, we can imagine that a very applied and specific piece of knowledge will have a much more skewed probability distribution over a narrower range with a higher maximum, corresponding to a greater probability of success.

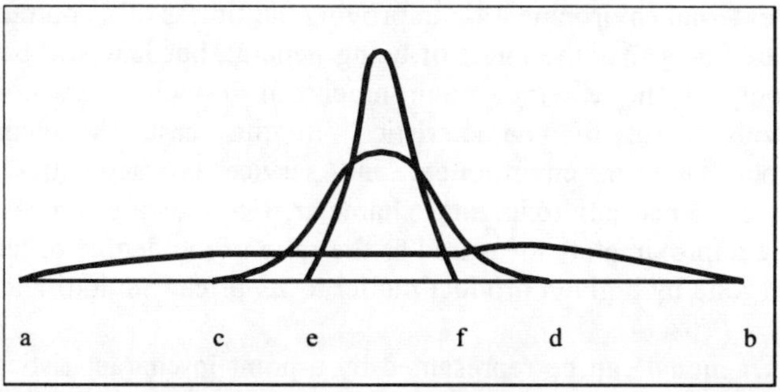

Figure 9.1 Range of search and probability of success for basic research (a–b), applied research(c–d) and development (e–f).

The advantage of this type of representation is that basic and applied R&D can be described by means of the same parameters: range and probability of success. Furthermore, we can hypothesise a life cycle that begins when a basic search first uncovers the fundamental concepts required to understand the new field. Subsequently, more applied search achieves partial, limited success (local peaks in the probability distribution of successful outcome), which leads to focusing on narrower ranges. Finally development improves on these successes by focusing on even narrower ranges, thus increasing the probability of success. In this chapter both the range and the probability of success are described in characteristics space.

The main outcome of search activities considered in this chapter is changes in product technology. Each product is represented by means of two sets of characteristics, one describing its internal structure (technical characteristics) and the other the services performed for their users (service characteristics) (Saviotti and Metcalfe, 1984). As a result of firms' search activities their KB grows, the characteristics of the products improve, and the cost at which such characteristics of the products can be provided falls. Among these characteristics, the ones that can determine the products' performances are service characteristics. The selection of products is made by their users, who choose the products to suit their requirements. Given that service characteristics are the only ones that affect users directly, successful products are those that are better adapted to their external environment. Of course, not all the components of the external environment are equally important for a firm. The users of its output are the most important component of the external environment. However, we can assume that not only firms, but all other organisations survive by adapting to their external environment. We can thus use the concept of fitness, defined as the capacity of an organisation to adapt to its external environment (Saviotti and Mani, 1995). The organisation adapts to its external environment by improving the fitness of its output. Such a definition of fitness has the merit of being general, but it would be easily applicable only if the external environment of a technology could be described with a set of characteristics. In this case the degree of correspondence between environment and service characteristics would measure fitness. Since environmental characteristics are rarely measurable, fitness can be approximately measured as the ratio of the degree of technical change undergone by a given product model to its price (Saviotti and Mani, 1993).

Each product model can be represented by a point in characteristics space (from now on 'X-space'). A technological population is the distribution of the technology's product models in X-space. Search activities contribute to change the position, shape and density of a technological population (Saviotti, 1991, 1994).

The following attempts to provide an analytical representation of the general concepts knowledge, learning and search presented in this section.

AN ANALYTICAL REPRESENTATION OF KNOWLEDGE AND OF SEARCH ACTIVITIES

As indicated in the previous section, the KB grows by means of search efforts. However, the final goal of search efforts is not only to learn but also to develop competitive products, that is, to increase the fitness of the product technology considered. Consequently:

$$\frac{dKB}{dSE} = \textit{rate of learning due to search efforts} \tag{9.1}$$

$$\frac{dF_i}{dSE} = \textit{rate of return on search efforts} \tag{9.2}$$

where: SE = search effort; KB = knowledge base; F_i = fitness of technology i.

Furthermore:

$$\frac{dF_i}{dKB} = \textit{technological opportunity of a given knowledge base} \tag{9.3}$$

The previous variables are related among themselves and to the probability of learning and to the range of learning:

$$\frac{dKB}{dSE} = \frac{dKB}{dF_i}\frac{dF_i}{dSE} \tag{9.4}$$

$$\frac{dF_i}{dSE} = \frac{dKB}{dSE}\frac{dF_i}{dKB} = p(SE) \tag{9.5}$$

That is, the rate of return from a technological search effort, *SE*, depends on the rate of learning within a given technology and on the opportunity of the technology itself. Neither fast learning in a technology with limited opportunity, nor slow learning in a highly applicable technology, will ensure market success. As was already evident to students of technological innovation in the1970s (Rosenberg, 1972), successful innovation requires a marriage of technological opportunity and market demand. Also, the rate of return on search efforts is equal to the probability *p*(*SE*) of obtaining the required outcome. In turn, since the absorptive/retrieval capacity of a given organisation is greater for external knowledge similar to that already possessed by the organisation, *p*(*SE*) depends: (1) inversely on the distance between the existing technological position in X-space and the position of the technology which is the object of the search, and (2) directly on technological opportunity:

$$p(SE) = \frac{b}{D(T_1, T_0)} = \frac{dKB}{dSE}\frac{dF_i}{dKB} \tag{9.6}$$

Hence:

$$b = \frac{dF_i}{dKB} \tag{9.7}$$

and

$$\frac{dKB}{dSE} = \frac{1}{D(T_0, T_1)} \tag{9.8}$$

That is, the rate of learning decreases with the distance between the positions of the existing and the searched technology. This is equivalent to restating the fact that knowledge has a 'local' character.

We can obtain a more detailed understanding of the relationship between fitness and search efforts if we introduce an approximate, but measurable, definition of fitness (Saviotti and Mani, 1993), according to which $F_i = TC_i/P_i$. In this case:

$$\frac{dF_i}{dSE} = \frac{d\left(\frac{TC_i}{P_i}\right)}{dSE} = \frac{1}{P_i}\frac{dTC_i}{dSE} + TC_i\frac{d\left(\frac{1}{P_i}\right)}{dSE} \tag{9.9}$$

the expansion of (9.9) gives:

$$\frac{dF_i}{dSE} = \frac{1}{P_i}\left(\frac{dTC_i}{dSE} - F_i\frac{dP_i}{dSE}\right) \tag{9.10}$$

From equation (9.10) it can be seen that the rate of return from search activities increases with the rate of growth of technical change and with the rate of fall in price determined by search activities. The first term in brackets on the right describes the change in quality of the technology considered and the second the change in the efficiency with which it is produced. Furthermore, we can see that the effect of the rate of price fall is greater the higher the initial fitness of the technology and that the overall effect of search activities is greater the lower the initial price of the product technology considered.

THE DYNAMICS OF SEARCH ACTIVITIES

In this chapter the goal of search activities is to develop a new technology T_1, different from the existing technology T_0. T_1 is different from T_0 if it occupies a different position in X-space. The different position can be in the same dimensions of X-space, in which case the new technology would be the result of incremental innovation or of specialisation, or in completely new dimensions, corresponding to a radical innovation. T_1 can be either a substitute or a different technology, but it has to compete with T_0, in other words, T_1 and T_0 must have some common service characteristics. The amount of resources allocated to a particular search activity is called its search effort *SE*(*t*). Search activities aimed at developing T_1 [$SE_1(t)$] proceed simultaneously with those aimed at improving T_0 [$SE_0(t)$]. However, the range of search γ in $SE_1(t)$ changes during the life cycle of the technology. The range of search is equal to the distance between the two technologies T_0 and T_1 when the new technology T_1 is being established. Once T_1 exists search activities start scanning a region of space internal to the new technological population T_1. Search becomes more incremental and the range, γ, becomes smaller than $D(T_0,T_1)$ (Figure 9.2).

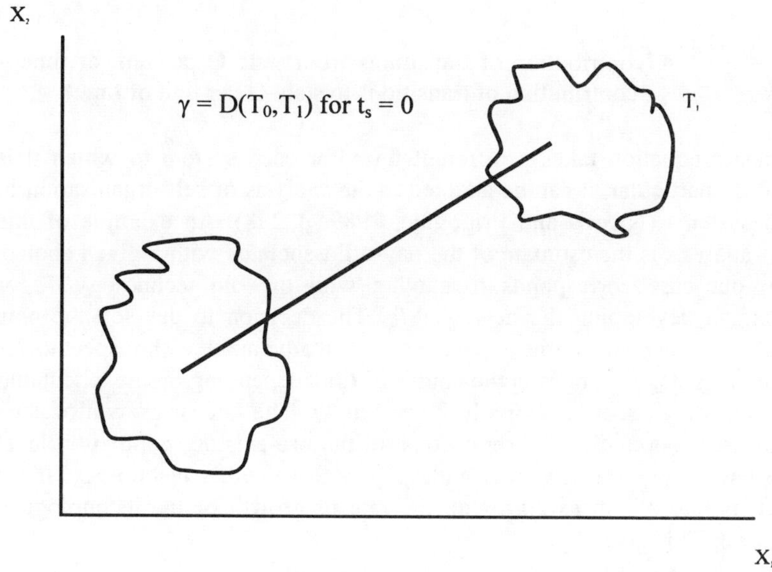

Figure 9.2 *The* range *of search γ is equal to the distance between the two technological populations only when the new technology T1 is established for search time* $t_s = 0$.

We can expect the level of search efforts to depend on: (1) the size of the existing and/or the potential markets, (2) on the extent of competition in the existing and/or the potential markets, (3) on the probability of actually being able to develop the innovation, and (4) on the differential advantage of the new with respect to the old technology. In terms of the present theoretical framework: (1) corresponds to the level of the technological population, either the existing or the expected one; (2) to the density of the technological population, either the existing or the expected one; (3) to the expected probability of finding the required outcome, $p(SE)$; and (4) to the relative attractiveness of the old and new technologies. The role of population density can be understood as follows: the higher density corresponds to a higher intensity of competition, which provides a motivation for producers to exit the core of the technology to establish themselves in a niche (Saviotti and Mani, 1993).

The allocation of search efforts to T_0 (incremental innovation) or to the creation of T_1 influences the size of the respective technological populations N_0 and N_1. In turn, as indicated above, the size of the population affects search efforts. The dynamics of search efforts can then be derived from that of the populations. Population dynamics can be derived from a master equation, which, in its most general form, can be written as:

$$\frac{dProb(Q,t)}{dt} = \text{(contribution of transitions from state Q per unit of time} - \text{contribution of transitions to state Q per unit of time)}$$

The master equation takes a different form for each system to which it is applied. In particular, it can be adapted to the analysis of self-organisation in human systems (Nicolis and Prigogine, 1989, p. 238). An example of this type of analysis is the estimate of the pay-off associated with a given choice, that in our case corresponds to staying with the old technology T_0 or investing in developing the new one T_1. The decision to develop the new technology T_1 depends on its expected or actual advantage with respect to T_0. Such an advantage changes in the course of time depending on the extent and on the success of search efforts in T_0 and in T_1. The rate of growth of each technological population is proportional to the pre-existing population level and to its relative attractiveness with respect to the other technology. If we neglect its rate of intrinsic growth, the rate of growth of the technological population, T_1 is given by:

$$\frac{dN_1}{dt} = aN_1\left(\frac{N_0 A_1}{A_0 + A_1} - \frac{N_1 A_0}{A_0 + A_1}\right) \tag{9.11}$$

where $A_1 / (A_0 + A_1)$ is the relative attractiveness of technology T_1, and $A_0 / (A_0 + A_1)$ is the relative attractiveness of T_0. A symmetrical expression can be written for N_0.

The absolute attractiveness of each technology is equal to the rate of return from search efforts. Thus:

$$A_0 = dF_0 / dSE_0 \text{ and } A_1 = dF_1 / dSE_1 \tag{9.12}$$

We have neglected the rate of intrinsic growth of technological population T_1 because the main aim of this chapter is to study the role of knowledge in the generation of discontinuities in technological evolution. The process of intrinsic growth, that is, of growth unperturbed by other technological populations, is unlikely to produce discontinuities.

The time path of search activities is linked to the evolution of populations by means of an equation like the following:

$$dSE_1/dt = kdN_1(t)/dt \tag{9.13}$$

where the constant of proportionality, k, will contain the effect of the range of search, of population density and of the technological opportunity of T_1. k could have, for example, the form:

$$k = b_1/\rho_1\gamma = p(SE)_1/\rho_1 \tag{9.14}$$

where ρ_1 is the density of the technological population T_1, b_1 is its technological opportunity, and γ is the range of search in X-space.

NUCLEATION THEORY AND BARRIERS TO TRANSITION

The factors influencing the probabilities of transition between two states can be understood in reference to nucleation theory (Nicolis and Prigogine, 1989). According to this theory, fluctuations occurring within a stable population, corresponding to a given state, can induce transitions to a different state. The fluctuations are required because the two states are separated by a barrier. This is true, even when the final state is more stable than the initial one. After the final state is established, fluctuations can occur within it, inducing the reverse transition to the initial state. The ratio of the populations of the two states depends on their relative stability, or attractiveness.

We can apply these considerations to two technological populations, T_0 and T_1, having different stabilities, or fitnesses. For example, they can have different unit costs, efficiencies, performance and so on. In order for the transition ($T_0 \rightarrow T_1$) to occur, a barrier must be overcome (Figure 9.3). Here it must be pointed out that the curve shown in Figure 9.3 has the shape commonly used in physics, where a stable state corresponds to a minimum of energy and, therefore, to a trough or to a valley in the diagram. In the case of either a technological or an economic population, the variable corresponding to energy in determining the relative stability of different populations is fitness. However, since stability increases with fitness, each stable population has to correspond to a local maximum, that is, to a peak. If we were to represent fitness on the vertical axis, the curve corresponding to that of Figure 9.3 would show a transition from a peak to a valley to another peak. Since the concept of 'barrier' is more easily represented as overcoming a hill, for the moment we have decided to keep using the conventional graphic representation. In fact, such a curve can be easily obtained for a technological or an economic population if we plot the reverse of fitness ($1/F_i$) on the vertical axis. A different treatment of fitness, implying the use of surfaces with hills and valleys, would be required in a more sophisticated modelling exercise.

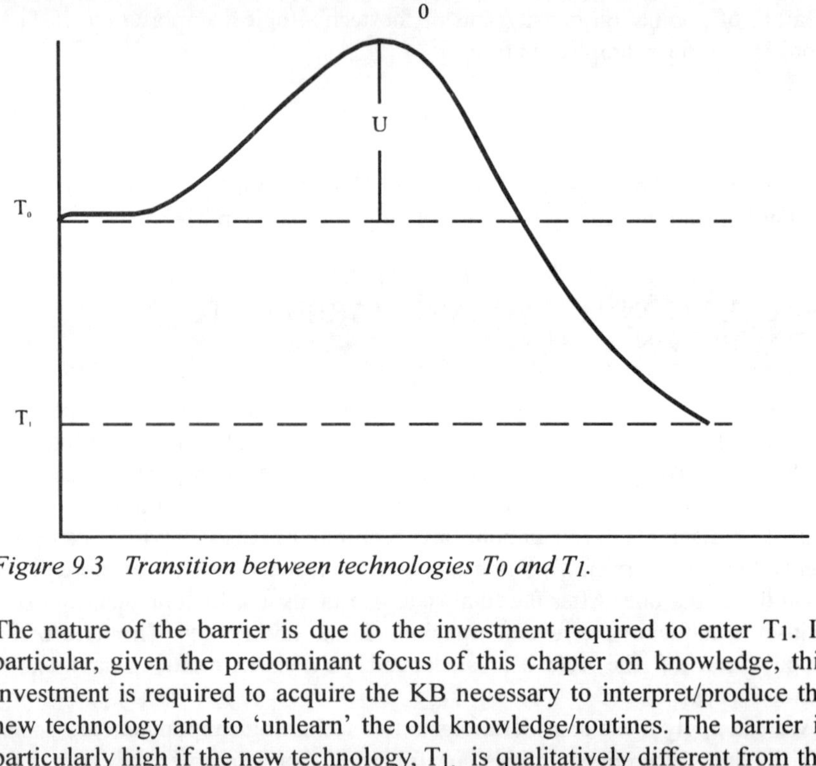

Figure 9.3 Transition between technologies T_0 and T_1.

The nature of the barrier is due to the investment required to enter T_1. In particular, given the predominant focus of this chapter on knowledge, this investment is required to acquire the KB necessary to interpret/produce the new technology and to 'unlearn' the old knowledge/routines. The barrier is particularly high if the new technology, T_1, is qualitatively different from the old one, that is, if it has a new internal structure, so that little or nothing of the old KB can be used to interpret/retrieve the new technology. As already pointed out, this transition would correspond to a competence disrupting technological change.

The variable represented on the vertical axis of Figure 9.3 is the inverse of the fitness of the technologies T_0 and T_1. *U* is the height of the barrier to be overcome if the transition has to take place.

Factors contributing to the height of the barrier are:

- The difference or distance, $D(T_0, T_1)$, between the two technologies in space. This reflects the local character of knowledge. Depending on how radical the innovation is, the new technology will either share some of the technical characteristics with the old one or will be in completely new dimensions of technical X-space. Therefore, a type of distance measurement is required which takes into account not only the distance in a Euclidean sense, but also the degree of commonality of variables. This distance could be considered a measure of the degree of competence disruption of the new technology, T_1.
- The supply (ST) of scientists and technologists capable of interpreting and understanding the new technology. The barrier could, for example, be represented by an expression such as the following:

$$U = U_0 \, exp[D(T_0, T_1)/ST] \tag{9.15}$$

The ratio $D(T_0, T_1)/ST$ would be proportional to the cost of overcoming the barrier to entry into the new technology. For example:

$$C(KB) \propto [D(T_0, T_1)/ST] \tag{9.16}$$

We can apply nucleation theory to the transition between two technologies as follows. At a given time most firms are at T_0. However, there are always fluctuations, represented by sporadic search efforts, which may lead one or a few firms (members of T_0 population) to overcome the barrier and to pass to T_1. The transition to T_1 is an innovation. If the innovation is successful there will be imitation. Imitation is an autocatalytic phenomenon, in the sense that the higher the rate of imitation the greater the incentive for other firms to imitate, at least up to a certain point. Imitation/autocatalysis accelerates the rate of transition $T_0 \rightarrow T_1$. In other words, the new technology, T_1, is stable only if there is imitation. This is at least partly an endogenous mechanism. Fluctuations can occur due to sporadic search efforts within the same technology. However, search efforts occurring within completely unrelated technologies can also have an important effect and give rise to transitions.

LOCK-IN, DOMINANT DESIGNS, TECHNOLOGICAL REGIMES, TECHNOLOGICAL PARADIGMS AND SO ON

The existence of barriers to transition can help to explain phenomena such as lock-in, dominant designs, technological regimes and paradigms, and so on.

In this sense it must be remebered that both the height of the barrier and the relative stability of the two technologies, T_0 and T_1, are not fixed once and for all, but can vary during the evolution of the technologies. For example, the barrier is likely to be higher at the very beginning of the life cycle of the new technology T_1, when the knowledge and the skills required to produce and to use it are very scarce. However, as imitation starts occurring, the greater demand for the new knowledge and skills is likely to induce the development of research, education and training in all the required fields. The barrier will be reduced by the greater availability of the human resources required to produce and use the new technology. Furthermore, the relative stability of the two technologies can change during their evolution. The efficiency and performance of a technology can change during its life cycle, as occurred, for example, during the evolution of motor cars, aircraft and computers. Moreover, improvements can be induced in the efficiency and performance of the old technology by the competition coming from the new one. Different combinations of these processes influencing the height of the barrier and the relative stability of the two technologies can reinforce situations of lock-in or dictate the end of a previously dominant design and paradigm. Two examples of different combinations are discussed below.

Example 1

The new technology T_1, not yet fully developed, is potentially superior to T_0. However, as T_1 appears, the efficiency of T_0 improves faster than the height of the barrier falls. In this case the net barrier to be overcome actually grows, thus reducing the probability of transition. A situation like this can occur if the rate of incremental innovation in the new technology is faster than the rate at which education and training in the new technology are developed. This situation reinforces the lock-in in T_0 and stabilises the previously dominant design and paradigm, even in the presence of a potential superiority of the new technology (Figure 9.4).

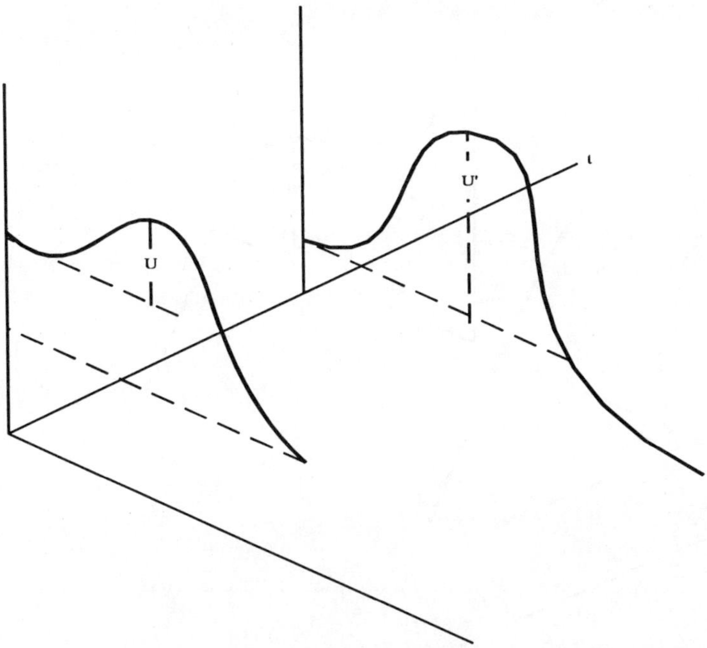

Figure 9.4 The barrier to the transition/innovation increases as the generalised efficiency for the old technology increases.

Example 2

Improvements in the two technologies, T_0 and T_1, proceed at a similar pace in such a way that their relative fitness is unchanged. Simultaneously there is a very fast development of education and training in the new technology, T_1. The barrier falls, increasing the probability of transition to the new technology, T_1. The old technology can become extremely unstable, to the point of disappearing (Figure 9.5).

SUMMARY AND CONCLUSIONS

In this chapter we have attempted to analyse the role of knowledge in the emergence and development of technological innovation. We have attempted to develop a formal treatment of some general concepts about technological knowledge which have emerged recently in the literature, such as the local character of knowledge, technological opportunity, search activities, rates of learning and the knowledge base of an organisation. Moreover, we have used

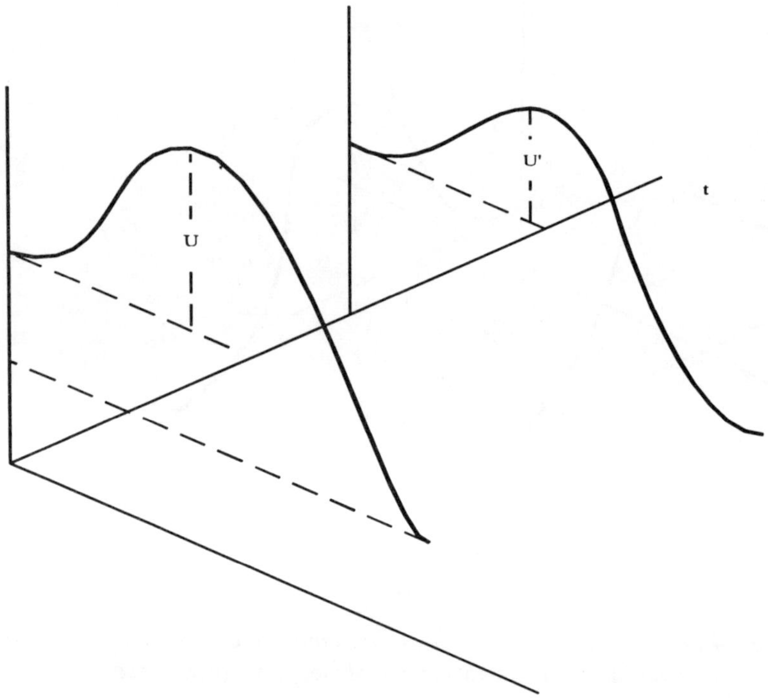

Figure 9.5 The barrier to the transition/innovation falls because during the diffusion of the technology the cost of acquiring the new knowledge it falls through teaching, training and search activities.

nucleation theory to show that the creation of an innovation, namely, the transition between two different technological populations, needs to overcome a barrier. We have discussed the factors influencing the height of the barrier, and therefore the probability of the transition to the new technology, and the relative stability, or fitness, of the two technologies. The combination of the effects of these factors can change relative stability and barrier height in such a way as to favour lock-in and the continued dominance of old designs and paradigms even in the presence of a potentially superior new technology, or the emergence of the new technology and the complete disappearance of the old one.

This chapter does not provide a fully worked out model of the role of knowledge in technological innovation. Rather, it is a first exploration in modelling such a role. Moreover, nucleation theory is used rather intuitively and not applied to explicit modelling. In other words, this chapter sets the ground for a more explicit modelling exercise of the role of knowledge in technological innovation based on evolutionary theories.

NOTES

1 INRA-SERD, Université Pierre Mendès-France, BP 47, 38040 Grenoble, Cedex 9, France. Tel: (33) 76.82.58.31; Fax: (33) 76.82.54.55; E-mail: saviotti@grenoble.inra.fr.
2 Department of Physics, University of Manchester, Manchester M13 9PL, UK. Tel: (0161) 275-4194; Fax: (0161) 275-4218.

BIBLIOGRAPHY

Abernathy, W.J. and J.M. Utterback (1975), 'A dynamic model of process and product innovation', *Omega*, **3** (6), 639–56.

Abernathy, W.J. and J.M. Utterback (1978), 'Patterns of industrial innovation', *Technology Review*, June/July, 41–47.

Cohen, M. and D. Levinthal.(1989), 'Innovating and learning: the two faces of R&D', *Economic Journal*, **99**, 569–96.

Cohen, M. and D. Levinthal (1990), 'Absorptive capacity: a new perspective on learning and innovation', *Administrative Science Quarterly*, **35**, 128–52.

Dosi, G. (1982), 'Technological paradigms and technological trajectories: a suggested interpretation of the determinants and directions of technical change', *Research Policy*, **11,** 147–62..

Nelson, R. and S. Winter (1977), 'In search of useful theory of innovation', *Research Policy*, **6,** 36–76.

Nelson, R. and S. Winter (1982), *An Evolutionary Theory of Economic Change*, Cambridge, MA: Harvard University Press.

Nicolis, G. and I. Prigogine (1989), *Exploring Complexity*, New York: Freeman.

Rosenberg, N. (1972), *Technology and American Economic Growth*, New York: Harper and Row.

Sahal, D. (1981), *Patterns of Technological Innovation*, Reading, MA: Addison Wesley.

Saviotti, P.P. (1988), 'Information, entropy and variety in technoeconomic development', *Research Policy*, **17**, 89–103.

Saviotti, P.P. (1991a), 'The role of variety in economic and technological development', in P.P. Saviotti and J.S. Metcalfe (eds), *Evolutionary Theories of Economic and Technological Change: Present State and Future Prospects*, London: Harwood Publishers.

Saviotti, P.P. (1991b), *Technological Evolution, Product Characteristics, Competition and Variety*, paper presented at 'Colloquium Management of Technology', conference Paris, 27–28 May.

Saviotti, P.P. (1994), *Knowledge, Information and Organisational Structures*, presented at the 11th congress of the International Economic History Association, Milan, 12–16 September.

Saviotti, P.P. (forthcoming), *Technological Evolution and the Economy*, Aldershot: Edward Elgar.

Saviotti, P.P. and G.S. Mani (1993), *A Model of Technological Evolution based on*

Replicator Dynamics, presented at the Conference on 'New Developments in Technology Studies: Evolutionary Economics and Chaos Theory', Amsterdam, 6–8 May.

Saviotti, P.P. and G.S. Mani (1995), 'Competition, variety and technological evolution', *Journal of Evolutionary Economics*.

Saviotti, P.P. and J.S. Metcalfe (1984), 'A theoretical approach to the construction of technological output indicators', *Research Policy,* **13**, 141–51.

Saviotti, P.P. and J.S. Metcalfe (eds) (1991), *Evolutionary Theories of Economic and Technological Change: Present State and Future Prospects,* London: Harwood Publishers.

Schumpeter, J. (1942), *Capitalism, Socialism and Democracy*, London: George Allen and Unwin, 5th edition, 1976.

Teece, D. (1981), 'The market for know-how and the efficient international transfer of technology', *Annals of the American Academy of Political and Social Science,* **458**, 81–96.

Tushman, M.L and P. Anderson (1986), 'Technological discontinuities and organisational environments', *Administrative Science Quaterly*, **31**, 439–465.

PART III

Trust and Organisational Learning

10. Trust and Organisational Learning During Inter-Firm Cooperation

Nathalie Lazaric and Edward Lorenz

This chapter considers why trust may be associated with the process of inter-organisational learning. We shall argue that the build-up of trust is an integral part of the process whereby firms involved in long-term cooperative relations establish mutually acceptable rules or principles to guide their response to the unanticipated. Trust is a kind of cement which allows partners to commit resources to collaborative endeavours in contexts where there remains an irreducible element of uncertainty over the outcome.

Before elaborating on this idea, we develop, in the first two sections, the distinction between individual and collective learning. Having defined collective learning as the process of creating and modifying a set of shared rules and procedures which allow individuals to coordinate their actions in the search for problem solutions, we argue that collective learning invariably has a political as well as a cognitive dimension. This is because the shared rules not only select, distribute and coordinate individual knowledge, but they also select who benefits from the returns to joint productive activity. We then consider whether the success of cooperation in collective learning can be accounted for by the force of reputation effects in self-fulfilling implicit contracts. We argue that in a world characterised by bounded rationality and unanticipated contingencies, the necessary conditions of unambiguous contractual terms and ability to monitor contract compliance are violated. This leads to our development of the notion of trust as the experientially based judgement that others will act in ways designed to further our interests when faced with the unanticipated.

KNOWLEDGE CREATION AND INDIVIDUAL LEARNING

Our discussion of learning starts at the level of the individual and with a consideration of how the individual's bounded rationality affects his representation or understanding of the environment around him. It will be useful to distinguish right from the start the notion of learning we develop here from the sort of informational dynamics developed in the game theoretic literature. It is common in game theoretic models to use the term 'Bayesian learning' for describing a situation of asymmetric information, where an individual is confronted with an increasing amount of information about the state of the world. The individual is assumed to hold prior beliefs concerning the expected utility associated with possible combinations of strategies. Through observing the actions taken by those around him, who are believed to be better informed, he updates his prior beliefs according to the algorithm provided by Bayes's theorem.

The underlying assumptions of this approach seriously limit what the analysis of learning amounts to. In Bayesian modelling, it is taken as given that individuals share a description of the possible states of the world which is complete for all decision-making purposes, and that they are able to attach unambiguous subjective probabilities to each possible state. The strong assumption here is that the individual's substantive rationality is such that he is theoretically capable of knowing the world perfectly, even if at any point in time he lacks the necessary information to determine precisely which among the set of possible states of the world currently obtains. This assumption precludes any analysis of what is one of the central problems in learning, namely how individuals construct and improve their understanding of the world, including the causal relations between actions and outcomes (see Marengo, this volume). In particular, the Bayesian approach precludes that individuals may be confronted with unanticipated events which call for a reinterpretation of their current representation of possible states of the world. Furthermore, the rules that are applied in determining individual choice – Bayes's rule and the maximisation of expected utility – are given *ex ante* as part of the individual's rationality. This precludes any consideration of the possibility that the rules or algorithms used may themselves be the object of learning and refinement.

The alternative approach which we adopt here is inspired by the work of Holland and his associates (1986) on inductive learning. In this vision of learning, individuals construct representations of the world as they discover regularities which are pertinent for decision-making. These models or representations of the environment, including the actions which particular events call for, are necessarily imperfect and open to ongoing interpretation and revision as experience accumulates. Unanticipated outcomes may throw into question the validity of the current representation. There is a trial-and-error aspect to this learning process given the individual's bounded rationality and hence limited experience with the full range of possible events, actions and associated outcomes. The learning process is by no means entirely random, however, since the direction of individual exploration is influenced by the nature of the problem and is limited by what the individual already knows. Because of bounded rationality, there is a tendency to search for new knowledge in the near proximity of current knowledge. As a consequence learning may display a path-dependent quality in which initial conditions influence its longer-term evolution.[1]

One feature that our approach to the problem of learning admits, which the Bayesian approach precludes, is that the world may be characterised by a diversity of individual representations. This poses a problem of inter-individual coordination in organisational or collective contexts. Organisations, on the purely cognitive level, can be understood as mechanisms for reconciling actual or potential conflict, due to the diversity of individual representations, through the creation of a base of common or shared knowledge (Lazaric, 1996; Marengo, 1995 and this volume). This shared knowledge is embedded and stored in the organisation's rules and procedures, both formal and informal, which select, distribute and coordinate individual knowledge and thus define the organisation as a collective actor. These considerations allows us to offer a preliminary definition of organisational learning, as the process of creating and modifying the set of common rules and procedures which allow individual members to coordinate their actions in attempting to resolve the problems they confront. The following section considers in more detail the nature of these rules.

ORGANISATIONAL LEARNING AS RULE INTERPRETATION AND MODIFICATION

Our understanding of organisational learning is influenced by the work of Argyris and Schön (1978). These authors define an organisation in terms of an 'action theory' which can be thought of as the set of rules which determine its representation of the environment and the actions to undertake on the environment in particular circumstances. Following Bateson (1977), Argyris and Schön define different levels of learning. 'Single-loop' learning consists of incremental increases in knowledge and performance that confirm the fundamental structure of the existing theory of action. 'Deutero' learning involves basic changes in the way members go about learning. Unlike single-loop learning, deutero learning involves the invention of new procedures for evaluating and modifying existing practices.

The notions of single-loop and deutero learning can be related to a dual classification of the rules which embody the shared knowledge of organisational members. On the one hand, there are relatively domain-specific rules which serve to model the environment and to determine the actions to be taken on the environment in particular circumstances. In the case of the firm, such rules determine, among other things, the way work is administered to produce a particular product. On the other hand, there are less domain-specific rules or procedures which determine the general ways an organisation goes about modifying its behaviour in an effort to improve its organisational performance.[2] These meta-rules provide guide lines for how the organisation should interpret and respond to unanticipated contingencies. They shape, for example, the way the firm goes about modifying its understanding of the market and modifying its behaviour when faced with unanticipated factor price changes or technological change.

From the perspective of this classification of rules, single-loop learning can be seen to amount to the incremental modification and improvement of the domain-specific rules that determine organisational decision-making at any point in time. Deutero learning, on the other hand, amounts to a change in the meta-rules which define the way the organisation goes about modifying and improving behaviour and performance. As an example, one can think of the process whereby a firm decentralises to shop level the responsibility for determining how production will be adapted to unanticipated changes in final demand. Such a decentralisation requires that a new set of shop-level procedures be established, possibly embedded in semi-autonomous work teams, for interpreting information and for establishing the rules that regulate employee behaviour at that level.

March (1991) has stressed that organisational learning is necessarily an interactive process. Individuals learn or are socialised to the organisation's existing rules or 'code', while at the same time the organisation learns from its members. One conclusion to draw from this is that an organisation can only learn from individuals who are not fully socialised to it, and whose knowledge deviates in some way from that embodied in the common rules. A similar point has been made in a recent article by Favereau (1995), who argues that the *sine qua non* of organisational learning is that the actors examine with a critical eye the rules which define them as a collective organisation. Without some effort to interpret and modify the rules in place, collective learning is an impossibility. The only learning that remains possible is the individual's socialisation to the rules in place.

There are good economic reasons for thinking that fundamental rule changes are relatively infrequent. First of all, the dedicated investments that go into learning the specific rules of the firm are non-salvageable, and consequently the costs of fundamental rule change are the costs of obsolescence. Second, bounded rationality and imperfect foresight mean that the returns to learning new rules are inevitably uncertain. As March (1990) has stressed, the uncertain evaluation of exploring new heuristics increases the attraction of sticking with established procedures and methods, something expressed in a tendency of organisations to develop knowledge in the near neighbourhood of current capabilities. Too much emphasis on the exploitation of existing knowledge to the detriment of the exploration of new knowledge, however, can result in a competency trap, where despite the diminishing returns to current practices the firm finds itself unable to undertake significant innovations.

RULES AND POLITICAL COMPROMISE

Much of the literature on organisational learning pays scant attention to the more political or conflicting dimensions of coordination within the firm. The rules which define an organisation, however, are more than cognitive benchmarks to facilitate the coordination of a diversity of individual representations. Rules and procedures also amount to political compromises which express the diversity of perceived interests and the search for common ground.

Rules reflect political compromises for a number of reasons. First, as Crozier's (1963) analysis of bureaucratic organisations persuasively argues, formal rules, while restricting individual liberty, also ensure subordinates a degree of protection from the arbitrary exercise of power by their immediate supervisors. Consider, for example, the now classic description by Aoki (1988) of the American firm, where minute details of the individual employee's work responsibilities are spelt out in lengthy formal contracts. Historical accounts of the emergence of this form of organisation during the interwar years and during the Second World War make clear that workers and their unions promoted such detailed shop-level regulation as a means of ensuring more impartial decision-making on matters of hiring and firing and the allocation of work (Jacoby, 1988). Correspondingly, any significant change in the rules is considered a matter for negotiations which take into account the diversity of interests and the individuals' concern for protection.

Rules should be thought of as political compromises for the arguably more fundamental reason that they are linked to a particular distribution of organisational quasi-rents. Consider again Aoki's (1988) description of the A-firm. Here the organisation of work is closely tied to a classification grade and wage scale. Promotion up well-defined job ladders in accordance with seniority rules determines salary progression. In the A-firm, what one does determines what one receives. The same general considerations apply for the radically different rules which regulate work organisation in the Japanese firm. Descriptions by Aoki (1988) and Coriat (1991) make clear that one's longer-term career opportunities in the J-firm are closely linked to the structure of internal labour markers which determine internal progression to better paid and more responsible positions. In both of these quite different forms of enterprise, organisation changes in the rules affect career opportunities and one's expected share of future quasi-rents.

More generally, any significant change in the rules which regulate the administration of work and the distribution of responsibilities in the firm will rearrange decision-making authority. As Stinchcombe (1986, p. 221) has pointed out: '... the right to take a decision is a property right because different decisions give profits to different people'.[3]

The general point that emerges from this discussion is that the rules which define the organisation not only select among the diversity of members' knowledge, but they also select who benefits from joint productive activity. The rules of the firm determine not only a particular way of distributing individual competencies, but also a particular way of distributing property rights in the general sense of rights to command over resources and rights to a share of present and future quasi-rents.[4]

This understanding of rules as both cognitive benchmarks for coordination and as political compromises points to the importance of trust for making the rule changes that are the substance of organisational learning. The problem is one of interpreting the intentions of others in future circumstances which cannot be fully anticipated, given our bounded rationality. Will others try to change the rules in ways that bring about a mutually beneficial improvement in organisation performance? Or, on the contrary, will they attempt to bring about changes which serve to redistribute organisational quasi-rents in their favour? Mistrust of the intentions of others may lead the members of an organisation to resist even relatively simple learning exercises promising mutual advantage. In the following section we propose a general definition of trust and consider how it comes about in relation to organisational learning.

TRUST AND ORGANISATIONAL LEARNING

Define the 'placing of trust' (by the trustor) as an 'action' that allows another (the trustee) to undertake actions that would not have been possible otherwise, possibly because resources are put at the trustee's disposal. Assume the context is such that, depending on how the trustee makes use of the new possibilities of action, the trustor will be better off or worse off than had they not been made available. Assume also that the context is one of risk for the trustor because the environment is marked by unanticipated contingencies that create ample scope for the trustee to interpret his obligations in a manner that shifts the distribution of returns in his favour. The inability of the trustor to anticipate all future contingencies precludes recourse to comprehensive contracting and third-party enforcement of contractual obligations.

In such contexts, the decision of an agent to place trust in another depends on her believing that he will act in a way that makes her better off rather than worse off. In general, when we say that an agent 'trusts' another we are referring to this background of 'belief' (Lorenz, 1988, 1993, pp. 308–11).

The above definition concerns one-sided trust between two individuals. The definition can be extended, however, to address situations of mutual trust in collective or organisational contexts. In a collective setting a group of individuals 'mutually place trust' when they decide to make the dedicated investments which go into learning a new set of collective rules and procedures. The mutual decision to learn a new set of common rules opens up new possibilities of collective action, for example the mastering a superior technology or a more efficient way of administering work. The risk each member of the group faces is that these changes, instead of bringing the promised mutual benefits, will provide the occasion for others to increase their share of organisational quasi-rents. Observe that our definition of organisational learning implies that all individuals have some power within the organisation, since the consistency of collective action depends on their mutual willingness to learn a shared set of rules. For this reason, the problem of trust in organisational settings is inevitably a reciprocal one.

To illustrate this point, consider the kinds of learning involved in the decision to decentralise operational decision-making power within the firm to the shop or team level. Such changes have become increasingly popular in the world of business (Levine and Tyson, 1990; Oliver and Wilkinson, 1992; Applebaum and Batt, 1994). The decentralisation of decision-making involves the development of new skills at the team level and new rules and procedures for ensuring the coordination of decision-making among teams and among shops. Such changes are usually initiated by the firm's management with a view to benefiting from the participation of shop-level employees in the process of product or process innovation. A common practice is for management to offer work teams a share in company profits and greater employment security in exchange for their commitment to the firm's goals. The risk the employees face is that the productivity improvements resulting from their participation will allow management to eliminate jobs, thus giving management an incentive to renege on their commitment to employment security. The risk that management faces is that employees will use their enhanced decision-making power to bid up their earnings rather than to seek improvements in enterprise productivity.

A possible response to the problem of trust raised above is that it can be adequately solved through the force of reputation effects in 'self-enforcing implicit' contracts. Intuitively one might suppose that cooperation can be sustained in such settings if the actors have sufficient interest in maintaining their reputation for being honest. If *ex post* breach of a promise by management leads to a loss of reputation, the firm will find it difficult to persuade future potential workers to participate or will have to pay a premium for this participation. Similarly, employees who renege on their commitments will find it difficult to gain employment in firms offering job security in exchange for their participation. The basic conclusion is that in so far as the expected value of future cooperation is greater than the one-time gain from reneging on one's commitment, both labour and management will have an incentive to behave honestly (Kreps, 1990a, pp. 101–6).

A formal difficulty with such reputation arguments is that it can be shown that cooperation will unravel if the end point of the sequence of relations between labour and management is known in advance. If the end point is known, then the employees will know that management will exploit them on the last move since they will have no interest in maintaining their reputation. Knowing this, they will also know that management will have no incentive not to exploit them on the next to last move in order to reap the benefits of future cooperation. By a logic of backward induction it can be concluded that cooperation will never get started.[5]

Kreps and Wilson (1982) and Milgrom and Roberts (1982), in a series of highly mathematical articles, have offered a solution to this apparent paradox based on the idea that if one side is imperfectly informed about the character of the other side, then it may be rational for the informed actor to invest in a reputation for being cooperative even when the end point of the game is known in advance. In the context of our example, the basic idea can be illustrated by assuming that the community of potential employees holds a small positive prior probability (say 0.001) that management at a particular firm is 'irrational' and behaves as a conditional altruist who always starts out by cooperating and is never the first to defect. As long as this prior belief is common knowledge, it can be shown that the rational thing for the employees to do is to give cooperation a try. Even if the management isn't really a conditional altruist, they will have an interest in mimicking this form of irrational behaviour in order to reinforce the employees' 'belief' that they may be irrational (a belief which the employees revise over time according to Bayes's rule). This deception, which can be interpreted as acting to create a 'reputation' for being cooperative, serves to keep cooperation alive to the benefit of all.[6]

While the argument provides a clever solution to the problem of backward induction, we are reluctant to identify the beliefs which figure in reputation arguments with the notion of trust. First of all, as Kreps (1990a, p. 119) has observed, reputation must be for something. The efficacy of reputation effects in enforcing implicit contracts depends on the contractual terms being unambiguous and on the wider community being able to observe if they are complied with. If this were not the case it would be impossible for community members to make judgements as to the honesty of their potential partners. In the case of contractual disputes they would be unable to make clear judgements as to whose claims were bogus. The inability of the wider community to make such judgements would clearly reduce the value to an individual involved in a contractual relation of always acting so as to maintain a good reputation. For example, in the case of implicit agreements over worker participation discussed above, if the terms of the agreement are ambiguous or unobservable, management may be tempted to renege on its commitments, to lay-off its current workforce, and to seek new recruits who are prepared to cooperate on the same terms as the previous employees.

As a rule, the requirement that commitments or contractual terms be unambiguous and observable is not met in the case of organisational learning. This is true because organisational learning involves mutual adaptation to the 'unanticipated' and, as Kreps (1990a, pp. 116–119) readily admits, if a contingency is truly unanticipated it will be impossible to specify 'unambiguously' in advance what we expect from others in adapting to it. This is one reason why we believe trust has an important role to play in sustaining organisational learning. Trust is the belief that our collaborators will act in a way designed to improve our situation rather than worsen it in situations of uncertainty.[7]

Compliance with the terms of organisational learning is difficult for the wider community to monitor for a related reason. Organisational learning is highly specific to particular organisations or groups and involves the creation of a specific language or code. It may also involve the development of informal understandings which members rarely feel the need to make explicit. For this reason it is often difficult for potential collaborators who are outside the group or organisation to make sense of internal conflicts and to draw useful judgements concerning the trustworthiness of a particular member. This helps to explain why, as Rivaud-Danset (this volume) has observed, when beliefs about the trustworthiness of an individual spread, this spreading has more the quality of a rumour than of certain knowledge.[8]

Equilibrium beliefs in reputation models are also different from trusting beliefs because the equilibrium depends on the extreme assumption of perfect foresight. The basic solution concept for dynamic games of this sort is a perfect Bayesian equilibrium which can be defined as a combination of strategies[9] and a series of beliefs such that at each point in time the players' strategies are the best responses to each other.[10] The solution requires that individuals have sufficient rationality to foresee all future contingencies and to anticipate in advance how their potential partners will revise their beliefs in response to observed actions. In the case of our illustrative example, it requires that management knows in advance how the employees will calculate the expected gains from cooperating at each point in time, and it requires that the employees know that management has the rationality to make this calculation. All the 'learning' is packed into pre-game calculation and the future holds no surprises.

In our view, trust is a belief that is closely linked to the notion of bounded rationality in the sense of the limited capacity of individuals to foresee future contingencies: Bounded rationality means that individuals can hope to explore only a small subset of the choices that will be available to them in the future and only a small subset of the consequences of any choice. Correspondingly they are not in a position to pick out their optimal strategies through comparing expected pay-offs over the entire space of strategy combinations. Faced with such limitations to their substantial rationality, individuals are forced to form 'judgements' about the trustworthiness of others based on their 'past' experience of interacting with them. Trust, then, may be defined as the experientially based judgement that those we cooperate with will seek to adapt to the unanticipated in ways that respect a fair division of joint-returns.[11]

This leads us to the following hypothesis concerning how trust comes about. At the risk of circular reasoning, we would argue that unanticipated contingencies are critical conjunctures for the formation of trusting beliefs. Trust is a belief that an agent forms with respect to others on the basis of his past experience with how they respond when confronted with unanticipated contingencies that offer possibilities for behaving opportunistically. Trust is the judgement one forms based on this learning process that in such circumstances others will act in ways intended to improve one's situation rather than worsen it. Not only are such judgements to a significant degree specific to the particular relationship, but they inevitably remain tentative and open to revision for the simple reason that evaluations of how others will react to the unanticipated and come to perceive their interests are inductive assessments rather than deductions based on a complete understanding of the environment.

This implies that trust may come about over time as part of a virtuous circle of organisational learning, mutual gains and revised judgements concerning the trustworthiness of others. This conception of the origins of trust merits two remarks concerning possible obstacles to its creation. First, the build-up of trust inevitably requires an initial risk since, as we have argued above, the sort of public information that forms the basis of reputation provides deficient indicators of what to expect when partners confront the unanticipated. Establishing trust inevitably requires some initial leap of faith. Second, there is no guarantee that trust will come about, since failed learning and mistrust may also prove mutually reinforcing. One cannot preclude a vicious circle of failed cooperation and mistrust.

The above remarks concerning obstacles to trust remain at the level of theory. In practice these obstacles are often overcome through careful initial crafting of the rules which guide collective response to the unanticipated. In the following empirical section, focusing on inter-firm learning, we point to three features of such rules which can tip the balance towards creating trust rather than mistrust. First, firms seek to establish principles which ensure an equitable sharing of the risks associated with unanticipated market change or technological complexity. Second, firms adopt rules which set limits to their mutual dependency and hence limit the possibility that environmental shocks which impact negatively on their performance might seriously jeopardise the performance of their partner. Third, firms contemplating long-term commitments begin by making small dedicated investments and, depending on the outcome, they risk progressively larger investments. This incremental procedure is another facet of the observation that trust can emerge through a process of learning over time.

BUILDING TRUST : CASE STUDY EVIDENCE

This section draws on two empirical studies. One study was undertaken by Lorenz between 1985 and 1990 on long-term subcontracting relations in the machine-building industry in the Lyon conurbation of the Rhone-Alpes region of France. The other study was undertaken by Lazaric during 1990–92 on technology agreements between robot-makers and automobile producers in France, Germany and Italy.[12] The subcontracting study was based on interviews with the management of ten equipment and industrial machinery producers ranging in size from a low of 39 employees in a firm producing industrial filters to a high of 500 employees in a firm specialising in machinery for the production of corrugated cardboard. Most of the firms were operating in internationally competitive markets, with exports often accounting for over half of their annual sales. The auto industry study was based on the analysis of eight technological agreements between robot producers and auto users over a period of ten years. With the exception of the agreement between Renault and Renault Automation and the agreement between Fiat and Comau, the agreements concerned independent companies. The principal aims of the agreements were the redesign of existing robot models to meet the specific configuration of a particular user's plant and the development of specific software adapting the opto-electronic control mechanisms of robots to the needs of a particular user.

The two case studies share the feature that inter-firm cooperation was motivated by the limited capacity of any single producer to explore all his relevant technological options or to provide for all his technological needs. The cases are dissimilar in that the technological alliances in the auto industry concerned firms with roughly comparable technological capacity and rather similar competencies. One might describe these relations as horizontal in nature. In the subcontracting study, on the other hand, the subcontractors had rather different skills than did the client firms and were, as a rule, relatively small and quite limited in their technological capabilities compared with the client firms. Client firms in Lyon sought long-term relations in order to benefit from the specialised metal-processing capabilities of subcontractors who had invested in computer numerical control technology. One might describe the relations as vertical in nature.

Technological alliances and long-term subcontracting relations are based on inter-firm organisational learning in the sense that their success depends on the creation of a set of common rules and procedures which allow the firms to coordinate their decisions and to solve the technological and organisational problems they encounter. Of course, not all organisational members are directly involved in the creation and modification of the rules which coordinate inter-firm relations. Invariably certain individuals or groups serve as boundary-spanners, acting on behalf of their respective organisations and indirectly implicating other services and functional divisions of the firms in relations of cooperation. In the case of long-term subcontracting relations, the direct locus of organisational learning may simply be the purchasing agent of the client firm and the sales agent of the subcontractor, who work together according to some more or less explicit rules and understandings. In technological agreements these boundary-spanning relations are generally more complex, involving teams of engineers, scientists and administrators from each firm.

In both types of inter-firm cooperation, the firms face risks due to the inherently uncertain nature of the learning process, which precludes the use of comprehensive contracting. In the case of the subcontractors, the main risk is that the client firm might prematurely terminate a contract after the subcontractor has made a generalised capacity expansion, solely because of the prospect of selling a large quantity of output to the particular client. The principal risk for the client firm is late delivery or the delivery of poor quality components. In the case of technological alliances, the principal risks are that the costs of the technological development will be unequally shared or that one firm will appropriate an unjustifiably large share of technological rents. There is also the risk of loss of proprietary technological information to competitors who may also enter into an alliance with one's current alliance partner.

Our basic argument is that the firms recognise the irreducible nature of the risks they face, and that they seek to cope with these risks by putting in place a system of more or less non-domain-specific rules which guide their response to the unanticipated and contribute to the build-up of trust. Although the rules have this common objective, their form tends to differ according to the nature of the risk faced. Consider first the rules that regulate the sharing of unanticipated costs in technological alliances. Cost-sharing can be a particularly contentious issue if the installation and maintenance costs of new robot models prove unexpectedly high. The firms seek to deal with this eventuality by specifying that the producer will bear specific installation and maintenance costs amounting to 30 per cent above contract price, and that costs above this amount will be shared equally. This rule serves the function of discouraging the producer from prematurely bringing new robot models on line and shifting the anticipated costs of this decision partially on to the user, while at the same time protecting the producer from bearing the full costs of truly unanticipated technological complications.

Another contentious issue in technological alliances in the auto industry concerns the dissemination of innovative solutions. Interests are often opposed here, with the robot producer favouring a rapid dissemination of the solution, while the auto user favours a slower dissemination allowing him to capture a larger share of the technological rents. In the case of specific software for robots, a typical procedure is to separate the general methodology of the solution from the details of the particular user's application. The former is transferred to other clients of the producer while the latter remains confidential.

One of the principal risks faced by the subcontractors in Lyon was excess capacity. Client firms in Lyon responded by offering their subcontractors partial guarantees as to the amount of work they would make available on a long-term basis. The guarantees took various forms. The client firms engaged in the production of agricultural machinery and haulage equipment provided annual guarantees to their subcontractors on the absolute amount of work they would provide in exchange for guarantees on price. Other client firms, including the producers of textile equipment and corrugated cardboard machinery, argued that the uncertainty they faced in their own markets precluded offering long-term guarantees on the absolute level of work, and they adopted a policy of guaranteeing their partners a fixed percentage of the work available. As a part of this system of guarantees, it was understood that subcontractors would not be instantaneously dropped by the clients if a differential in terms of price or quality of delivery time emerged with respect to competitor subcontractors. Rather, a reasonable amount of time would be allowed for the subcontractor to match the competition.

A second type of rule, which concerned only suppliers in the subcontracting study, responds to the problem of a subcontractor becoming excessively dependent on a particular buyer.[13] In the case of the Lyon machine-building sector, this problem was regulated by the client firms applying what they called the '10 to 15 per cent' rule. This rule sets the value of a client's orders at between 10 per cent and 15 per cent of a subcontractor's total sales. The maximum is set at 15 per cent to avoid the possibility of the client firm's own market difficulties having a crippling effect on the subcontractor. Any figure less than 10 per cent, however, would imply too insignificant a position in the subcontractor's order book to warrant the desired consideration. The 10 to 15 per cent rule ensures the client firm a certain flexibility, while at the same time making an ongoing relationship of interest to the subcontractor. This procedure contrasts with the prior preference of many client firms for highly dependent subcontractors which lacked bargaining power in price negotiations.

A third type of rule, which is common to our two case studies, is that the firms started by making small commitments to each other and then progressively increased their commitments depending on the quality of their exchange. For example, in the case of long-term subcontracting relations in Lyon, a typical procedure was for a client firm to start by demanding details over the phone of the subcontractor's capacity, equipment and particular areas of expertise. This was followed by a personal visit to verify the information and negotiate an initial small order, with the assurance that a longer-term contract would follow, depending on performance. A second visit was made while the components were being produced in order to assess the subcontractor's methods, including quality control. Successful completion of the first order was followed by a somewhat larger second order and, contingent on performance, a third, after which the subcontractor was made a partner. Most of the firms stated that this process required a minimum of a year.

In the case of technological alliances, the learning process is similarly incremental in nature. Firms generally began their cooperation by focusing on some rather minor technological problem that was not central to the user's need. Collaborative activity may have been located in a research laboratory at some distance from the user's main production site. The relation only began to take on the quality of a trusting partnership when the robot producer was involved in the technological developments associated with the launching of a new auto model. It may take as long as three or four years, however, before a robot producer is truly integrated into the design of new robots and software. Success in this initial cooperative endeavour is almost always a signal that the robot producer will be involved in the development of the next auto model.[14]

In short, trust is built-up through an incremental learning process. Small risks are followed by larger ones, contingent on the success of cooperation. The importance of time and experience in deciding whether to cooperate or not points to the limits of the argument discussed above, that a concern for one's reputation will automatically ensure the success of cooperation. The firms in our case studies clearly doubted the efficacy of reputation effects alone to motivate the desired forms of cooperative behaviour on the part of their potential partners. Given the impossibility of specifying in advance exactly what they expected from a partner if a good reputation were to be maintained, the firms felt the need to learn how their collaborators would respond to the unanticipated before undertaking the risk of a long-term commitment. In this manner they increased the probability that trust would come about as part of a virtuous cycle of learning, mutual gains and revised judgements about the trustworthiness of others.

CONCLUSION

Our aim in this chapter has been to link the processes which increase what organisations know how to do, with the processes whereby trust is built-up among them. In most analyses of organisational behaviour, one aspect of the matter is ignored or underplayed, something which reflects the competing visions of the firm that one finds in organisational literature. Either the firm is presented as a purely cognitive entity, driven by market selection forces to accumulate competencies and to improve its performance, or it is conceived of as a political device for solving agency problems through some combination of incentives and authority.

We believe, along with others in the profession, that there is a real need for a more integrated conception of the firm, one that recognises both its cognitive and political dimensions. But most efforts in this direction, however commendable, seem wanting in analytical depth. At the level of first principles they often amount to little more than the assertion that routines or rules serve multiple purposes.

We offer this chapter as a modest contribution to a more integrated vision of the firm by exploring the links between trust and organisational learning understood as the process of creating and modifying the shared rules which embody organisational knowledge and competencies. These shared rules not only draw individuals into particular forms of coordination but also implicate them in particular distributions of organisational quasi-rents. Rule changes, the very substance of organisational learning, are potentially contentious episodes, since there is no guarantee that such periods of relative fluidity in the organisation's structure will not provide an occasion for others to improve their situation at one's expense.

We have suggested that firms may seek to cope with this uncertainty by agreeing from the outset on a set of meta-rules for guiding their response to the unanticipated. This should not be interpreted as an argument that there is some sure formula for building up trust between firms. The meta-rules we have identified are relatively non-domain-specific and there is ample scope for partners to interpret them in conflicting ways. Clearly there are no guarantees in inter-firm cooperation, and one cannot eliminate all risk. Nonetheless, the two case studies presented provide empirical support that carefully crafted rules to regulate response to the unanticipated, can contribute to the build-up of the trust that promotes successful inter-firm cooperation.

NOTES

1 A good example of this context-embedded approach to learning is Herbert Simon's work on bounded rationality, where individuals with limited information and limited calculative ability establish 'satisficing' rules for decision-making appropriate to the particular conditions of the problems they confront.
2 The distinction we are making here has much in common with that made by Holland *et al.* (1986, pp. 41-5) who distinguish between empirical and inferential rules. In their approach, a cognitive system's representation of the environment is formed and altered by the application of condition-action rules which take the general form of: if (condition 1, condition 2, ... condition n) then (action). Empirical rules describe the environment and prescribe the actions to be taken on it. In so far as a rule serves to describe the environment, the 'action' part of the rule calls for a modification of the state of knowledge of the system. In the case of procedural rules, the action part is some modification of the empirical rules.
3 This link between the distribution of power and the distribution of quasi-rents is central in the recent work by Freeman and Rodgers (1993) and Freeman and Lazear (forthcoming) on granting employees co-decision rights through· mandatory works councils. Despite the productivity-enhancing effects of such institutions, the authors argue that they will not be voluntarily adopted by management because they lead to a redistribution of quasi-rents to the favour of labour.
4 See Favereau's (1994) related discussion about the relation between equity and efficiency in rule creation.
5 This, of course, is just a version of the 'chain-store paradox' discussed by Selten (1978).
6 See Kreps (1990b) for a discussion and a formal proof. This line of reasoning should not be confused with an 'invisible hand'-type argument where cooperation emerges as the unintended consequence of the pursuit of individual interest. Even if the subcontractors know for certain that the client firm is only pretending to be a conditional altruist, cooperation can be sustained as long as this is not common knowledge. Suppose the subcontractors know that the client firm is pretending but the client firm is uncertain of this and holds a small probability (0.001) that the subcontractors believe to be truly a conditional altruist. Given this prior, the client will have an interest in acting as if believes the subcontractors are certain is an altruist and the subcontractors will have an interest in reinforcing this prior believe by acting as if they do belief this to be the case. Hypocrisy is the 'cement' which holds together the social order.
7 For a related discussion of the relation between contract, reputation and trust, see Deakin and Wilkinson (1996).
8 This can also help to explain why beliefs about trustworthiness may more easily generalise within an organisation than without. The organisational specific knowledge of the members of an organisation may allow them to draw valid inferences about the trustworthiness of other members where outsiders cannot.
9 A strategy is defined as a rule which tells a player how to act at each instant of the game.
10 In other words, each player's strategy must give him the maximum pay-off given the strategies and beliefs of the other players (see Rasmusen, 1989, p. 110).
11 Our definition of trust in terms of experientially based judgements distinguishes our position

sharply from that of O.E. Williamson (1993, pp. 469, 486) who would appear to believe that individuals can adequately deal with uncertainty through calculating the expected utility associated with different available choices or strategies. Correspondingly, he would relegate the notion of trust to non-calculative interpersonal relations, defined by the criteria that an agent who trusts is predisposed to ascribe good intentions to another even when things go wrong. His discussion, however, entirely avoids the problem of truly unanticipated contingencies.

12 Our aim in this empirical section is not to provide a complete picture of the activities of the case study firms, but rather to focus more narrowly on the procedures adopted by the firms to cope with uncertainty. For more thorough presentations of the case study evidence, see Lazaric (1993) and Lorenz (1988, 1993).

13 The lack of specific rules regulating supplier dependency in the auto industry study presumably reflects the greater financial strength and market opportunities of robot producers compared with the small metal-working firms supplying components to machine-building clients in the Lyon region.

14 The only exception to this rule is the case of Renault and ABB, which have not renewed their alliance despite the apparent success of the technological solutions that emerged from their cooperation. ABB and Renault entered into an alliance with comparatively little prior collaborative experience, and this may account for the organisational problems the firms encountered. It would appear that the firms had difficulty adapting to each other's quite different ways of organising research and development, and were reluctant to make the necessary internal rule changes. The experience of Renault and ABB provides *'prima facie'* evidence in support of our position that the rule changes necessary for successful inter-firm cooperation depend on the incremental build-up of trust. For more details on this interesting case, see Lazaric (1993).

BIBLIOGRAPHY

Aoki, M. (1988), Information, *Incentives and Bargaining in the Japanese Economy*, Cambridge: Cambridge University Press.

Applebaum, E. and R. Batt (1994), *The New American Workplace*, Ithica: IRL Press.

Argyris, C. and D.A. Schön (1978), *Organizational Learning*, Reading MA: Addison-Wesley.

Bateson, G. (1977), *Vers une Ecologie de l'Esprit*, Paris: Seuil.

Coriat, B. (1991), *Penser à l'Envers*, Paris: C. Bourgois.

Crozier, M. (1963), *Le Phénomène Bureaucratique*, Paris: Seuil.

Deakin, S. and S.F. Wilkinson (1996), 'Contracts, cooperation and trust: the rôle of the institutional framework', in D. Campbell and P. Vincent-Jones (eds.*), Contract and Economic Organisation: Socio-Legal Initiatives*, Aldershot: Dartmouth.

Favereau, O. (1994), 'Règles, organisation et apprentissage collectif: un paradigme non standard pour trois théories orthodoxes', in A. Orléan (ed.*), Analyse Economique des Conventions*, Paris: Presses Universitaires de France, 113–138.

Favereau, O. (1995), 'Apprentissage collectif et coordination par les règles: application à la théorie des salaires', in N. Lazaric and J.M. Monnier (eds), *Coordination Economique et Apprentissage des Firmes*, Paris: Economica, 23–38.

Freeman, R. and E. Lazear (forthcoming), 'An economic analysis of works councils', in J. Rodgers and W. Streeck (eds), *Employee Participation in Works Councils*, Chicago: University of Chicago Press.

Freeman, R. and J. Rodgers (1993), 'Who speaks for US? Employee representation in a non-union labor market', in B. Kaufman and M. Kleiner (eds*), Employee Representation Alternatives and Future Directions*, Madison: Wisconsin Industrial

Relations Research Association.
Holland, J., K. Holyoak, R. Nisbett and P. Thagard (eds) (1986), *Induction, Processes of Inference, Learning and Discovery*, Cambridge MA: MIT Press.
Jacoby, S. (1988), *Employing Bureaucracy*, New York: Columbia University Press.
Kreps, D. (1990a), 'Corporate culture and economic theory', in J.E. Alt and K.A. Shepsle (eds), *Perspectives on Positive Political Economy*, Cambridge: Cambridge University Press, 90–138.
Kreps, D. (1990b), *A Course in Microeconomic Theory*, Princeton University Press.
Kreps, D. and R. Wilson (1982), 'Reputation and imperfect information', *Journal of Economic Theory*, **27**, 253–79.
Lazaric, N. (1993), '*Les Interactions entre Utilisateurs et Producteurs d'Equipement. Comparaisons Internationales et Evaluation de l'Apprentissage Interactif*', Etude MRE, October.
Lazaric, N. (1996), 'Organisational learning and combinative capacity during technological agreements: some empirical evidence in the robotic sector', *Revue Internationale de Systémique*, **10** (3), 201–21.
Levine, D. and L. Tyson (1990), 'Participation, productivity and the firm's environment', in A. Blinder (ed.), *Paying for Productivity*, Washington, D.C.: Brookings Institute, 183–243.
Lorenz, E. (1988), 'Neither friends nor strangers: informal networks of subcontracting in French industry', in D. Gambetta (ed.), *Trust: Making and Breaking Cooperative Relations*, New York: Basil Blackwell, 194–210.
Lorenz, E. (1993), 'Flexible production systems and the construction of trust', *Politics* and Society, **21**, (3), September, 307–24.
March, J.G. (1990), 'Exploration and exploitation in organizational learning', *Organization Science*, **2** , 71–87.
Marengo, L. (1995), 'Learning, competences and coordination in organisations', in N. Lazaric and J.M. Monnier (eds), *Coordination Economique et Apprentissage des Firmes*, Paris: Economica, 3–22.
Milgrom, P. and J. Roberts (1982), 'Predation, reputation and entry deterrence', *Journal of Economic Theory*, **27**, 280–312.
Oliver, N. and B. Wilkinson (1992), *The Japanisation of the British Economy*, London: Basil Blackwell.
Ramussen, E. (1989), *Games and Information*, Oxford: Basil Blackwell.
Selten (1978), 'The chainstore paradox', *Theory and Decision*, 9, 127–59.
Simon, H.A. (1978), 'Rationality as process and as product of thought', *American Economic Review*, **68** (2), 1–16.
Stinchcombe, A. (1986), *Stratification and Organisation*, Cambridge: Cambridge University Press.
Williamson, O.E. (1993), 'Calculativeness, trust and economic organization', *Journal of Law and Economics*, **XXXVI**, April, 453–87.

11. Knowledge Distribution and Coordination in Organisations

Luigi Marengo[1]

INTRODUCTION

In this chapter I will briefly discuss, by means of a simple simulation model, a basic dilemma which is faced by every economic organisation, that is, the dilemma between commonality and diversity of knowledge. Organisations whose members share a perfectly homogeneous knowledge basis do not face any 'cognitive' obstacles to effective coordination, but are likely to present little scope for learning and adaptation, as mutual learning is not possible. On the other hand, diversity of knowledge allows such learning but makes coordination more problematic.

This view of economic organisations as 'loci' of the division of knowledge and social learning is not developed in neoclassical theory, which assumes that the knowledge required in production is already available to the society in perfectly coherent pieces, and that the economic problem of organisations is only one of inducing people to use it in an appropriate manner. On the contrary, I assume that the main economic task of organisations is to generate a collective knowledge basis by means of a set of cognitive, incentive, power and control mechanisms. In this chapter I shall concentrate only on the cognitive mechanisms: a major area for future development will be to provide a unifying framework for the analysis of all these mechanisms, and of the organisational forms to which they give rise, in terms of their capabilities of generating and modifying organisational knowledge.[2]

This cognitive approach to organisations has much in common with the views expressed by F.A. Hayek, who in 1945 claimed that: '... the problem of a rational economic order is determined precisely by the fact that knowledge of the circumstances of which we must make use never exists in concentrated or integrated form, but solely as the dispersed bits of incomplete and frequently contradictory knowledge which all the separate individuals possess'.

From this perspective, the fundamental purpose of economic organisations is to coordinate distributed knowledge.[3] Here is a clear similarity with the problem of distributed computation, which is the subject of intensive research in computer sciences, but with some fundamental differences: in social organisations, tacitness is deeper and more widespread, and interpretation and meaning seem to be much more problematic than in communities of computers. A relevant part of the knowledge possessed by the individual members of an organisation is tacit in nature and can neither be effectively transferred nor effectively communicated across agents.

However, tacitness has a much deeper dimension than that usually considered in the literature on technological change, where it is usually seen in connection with skills acquired through repeated practice, when the components required for a good performance are never entirely transparent, even to the executor. The examples which are usually referred to are those of skilful physical activities, such as riding a bicycle or playing soccer: it is evident that nobody will ever learn to ride a bicycle or become a good soccer player just by studying a handbook, however detailed and complete it may be. However, as Polanyi has forcefully emphasised, there is a more fundamental sense in which knowledge has a tacit component well beyond skilful physical activities. This has to do with the tacit component in every act of interpretation and meaning attribution: '... while tacit knowledge can be possessed by itself, implicit knowledge must rely on being tacitly understood and applied. Hence all knowledge is either tacit or rooted in tacit knowledge' (Polanyi, 1969, p. 44).

Categories through which individuals interpret and process signals have a tacit and idiosyncratic dimension which prevents groups from ever exactly sharing meaning. Economic organisations are therefore systems of interpretation and meaning (March, 1988a), where interpretation of past experience: '... is captured by routines in a way that makes the lessons [of history], but not the history, accessible to organisations and organisational members who have not themselves experienced the history' (Levitt and March, 1988).

Organisational routines, practices and procedures (Nelson and Winter, 1982; Cohen *et al.*, 1995) are systems of interpretation and meaning which encode past experience, store interpreted experience in the organisational memory and direct organisational decision-making through a logic of appropriateness.[4]

Firms – and for that matter every economic organisation – are therefore characterised by the collective distributed knowledge they embody (Winter, 1982). Such knowledge encompasses not only (and not even primarily) knowledge of technologies *stricto sensu*, but also knowledge of all the other characteristics of both the external and the internal environments: organisational and bureaucratic practices, relationships with markets and financial institutions, and so forth. This set of collective distributed knowledge can be called 'organisational competencies'. In this chapter, I shall suggest that organisational competencies are the emergent property of the interaction among individual and collective learning processes. I shall also argue that the structure of the organisation[5] plays a fundamental role in shaping and driving this path-dependent collective learning process, by defining the interaction mechanisms which control the exposure to information of individuals and groups, and thus the scope of their learning activity, and whether and how such learning can be embodied into new organisational routines and practices.

THE KNOWLEDGE DISTRIBUTION DILEMMA IN ORGANISATIONAL LEARNING

In every kind of economic organisation, be it an organisation *stricto sensu*, a network of organisations and/or individuals, or a market, there exists a trade-off between commonality and diversity of knowledge. Sharing a common and homogeneous knowledge basis is a necessary condition for agents to communicate and coordinate their actions. However, if all the members of an organisation shared exactly the same body of individual knowledge, no form of collective learning from each other would be possible and the organisation would ultimately lose its capability for learning and adapting to new environmental conditions.

In economic organisations, this trade-off between commonality and diversity of knowledge is also strictly connected to the trade-off between exploitation and exploration (March, 1991): organisations always face the dilemma between concentrating their resources on the exploitation of the knowledge which is already available to them and the exploration of new possibilities. Both exploitation and exploration are necessary for the survival of an organisation. Without exploration of new possibilities, the organisation would find itself trapped into sub-optimal states and would eventually become ill-adapted to changing environmental conditions. However, organisations which devote all of their resources to the exploration of new possibilities will face too high a degree of risk, and even in the case of successful discoveries they will fail to exploit the knowledge they acquire and will systematically perform worse than followers and imitators.

March stresses the importance of the social context in which organisational learning takes place:

> [A] distinctive feature of the social context ... is the mutual learning of an organisation and the individuals in it. Organisations store knowledge in their procedures, norms, rules, and forms. They accumulate such knowledge over time,

> learning from their members. At the same time, individuals in an organisation are socialised to organisational beliefs. (March, 1991, p. 73)

Within organisations, these two processes normally coexist and interact at different levels. One of the strengths of organisations is their capacity to combine flexibly procedures for selection and procedures for innovation. Fast-learning and slow-learning individuals and departments can coexist. Innovation itself can become a largely routine process, though uncertain in its outcome. Learning-by-doing can add exploratory value to normally exploitative activities.

Mutual learning and the distribution of knowledge are fundamental factors which determine an organisation's balance between the processes of exploration and exploitation. A high degree of differentiation of knowledge among the members of an organisation increases the total amount of knowledge possessed by the organisation. But differentiation makes coordination more difficult and ultimately can inhibit the social exploitation of this broad knowledge base. On the other hand, a body of organisational knowledge which is commonly shared by all the members may facilitate coordination while reducing the scope for decentralised experimentation, which could prove a vital source of organisational learning.

Hence there exists a tension between centralisation and decentralisation in the organisational learning process. Firms require both centralisation and decentralisation to operate successfully in changing environments. Decentralisation in the acquisition of knowledge is a source of variety and experimentation, and, hence a fundamental source of learning. But, ultimately, knowledge has to be made available for exploitation by the entire organisation. When agents differ with regard to their representations of the environment and their cognitive capabilities, there must exist an organisational body of knowledge which guarantees the coherence of the various learning processes. In order to cope with changing environments, the process of generating and modifying such a body of knowledge, although fed by the decentralised learning processes, has to undergo some form of centralisation. Thus a tension inevitably arises between the forces which assume the coherence of the organisation and the forces which promote decentralised learning.

The following sections put forward a preliminary investigation of these issues by means of a few simulation experiments which make use of a methodology similar to the so-called 'classifiers systems'. Section 3 outlines a very basic organisational decision-making problem and the simulation methodology which can model substantive learning and the formation of collective knowledge and languages. Section 4 will briefly describe a few simulations of this model in which the adaptive performance of different organisational designs – characterised by different modes of intra-organisational distribution of knowledge – will be tested against simple environments characterised by different degrees of variability and predictability. Section 5 concludes.

A COMPUTATIONAL MODEL OF ORGANISATIONAL LEARNING AND DECISION-MAKING

Let us begin by considering a standard problem of individual decision-making, which will then be extended to a collective one. Let:

$$[S = \{s_1, s_2, \ldots\ldots\ldots, s_n\}]$$

be the set of *n* possible states of nature and:

$$[A = \{a_1, a_2, \ldots\ldots\ldots, a_k\}]$$

the set of *k* possible actions the decision-maker can undertake.

The pay-off to the agent is given by a function:

$$[P = A \times S \rightarrow R]$$

where the agent's pay-off to action a_i when the state of the world s_h occurs will be indicated by P_{ih}.

The action the agent chooses obviously depends on the level of his or her knowledge about the state of the world. The agent's state of knowledge (or 'information-processing capabilities') can be represented by a collection of subsets:

$$[P(s_i) \subseteq S]$$

where $P(s_i)$ is the set of states of the world which the agent considers as possible (or cannot tell apart) when the real state is s_i. The set of subsets $P(s_i)$ represents a sort of collection of categories which the agent employs in order to classify the environment and to find in it those regularities which can usefully be exploited by his or her actions.

Standard Bayesian decision theory and game theory postulate that the collection of such categories forms a partition of the set of states of the world, ruling out in this way the possibility of substantive ignorance or partial knowledge[6] of some parts of the environment. Bayesian modelling precludes ignorance which cannot be reduced by simply acquiring new information, but rather requires modification the very categories on which information collection and interpretation are based (more on this can be found in Marengo, 1995). However, excluding substantive ignorance implies excluding the possibility of substantive learning or the construction of new, more useful mental models for the interpretation of reality. Substantive learning cannot be reduced to simple probability updating (that is, the acquisition of new information within a constant model of the world).

More general representations of the agent's information-processing capabilities than the probabilistic one can be found in the theories based on the concept of 'fuzzy sets' (cf., for instance, Shafer, 1976; Dubois and Prade, 1988). In these theories the information-processing capabilities of decision-makers are more generally represented by subsets of the 'power set' of *S* (partitions being a special case). Substantive ignorance, surprise and inconsistencies can be naturally modelled in this framework. Learning, seen as category modification, can therefore be represented as a search in the space of subsets of the power set of S (that is, the space of models of the world).

The computational model which is described here is just one of the (infinite) possible models which consider learning as a movement in this space. It is based on 'classifiers systems' (cf. especially Holland, 1975, 1986; Holland *et al.*, 1986), but with some substantial differences and simplifications.

The basic component of this learning system is a condition–action rule, where the execution of a certain action is conditional upon the agent's perception that the present state of the world falls into one of the categories he or she has defined in his 'mental model'. The condition part is a 'category', that is, a subset of the states of nature, and is activated when the last detected state of the world falls into such a subset. Practically, the condition is a string of *n* symbols (as many as the states of the world) over the alphabet {0,1} and it is satisfied whenever the last state of the world corresponds to a position where a '1' appears. All in all, the condition:

$$[c_1, c_2, \ldots\ldots\ldots, c_n \quad \text{with} \quad c_i \in \{0,1\}]$$

is satisfied when, if s_k is the last observed state of the world, we have:

$$[c_k = 1]$$

Thus a set of conditions defines a 'subset of the power set of *S*'. It is important to notice that each condition defines one subjective state (or category) of the world, as perceived by the agent, and defines its relationship with the objective ('true') states of the world. This relationship remains anyway unknown to the decision-maker, who only 'knows' the subjective states.

This important point deserves an example: suppose there exist three 'real' states of the world:

$$[S = \{s_1, s_2, s_3\}]$$

and the agent's state of knowledge is represented by the following two conditions:

$$[\upsilon_1\text{: } 110]$$

$$[\upsilon_2\text{: } 101]$$

The agent conceives two 'subjective' states of the world, υ_1 and υ_2. The agent thinks he or she is in the former when the real state of the world is either s_1 or s_2, whereas the agent believes he or she is in the latter when the real state is either s_1 or s_3. This correspondence between subjective and objective states can only be described by an omniscient external observer and is not actually known by the agent, who is unaware of the existence of the elements of the set *S*. All he or she knows are the two υs.

The action part is a string of length *k* (the number of the agent's possible actions) over the same alphabet and with the following straightforward interpretation:

$$[a_1, a_2, \ldots\ldots\ldots, a_k \quad \text{with} \quad a_i \in \{0,1\}]$$

has one, and only one, position which equals '1':

$$[a_h = 1]$$

and $a_i = 0$ at every other position, meaning that the action '*h*' is chosen.

The decision-maker can therefore be represented by a set of such condition-action rules:

$$[R = \{R_1, R_2, \ldots\ldots\ldots, R_q\}]$$

where:

$$[R_j: c_1,c_2,\ldots\ldots\ldots,c_n \Rightarrow a_1,a_2,\ldots\ldots\ldots,a_k \quad \text{with} \quad c_i,a_i \in \{0,1\}]$$

In addition, each rule is assigned a 'strength' and a 'specificity' measure. The 'strength' measures the past usefulness of the rule, that is, the pay-offs cumulated every time the rule has been applied (minus some other quantities which will be specified later); the 'specificity' measures the strictness of the condition: in our case the highest specificity (or lowest generality) value is given to a rule whose condition has only one symbol '1' and therefore is satisfied when, and only when, that particular state of the world occurs, whereas the lowest specificity (or the highest generality) is given to a rule whose condition is entirely formed by '1's and is therefore always satisfied by the occurrence of any state of the world.

At the beginning of each simulation, the decision-maker is supposed to be completely ignorant of the characteristics of the environment he or she is going to face: all the rules initially generated have the highest generality, meaning that all their conditions are formed entirely by 1's. The action parts, however, are instead randomly generated to represent the fact that, because of the condition of absolute ignorance, the decision-maker does not have any reason to prefer one action over another.

The decision-maker is also assumed to have limited computational capabilities, therefore the number of rules stored in the system at each moment is kept constant and relatively 'small' in comparison with the complexity of the problem which is being tackled.

This set of rules is processed according to the following steps throughout the simulation process:

1. *Condition matching*: a message is received from the environment which informs the system about the last state of the world. Such a message is compared with the condition of all the rules, and the rules which are matched (that is, those which apply to such a state of the world) enter the following step.
2. *Competition among matched rules*: all the rules whose condition is satisfied compete in order to determine the one which is allowed to execute its action. To enter this competition, each rule makes a bid based on its strength and on its specificity. In other words, the bid of each matched rule is proportional to its past usefulness (strength) and its relevance to the present situation (specificity):
   $$[Bid(R_j,t) = k_1\,(k_2 + k_3 Specificity(R_j))\,Strength(R_j,t)]$$
   where k_1, k_2 and k_3 are constant coefficients.
   The winning rule is chosen randomly, with probabilities proportional to such bids.
3. *Action and strength updating*: the winning rule executes the action

indicated by its action part, and has its own strength reduced by the amount of the bid and increased by the pay-off that the action receives, given the occurrence of the 'real' state of the world. If the *j*th rule is the winner of the competition, we have:
[$Strength(R_j,t+1) = Strength(R_j,t) + Pay\text{-}off(t) - Bid(R_j,t)$]

4. *Generation of new rules*: the system must be able not only to select the most successful rules, but also to discover new ones. This is ensured by applying 'genetic operators', which, by recombining and mutating elements of the already existing and most successful rules, introduce new ones which could improve the performance of the system. In this way new rules are constantly injected into the system and scope for new opportunities is always made available.

Genetic operators generate new rules which explore other possibilities in the proximity (in a sense which I am going to define precisely) of the presently most successful ones, in order to discover the elements which determine their success and exploit them more thoroughly: the search is not completely random but is influenced by the system's past history. New rules so generated substitute for the weakest ones stored in the system, so that the total number of rules is kept constant.

Two genetic operators have been used for the condition and one for the action part. The latter can be defined 'local search' and is simply a mutation in the vicinity: the action included in the newly generated rule is chosen (randomly) in the close proximity of the one included in the parent rule. The interpretation of this operator is straightforward: decision-makers tend to explore alternatives in the vicinity of the ones already employed.

The two operators used for the condition part deserve more attention because of their role in modelling the evolution of the state of knowledge embedded into the system. They operate in opposite directions:

- *Specification*: a new condition is created which increases the specificity of the parent one: wherever the parent condition presents a '1', this is mutated into a '0' with a given small probability.
- *Generalisation:* the new condition decreases the specificity of the parent one: wherever the latter presents a '0', this is mutated into a '1' with a given small probability.

Specification and generalisation are two possible cognitive strategies which tend to drive the learning system towards, respectively, specific rules which apply to more specific states of the world, and more general rules which instead cover a wider set of states of the world. Different degrees of specification and generalisation can be simulated 'both by means of different' combinations of these two genetic operators and by varying the coefficient k_3 with which specificity enters the bid equation: the higher this coefficient, the more highly specific rules will be likely to prevail over general ones. The simulations discussed in the rest of the chapter will use a 'specificity coefficient' to summarize the overall inclination of the system towards the search for specific rules: such a coefficient will represent both the value k_3 in the bid equation and the probability of the application of the genetic operator 'specification' every time the genetic operators routine is called.

HOMOGENEITY VS DIVERSITY OF KNOWLEDGE IN ORGANISATIONAL LEARNING: SOME SIMULATION RESULTS

This section employs the computational model of learning outlined in the previous section in order to analyse, by running a few simulations, how different modes of knowledge distribution within an organisation can influence the direction and speed of collective learning.

As already mentioned in the introduction, organisations face a trade-off between the need for coordination, which enables the exploitation of the available knowledge, and the need for expanding and modifying the available knowledge, which is an essential condition for search and exploration of new possibilities.

Coordination requires a collective knowledge basis, consciously shared by the agents involved in a given interaction. In a world – such as the one postulated by standard neoclassical economics – where agents share the same model of the world or know each other's model, the only obstacle to effective coordination derives from some form of lack, bias or strategic use of information. On the other hand, in a world where decision-makers do not entirely share a given model and do not know *a priori* each other's models, the first issue becomes that of building a collective knowledge basis which enables them to communicate effectively and eventually achieve coordination. If, for instance, one individual or part of the organisation communicates to another that, to the best of their knowledge, the present state of the world is *X* and such communication is faithful (and known as such to the other), the meaning of such a piece of information can still be misunderstood because the receiver has different information-processing capabilities from the sender. For example, the proposition 'the state of the world is X' can have a different meaning for the receiver(when the considered subset of the states of the world's power set is not the same for the two agents) or even no meaning at all (when *X* does not exist in the receiver's information-processing capabilities).

If allowing for diversity of knowledge creates new problems for organisational design and is a possible source of inefficiency (see also the so-called 'loss of control' literature, for example, Calvo and Wellisz, 1978), it is also a fundamental source of new ideas and new bodies of knowledge which can be acquired and exploited by the entire organisation. The model outlined in the previous section can help cast some light on this dilemma.

Consider the following coordination problem faced by an organisation: the organisation (a firm, for instance) has to respond to an exogenous environment by implementing some collective action. Suppose, for instance, that a firm can produce a certain number of product types, which are demanded by an exogenous market, and that the production process is divided into several parts, each carried out by a different shop. The problem is therefore to detect correctly which product type is being demanded (state of the world) and to coordinate the actions of the different shops so that the correct production process is implemented.

More specifically, suppose that there exist eight possible product types (states of the world), called respectively '1', '2', ...'8'. The firm's production possibilities set is represented by sequences of operations which can be of two types (A and B). Such sequences all have the same length and map into a product type, which is conventionally designated by the number of operations of type A which are utilised in its production. For example, the product of type '8' is produced by all, and only, the production processes which contain eight operations of type A. Each production process is divided into two parts (of the same length) which are carried out separately by each of two shops. The problem of the firm is therefore to forecast the product type which will be demanded by the market and to implement the correct production process by coordinating the operations of the two shops. The pay-off is the following: if the firm produces the correct product type it receives a pay-off of 5 units; if it does not produce the correct output it receives a negative pay-off, given by the distance of the actual product type from the required one (for example, if the market demands type '7' but the firm produces type '5', it will receive the pay-off '–2').

This is a rather naive model, but it already represents quite a complex coordination problem. In game theoretic terms we have two players (the two shops) who have four possible strategies each (that is, implementing a production process with a number of operations of type A which can vary from one to four) and who can play one of eight possible different games, each with a different pay-off matrix.

Suppose that all the decision-making units of which the organisation is made are represented by agents whose knowledge of the state of the world evolves exactly in the way presented in the previous section. Their state of knowledge is represented by a subset of the power set of the set of states of the world. Moreover, they are completely ignorant at the outset (they cannot distinguish among the eight possible states of the world), and they refine their knowledge structure according to their experience and their cognitive capabilities.

The following simulations will test the behaviour of a simple, but quite general, organisational structure (visualised in Figure 11.1), composed of a 'management' and two shops. The management observes the environmental message (the last state of the world), interprets it according to its evolving 'model of the world', and sends a message to the two shops.

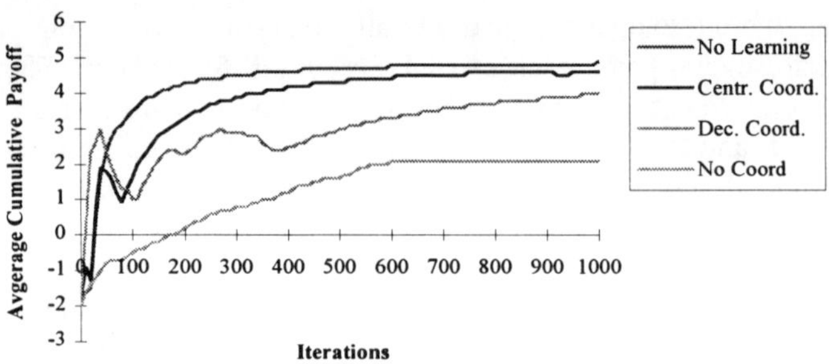

Figure 11.1 Organisational information flows

Each of the two shops can, in general, observe three kinds of signal and develop an interpretive model for each of them. These signals are, respectively, the environmental signal (last observed state of the world), the message sent by the management (and based on its own interpretation of the environment), and the signal sent by the other shop (that is, its last action). The latter two messages are, respectively, centralised and decentralised coordinating devices which allow the shops to coordinate their action, whereas the former message allows the two shops to form their own independent (from the management's) model of the world.

The weights with which these three types of message enter the shops' decision processes define the organisational balance between differentiation and commonality of knowledge. In our model, such weights are represented by the 'specificity coefficients' which express the agent's search for a precise model which interprets the corresponding type of message.

A high specificity coefficient for the shops' condition parts, which classify messages coming from the environment (messages of type 1B in Figure 11.1), implies that shops are seeking to build a detailed individual model of the world. A low coefficient implies that shops do not care to 'understand' the environment. When the coefficient is equal to zero we have an organisation in which shops do not form any autonomous model of the world but rely entirely on the interpretation of the world given by the management (messages of type 1 and 2).

A high specificity coefficient for the condition part which classifies messages coming from the management (messages of type 2 in Figure 11.1) implies that shops attribute great importance to the correct interpretation of the coordinating messages which are sent by management. A low coefficient implies that shops are not seeking careful coordination on the basis of centralised information flows. When the coefficient is equal to zero, we have an organisation without any form of centralised coordination (that is, the management has no role).

Finally, a high specificity coefficient for the condition part which classifies messages coming from the other shop (messages of type 3 in Figure 11.1) implies that shops are attaching high importance to mutual, decentralised coordination. When the coefficient is equal to zero we have an organisation without any form of decentralised coordination (that is, no inter-shop communication).

Thus by designing experiments with different combinations of the three specificity coefficients, it is possible to test the performance of different organisational balances between centralised and decentralised mechanisms of coordination and knowledge distribution.

Simulation 1

Let us first consider a stationary environment with a constant state of the world. Simulations show that:

- Coordination can be achieved with no model-learning at all (that is, specificity coefficients are all equal to zero) due to the action of selection mechanisms. Agents do not 'understand' anything about the environment in which they operate, but randomly select actions until they find the good ones, which they subsequently stick to. This appears, in our simple example, as the fastest way to achieve coordination in stationary environments.
- Coordination can be equally achieved, although after a greater number of iterations, when either the management or the shops are learning about the environment, provided this learning is paralleled by learning about how to interpret coordinating messages, either centralised or decentralised.
- Coordination cannot be properly maintained when agents are individually learning about the environment but not about any of the coordinating devices. In this case, selection mechanisms tend to make coordination emerge temporarily, but this action is counteracted by individual search, which constantly undermines such coordination.

To summarize, agents can coordinate – in stationary environments – by randomly selecting among actions and by sticking to a good one when it has been selected, without building any model of the environment. If instead, they try to learn (that is, to build such a model and to improve it constantly), they also need to build a model for the interpretation of coordinating messages: messages 1 and/or 1B are not sufficient, and messages 2 or 3 are also needed. Figure 11.2 summarizes these results by plotting the average cumulated pay-off of the different organisational set-ups, with different specificity coefficients on different messages.

Figure 11.2 Stationary environment

Simulation 2

A sudden and big environmental shock is introduced in a previously stationary environment. The experiment is designed in the following way: for the first 500 iterations, product type '3' is constantly demanded. At iteration 501, demand suddenly switches to type '7' and subsequently remains there. The problem therefore is radically to reorganise the routines which, after 500 iterations with the same product type, are already deeply embedded in the organisation.

Simulations (see Figure 11.3) show that a search for specific rules is in this case necessary to respond to the environmental change. In particular, a high specificity coefficient for the conditions which classify the environmental message is essential for speeding up the adaptation process. Figure 11.3 plots these results.

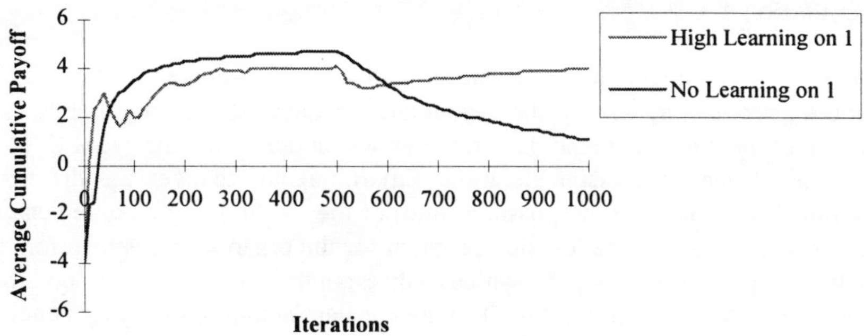

Figure 11.3 Environmental shock

Simulation 3

The previous experiment considered a single environmental shock which required a radical change of organisational routines. Now we shall consider an environment that is changing continuously according to a regular pattern. The experiment presumes that the product type in demand switches back and forth from '3' to '4' at successive iterations.

Simulations (see Figure 11.4) show that only when the specificity coefficients on the shops' conditions that classify environmental messages are high, can the organisation exploit the environmental regularity. Otherwise, the organisation cannot exploit this regularity and settles into constantly producing either of the two types, with an average pay-off of 2.

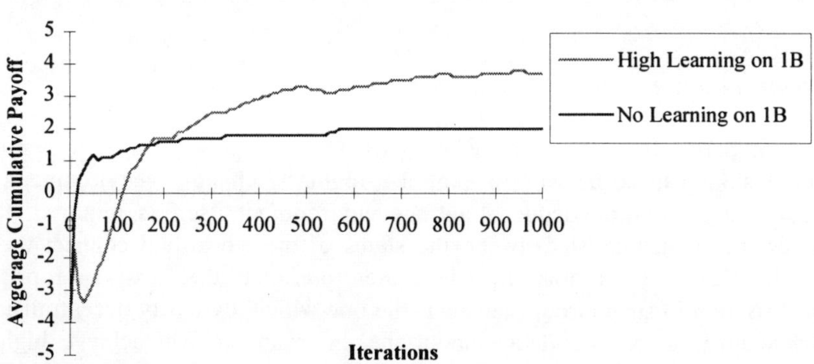

Figure 11.4 Predictably changing environment

Simulation 4

Let us now consider continuous but unpredictable environmental changes, so that a precise forecast of the demanded product type is impossible.The product type which is being demanded varies randomly among types '3', '4' and '5' at each successive iteration. Environmental changes are therefore confined to a subset of the possible states of the world, but are unpredictable inside such a subset; the learning problem for the organisation is therefore to define an 'internal state' which corresponds to the three possible environmental states and to link it to the constant action of always producing type '4'.

Contrary to the previous case, high specificity coefficients on the shops' conditions which classify environmental messages reduce organisational performance, which may be increased by high specificity coefficients on the shops' conditions which classify managerial signals. The results are reported in Figure 11. 5.

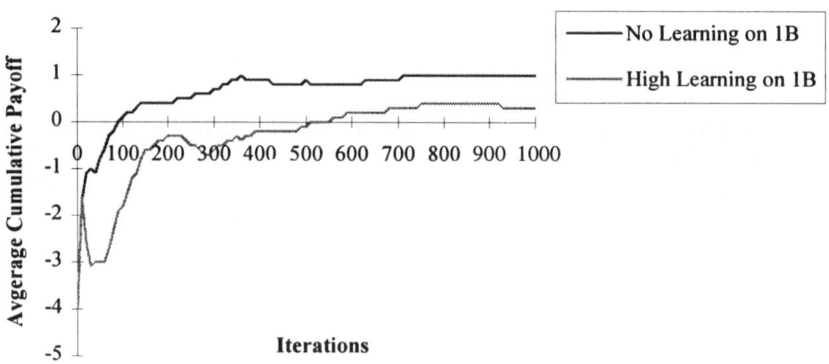

Figure 11.5 Randomly changing environment

By comparing the results of the previous two simulations, some interesting conclusions can be drawn. To exploit a regularly changing environment, a high amount of knowledge about the environment itself is required: the model must distinguish between the states of the world and connect them diachronically. It is not surprising, therefore, that the most appropriate organisation in such circumstances is the one which, by partly decentralising the acquisition of knowledge about the environment, can achieve higher levels of sophistication in its model of the world, provided the coordination mechanisms – which are here centralised – are powerful enough to enable the organisation to solve conflicts of representation

On the other hand, this very decentralisation of the acquisition of knowledge can be a source of loss when it is more profitable for the organisation to stick to a robust and stable set of routines. This situation requires strong coordination in order to make the entire organisation implement coherently such a set of routines. Autonomous and decentralised experimentation can only disrupt such coherence.

CONCLUSIONS AND DIRECTIONS FOR FURTHER RESEARCH

This chapter has presented a preliminary investigation of the trade-off which arises in every collective learning process between centralisation and decentralisation of knowledge bases and learning processes. It has been argued that such a dilemma has deep connections with the trade-off – which is present in every evolving system – between exploitation of the available knowledge and exploration of new possibilities. Organisations require both centralisation and decentralisation to operate successfully in changing environments. Decentralisation in the acquisition of knowledge is a source of variety, experimentation and, ultimately, a fundamental source of learning. However, eventually, knowledge has to be made available for exploitation to the entire organisation. As shown by the simulations of the previous section, when agents differ with regard to their representations of the environment and their cognitive capabilities, there must exist an organisational body of knowledge which guarantees the coherence of the various learning processes. The simulations have also shown that, in order to cope with changing environments, the process of generation and modification of such a body of knowledge, although fed by the decentralised learning processes, requires the existence of some form of centralisation of such learning processes.

Although these results seem general enough, some caveats are due on the nature of the simulation model developed in this chapter. First, the model employed here reduces learning to a mere classification of environmental and organisational signals and to the selection of a proper action for each class.

Representations and organisational codes are here only sets of labels which are attached to subsets of input signals, where syntactical links between such categories are completely lacking. A learning model should also include the dynamics of the latter, but this seems feasible only by imposing some arbitrary grammar and losing the generality and flexibility of the model (cf. Holland, 1986).

A second important limitation concerns the fact that the learning model which has been employed in this chapter is strictly adaptive: learning is modelled as a search for quasi-pay-off-equivalent classes of input signals. Thus the basic driving force for learning is the pay-off received from the environment, and no autonomous learning is possible which is not driven by pay-off differentials. Moreover, no learning takes place outside the set of signals actually experienced by the learning system. In other words, though classifiers systems are much richer than simple stimulus–response models, the artificial learning agent is still endowed only with an extremely primitive set of reasoning skills. Progress in this direction is badly needed (see Riolo (1990) for a preliminary attempt in the direction of embodying richer reasoning skills within a classifiers system framework).

NOTES

1 Dipartimento di Economia; Università di Trento; Via Inama, 1; 38100 TRENTO; ITALY. Tel: +39-461-882201; Fax: +39-461-882222; email: lmarengo@risc1.gelso.unitn.it.
2 A preliminary investigation in this direction can be found in Coriat and Dosi (1994).
3 To be precise, knowledge is said to be distributed when a set of agents 'know' something that no single agent (fully) knows. This can be expressed in the formalism of epistemic logic: if we indicate by $K_i p_i$ the proposition that agent *i* knows proposition *i*, we say that the a set of *n* agents has the distributed knowledge of a proposition *q* (and we indicate it by *Dq*) when: $K_1 p_1 \wedge K_2 p_2 \wedge \ldots\ldots \wedge K_n p_n \Rightarrow Dq$ with $q \neq p_i$ for every *i*.
4 Appropriateness, as logic for action, means that action is not so much driven by rational calculation of the value of the consequences to alternative courses of action, but rather by recognition of familiar patterns in the present state of the world and application of known 'appropriate' procedures (Cyert and March, 1963; Nelson and Winter, 1982; Levitt and March, 1988).
5 In the definition given by Herbert Simon, the structure of an organisation, 'designates for each person in the organisation what decisions that person makes, and the influences to which he is subject in making each of these decisions' (Simon, 1976a, p. 37).
6 Among the phenomena which standard decision theory rules out with the partition postulate are surprise in the sense of Shackle (that is, a state of the world occurs which was not even conceived), systematic mistakes (that is, excluding the state s_i when it occurs, although such a state is considered as possible in other cases), and categories which partially overlap and are not necessarily disjoint.

BIBLIOGRAPHY

Aoki, M. (1986), 'Horizontal vs vertical information structure of the firm', *American Economic Review*, **76**, 971–83.

Arrow, K.J. (1974), *The Limits of Organisation*, New York and London: W.W. Norton and Co.

Arrow, K.J. (1985), 'Informational structure of the firm', *American Economic Review*, **75**, 303–7.

Calvo, G. and S. Wellisz (1978), 'Supervision, loss of control, and the optimal size of the firm', *Journal of Political Economy*, **87**, 943–52.

Clark, H.H. and C.R. Marshall (1981), 'Definite reference and mutual knowledge', in A.K. Joshi, B.L. Webber and I.A. Sag (eds), *Elements of Discourse Understanding*, Cambridge, MA: Cambridge University Press, pp. 10–63.

Coase, R.M. (1937), 'The nature of the firm', *Economica*, **4**, 386–405.

Cohen, M.D. (1984), 'Conflict and complexity: goal diversity and organisational search effectiveness', *American Political Science Review*, **78**, 435–54.
Cohen, M.D. (1987), *Adaptation of Organisational Routines*, Ann Arbor, Institute of Public Policy Studies, University of Michigan, mimeo.
Cohen, M.D. (1991), 'Individual learning and organisational routine: emerging connections', *Organisation Science*, **2**, 135–9.
Cohen, M.D., R. Burkhart, G. Dosi, M. Egidi, L. Marengo, M. Warglien and S.G. Winter (1995), *Routines and Other Recurring Action Patterns of Organisations: Contemporary Research Issues*, Santa Fe, NM: Santa Fe Institute Working Chapter.
Coriat, B. and G. Dosi (1994), *Learning How to Govern and Learning How to Solve Problems*, Laxenburg, Austria, IIASA Working Paper.
Crémer, J. (1990), 'Common knowledge and the co-ordination of economic activities', in M. Aoki, B. Gustafsson and O.E. Williamson (eds), *The Firm as a Nexus of Treaties*, London: Sage Publications.
Cyert, R.M. and J.G. March (1963), *A Behavioral Theory of the Firm*, Englewood Cliff, NJ: Prentice Hall.
Dosi, G. and L. Marengo (1994), 'Toward a theory of organisational competencies', in R.W. England (ed.), *Evolutionary Concepts in Contemporary Economics*, Ann Arbor: University of Michigan Press, pp. 157–78.
Dubois, D. and H. Prade (1988), 'Modelling uncertainty and inductive inference: a survey of recent non-additive probability systems', *Acta Psychologica*, **68**, 53–78.
Geanakoplos, J. (1990), Game Theory without Partitions, and Applications to Speculation and Consensus, Santa Fe Institute, Working Paper 90–018.
Gordon, J. and E.H. Shortliffe (1984), *A Method for Managing Evidential Reasoning in a Hierarchical Hypothesis Space*, Stanford University, Department of Computer Science, Report STAN-CS-84-1023.
Hammond, T.H. (1990), *The Agenda of the Firm: Structure and Incentive in Institutional Design*, presented at the Conference on 'Fundamental Issues in Strategy: A Research Agenda for the 1990s', December, Napa, California.
Hayek, F.A. (1945), 'The use of knowledge in society', *American Economic Review*, **35**, 519–29.
Holland, J.H. (1975), *Adaptation in Natural and Artificial Systems*, Ann Arbor: University of Michigan Press.
Holland, J.H. (1986), 'Escaping brittleness: the possibilities of general purpose learning algorithms applied to parallel rule-based systems', in R.S. Michalski, J.G. Carbonell and T.M. Mitchell (eds), *Machine Learning II*, Los Altos, CA: Morgan Kaufmann, pp. 593–623.
Holland, J.H., K.J. Holyoak, R.E. Nisbett and P.R. Thagard (1986), *Induction: Processes of Inference, Learning and Discovery*, Cambridge, MA: MIT Press.
Levitt, B. and J.G. March (1988), 'Organisational learning', *Annual Review of Sociology*, **14**, 319–40.
Lounamaa, P.H. and J.G. March (1987), 'Adaptive coordination of a learning team', *Management Science*, **33**, 107–23.
March, J.G. (1988a), *Decisions and Organisations*, Oxford: Basil Blackwell.
March, J.G. (1988b), 'Variable risk preferences and adaptive aspirations', *Journal of Economic Behavior and Organisation*, **9**, 5–24.
March, J.G. (1991), 'Exploration and exploitation in organisational learning', *Organisation Science*, **2**, 71–87.
Marengo, L. (1992), 'Coordination and organisational learning in the firm', *Journal of Evolutionary Economics*, **2**, 313–26.

Marengo, L. (1995), 'Structure, competence and learning in an adaptive model of the firm', in G. Dosi and F. Malerba (eds), *Organisation and Strategy in the Evolution of the Enterprise*, London: Macmillan

Nelson, R.R. and S.G. Winter (1982), *An Evolutionary Theory of Economic Change*, Cambridge, MA: Harvard University Press.

Polayni, M. (1962), *Personal Knowledge: Toward a Post-Critical Theory*, New York: Harper Torchbooks.

Riolo, R.L. (1990), *Lookahead Planning and Latent Learning in a Classifier System*, University of Michigan, mimeo.

Shafer, G. (1976), *A Mathematical Theory of Evidence*, Princeton: Princeton University Press.

Simon, H.A. (1976a), *Administrative Behavior*, New York: The Free Press, 3rd edition.

Simon, H.A. (1976b), 'From substantive to procedural rationality', in S.J. Latsis, (ed.), *Method and Appraisal in Economics*, Cambridge, MA: Cambridge University Press, pp. 129–48.

Simon, H.A. (1979), 'Rational decision making in business organisations', *American Economic Review*, **69**, 493–513.

Teece, D.J., R. Rumelt, G. Dosi and S.G. Winter (1994), 'Understanding corporate coherence: theory and evidence', *Journal of Economic Behavior and Organisation*, **23**, 1–30.

Vardi, M.Y. (ed.) (1988), *Theoretical Aspects of Reasoning about Knowledge*, Los Altos, CA: Morgan Kaufmann.

Williamson, O.E. (1985), *The Economic Institutions of Capitalism: Firms, Markets, Relational Contracting*, London: Macmillan.

Winter, S.G. (1982), 'An essay on the theory of production', in H. Hymans (ed.), *Economics and the World around It*, Ann Arbor: University of Michigan Press, pp. 55–93.

Winter, S.G. (1987), 'Knowledge and competence as strategic assets', in D.J. Teece (ed.), *The Competitive Challenge*, Cambridge, MA: Ballinger, pp. 159–84.

12. Trust and Organisational Learning

Bertrand Moingeon[1] and Amy Edmondson[2]

INTRODUCTION

As organisations become flatter, more geographically dispersed and more prone to reorganisation, traditional notions of 'control' are being updated to reflect an increased need to 'trust' individuals and groups to carry out critical organisational tasks without close or frequent supervision (Handy, 1995). Thus, as others in this volume have noted, the ways in which organisations are currently changing highlight the role of trust. Along the same lines, trust plays a critical role in organisational situations in which collective learning is required. As Sako (this volume) points out, in the absence of uncertainty or imperfect information about the future, there is no need for trust, and 'organisational learning' is required in situations in which much is unknown and uncertain (Senge, 1990). This chapter explores the ways in which trust functions in organisational learning, and presents a framework to facilitate analysis of relationships between these two management constructs. The intervention work of Chris Argyris is used as an exemplar of implementing organisational learning, to illustrate relationships within this framework. The chapter draws from the literature and from data collected in interviews conducted by the authors with Argyris, and with the consultants and directors of a firm in which Argyris intervened to promote organisational learning.

Trust is a belief (Lazaric and Lorenz, this volume) related to likely outcomes, a belief that reflects an actor's cognitive representations of situational contingencies. Organisational learning shall be defined below as an iterative process of reflection and action that occurs infrequently without intervention. Does trust promote learning in organisations, or does learning promote trust? This chapter explores current notions of organisational learning and trust, and proposes an affirmative response to both of these questions. Not only does trust play a role in facilitating learning behaviours, trust can be an outcome of such behaviours. Thus the purpose of this chapter is to suggest some of the ways in which 'trust, cognitions' and 'learning behaviours' may be related in mutually reinforcing ways. In the next section, trust in an organisational context is briefly discussed, and then concepts of organisational learning are reviewed. The second half of the chapter will examine relationships between these two constructs and will discuss the aspects of trust introduced in the next section more fully.

Definition and Preliminary Discussion of Trust

Forty years ago, social psychologists identified trust and trustworthiness as necessary conditions for persuading others to change their views (Hovland, Janis and Kelley, 1953). More recently, trust has been implicated as vital to the maintenance of productive supplier relationships (Lorenz, 1988) and as essential in implementing self-managed work teams (Lawler, 1992). We define trust as the belief that relinquishing some degree of control over a situation to one or more others will not lead to personal loss or harm – a definition similar to those presented in Lorenz (1993) and in Mayer, Davis and Schoorman (1995).[3] We adhere to the helpful distinction made by Lazaric and Lorenz (this volume) between the 'cognitive state of trust' and the 'action of placing trust'. The latter involves risk, the former merely the willingness to risk. Thus trust – as a cognitive state – is the willingness to place resources at others' disposal; this willingness is based on an expectation that they will not be used in a way that will make the trustor worse off. Trust can function as a substitute for other, more explicit, controls (Larson, 1992), and thus is a source of efficiency (Arrow, 1974). Sako (this volume) includes reciprocity in her definition of trust as the, 'mutual expectation that partners will not exploit vulnerabilities'. Although our definition differs slightly from hers, we agree with the implicit proposition that trust is frequently mutual, existing simultaneously within the minds of two or more interdependent actors. This mutuality will be revisited at the end of this chapter.

The above definition leaves flexibility about the nature of the situation in which trust applies. Managers who say they trust a subordinate, or team members who trust each other, may mean quite different things, such as belief that another is capable of producing a desired outcome or, in contrast, belief that another can be relied upon to behave in ways that support the interests of the trustor. The former involves 'trust in competence' and the latter, 'trust in intentions'. Although these two types of trust may often co-occur, they are conceptually distinct. Trust in competence refers to the belief that another has the ability to perform a task or fulfil a responsibility, while trust in intentions refers to the belief that another is sincere in his or her espoused commitment to carry out a task or responsibility. This distinction is similar to that made by Sako (this volume) between 'competence trust', 'contractual trust' and 'goodwill trust'; 'trust in competence' here is essentially the same as her competence trust, while 'trust in intentions' blends aspects of Sako's contractual and goodwill types, specifically the expectation that promises will be carried out, together with a general sense of the trustee's integrity and shared commitment to mutual goals. Finally, we have found it helpful to avoid treating trust as dichotomous and to consider instead levels of trust. The rationale for, and implications of, this distinction are explored in the second part of this chapter, which discusses the role of these two kinds of trust in organisational learning. First, we review existing perspectives on 'organisational learning' and the 'learning organisation'.

ORGANISATIONAL LEARNING AND THE LEARNING ORGANISATION

The first obstacle to understanding relationships between organisational learning and trust is the array of conflicting definitions and differing perspectives related to the notion of organisational learning. Existing definitions of organisational learning include such different constructs as 'diffusion of information' in an organisation (Huber, 1991) and the cognitive phenomenon of 'interpretive processes' (Daft and Weick, 1984). In some conceptions, organisational learning is prescriptive (for example, Hayes, Wheelwright and Clark, 1988; Senge, 1990; Argyris, 1993), and elsewhere is the basis of descriptive theory that documents factors influencing or impeding organisational adaptation (for example, Levitt and March, 1988; Huber, 1991). This section briefly reviews the literature on organisational learning using a two-by-two framework to organise its diverse contributions. Integral to this framework is an explicit distinction between 'organisational learning' and the 'learning organisation' (Edmondson and Moingeon, 1995): the term 'organisational learning' encompasses a broad range of phenomena, including, but not limited to, desired processes of individual development and organisational adaptation, while those who focus on 'the learning organisation' comprise an explicitly normative subset of the literature. Finally, we present a normative, process-oriented definition of organisational learning. This review does not attempt to be exhaustive, but rather to identify and illustrate distinctions in the literature, to set the stage for a subsequent discussion of the role of trust.

Dimensions of Organisational Learning

The organisational learning literature encompasses multiple constructs and a notable lack of cross-fertilization among differing perspectives (cf. Shrivastava, 1983; Fiol and Lyles, 1985; Huber, 1991). The primary unit of analysis – or the entity seen as 'learning' – provides one distinction in the organisational learning literature; the research objective provides another (Edmondson and Moingeon, 1996). This distinction does not describe the object of research, but rather points to the entity viewed as doing the learning. In short, some researchers focus on how organisations learn – that is, how such social systems may adapt, or change, as a function of factors such as individual cognitive properties or organisation policies. Other researchers primarily examine how individuals learn – that is, how individuals embedded in organisations develop, adapt or update cognitive models.

At the same time, in both groups, some authors primarily attempt to describe relationships among variables. The intended research product is a description of a phenomenon or a model of causality. Others undertake research primarily aimed at creating or assessing organisational change strategies, in efforts to create learning organisations. The research objective is to identify managerial actions that improve organisational effectiveness. A two-by-two matrix depicts the resulting categories of learning phenomena (Figure 12.1). These are: (1) 'residues' (organisations as residues of past learning); (2) 'communities' (organisations as collections of individuals who can learn and develop); (3) 'participation' (organisations as increasing their capacity for change through widespread intelligent activity by their employees), and (4) 'accountability' (organisational effectiveness as dependent upon individuals gaining awareness of personal causal responsibility and developing interpersonal skills).

Residues: Descriptive Research at the Organisational Level of Analysis

Organisational learning in this category encompasses phenomena such as how routines shape organisational behaviour, how knowledge is acquired and the role of interpretive processes. For some scholars, organisational learning describes the role and stability of routines in organisations (for example, Levitt and March, 1988). Learning is thus a mechanism that accounts for the status quo, in that processes such as imitation and trial-and-error explain existing patterns of organisational behaviour. In contrast to the normative approaches discussed below, learning is seen as a faulty mechanism, because the lessons of the 'past' (embodied in current routines) dominate organisational life. Organisational routines are over-learned, as organisational actors are more habit-driven and imitative than rational. For example, Levitt and March (1988) note that organisations as entities stop actively seeking alternatives once they have built up experience in known routines. Such built-in barriers to adaptation as 'superstitious learning' (viewing desired outcomes as a result of well-reasoned organisational actions) and 'competency traps' (beliefs that current practices are better than potential alternatives, leading to the continuity of inferior work processes) explicitly function at the organisational level of analysis. Organisational learning is thus the accumulated residue of past inferences.

RESEARCH OBJECTIVE	PRIMARY UNIT OF ANALYSIS: *Organisation*	PRIMARY UNIT OF ANALYSIS: *Individual*
Descriptive research	RESIDUES organisations as embodiments of past learning	COMMUNITIES individual learning and development in organisations
Intervention research	PARTICIPATION organisations increasing the capacity for change through active, intelligent participation	ACCOUNTABILITY individuals gaining awareness of personal causal responsibility and interpersonal skill

Figure 12.1 A typology of organisational learning research

Other scholars define organisational learning as a process by which an organisation expands its repertoire of actions, focusing on how knowledge is acquired and distributed. For example, Huber defines 'learning' as a process that enables an entity to increase its range of potential behaviour through its processing of information. 'Organisational learning' is defined as occurring when any of an organisation's units acquires knowledge that the unit recognizes as potentially useful to the organisation (Huber, 1991). Finally, others in this category examine how interpretive processes can inhibit perception of the need to change (Weick, 1979). Processes of social construction are at the root of such organisational dilemmas; shared perceptions of the appropriateness of current practices preclude effective adaptation (Daft and Weick, 1984).

Communities: Descriptive Research at the Individual Level of Analysis

This category includes descriptions of individual learning in organisations, models that specify conditions enabling employee learning, and models that describe beneficial outcomes of individuals engaging in learning. Brown and Duguid (1991, p. 48) describe learning as becoming 'an insider' by acquiring tacit or 'noncanonical' knowledge. Although Brown and Duguid studied how work groups became communities of learning, it is the individuals who learn, become insiders and contribute to differences among groups.

Others in this category show how organisational environments affect the learning and development of individuals. For example, flatter organisational structures create a tension that elicits personal development by employees, and this individual learning contributes to a process of continual transformation of the organisation (Pedler, Boydell and Burgoyne, 1988; Pedler, Burgoyne and Boydell, 1990). New interpersonal challenges encountered in less hierarchical, team-based organisations encourage individuals to engage in developing communication and other interpersonal skills, which creates a kind of institutionalized learning or 'organisational capability' (Pettigrew and Whipp, 1991). According to these perspectives, when its members learn, an organisation's capability is enhanced; however, they are distinguished from intervention research in that they do not focus on strategies for implementing change. In contrast, researchers in the following two sections have embraced this objective.

Participation: Intervention Research at the Organisation Level of Analysis

Researchers in this category explore questions of what policies can be employed to create flexible and responsive (learning) organisations and to overcome resistance to change. They propose human resources or manufacturing policies to improve organisational responsiveness. For example, Hayes, Wheelwright and Clark (1988) advocate implementing just-in-time production systems as a way of creating learning organisations. Making critical information accessible and transparent by increasing the interdependencies among workers is one element of increasing both the importance and chances of relevant problem-solving by individuals, who thereby contribute to creating flexible, efficient organisations. Fostering the participation of employees and utilising their analytic capacity to benefit the organisation is described as essential for organisational adaptiveness. In contrast to those in the fourth category, here the organisation learns when its members participate fully by solving problems and communicating with each other about substantive issues.

Accountability: Intervention Research at the Individual Level of Analysis

In this category, when individuals learn – as a result of interventions designed to foster self-reflection – their organisations become more effective. Thus individual cognition is seen as critical to organisation effectiveness. Organisational learning is a phenomenon in which individuals in organisations develop and refine their cognitive maps – their 'theories-in-use' (Argyris and Schön, 1974) or 'mental models' (Senge, 1990) – and thereby become more effective decision-makers. The goal of these researchers is to develop intervention strategies to facilitate this process. For example, John Seely Brown at Xerox describes the use of laboratories in which employees experiment with computerized simulations designed to help them develop new mental models of how the business operates (Brown, 1991). Similarly, Senge (1990) argues that teams of managers can learn to understand their organisations as dynamic systems in 'learning laboratories' guided by a facilitator. Moreover, 'action science' (Argyris, Putnam and Smith, 1985) presents organisational learning as a vital but rarely-occurring activity, constrained by a core dilemma. Individuals must learn for their organisations to be effective, yet organisational environments typically preclude learning. According to Argyris (1990), interpersonal competence is generally so low that communication of information in the presence of any 'face threat' (Goffman, 1959) involves distortion, and yet many important organisational interactions are characterized by such subtle threats to 'face'. In these situations, individuals' implicit theories, or 'theories-in-use', lead them to behave in ways that produce outcomes exactly contrary to what they hope to produce in interpersonal interactions (Argyris, 1982). Moreover, these theories-in-use (called by Argyris and Schön (1978) 'Model I') systematically preclude learning about ways to escape their counterproductive effects. Analogous to Levitt and March's competency traps, these factors constitute built-in impediments to learning at the micro-level of individual reasoning processes.

Summary and Discussion

Some authors describe how organisations learn whatever it is they learn, while others view learning as something that needs to be created. Those who describe the 'learning organisation' tend to advocate strategies to improve organisations; the term represents an ideal type, a kind of organisation to be pursued. Within this normative subset, two levels of analysis represent two theoretical views. Those in the 'participation' category view organisational effectiveness as an outgrowth of policies that engage individuals in contributing to the organisation, while those in the 'accountability' category view effectiveness as dependent upon properties of individual cognition.

Accountability strategies for creating learning organisations
Researchers in the accountability category identify 'self-sealing' dynamics that stem from the way people in organisations think about their environments. Organisational learning, therefore, cannot occur without intervention to help people see how their own thinking may be contributing to current problems. A common theme shared by the intervention strategies is helping people see how their own actions can lead to the undesired results that they typically attribute to exogenous factors. For example, in Senge's learning laboratories, managers learn how their own decisions can create unintended negative consequences for their organisation. Similarly, Argyris argues that people are unaware of the way their own theories-in-use cause problems they attribute to others. With the help of a skilled interventionist, people can learn new theories-in-use ('Model II'). This is a process of learning how one's own ways of thinking can be counterproductive, while learning new Model II interpersonal skills of balancing 'advocacy' with 'inquiry', testing inferences and illustrating conclusions with 'directly observable data' (Argyris, 1993). This process is 'double-loop learning', because it involves inquiry into rules and values that shape organisation members' actions, not just correcting the actions themselves (see also Lazaric and Lorenz, this volume). Engaging in such a process requires considerable commitment and practice, but can result in members of an organisation significantly improving their effectiveness and ability to learn in difficult interpersonal exchanges. Argyris (1993) provides an in-depth description of a five-year change project in a consulting firm, which led to significant behavioural changes. Recently, we conducted interviews with directors and senior consultants at this organisation, to learn more about the role of trust in the learning process. As described in the next section, trust can play a critical role in facilitating such a process.

Organisational learning defined and discussed.
The centrality of cognition in these approaches suggests a definition of organisational learning as a process in which an organisation's members actively use valid data to guide behaviour in such a way as to promote the ongoing adaptation and innovation of the organisation. Organisational learning is thus defined as a process that requires individual and collective reflection and supports organisational adaptiveness. It is an iterative process of acting, assessing and acting again – an ongoing cycle of reflection and action that cannot be taken for granted in organisations, noted for their

adherence to routine. However, as thus defined, organisational learning is a process that can be initiated, encouraged and practised. The premise that engaging individuals in reflecting upon, and developing, their own thinking processes is an essential component of creating learning organisations underlies this definition. Finally, engaging an organisation's members in such a learning process typically requires intervention from a consultant or researcher.

RELATIONSHIPS BETWEEN ORGANISATIONAL LEARNING AND TRUST

We have identified three distinct roles played by trust in efforts to implement organisational learning: 'trust as a prerequisite' to intervention, 'trust as an outcome' and – at first glance paradoxically – 'trust as an obstacle'. Each of these will be explained below in the context of organisational learning for both competence and intentions types of trust, thereby introducing six ways in which trust plays a role in organisational learning (Figure 12.2). We argue that levels of trust (for both intentions and competence) are both important influences on, and outcomes of, organisational learning. In preparation for undergoing an organisational learning intervention, levels of trust can be assessed both among organisation members and between the organisation and a facilitator or consultant (see Figure 12.3). Argyris's (1993) intervention in a consulting firm will be used below as an example to illustrate these relationships.

Levels of Trust: Competence and Intentions

Trust is required in situations in which one has to make a decision or act in the face of some degree of uncertainty. For some authors, this uncertainty is related to the unpredictability of others' behaviour, such that, 'trust presupposes decision-making in a situation of risk, where the risk is attributable to the strategic behaviour of others or to the possibility that they will behave opportunistically' (Lorenz, 1988, p. 197). The cognitive state of trust decreases the level of perceived uncertainty for the trustor, 'while environment uncertainty is exogenous, the behavioural element of uncertainty is reduced in trust relations' (Sako, this volume). Thus we argue that a given action will not be implemented until the uncertainty reaches a level considered low enough by the actor to justify the risk. This decrease in perceived uncertainty is related to an increase in trust; thus it is sensible to discuss the 'level of trust' required to act.

Awareness of trust as a continuum precludes an 'all or nothing' (trust/no trust) analytical approach, and allows us to make distinctions that are relevant to taking action. We illustrate this point with a simple example. Imagine that John and Bill work in the same office, and Bill has a laptop computer that John wants to borrow. Bill refuses John's request, saying that he needs to use the computer.

Within firm or between firm and others	Trust as prerequisite	Trust as outcome	Trust as obstacle
Trust in competence			
Trust in intentions			

Figure 12.2 A framework of relationships between trust and organizational learning.

A third colleague, Mary, observing this exchange, knows that Bill will be in meetings all day and will not need his computer. After John leaves, Mary asks Bill about his real reasons for not lending his computer to John. Bill responds, 'I don't trust John'. Such usage, typical of everyday conversation, suggests that trust is dichotomous. However, to continue with this simple example, we can illustrate the importance of levels of trust. If John had asked Bill for a pencil instead, Bill would have readily agreed to the loan. There is an implicit two-step cognitive process in these decisions. First, in each case Bill must assess the minimum level of trust required to lend his computer (or pencil) – a 'trust threshold' – and then compare the threshold with his level of trust in John. For the computer, the trust threshold is higher than his trust in John, precluding agreement; for the pencil, the threshold is sufficiently low to allow the action of placing trust.

Not only is it important to recognise levels of trust, but it is also important to distinguish between trust in intentions and trust in competence. In this example, Bill's unwillingness to lend his computer may be due to a lack of trust in John's ability to use a computer without damaging it, involving an assessment of John's expertise. On the other hand, his reluctance may be due to a lack of certainty about John's character and intentions – about his commitment to care for the computer as carefully as if it were his own, or to return it promptly or, for that matter, to return it at all! Unlike trust in intentions, trust in competence applies to oneself ('self-trust') as well as others (such as John).

Example 1: Engaging a consultant to facilitate an organisational learning process

Firm members' trust in consultant	Trust as prerequisite	Trust as outcome	Trust as obstacle
Trust in competence	If members believe consultant is capable of helping firm, they will agree to participate	After exposure to consultant's skills members' trust in his/her competence increases	Excessive dependence on consultant can inhibit taking responsibility for own learning
Trust in intentions	If members believe consultant will not betray the firm or its members they will participate	As a result of working together, members become increasingly comfortable with goodwill and integrity of consultant	Blind trust in his/her intentions leads members not to challenge or confront consultant thereby reducing opportunities to further their own learning

Figure 12.3 Applications of the trust framework

Example 2: Effects of within-firm relationships on organisational learning

Firm members' trust in each other	Trust as prerequisite	Trust as outcome	Trust as obstacle
Trust in competence	If members believe that their colleagues have the ability to learn new skills they agree to participate	Practising learning new skills increases the confidence firm members have in each other's competence	Excessive confidence in each others' competence creates complacency and thus lack of motivation to change
Trust in intentions	If members are willing to be vulnerable with colleagues – as necessary for learning – they agree to participate	As a result of learning and exploring new territory members are increasingly comfortable with the goodwill and integrity of colleagues	Blind trust in intentions can preclude reflecting critically about each others' statements

Figure 12.3 Applications of the trust framework

Functions of Trust

In terms of organisational learning, both types of trust can function in three ways. First, trust is a 'prerequisite' to embarking in a project of enhancing organisational learning (Good, 1988; Lorenz, 1988). A minimal level of trust in competence and in intentions is required for an organisation's members to enter into this learning process. Second, gaining a certain level of trust can be an 'outcome' of an intervention designed to create a learning organisation. Third, excessive trust can create an 'obstacle' to building a learning organisation, through complacency or dependence which inhibit taking responsibility for change and learning.

Trust as prerequisite.

Lorenz notes that: 'The "action" of placing trust (by the trustor) allows another (the trustee) to undertake actions that would not have been possible otherwise, possibly because resources are put at the trustee's disposal' (1993, pp. 307–8).

This is especially true in efforts to create a learning organisation. For executives to ask an external consultant to intervene in their organisation, they must have trust in both the ability and intentions of the consultant. An organisation's members will engage in such a learning process only if their level of trust in the competencies and the intentions of the consultant reaches the threshold required for such exposure. The first task of the consultant is to obtain this level of trust (Schein, 1988; Schwartz, 1994; Moingeon and Ramanantsoa, 1995).

Trust in competence is highly influenced by organisation members' view of the consultant's capacity to understand their organisation, and to take into account its unique attributes and concerns. For example, in an interview with the authors, one of the directors of the firm in which Argyris (1993) intervened explained that he decided to commit himself and to allocate part of his most scarce resource (his time) to the organisational learning process after seeing Argyris present a diagnostic map that illustrated the interpersonal and organisational dynamics of the firm. The competence embedded in the accuracy and insight of this 'action map' (which is described in Argyris, 1993, pp. 98–9) convinced the director to participate fully. Trust in competence also matters for relationships among the organisation's members (Argyris, 1985, p. xii). If they mutually believe that others are not competent enough to change their behaviours, or if the consultant receives such an impression of the organisation's members, the intervention will probably not succeed, or will not be undertaken.

Reaching a threshold level of trust in competence is necessary but not sufficient. A threshold level of trust in intentions is also needed for organisation members to risk the vulnerability that participation in an organisational learning intervention implies. For example, members' willingness to surface and discuss basic assumptions they hold about their organisation requires a high level of trust in the consultant's intentions (Schein, 1992). Also, for an organisation's members to have sufficient trust, a consultant must somehow demonstrate that she does not work solely for the CEO's interests but rather to serve the whole firm's interests. It follows, then, that members must trust the CEO's intentions; if they do not, the change process could be perceived as an attempt to manipulate them. Similarly, for trust in intentions to be present, members must believe that confidential company issues will not be revealed to others, and so the consultant must stress that confidentiality is very important both externally and within the firm. However, this is not without a potential risk. On the one hand, ensuring confidentiality increases the level of trust between the organisation's members and the consultant; on the other hand, it may contribute to maintaining a low level of trust within the organisation (among the organisation's members) if it discourages openness (Schwartz, 1994, p. 271). Finally, to be effective, the consultant must trust the organisation members' commitment to engage in the learning process.

Argyris (1995, in an interview with the authors) uses three 'structural devices' to help establish trust in both competence and intentions before engaging in an organisational learning intervention. First, when the CEO invites him into the organisation, he asks for a meeting with other senior executives to give them an opportunity to critique the proposed process, and then to choose whether or not to participate; 'that way they can't say this was the CEO's idea', but instead must take responsibility for their participation. Second, he tells the group explicitly that, 'if they ever hear that I am bad mouthing them, or feel I am not behaving in a way that is consistent, to bring it out in the open, publicly'. Third, is a '50-second contract – in 50 seconds they can kill it, or I can kill it ... These are all structural devices to build trust'.

Argyris's approach involves building both competence and intentions types of trust. For the latter, he explains that he is careful not to appear to 'take sides' with the CEO in meetings, and to illustrate by his behaviour that he is working to help everyone. He tells participants repeatedly that he wants to be confronted by them if they have any concerns or doubts. His core strategy for building trust is to try to demonstrate competence by acting in ways that are consistent with Model II, even under some degree of stress (Argyris, 1995). That is, the primary mechanism for building trust is, 'through my actual behaviour in the seminars, especially when I say things that would be somewhat embarrassing or threatening to them, such as about the way they manipulate each other, and they can see that I am consistent with Model II in these situations'. The key is to maintain a Model II learning orientation in difficult situations: 'When I was challenging them and they were challenging me, how I challenged them and how I dealt with their challenge was critical – that is, did I maintain a learning orientation, or did I become as Model I as they did?'.

In sum, a low level of trust within an organisation is an obstacle to learning. Lack of trust can create a self-sealing situation, because the existence of this lack of trust as an obstacle cannot be discussed undiscussable (at least without the help of an interventionist) (Argyris, 1993). Making the lack of trust discussable requires a high level of trust – which, of course, presents a dilemma. A skilled interventionist can make this issue discussable, allowing this obstacle to implementing an organisational learning process to be surmounted.

Trust as outcome

Increasing trust is one of the outcomes of interventions designed to create learning organisations (Argyris, 1990, 1993). When people embedded in a social system together examine values and norms that shape behaviour in that system, and also envision new values, the result can be increased understanding and trust (Lazaric and Lorenz, this volume). Members of an organisation or team involved in a significant learning process are likely to increase their levels of trust in both competence and intentions. A virtuous loop is thereby created; improvement contributes to a higher level of trust (mutual trust, self-trust and trust in the consultant), which further supports commitment to the learning process. In contrast, an insufficient level of trust in competence can lead to a self-fulfilling prophecy and thus a vicious cycle (Moingeon, 1994). A learning process can be successful only if the people involved increase their trust in their competence in such a way that they can continue the ongoing learning process without the help of a consultant.

Trust in intentions grows as data show that initial trust was merited. The consequence of this self-reinforcing process is a decrease in transaction and control costs within the organisation (Arrow, 1974; Larson, 1992). Thus over time, trust among interdependent others becomes more precisely reciprocal (cf. Sako, this volume.) We interviewed another consultant from the firm discussed above, who focused on the internal efficiencies his firm has gained from diagnosing behavioural dynamics and being able to avoid the unproductive internal competition that, in his words, 'is typical of professional service firms. We are better at working out problems internally because we can diagnose them and figure out ways to avoid them', he explained. He observed that their new ability to examine 'unproductive frames', that is, to examine causes of interpersonal tension, as well as to experiment with implementing new behaviours, gives rise to sizeable savings in consultants' time. And, as he concluded, 'being stuck in behavioural dynamics costs money'. Along similar lines, a director we interviewed explained that, 'several years ago, we found ourselves faced with classic professional-services-firm nastiness, and we decided to try to change it'. Through working with Argyris, 'we learned – and are still learning – how to diagnose and fix these dynamics, which are a significant source of ineffectiveness.' The intensity of a process of reflecting upon values and rules that shape behaviour in an organisation – if conducted skilfully and with reliance on directly observable data – contributes to an increase in the level of trust in intentions among firm members (Argyris, 1993; Lazaric and Lorenz, this volume). This is in part because, as people learn to see the encompassing, subtle forces governing behaviour in the organisation, they can no longer embrace simplistic attributions about others' negative motives for acting in certain ways.

This self-reinforcing (virtuous) cycle also applies to relationships between an organisation and its suppliers, customers, or other external partners. A high level of trust among an organisation's members, on the one hand, and the organisation's capacity to build trust-based relationships with its environment, on the other, are intangible assets that can be used as a source of competitive advantage (Collis, 1996; Nanda, 1996).

Trust as obstacle

As discussed previously, there is a threshold below which the level of trust is insufficient to implement an organisational learning process successfully. However, it is important to note that an excess of trust can also preclude the implementation of such a process. If an organisation's members have too much trust in an interventionist's competencies, they become subject to a risk of becoming dependent on them. They may fail to reflect critically on the process, as necessary to be fully accountable as participants in implementing organisational learning. Consultants are likely to make mistakes and to misunderstand some of the data they obtain, requiring full and equal participation in the process by members to detect and correct such errors (Argyris, 1995). Likewise, within an organisation, too much trust in competence has already been identified as a source of organisational resistance to change; the 'competency trap' (Levitt and March, 1988) involves an inability to change routines or to innovate. As discussed previously, an organisation's members who are overly confident in the appropriateness of existing routines are not aware of this error. By surfacing tacit assumptions (Schein, 1992) and examining cognitive maps, an interventionist can help them to become aware of this implicit trust in current organisational competence. This allows members to become aware of the impact of excessive trust, or complacency, on how their organisation functions, as well as to understand the ways in which they have unknowingly colluded with the status quo (Argyris, 1993).

Similarly, excessive trust in intentions can create an obstacle to organisational learning. This stems from relationships among organisation members, and between them and the interventionist, in which an excess of trust can create blindness. For example, if the consultant has too high a level of trust in the CEO's intentions, he might fail to reflect critically on the CEO's behaviour, naively assuming his motives and goals to be the same as the consultant's own. Similarly, organisation members must take responsibility for the intervention not being used for political purposes. It is possible for executives publicly to advocate the benefits of the intervention for the firm when their actual intentions are to gain power to manipulate others. In sum, excessive trust can take the form of complacency or dependence (see Figure 12.3).

CONCLUSION

This chapter discusses the different functions played by two types of trust (competence and intentions) in efforts to implement organisational learning. Three functions of trust were presented: trust as a prerequisite, trust as an outcome and trust as an obstacle, along with a framework that highlights six opportunities for organisational assessment and self-reflection regarding levels of trust, relevant to engaging in an organisational learning process. A case of an organisational learning intervention conducted by Argyris (1993) is used to demonstrate how trust can function in undertaking such a process.

Researchers have tended to have difficulty separating antecedents and outcomes of trust (Mayer, Davis and Schoorman, 1995), a confusion we attribute in part to the self-reinforcing dynamic described in this chapter. As with many variables of interest in organisational behaviour, trust functions as both an antecedent and an outcome. This dual role is especially salient for learning phenomena.[4]

We conclude, along with others in this volume, that both trust and organisational learning are central issues in management and organisational behaviour which will require further, multidisciplinary research if scholars and practitioners are to develop practical, actionable knowledge relevant to improving organisations. A single case study was used in this chapter to illustrate both the critical roles of trust in organisational learning and the importance of organisational learning for firm effectiveness. However, we believe that systematic empirical research must be undertaken further to understand the inter-relationships and effects of both trust and learning for organisations.

NOTES

1 Bertrand Moingeon is Associate Professor of Strategic Management at HEC Paris (78350 Jouy-en-Josas, France).

2 Amy Edmondson is Assistant Professor of Technology and Operations Management at Harvard Business School (Harvard University, Boston, MA 02163, USA).

3 We also wish to acknowledge Chris Argyris's input to this definition. In a recent meeting with the authors to discuss the role of trust in 'action science' interventions, he defined trust

as willingness to give control to another.

4 This observation was also contributed by Argyris, in a recent meeting with the authors.

BIBLIOGRAPHY

Argyris, C. (1982), *Reasoning, Learning and Action: Individual and Organizational*, San Francisco: Jossey-Bass.

Argyris, C. (1985), *Strategy, Change and Defensive Routines*, Boston: Pitman.

Argyris, C. (1990), *Overcoming Organizational Defenses Facilitating Organizational Learning*, Boston: Allyn and Bacon.

Argyris, C. (1993), *Knowledge for Action. A Guide to Overcoming Barriers to Organizational Change*, San Francisco: Jossey-Bass.

Argyris, C. (1995), taped interview with B. Moingeon and A. Edmondson, Boston, 8 November.

Argyris, C. and D.A. Schön (1974), *Theory in Practice*, San Francisco: Jossey-Bass.

Argyris, C. and D.A. Schön (1978), *Organizational Learning: A Theory of Action Perspective*, Reading, MA: Addison-Wesley.

Argyris, C., R. Putnam and D.M. Smith (1985), *Action Science : Concepts, Methods, and Skills for Research and Intervention*, San Francisco: Jossey-Bass.

Arrow, K.J. (1974), 'Limited knowledge and economic analysis', *American Economic Review,* March, 1–20.

Brown, J.S. (1991), 'Research that reinvents the corporation', *Harvard Business Review,* January-February.

Brown, J.S. and P. Duguid (1991), 'Organizational learning and communities of practice: toward a unified view of working, learning, and innovation', *Organizational Science,* **2** (1), 40–57.

Collis, D. (1996), 'Organizational capability as a source of profit' in B. Moingeon and A. Edmondson (eds), *Organizational Learning and Competitive Advantage*, London: Sage.

Daft, R.L. and K.E. Weick (1984), 'Toward a model of organizations as interpretation systems', *Academy of Management Review*, **9**, 284–95.

Edmondson, A. and B. Moingeon (1995), 'The learning organization: an integrative approach', in A. Alkhafaji (ed.), *Business Research Yearbook: Global Business Perspectives II*, Lanham: University Press of America, pp. 315–19.

Edmondson, A. and B. Moingeon (1996), 'When to learn how and when to learn why: appropriate organizational learning processes as a source of competitive advantage', in B. Moingeon and A. Edmondson (eds), *Organizational Learning and Competitive Advantage*, London: Sage.

Fiol, C.M. and M.A. Lyles (1985), 'Organizational learning', *Academy of Management Review*, **10** (4), 803–13.

Goffman, E. (1959), *The Presentation of Self in Everyday Life*, New York: Doubleday.

Good, D. (1988), 'Individuals, interpersonal relations, and trust', in D. G. Gambetta (ed.), *Trust*, New York: Basil Blackwell, pp. 131–85.

Handy, C. (1995), 'Trust and the virtual organization', *Harvard Business Review*, May-June, 40–50.

Hayes, R., S. Wheelwright and K. Clark (1988), *Dynamic Manufacturing: The Making of the Learning Organization*, New York: The Free Press.

Hovland, C., I. Janis and H. Kelley (1953), *Communication and Persuasion*, New

Haven: Yale University Press.
Huber, G.P. (1991), 'Organizational learning: the contributing processes and the literature', *Organizational Science,* **2** (1), 88–115.
Larson, A. (1992), 'Network dyads in entrepreneurial settings: a study of governance of exchange relationships', *Administrative Science Quarterly*, **37**, 76–106.
Lawler, E. (1992), *The Ultimate Advantage: Creating the High Involvement Organization*, San Francisco: Jossey-Bass.
Levitt, B. and J. March (1988), 'Organizational learning', *Annual Review of Sociology,* **14**, 319–40.
Lorenz, E.H. (1988), 'Neither friends nor strangers: informal networks of subcontracting in French industry', in D. Gambetta (ed.), *Trust. Making and Breaking Cooperative Relations*, New York: Basil Blackwell, pp. 194–210.
Lorenz, E.H. (1993), 'Flexible productions systems and the social construction of trust', *Politics & Society*, **21,** September, 307–24.
Mayer, R.C., J.H. Davis and F.D. Schoorman (1995), 'An integrative model of organizational trust', *Academy of Management Review*, **20** (3), 709–34.
Moingeon, B. (1994), 'L'auto-analyse stratégique: un service délicat', *L'Expansion Management Review,* **74**, 83–7.
Moingeon, B. and B. Ramanantsoa (1995), 'L'apprentissage organisationnel: éléments pour une discussion', in C. Argyris (ed.), *Savoir pour Agir. Surmonter les Obstacles à l'Apprentissage Organisationnel*, Paris: InterEditions, pp. 295–317.
Nanda, A. (1996), 'Resources, capabilities and competencies', in B. Moingeon and A. Edmondson (eds), *Organizational Learning and Competitive Advantage*, London: Sage.
Nelson, R. and S. Winter (1982), *An Evolutionary Theory of Economic Change,* Cambridge, MA: Harvard University Press.
Pedler, M., T. Boydell and J. Burgoyne (1988), *Learning Company Project: A Report on Work Undertaken,* October 1987 to April 1988. Sheffield: Training Agency.
Pettigrew, A.M. and R. Whipp (1991), *Managing Change for Competitive Success*, Oxford: Blackwell.
Schein, E.H. (1988), *Process Consultation, Volume I: Its Role in Organization Development* (second edition ed.), Reading, MA: Addison-Wesley.
Schein, E.H. (1992), *Organizational Culture and Leadership,* San Francisco: Jossey-Bass, revised edition.
Schwarz, R.M. (1994), *The Skilled Facilitator. Practical Wisdom for Developing Effective Groups*, San Francisco: Jossey-Bass.
Senge, P. (1990), *The Fifth Discipline: The Art and Practice of the Learning Organization*, New York: Doubleday.
Shrivastava, P. (1983), 'A typology of organizational learning', *Journal of Management Studies*, **20** (1), 7–28.
Weick, K.E. (1979), *The Social Psychology of Organizing,* Reading, MA: Addison-Wesley.

13. Organisational Trust, Learning and Implicit Commitment

Pierre Livet[1] and Bénédicte Reynaud[2]

INTRODUCTION

The notion of trust is used with increasing intensity in current economic theory.[3] K. Arrow's remarks in *The Limits of Organizations* (1974, p. 23), where he describes ethical and moral principles, including trust, as 'an invisible institution', have had an incredibly wide influence. Despite being a 'fuzzy' category (and foreign to at least neoclassical theory), economists are now given to importing it into their work, but without any systematic rigour. In this respect, we do not share André Orléan's optimism when he writes:[4] 'Despite the fact that this notion was never entirely neglected by economists, ... it nevertheless remained a difficult category to grasp. Recent theory has tried to overcome this, in order to give the notion a clearly defined place within the analytic framework specific to economics' (1994, p. 17).

The idea of trust is used in three different contexts. First, there is an attempt to give it a theoretical status in relation to one of the fundamental principles of economics: the calculation of individual interests. This problem is well formulated by André Orléan (1994, p. 17): 'Is trust the result of rational calculation of reciprocal interests or does it define a specific modality of interaction which directly links people to one another beyond the calculation of interest?'.

Second, it has a role in the acceptance of money as a medium of exchange.[5] Third, it is alternatively argued that trust is superfluous[6] or indispensable in explaining why exchange occurs.[7]

Theorists often endorse a functional view of trust, relying on description rather than definition. Laurent Cordonnier (1995, p. 6) sees it as 'the psychological structure, ... which causes others to cooperate'. But in our opinion, it is just this 'psychological structure' or, as K. Arrow (1974, p. 23) calls it this 'lubricant of the social system' that needs to be defined in terms of systems of interactions.

These remarks should not be taken to mean that we favour a conceptual 'protectionism'. If economics is to be more than just an experimental field for mathematicians, economists must integrate such principles as trust, loyalty and fairness into their reflections, but to remain meaningful, they must be used with care. Although it is illusory to expect trust in the strong sense of the term to be integrated into economic theory, we can reasonably hope to integrate some more moderate notion of the concept.

The first part of this chapter is devoted to a discussion of the notion of trust in economics. We show first of all that in the strong trust sense it is 'undecidable'. We move on to a general discussion of trust based on several different definitions: trust in the strong sense, contractual trust, and organisational trust and analyse the way in which models in economics refer to one or other notion of trust. In the second part we present our concept of organisational trust, showing that it requires two conditions: implicit commitments and the creation of a space of undecidability. In conclusion we show that these implicit commitments link organisational trust to organisational learning.

THE NOTION OF TRUST IN ECONOMICS

The Undecidability of Trust in the Strong Sense

Trust, in the absolute and strong sense of the term, is undecidable.[8] There are two possible ways of reasoning when deciding whether to trust someone in the strong sense, and both of these lead to a dead end. On the one hand, to trust someone absolutely implies not caring about their precise intentions, and trusting them without further inquiry. This is implicit in point (2) of Williamson's definition of trust: 'X reposes personal trust in Y if X 1) consciously refuses to monitor Y; 2) X is predisposed to ascribe good intentions to Y when things go wrong; and 3) treats Y in a discrete structural way' (1993, p. 483).

But surely it is absurd not to worry about the other's intentions, for trust concerns just these intentions!

On the other hand, we could base our trust on what we know or anticipate of the other's intentions. We may substantiate our interpretation of their intentions by requiring some warranty from them. Most of the time we expect promises, which are a sort of guarantee. But here lies a dilemma. Is a promise a guarantee of the other's intention, and so worthy of our trust, or is it just the expression of an intention to guarantee, and so possibly open to question? We cannot decide between the two interpretations. The utterance of a promise expresses an intention to guarantee, but even an expressed intention is not inherently anything more than an intention. It is not a real guarantee.[9]

Of course we could use some more concrete warranty, such as Williamson's hostages, but this implies that trust is excluded. So either we try to get a decidable warranty or we accept this undecidable intended guarantee. But we need not interpret the situation negatively; just as we cannot decide that a promise will be fulfilled, so we cannot decide that it will not be fulfilled. Trying to find decisive evidence for one interpretation over the other is hopeless, but some (non-decisive) evidence is available.

As a way of arriving at a reasonable and moderate notion of trust, we ask the question: what are the contextual features of the situation of promising that make it reasonable for someone to accept a positive interpretation?

Three Notions of Trust Within a Common Framework

Within the literature trust is seen as opposed to calculation. For example, Williamson describes 'personal trust as nearly non-calculative'. He claims that, 'calculated trust is a contradiction in terms' and that 'user-friendly terms, of which "trust" is one, have an additional cost, since only innocents are taken in' (1993, p. 485). But calculation can be qualified. Totally putting it aside is characteristic of *personal* trust, or trust in the strong sense. Calculation can be implicit and, perhaps unconsciously, restricted by the limited and situated rationality of agents; this is characteristic of *organisational* trust and is based upon implicit commitments. *Contractual* trust is intimately related to distrust as it requires explicit guarantees. We do not need explicit contracts when we are confident that we can trust our partners. When X requires an explicit contract with Y, he manifests his need for some assurance that Y will honour their agreement.

Thus trust is a wide-ranging concept. The greater the trust, the less one needs to specify the commitments and refer to them in litigation. Thus when economists define trust by establishing different degrees: strong, weak, conditional, and so on,[10] they describe one characteristic form of trust among the many that exist.

A general definition of trust

The three notions of trust are all variations of one general type. Their differences can be made explicit by considering the following four examples. X reposes trust in Y for some action A if:

1. X expects Y to do A in those circumstances in which doing A is possible and expected.
2. X and Y accept that there could be some uncertainty regarding whether Y will do A (this is assumed but not necessarily made explicit).
3. X acknowledges that this uncertainty has an element of irreducibility. He accepts that there are limits to his efforts to reduce it (whether by placing

extra constraints on Y or by trying to get probabilistic confirmation of Y's intentions on the basis of assumed subjective probabilities).

4. X acts as if Y will do A in the required circumstances.

Some comments upon this definition are needed in order to avoid possible misunderstandings:

1. Reciprocal trust requires that Y satisfies the same conditions, but X can trust Y without Y trusting X. Uncertainty is always presupposed, even in cases of personal or strong trust. Undecidability is a limiting case of uncertainty which occurs when the very means of getting rid of the uncertainty (making promises, reinforcing some particular interpretation) reintroduce it. In the case of strong trust, uncertainty is simply put aside and appears to be forgotten (but we will see that it is not).
2. Incomplete or imperfect information creates uncertainty, but uncertainty is reduced when hypotheses are confirmed or refuted by revision of prior probabilities in accordance with new evidence. Trust limits this search for confirmation. For example, there could be some period for which variation in the other's behaviour is not taken into account.
3. We might think that legal constraints are all that are needed by way of 'extra constraints' to ensure contractual trust but if this were the case, contractual trust would not be trust at all, as condition (3) above would not be satisfied. As a contract is an explicit commitment, legal constraints are supposed to be anticipated by each of the partners.

Contractual trust is, then, only subject to three kinds of uncertainty: first the possibility that the other person will break his promise despite penalties; second, bad luck and contingencies (the case of '*force majeure*'); and, third, the parties to the contract may each interpret it differently. We will now examine contractual and strong trust in more detail before turning to a discussion of organisational trust..

Contractual trust

Trust requires either written or verbal guarantees even if they do not have a decidable interpretation. However, the fact that these guarantees have been uttered or written is itself decidable. If my partner doesn't act according to his promise, I can blame him (if the promise is not a legal contract) or I can take an action against him (if it is). If he fulfils his promise, I still cannot be sure that he acted purely with the intention of keeping his promise, and not for some other more questionable motive. But I ignore this uncertainty (due to undecidability) by disregarding his motives. Consequently, X expects that Y will do A, and Y expects that A will do the corresponding X. Condition (3) still holds, but is made relative: X has got Y to express certain intentions to provide guarantees, but has not obtained a physical limitation on the possible actions of Y. Nonetheless, X does not seek supplementary constraints on Y.

The labour contract of traditional economic theory, by which people contract to exchange services for a wage, is one prototype of contractual trust (or of contractual distrust). The wage contract creates a reciprocal commitment between employer and employee, though this does not mean that the content of the commitments is equal. A fifth condition should, thus, be added to the general definition in this case (that is, (1) to (4) apply reciprocally to Y).

Thus X, the employer, expects Y, the employee, to perform a number of tasks, and Y in turn expects that X will pay him. The employee acts as if the employer really will pay up. When it comes to contracts, however, trust and distrust are opposite sides of the same coin. Distrust comes from the fact that the labour contract is characterised by the conflicting interests of employer and employee and, at the same time, by an authority relationship (or relation of subordination). The only way to overcome distrust is through a contract. According to the legal expert, Paul Durand:

> ... the labour contract is defined as a convention by which a person, called a worker or an employee, commits himself to perform physical acts ... for the benefit of another person, called an employer, by putting himself into a situation of subordination, against some remuneration given in money and called a wage. (1947, t. 2, p. 223)

In a sense, any wage relation expresses contractual trust, particularly when it relies on promises (for example, promotion scales and wage agreements that stipulate lower wages in return for stability of employment), or when it relies on rules that have not yet been applied (for is not an as yet unapplied rule a kind of promise?).

Strong trust

Strong trust is reciprocal. Condition (3) is satisfied, as is condition (2). But uncertainty is treated in a peculiar way. For an external observer, the level of uncertainty could appear rather high, but the partners simply ignore it. They just 'bracket' or 'suspend' it. In situations of contractual trust, where explicit guarantees could be called for, people linked by strong trust avoid asking for them. For example, friends lend money to each other without contract, and if one of them were to propose a contract the other would refuse it. This is not to suggest that there is no need for evidence, but refusal to worry about guarantees is in itself the kind of evidence required to establish strong trust. If Y gives some evidence of trustworthiness to X, X may consider it sufficient, but not necessary, for him to trust Y. If Y gives no such evidence then, with a considerable lapse of time, evidence will become necessary for X to trust Y.

In the case of strong trust, if one person's behaviour fails to coordinate with another's, the latter does not immediately assume that trust is broken. As Williamson says in his condition (2), X is predisposed to ascribe good intentions to Y when things go wrong. Indeed, X considers himself committed to restore the defective coordination by cooperating with Y. Of course, even strong trust is undermined when one person explicitly expresses a desire to quit the common action or when he requires contractual guarantees.

As an example, consider the following practice common in Japanese firms.[11] If a worker makes a mistake he is helped to correct it, and mutual aid is considered normal. The founder of 'Toyotism', T. Ohno (1978, p. 36), insisted upon the importance of cooperation:

> ... supervisers have to lead workers by their hand and to teach them what they have to do. This is the way for them to obtain the workers' confidence. The operators in the same line have to learn that they depend upon each other and so must help each other. (1978, p. 36)

As Magaud and Sugita observed:

> '... mistakes, failures, dysfunctionings are normal and integral to the normal production process' (extract from his diary, quoted in J. Magaud and K. Sugita (1990)).

It is for this reason that people look for quick solutions rather than resorting to sanctions.

Strong trust is, in a sense, less demanding than either contractual trust or organisational trust, as it requires no evidence. In another sense, however, it is more demanding: you cannot allude to contracts, you have to forgive failures in coordination, you must acknowledge your own mistakes, and sometimes you must take charge of some part of the other's actions.

In economic relations, strong trust is scarce and limited to very close interactions. Paternal relations, which existed in some firms until the end of the 19th century (but only the 'truly' paternal ones: those exhibiting more protection than exploitation, and based upon the charisma of the boss), could be a limiting case of strong trust.

Forms of Trust in Economic Theory

Akerlof's model of 'labour gift exchange': a mix of the three notions of trust

Akerlof's model of the 'Labour contract as partial gift exchange' (1982) could be understood as a combination of the three notions of trust. Akerlof provides the first 'sociological explanation' of efficiency wage models. Most of these models accept that the firm may find it unprofitable to cut wages even in the presence of involuntary unemployment. They are based on 'the efficiency wage hypothesis', according to which labour productivity depends on the real wage paid. Thus cutting wages could result in rising labour costs. Nevertheless, each type of theory offers different rationales for wages paid in excess of the market-clearing rate. In sociological models, wage rigidity is due to social conventions (Solow, 1981) or group behaviour (Akerlof, 1982).

In the latter theory, Akerlof uses sociological evidence to explain two related phenomena:

1. The way in which a firm raised group work norms by paying wages in excess of the market level at a time when most of the workers of the firm exceeded the minimum work standards by an average of 17 per cent.
2. And why, subsequently, neither the workers nor the firm changed their behaviour: the workers neither expected nor asked for a promotion or a wage increase in return for their effort; the employers did not raise the minimum standard.

One part of this example could be analysed in terms of contractual trust. Employees make a 'gift' to the employer by working more than the norm and, in return, the employer pays a higher salary than the market-clearing wage. In treating the extra work as a gift the employer ignores motives and expects work at this level, and does not use physical mechanisms (such as changing machine speeds) to enforce it. In return, the workforce expects to receive an above market-level wage.

Another plausible interpretation is in terms of strong trust. Employees continually give signs of cooperation. The employer does not expect these signs at every moment in time, but just frequently enough to justify the gift of a salary higher than the market-clearing wage. If the norm is not attained in one period, the employer may overlook this if earlier experience leads him to interpret the failure as a simple 'accident' and not as a change in strategy. This could be because of strong trust which is founded on a temporal lag in the interpretation of signs. But if in a further period the normal minimum is still not attained, evidence of trustworthiness will become necessary. The employer will fall back on implicit commitments and the evidence for them: the constraints imposed by workers on themselves.

Strong trust seems to be present in another part of this example: solidarity between workers. According to Akerlof, solidarity allows the group to avoid the sentiment of collective failure which could arise if one of the group members did not attain the norm.

Organisational trust is also relevant. Let us imagine that the employer pays a wage in excess of the market-clearing wage in return for an implicit future commitment. In this scenario, the implicit commitments associated with the efficiency wage represent an improvement over those of the 'captive' variety[12] for which workers, attracted by the wage and not the job, are offered only the market-clearing wage. The difference between the market-clearing wage and the efficiency wage is supposed to improve the level of implicit commitment, leading to work of a greater intensity and superior quality (in Akerlof's theory) and providing an incentive not to shirk (in that of Shapiro and Stiglitz, 1984).

Organisational trust is also relevant to understanding the level of effort obtained from workers. Trust physically affects workers' actions by establishing possible modes of coordination (one does not substantially exceed a norm without a minimum of consensus).

The wage contract in non-standard economic theory: contractual and organisational trust

H. Simon (1951) gave new life to the analysis of the notion of the wage contract by applying a non-standard perspective to it. According to Simon, the distinctive feature of the wage relation (as opposed to the labour contract of traditional economic theory) comes from the fact that the worker undertakes the performance of a certain subset of tasks selected from a larger possible set at some future point in time. In his article, Simon shows that, in a situation of uncertainty for the producer, a labour contract is superior to a sales contract because the decision over which tasks should be performed can be delayed until his real needs are known. The employer is prepared to pay for flexibility from the worker as this is the only way to respond to fluctuations in demand. According to Edward Lorenz (1994), the labour contract is necessarily incomplete and the worker confers on the employer the right to determine how to adapt to unanticipated events.

Let x be an element of the set of all possible behaviours, B the employer ('Boss') and W the employee ('Worker'). According to Simon:

> We will say that B exercises authority over W, if W permits B to select x. That is, W accepts B's authority over W when his behaviour is determined by B's decision. In general, W will accept authority only if x_0, the x chosen by B, is restricted to some given subset (W's 'area of acceptance') of all possible values ... W will be willing to enter an employment contract with B only if it does not matter to him 'very much' which x (within the agreed upon area of acceptance) B will choose. (1951, pp. 294–5)

One may interpret the labour relation developed by Simon in terms of contractual and organisational trust. The same goes for other models which refer to the radical incompleteness of the labour contract. The labour contract, like any other, is an explicit commitment between parties. But it also refers (implicitly) to some region of implicit commitment: the coordination of tasks assigned by the employer during production. Implicit commitments ensure flexibility, and explicit commitments ensure long-term stability. The defeasibility of the implicit commitments is not cancelled out but is reduced. There are some demands that an employer might conceivably make which are implicitly unacceptable, such as requiring a worker to risk his life or to act in a way which endangers others. Such demands should not be included in a contract as they would be illegal. Apart from legal constraints, and cases of '*force majeure*', explicit commitments remain valid even if there is some change in circumstances. They can be overturned only when a condition mentioned in the explicit commitments is no longer satisfied. Thus explicit commitments ensure the stability of implicit commitments.

The labour contract is asymmetric because the employee's implicit commitments are dictated by the employer. A symmetric contact is one in which implicit commitments are determined either by both partners, by some third party, or by the environment.

Incompleteness is a property of every contract. Even contracts to buy or sell imply some domain of implicit commitment: the financial network, the domain of production, the domain of consumption. Contracts are explicit commitments which presuppose stability in the domains of implicit commitment. Labour contracts, for instance, presuppose stability in the domain of the technologies provided by the employer.

ORGANISATIONAL TRUST

Organisational trust presupposes both conventions and contractual trust, but for the most part it relies upon what we call implicit commitments (that is, commitments that emerge from the effective practices of coordination in the workplace). Thus we need a definition of implicit commitment, and then we will see that, as a consequence, organisational trust also requires the existence of intervals of undecidability.

First Condition: Implicit Commitments and 'Reasonable' Commitments

Suppose that action A_n is a part of a collective action, A. A cannot be successful if A_n and its parts, A_i and A_n are not realised. X can do A_n or some A_i. He can also do other actions unrelated to A. He knows, or he believes, that Y can do A_n or A_i or other actions unrelated to A. X is not sure that Y is willing to take part in collective action A, as it would exclude him from other preferred actions (that is, Y's doing some A_i restricts his possible range of action). As there are insufficient people for each to do only one part of the collective action, they must each perform several of its parts, A_i, sequentially. In this type of situation, when X sees Y doing an A_i, he can reasonably believe that Y is 'implicitly committed' to taking part in the collective action, A, and to coordinating his actions with those performed by others. The same holds for Y if she observes X doing some A_i.

This kind of commitment is only an implicit one, as there was no explicit announcement of an intention to coordinate. Take the example of a car in a ditch: I see people grasping the right front of the car, others grasping the left front, so I myself take the left back, and some others the right back. I consider that we are implicitly committed to pushing the car out of the ditch.

What counts as either a possible collective action or a possible part in a collective action? A possible action is: (1) a possible transformation of the state of the world, that is (2) caused, at least partially, by an agent, who (3) intended to cause the transformation in this, or in some similar, way. 'Possible' also has an evaluative meaning in this context. The new state of the world caused by the agent's action should not be less preferred by the agent than the previous one. So only those actions that produce states of the world that are not less preferred to the initial ones count as 'possible actions' for a reasonable commitment. Even this definition leaves us with many different ways of shaping some sequence of movements into actions. But remember that we are talking about actions that are possible objects of ascription. Thus the huge class of 'actions' is reduced to a much smaller one: the class of 'actions recognizable by others'.

Now we can turn to the machinery of implicit commitment. Remember that implicit commitments are defeasible ones. The conditions that the collective action imposes on you could be different from the ones that you anticipated. The initially anticipated conditions may have been 'reasonable' ones, but the action may not have turned out to be as flexible as expected and another option may now seem preferable. Thus the commitment is suspended.

Implicit commitment is an attributive notion (that is, it is ascribed to you by others, or to others by you). It may not be a real commitment from the point of view of the supposedly committed. If belief in this commitment is mistaken, then subsequent actions will not be as expected and the ascribed 'commitment' will be cancelled out.

Explicit commitments are needed to ensure more stable commitments. An explicit commitment is supposed to be immune to any modification of conditions not anticipated or explicitly mentioned at the time of the agreement (leaving aside cases of '*force majeure*').

The reasonability condition

Remember that we are only looking for a method for assigning 'reasonable' implicit commitments to other people. We use this mainly when we ask ourselves whether someone will remain a participant in a collective action in which we are involved. We are endowed with limited rationality, so we proceed lexicographically, step by step, stop as soon as possible, and keep on only if there is some evidence of a difficulty. The reasonability condition can be spelt out in five sub-conditions. First, there must be a web of coordinated actions of which X's current action is one, and such that X cannot be supposed to hope to gain any utility or pleasure from his isolated action, A_i, if the coordination does not succeed. Suppose we are sure that X needs to undertake his part of the outcome of the collective action in order to survive. Then his commitment is beyond question. On the other hand, if we know that he can earn his living by doing another job and is worried about his commitment, we have to ensure that our collective action gives him other advantages. The following order seems quite intuitive: we first care about our survival and the satisfaction of basic needs; second, we worry about our liberty of choice; third, we worry about our level of responsibility; and fourth, we worry about aesthetic features imminent in the action (such as its complexity).

Freedom of choice is spelt out in two ways: the richness of future possibilities that the present action opens up (the 'fan out'), and the possibility of substituting some part for another during the course of action (flexibility). Richness has to be taken into account before flexibility so – the second sub-condition – we have to ensure that the collective action offers X the best 'fan out' (for example, by ensuring that his part of our collective action leaves him with more leisure time). We could do this by giving him higher wages: receiving more money is effectively having a larger set of possible consumption actions.

Say we observe that X is a bit bored by his present job. His alternatives might not give him more leisure time, but if we are nonetheless worried about his commitment, then – third sub-condition – we have to give him more opportunities for change or more flexibility (giving him more money would not be sufficient, for between two jobs giving the same income, he chooses the more flexible one, and the possibilities of choice that money can give are limited by the time that is left after work). However, if we cannot give him more flexibility we try to make him conscious of the fact that he is the only person whose abilities meet the complex needs of our collective action. Thus – fourth sub-condition - we pay attention to the 'fan in' of the structure of coordination: the number of different individual actions that converge towards his own part (the higher the 'fan in', the higher the collective responsibility you have). Finally, – fifth sub-condition – X could give some 'aesthetic value' to the complexity of the structure of coordination. This aesthetic value results from the fine-tuning of the coordination between actions – such as, for instance, when X's choosing to do an action A_i implies doing action A_j for some Y. In some cases flexibility and fine tuning are incompatible features.

Notice that we are close to the notion of liberty introduced into economics by Sen (1992). At some point X is confronted with different sets of possible actions (Sen speaks of 'sets of functionings'). To each option is appended a string of future actions, or even a tree of possible future options between strings of future actions. Some of these will be individual actions, the outcomes of which can be obtained by X alone. Their value is given by the intrinsic value X assigns to the action A, plus the expected value of the outcome of A. Others will be collective actions, the outcomes of which cannot be obtained by X alone without cooperation with others. In this case, each anticipated partial action, A_i, of X is given an extra value, in addition to the intrinsic value that X assigns to the action A. This extra value is some part of the value of the collective outcome considered as a public good (putting aside the cases where there are public good dilemmas). In addition, X gives extra value to the diversity of the set of possible future alternatives that each tree of possible actions offers to him;[13] he assigns extra value to the 'fan out' of the collective action (the collective or individual action offers several possibilities for branching into other future actions of interest). He also assigns an extra value to flexibility, the possibility of being able to choose either some part, A_i or some other part, A_j over the 'fan in' of the collective action and its fine-tuning.

Reasonability conditions could be seen as explanations of what Rawls calls the 'Aristotelian principle': '... other things being equal, human beings enjoy the exercise of their realised capacities, and this enjoyment increases the more the capacity is realised or the greater its complexity' (Rawls, 1971, p. 426).

For example, we studied a situation where 'organisational trust' was called for: workers belonging to the same team in a maintenance workshop of a transport company had to cooperate to obtain a bonus. Management instigated a salary formula by which a bonus was paid to each member of any team whose combined output exceeded a certain threshold. The bonus varied linearly within fixed bounds in accordance with output: a worker received nothing if the team's output remained below a minimum output, and received the maximum bonus if his team attained or exceeded an upper threshold (that is, the ceiling output level). Each worker had to decide the degree to which he would cooperate in accordance with the amount of the bonus he sought.[14]

As in all cases where reasoning about the decisions of others is called for, each worker's representation of the collective action, A, may have been different. Uncertainty stems from the possible differences in each individual's understanding of what A involves, and the possibility of a modification in both the individual's commitment to A and his representation of it. However, mutual observation helps to ensure cooperation. Suppose that actions A' are of the curative type performed in the workshop, and that actions A" are of the preventive kind. Logistics fixes the order of priority of the A's and A"s in accordance with needs. Workers are not indifferent between the two: curative tasks are always preferred to preventive ones, which are considered repetitive and dirty.

These features permit an evaluation of the level of implicit commitment and degree of organisational trust. If worker X observes that Y respects the current work priorities which oblige him to do the disliked, preventive tasks A", then X may conclude that: (1) Y is implicitly committed to the team, and (2) Y is, in this sense, reasonable. It appears that the observation of the performance of A" places an objective constraint on the interpretation of Y's intentions.

Notice that our five steps (comparing outcomes, comparing 'fan out', comparing flexibility, comparing 'fan in', and comparing the fine-tuning) can be used to divide implicit commitments into two classes: the first two steps correspond to captive implicit commitments, the last three steps to motivating implicit commitments. Captive commitments are based upon features of events and things outside the scope of the present action, while motivating commitments are based upon features of events and things internal to the present action. In captive commitments, action has only an instrumental value, but in motivating commitments it has an intrinsic value as well (or certain features of this action have intrinsic value). When we choose to do a job merely for money our commitment is a captive one (in this case, an explicit one as well). When we are engaged in some collective action because of its flexibility or its fine-tuning, or because of any other intrinsic property of either the collective action or our own part in it, we are engaged by a motivating commitment (which, most of the time, is an implicit one).

In organisations, trust is generally founded on implicit commitments. Contractual trust or explicit commitments define the general framework which ensures that people will keep on working together. But when we expect that our partner will play his part in a coordinated action, we do not rely upon contractual trust, but on implicit commitments; that is, on organisational trust. The level of trust ensured by implicit commitment cannot be lower than that guaranteed by contractual commitments, and most of the time it is higher. Implicit commitments ensure solidarity among workers, contractual commitments ensure only the stability of the relation between workers and employer. Implicit commitments are more defeasible but stronger when not revised. Global trust is lower, local trust is higher. In contractual commitments, which are remedies against defection, global trust is reinforced but local trust is lower.

Implicit commitments trap us in social coordination. There is a double ruse involved: (1) coordination is attractive because the 'fan out' of an individual action is higher when it is part of a collective action, and because some outcomes cannot be reached without collective action; and (2) implicit commitments are ascriptions. Imagine encountering a group of people faced with an action that none of them can carry out individually. Features of their behaviour will hint that they consider one another implicitly committed to coordinating their individual actions in a collective one, but they may also ascribe an implicit commitment to anyone who looks at them sympathetically.

So what do you do if they ascribe such an implicit commitment to you? You have not planned on undertaking this activity but it is an opportunity to obtain some unanticipated collective result. If you are not in a hurry, it is reasonable to cooperate, but you might then find that your set of possible actions changes. For example, the collective action might take longer than expected. At some point you have to choose between remaining or forsaking the collective action in favour of some previously planned individual action. However, forsaking the collective action would lead to a diminution of your set of possible actions because the future benefit of the collective action would be lost. Only by remaining do you make sense of your previous contributions to the collective effort. Even if the immediate choice is between an individual action on behalf of the collective and one for your own private purposes, you must take into account the fact that, partly as a result of your past actions, the collective action is already partially performed. The collective action counts as numerous possible actions in a single option. Even if all but one of these actions is already realised, they are all part of the same sequence or members of the same set. Moreover, you might prefer to choose the option which opens to you the larger set of possible actions.

This could be a way to vindicate decisions that run foul of the 'sunk cost' fallacy. The ascriptive character of implicit commitments makes a step-by-step involvement in social coordination based on a sequence of reasonable arguments possible – even if we had been able to anticipate the final state and compare it with every possible alternative, the rational choice would have been different. The implication is that social coordination is often a result of our limited power of anticipation and the fact that the reasonableness of actions is not transitive.

Implicit commitments can also explain why most people cooperate in cases of public good dilemmas. Suppose that they are used to being involved in very complicated collective coordinations, for example shipowners are used to complex exchanges with many harbour authorities, but some of their ships happen to sink because there is no lighthouse at the mouth of a particular river. Thus there is a breakdown in their complex coordination. Then it is reasonable to pay to build a lighthouse even if some other shipowners will benefit from it without paying for it. The paying shipowner maintains his set of possible actions, the complexity of which is strongly decreased, and even adds to it the action of building the lighthouse. Each shipowner can be sure that every other shipowner who has seen one of his ships sink, or is anxious about this possibility, will cooperate reasonably. So there is no longer a public good dilemma.

Since contracts require cooperation they are subject to a prisoners' dilemma. Remember that contracts are explicit commitments. We need explicit commitments, rather than implicit ones, when the complexity of the coordination requires that no participant defects. So explicit commitments ensure that every participant is aware that, were someone to defect, the collective result would not be realised. Explicit commitments are made so as to prevent breakdowns of coordination. They anticipate problems such as public good dilemmas or prisoners' dilemmas, and to solve them they exploit reasonable implicit commitments. In this way, explicit commitments rely on implicit ones.

In organisations and firms, trust depends on implicit commitments which are revealed by the constraints that people accept for the sake of coordination. Even contractual, explicit commitments are based upon implicit ones. Explicit commitments need a background of implicit commitment to ensure organisational trust, implicit commitments cannot make cooperation certain because they are defeasible, but since coordination is a device for generating implicit commitments, it compensates for this uncertainty.

Second Condition: Undecidability Intervals

We noted that implicit commitments can be of two kinds: motivated, where the positive part of the final balance is endogenous to the collective action; or captive, where the positive part of the final balance is exogenous to the collective action (for example, when we engage in some coordination because of the wage we will earn and the possibilities this opens up). Suppose that in a certain firm we have workers with both kinds of commitment. We cannot expect the same intensity of work from the captive ones as from the motivated ones. So could we try to impose on every worker some additional 'motivation', either by threatening the captive ones with redundancy or by adding to their wage incentive? This would simply transform the motivated workers into captive ones! In any case, one cannot tell whether some worker who is not working intensely is a motivated one resisting the constraints on his liberty, or a captive one just working at the level of intensity necessary to avoid being made redundant.

This is a consequence of the reasonableness of implicit commitments. It is reasonable for a worker to decrease the intensity of his work when the collective result is not at stake. Were we to try to prevent this behaviour we would be denying him the right to base his implicit commitments on an assessment of their reasonableness. So we would deny him the very possibility of reasonable implicit commitments. This would undermine even explicit commitments, for they depend upon a background of implicit commitments. We have to acknowledge the impossibility of transforming every agent into a motivated (or a captive) one.

Similarly, there is no definitive way to decide whether a worker's decrease in work effort is a sign that he is reluctant to work and that he is revising his implicit commitments, or a sign that he is a motivated worker who has noticed that the collective result will be exceeded. If we want to rely upon implicit commitments we have to admit this undecidability. Of course, there are lower and upper limits to this interval of undecidability. Below the lower limit the implicit commitment of the worker to others is broken, above the upper limit the worker is working too hard for others to reciprocate, so once again the implicit commitment is broken.

Notice that implicit commitments are possible only among members of a working community (the workers), while explicit commitments are possible between the workers and the employer as well, even though the latter might not be involved directly in the coordination and could just be the supplier of production tools and raw materials. In establishing explicit commitments an attempt is sometimes made to specify the lower and upper limits of these undecidability intervals, but most of the time they are settled by reciprocal adjustments of implicit commitments in the course of coordinating actions.

CONCLUDING REMARKS

It might be useful to relate the notion of implicit commitment to the notion of organisational learning as developed by Argyris and Schön (1978). In some sense, the web of implicit commitments we find in an organisation is the real content of what Argyris and Schön call a 'theory-in-use'. A theory-in-use is made up of practices and representations. The practices provide evidence for implicit commitments, while the representations provide the background of belief required to estimate the reasonableness of the commitment. Primary learning or single-loop learning is nothing but the revision of the conditions of implicit commitment that occur continuously during coordinated action in an organisation. All that we require in order to ascribe (revised) implicit commitments to people with changes in the conditions of coordinated action is that they continue to cooperate with others.

Deutero-learning requires awareness that some features of the theory-in-use are obstacles to improvements. It also requires that people in the organisation are implicitly committed to the coordinated search for these obstacles and the revision of this theory in use. Thus deutero-learning is not simply a matter of forming second-order representations about the theory-in-use (or making it explicit), but of shifting implicit commitments to this new and second-order task of revising the theory-in-use. As implicit commitments and limited rationality are linked together, deutero-learning is no more immune to cognitive biases than primary learning. The difficulty in moving from primary learning to deutero-learning lies in the requirement that people are able to identify the different parts of the collective action of theory revision.

We have seen that implicit commitments are flexible and can be maintained, even when the coordination task is changing. We change our expectations about others when the structure of the task is revised, but implicit commitments hold stable as long as the new circumstances do not undermine the reasonableness of the initial implicit commitment. This is the basic assumption: that we revise only if some salient event makes us aware that some basic condition of reasonableness is no longer satisfied.

NOTES

1 CREA/Ecole Polytechnique et Université d'Aix-Marseille I; e-mail: livet@romarin.univ-aix.fr.
2 CREA/Ecole Polytechnique et CNRS; 1, rue Descartes – 75005 Paris; Tél: (1) 46.34.36.20; Fax: (1) 43.25.29.44; e-mail: reynaudb@poly.polytechnique.fr.
3 This observation was recently made again in connection with other ethical or moral notions such as loyalty, equity and reputation: cf. H. Zadjela (1994, p. 70) and A. Orléan (1994a, p. 17).
4 Is it not significant that H. Zadjela (1994, p. 69) calls them 'nomadic concepts, emanating from heterodox theories or other social sciences'?
5 Cf. M. Aglietta and A. Orléan (1982), M. Aglietta (1994), M. Aglietta and A. Orléan (1995) and A. Orléan (1992a, b).
6 O. Williamson (1993).
7 Mark Anspach (1994) offers the following comments on Mauss' view: 'In Mauss' view, the problem of exchange is the problem of reciprocal trust. What allows us to hope that the man to whom we give a present today will be generous to us tomorrow'.
8 On undecidability, cf. P. Livet (1994, Chapters 1 and 4).
9 Notice that although this undecidability produces uncertainty, it is not a consequence of uncertainty. Even the one who promises is not able to say whether his promise is really a guarantee or merely an intention to guarantee. There is an apparent paradox here. Even were we each to know all there is to know (the behaviour, the expressed intentions and, if it's possible, the intentions of others), we would still be confronted by this indecision. Undecidability is compatible with the full knowledge of the circumstances that create it. So we should resist the idea of identifying undecidability with radical uncertainty in the sense of an incomplete description of possible states of the world.
10 Cf, for example, M. Servet (1994a, b).
11 Cf. B. Reynaud (1994a).
12 For the difference between captive and motivated implicit commitments, see p. 278.
13 He takes into account only the relevant alternatives. He can count an option as relevant only if it includes some possibilities for action on its own, or some outcome to which he assigns an intrinsic value. In this way we avoid saying that the value of a set of alternatives could be

increased by the addition of irrelevant options, or by a redescription of the set of options.
14 The choice was not just between a maximum and minimum bonus. Moreover, the worker knew that he could not determine the collective output or the final level of the bonus.

BIBLIOGRAPHY

Aglietta, M. (1994), 'Ordre monétaire et banques centrales', in A. Orléan (ed.), *Analyse Economique des Conventions*, Paris: PUF.

Aglietta, M. and A. Orléan (1982), *La Violence de la Monnaie*, Paris: PUF.

Aglietta, M. and A. Orléan (eds) (1995), *Souveraineté, Légitimité de la Monnaie*, Association d'Economie Financière,Paris : Caisse des Dépôts.

Akerlof, G. (1982), 'Labour contracts as partial gift exchange', *The Quarterly Journal of Economics*, **97**, November, 543–69.

Anspach, M. (1994), 'La monnaie, la confiance, la transcendance: sacrifiant et paiement dans l'Inde ancienne', in M. Aglietta and A. Orléan (eds), *Souveraineté, Légitimité de la Monnaie*, Association d'Economie Financière, Paris: Caisse des Dépôts, pp. 133–47.

Argyris, C. and D. Schön (1978), Organizational Learning: A Theory of Action Perspective, Reading, MA: Addison Wesley.

Arrow, K. (1974), *The Limits of Organizations*, New York and London: W.W. Norton and Company.

Cordonnier, L. (1995), *L'Echange, la Coopération et l'Autonomie des Personnes*, paper submitted to the 'Séminaire Marchés et Organisations', Paris, Institut International La Défense, 3 February.

Durand, P. (1947), *Traité de Droit du Travail*, Paris: Dalloz.

Edwards, R. (1979), *Contested Terrain*, London: Heinemann.

Livet, P. (1994), *La Communauté Virtuelle*, Paris: Editions de l'Eclat.

Lorenz, H. (1994), '*Systèmes de Production Flexibles et Construction Sociale de la Confiance*', paper presented to the 'Séminaire Marchés et Organisations', Paris, Institut International La Défense, October.

Magaud, J. and K. Sugita (1990), *Angers-Nagano. Une comparaison France-Japon*, Working paper, April.

Ohno, T. (1978), *L'Esprit Toyota*, French translation 1989, Paris: Masson.

Orléan, A. (1992a), 'L'origine de la monnaie – I', *Revue du MAUSS*, **14**, 126–52.

Orléan, A. (1992b), 'L'origine de la monnaie – II', *Revue du MAUSS*, **15–16**, 111–25.

Orléan, A. (1994), 'Sur le rôle respectif de la confiance et de l'intérêt dans la constitution de l'ordre marchand', *A qui se fier?*, *Revue Semestrielle du Mauss*, **4**, 17–56.

Orléan, A. (ed.) (1994), *Analyse Economique des Conventions*, Paris: PUF.

Rawls, J. (1971), *Theory of Justice*, Cambridge, MA: MIT Press.

Reynaud, B. (1992), *Le Salaire, la Règle et le Marché*, Editions C. Bourgois, collection Cibles XXI.

Reynaud, B. (1994a), 'Les règles de salaire au Japon: un vecteur de connaissance distribuée?', *Japon in Extenso*, **32–33**, June–Septembrer, 97–105.

Reynaud, B. (1994b), *Les Théories du Salaire*, Paris: La Découverte, collection Repères.

Sen, A. (1992), *Inequality Re-examined*, Oxford: Clarendon Press.

Servet, J.M. (1994a), 'Paroles données', *A qui se fier?*, *Revue Semestrielle du Mauss*, **4**, 37–56.

Servet, J.M. (1994b), '*Six Hypothèses pour Définir la Confiance*', Working paper du Centre Auguste et Léon Walras, Maison Rhone-Alpes des Sciences de l'Homme, **168**, December.

Shapiro, C. and J. Stiglitz (1984), 'Equilibrium unemployment as a worker discipline device', *American Economic Review*, **74** (3), June, 433–44.

Simon, H. (1951), 'A formal theory of the employment relationship', *Econometrica*, **19** (3), July, 293–305.

Solow, R. (1981), 'Another possible source of stickiness', *Journal of Macroeconomics*, **1**, Winter, 433–44.

Williamson, O. (1993), 'Calculativeness, trust, and economic organization', *Journal of Law and Economics*, **XXXVI**, April, 453–87.

Zadjela, H. (1994), 'Que nous apprend la nouvelle économie du travail?', *Pour une autre économie, Revue Semestrielle du Mauss*, **3**, 60–76.

Index